Postfach 30 03 07 | 50773 Köln
Pellenzstraße 39 | 50823 Köln

Fon +49 (0)221 599 56 47
Fax +49 (0)221 599 10 24

dachverband@kritischeaktionaere.de
www.kritischeaktionaere.de

BASF SE
Zentralabteilung Recht, ZRR – D100
67056 Ludwigshafen
Deutschland
Telefax: +49 621 60-6641475
oder +49 621 60-6643693
oder per E-Mail: hv2015@basf.com

Counter Proposal
Association of Ethical Shareholders Germany
Annual General Meeting BASF SE, April 30, 2015

Counter Proposal Re. Agenda item 3

The Association of Ethical Shareholders disapproves the actions of the board members of BASF SE for the business year 2014.

Rationale:
BASF SE board members didn't fulfill their responsibility within the supply chain in the case of Lonmin. In the reports of the worldwide 3rd biggest Platinum enterprise Lonmin, BASF is declared, besides Mitsubishi, to be the main customer of the Lonmin enterprise (operating in South Africa, based in England). Lonmin characterizes BASF as „principal customer for PGMs". BASF Catalysts LLC and Lonmin are furthermore members of the International Platinum Group Metals Association. Thus, a close and long term commercial relationship is evident.

Now, the process of taking of evidence of the massacre of Marikana (16th August 2012) in the framework of the state appointed (Oct. 2012) "Marikana Commission of Inquiry" provides clear and extensive evidence, that Lonmin is – indirectly as well as directly – co-responsible for the massacre. On a concrete level Lonmin is accused to be co-responsible

1. for the killing of 34 mine workers on the 16 August 2012 and for the 70, partly sustained, injured
2. for escalation of violence and the killings prior to the massacre
3. for the unacceptable, partly inhuman living, working and environmental conditions which the workers and their communities have to suffer for decades – the major part of the Lonmin workers are living in shack-slums without running water, electricity and access to proper municipal services. Out of a total workforce of 30,000 employees, Lonmin provide accommodation for just 2,500 while 27,500 are offered a living allowance of R 1,850 a month. They end up living in shacks.

The evidence leaders of the Marikana Commission of Inquiry accuse Lonmin that it has often and repeatedly ignored and broken its legal obligations towards the workers and the local community. In 1999 Lonmin built 1,149 houses and in 2006 promised to build another 5,500 new houses by 2011. This did not materialize. Indeed merely three show houses were built for more than a decade. These empty promises, the miserable infrastructure and the low wages led to the strike in August 2012. Lonmin refused consequently to meet a very simple request of the workers: to talk with them. This was a catastrophic response and set the course of what was to follow. Lonmin, in contrary, gave logistic and infrastructural support to the highly militarized police operation, which led ultimately to death of three workers in one day and – as has been proven: this should have been foreseeable to Lonmin – to the killings on the August 16. This is a crucial reason why some persons of the Lonmin management are accused for murder and culpable homicide. Furthermore Lonmin Security guards are responsible for first escalation of violence and shootings of strikers, which is classified by the evidence leaders as unjustified.

More than two and a half years after the biggest massacre on civilians in South Africa since the end of apartheid, Lonmin meets rather idly and not at all levels its responsibility towards the families of the murdered and injured mine workers. All these documented delicts are strictly incompatible with the principles of the BASF management – e.g. as founding member of the UN Global Compact. BASF promises to demand these principles as well from its suppliers. The "standards of the value-added chain" and the "management of the supply chain", to which BASF committed itself, has a need of improvement in the case of Lonmin.

In order not to loose its reputation, BASF should take its own responsibility as main customer of Lonmin seriously and support and get Lonmin to financially compensate through reparation payments for the families of the 44 killed people of August 2012 (and the sustained injured) as well as with sustainable improvements of the local infrastructure. For example mining houses use a lot of water and in turn pollute water systems and especially underground water that communities are dependent upon. Lonmin should apply the UN Guiding Principle on Business and Human Rights and respect people and the environment in which they operate and demonstrate remedial actions they are taking.

BASF should organize its own fact finding mission around Lonmin operations to get an own impression of the living, working and environmental conditions of the Marikana communities.

As a publicly visible symbol of a prompt and consistent realization of its promises and strategies in the context of its "responsibility within the supply chain" BASF should install a fund of 1 million rand for each of the 44 persons who died in August 2012 in Marikana to be forwarded to the persons directly concerned (families of killed persons). The third anniversary of the massacre, 16 August 2015, would be an appropriate date for the handover of this fund.

Cologne, April 15, 2015

Markus Dufner
Managing Director Association of Ethical
Shareholders Germany

Dachverband
KRITISCHE AKTIONÄRE
Postfach 300307 | 50773 Köln
Fon +49 (0)221 599 56 47
www.kritischeaktionaere.de

From Marikana to Ludwigshafen: Along the platinum supply chain

◄ **Cover, flap, pp. 1, 2/3** Pictures secretly taken in the Marikana platinum mines of the underground work at a depth of approx. 1,000 meters. The only lighting in the shafts is the workers' headlights.

◄ **pp. 4, 6/7** Day and night: View from the informal settlement Nkaneng looking onto Lonmin's neighbouring Base Metal refinery. In the foreground on the left: one of the few measures taken after the Marikana massacre. In 2016 Lonmin ordered a large quantity of toilet houses, which can be placed on top of a hole in the floor.

◄ **pp. 8/9** Water is supplied to the informal settlements around Marikana through water tanks or individual, collectively used taps. This water point close to Nkaneng was installed in 2016. Women do the reproductive labour. In the background is one of the numerous ventilation systems for underground shafts.

◄ **pp. 10/11** Tree in Marikana. In the background: a transformer station and power lines that supply Lonmin's premises with electricity. Most of the inhabitants of the surrounding settlements, the Lonmin workers, have no electricity connection.

◄ **pp. 12/13** Counter motion of the ethical shareholder association *Dachverband der Kritischen Aktionärinnen und Aktionäre Deutschlands* not to grant discharge of liability to the Executive Board of the chemical group BASF for the financial year 2014, as it did not fulfil its responsibility in the supply chain in the case of Lonmin. Submitted on 15 April 2015 to BASF's shareholders' meeting on 30 April 2015 in Mannheim.

◄ **pp. 14/15** Bishop Jo Seoka, representative of Marikana's miners, speaks at the BASF shareholder meeting in Mannheim on 30 April 2015. To his left is Markus Dufner, Managing Director of the *Dachverband der Kritischen Aktionärinnen und Aktionäre Deutschlands*.

◄ **pp. 16/17** Late summer 2017 on the Willersinnweiher beach, a popular local recreation area in Ludwigshafen. Between the trees: a view of BASF operating under full capacity.

CONTENTS

22	**Foreword** *Bishop Jo Seoka*
28	**1. Introduction** *Britta Becker, Maren Grimm and Jakob Krameritsch*
46	**2. The convergence of corporate and government interests** The unfinished business of the Marikana massacre *Jakob Krameritsch and Maren Grimm*
62	**3. 'Only the stupidest countries stick to the economic boycott'** Germany, Switzerland and Austria as profiteers and pillars of the apartheid system *Simone Knapp, Jakob Krameritsch, Barbara Müller and Walter Sauer*
84	**4. Lonmin in context** The political economy of the South African platinum industry *An interview with Gavin Capps*
104	**5. There is no change in Marikana** The perspective of women *Asanda Benya and Judy Seidman*
130	**6. Confrontations with BASF** Additions to the company history and the Plough Back the Fruits campaigns *Maren Grimm and Jakob Krameritsch*
162	**7. Are we requesting too much?** Speech at the BASF AGM, Mannheim, Germany, 12 May 2017 *Mzoxolo Magidiwana*
166	**8. The theatre of irresponsibility** Cynicism and profitability *María do Mar Castro Varela*
182	**9. Hard rocks – soft rules** Human rights violations, the destruction of nature and the role of the state and corporations in international mining *Michael Reckordt*

196	**10. Horizons of responsibility**
Franziska Dübgen
212	**11. The limits of voluntary initiatives**
How business stands in the way of binding human rights standards
Sarah Lincoln
222	**12. The UN treaty on business and human right**
South Africa's role
Akhona Mehlo
240	**13. Rather part of the problem than the solution**
On the functions and effects of social audits
Carolijn Terwindt
258	**14. Power and the politics of corporate responsibility on the Platinum Belt**
A conversation with Dinah Rajak
276	**15. The chemistry is right**
The corporation and politics
Jan Pehrke
294	**16. Corporate structures and tax avoidance by BASF**
The platinum perspective
Christoph Trautvetter
312	**17. From BASF to Volkswagen and the World Bank**
German fingerprints at the scene of Lonmin's Marikana massacre
Patrick Bond
334	**18. Imperialist raw materials strategies in EU politics**
Boniface Mabanza
352	**19. Discourse (as) opposed to the facts**
Germany's links to the Marikana massacre have long gone unnoticed
Stefan Buchen
364	**20. Bared life**
Colonial and neo-colonial depictions of South African miners in the public imagination
Rosemary Lombard

378	**21. Postcolonial internationalism**	

378 **21. Postcolonial internationalism**
Thoughts on redefining global North–South solidarity in the twenty-first century
Alexander Behr and Trevor Ngwane

394 **22. 'The right to have rights'**
Global social rights as a tool against the power of transnational corporations and capitalist exploitation
Boris Kanzleiter and Britta Becker

416 **23. The real issues**
Politics against 'not wanting to know'
Stephan Lessenich

430 **24. A better life for all?**
Speech at the General Assembly, Berlin, 4 November 2017
Thumeka Magwangqana

434 **About the authors**
437 **Index**
444 **Credits, picture credits and video stills, thanks**

FOREWORD

Bishop Jo Seoka

The mining industry has always been the backbone of South African economy, and it still is. A healthy and sustainable mining sector accordingly should form part of the focus of our efforts to heal this country and its people. Nevertheless, the history of mining in South Africa has been and continues to be characterised by oppression and exploitation of the workers under the policy of the migratory system. Most of the miners are people with no education or a very elementary one that helps them take instructions from the employer. The new dispensation of 1994 did not assist much in changing the conditions at the mines, as there is still dissatisfaction with living and working conditions and with wages.

The Bench Marks Foundation, whose chairperson I have been since it was founded and launched in 2001, has been researching the Platinum Belt in the North West Province of South Africa. In 2003 we started to examine the transnational corporations that have operated in South Africa since 1994. In 2007 we produced the first report in a series popularly known as the 'Policy Gap', which focused on mining corporations such as Lonmin, the main platinum supplier of BASF, the biggest chemical enterprise worldwide, which is the focus of this book.

The Bench Marks Foundation had predicted mayhem on the Platinum Belt and around Lonmin. We warned the mining houses that a more difficult situation could be expected. Already in 2011, Lonmin was experiencing community protests resulting from frustrations and anger at the mining house's failure to heed the community's demands, such as the provision of employment opportunities for the local youth and the improvement of the appalling living conditions which, among other things, cause chronic sicknesses among children.

Therefore, there was already tension around the Platinum Belt and workers were talking about fighting for their labour to be compensated accordingly, since they worked under very tiring and dangerous conditions. For a period of twenty years, super-profits involving a return on investment of 30 per cent, way above the world benchmark of 8 per cent, enriched the shareholders and investors but impoverished the workers and surrounding communities.

In 2011 we decided to revisit the first edition of the 'Policy Gap' report and review whether there had been any changes in the behaviour of these corporations towards communities, and whether the mining houses had taken up any of the recommendations of the Bench Marks Foundation.[1] Lonmin was one of the mining houses whose challenging problems were highlighted in the report – such as high level of fatalities, poor living and working conditions for the miners, negative impact on small-scale farming, outsourcing of workers and environmental destruction.

We released a damning follow-up report on 14 August 2012. In a press release we outlined the outcomes of our report: 'The platinum mining companies appear on the surface to be socially responsible, respectful of communities and workers and contributing to host community development. Nothing can be further from the truth.'[2] Two days afterwards, on 16 August 2012, 34 mineworkers – on strike for better living and working conditions – were brutally killed by the South African police near the Lonmin-owned platinum mine in Marikana.

On 9 August 2012, the rock drill operators (RDOs) at Lonmin had begun their strike action to demonstrate their unhappiness with the mine management's refusal to negotiate a living wage. The RDOs led a march to Lonmin Platinum Division where the offices of Lonmin are located. There they were met with hostility from the mine management, who threatened the strikers with dismissal. In the following days, shooting was reported by various media – television, radio and print. People were killed, both mineworkers and policemen.

By 16 August, tension and conflict had escalated and there were fears that conflict might break out between the police and the striking miners. It was on this day that I decided to visit Marikana because it was within my episcopal jurisdiction and at the time I was also the president of the South African Council of Churches. My intention was to find out how we could defuse the volatile atmosphere that could lead to more people being killed. This I believe was prophetic since on that very day in the afternoon the police shot and killed 34 unprotected workers. The massacre happened when I had just relayed the message to Lonmin of the need for management to go and address the workers on the *koppie* (hill) about their demands. I had not yet taken the negative response of management back to the workers when the police opened fire on them after instructing me to leave the Lonmin area.

This is how my involvement began. Subsequently I met Maren Grimm and Jakob Krameritsch, two of the editors of this book. Our work together (and with many others) in challenging BASF – who claim that they are leaders when it comes to supply chain responsibility – has touched the nerve of corporations that have business interests on the African continent and especially in southern Africa. The campaign 'Plough Back the Fruits' (basflonmin.com) emerged in 2015 from our common discussions and research work – and from the understanding that we have to understand the larger picture of the supply chains that connect us globally in our struggle.

Our persistence, in attending and raising critical questions at the BASF AGM since 2015, has pushed the boundaries of engagement with BASF and Lonmin to a point where their business relations are strained and threatened. Not that our 'Plough Back the Fruits' campaign has called for BASF's withdrawal; instead it has always encouraged them to take full responsibility in ensuring that their supply chain be accountable and to admit direct and indirect responsibility for the 2012 massacre when innocent people's lives were sacrificed on the altar of capital.

I therefore consider it an honour to have been asked to write a foreword for this inspiring collaborative work. All the writers participating in this project are people committed to social justice, about which I am passionate. They have an amazing zeal and energy, having ventured where most fear to even talk about the situation and the issues that affect people's lives – human dignity and the integrity of the environment.

This publication, which starts by examining the long-term business relations between BASF and Lonmin, goes on to drill deeper – if I may use this metaphor here –into the hard rock of the persistent structures of inequality. By doing so we will understand that Marikana is not the tragic failure of an otherwise improving economic system but rather a calculated form of collateral damage.

Notwithstanding, it is never too late to mend what has been broken and to make amends for past failings. Like Nelson Mandela at his inauguration as president in 1994, we too hope that 'Never, never and never again shall it be that this beautiful land will again experience the oppression of one by another and suffer the indignity of being the skunk of the world.'

I trust the various chapters of this book will inspire and challenge the reader to take an active role in the campaign to change the attitudes and behaviour of the transnational corporations in former colonised countries. May this work challenge us to take a stand against injustices that undermine the dignity of workers and the integrity of Creation. So let us work together to eliminate oppression, exploitation, poverty and violence against workers, child labour and the abuse of women.

Aluta continua!

Johannesburg, December 2017

Notes

1 Jo Seoka, Policy Gap 6, 2011, www.bench-marks.org.za.
2 Press release by the Bench Marks Foundation, 14 August 2012, www.bench-marks.org.za.

▶ **pp. 26/27** Group photo with the women's organisation Sikhala Sonke in Nkaneng. Sikhala Sonke was founded on the day of the Marikana massacre – in an attempt to prevent it. Since then, the group has been working on campaigns to improve working and living conditions for people affected by mining. In the background: Lonmin's Base Metal Refinery.

1. INTRODUCTION

Britta Becker, Maren Grimm and Jakob Krameritsch
Translated by Joanna Mitchell

Nothing common is possible unless we refuse to base our life and our reproduction on the suffering of others, unless we refuse to see ourselves as separate from them.
– Federici and Henninger, 2012

On 16 August 2012, when 34 striking miners were shot by the South African police, four television channels and numerous photo journalists were on the ground.[1] Their images were sent around the world, shocking the global public. But apart from shock, what else do these images trigger? Do they shed any light on the events? Do they provide any aid or comfort to the affected families?

BASF and the Marikana massacre

Susan Sontag considers visual depictions of atrocities to have only limited emancipatory power, especially when they come from the global South and are received in the global North. In most cases, Sontag notes, these images 'confirm that this is the sort of thing which happens in that place. The ubiquity of those photographs, and those horrors, cannot help but nourish belief in the inevitability of tragedy in the benighted or backward – that is, poor – parts of the world' (Sontag and Kaiser, 2003). Sophisticated analyses, along with the structural causes and the transnational entanglements in violence, exploitation and suppression in the global South, retreat into the background of these images. This 'shared history'[2] is more often than not overlooked, while colonially shaped patterns of perception and hierarchies are left unchallenged.

In this sense, the photographs in this book have been selected with the purpose of contributing to a shared and common history. The images serve as more than simple illustrations or evidential material of the arguments put forth in this volume. They are, far more, documents which stand and speak for themselves in many regards, while simultaneously acting as testimony to transnational solidarity and cooperation.

In Europe, the Marikana massacre was widely perceived as an event confined to South Africa, while the transmitted photographs perpetuated the image of Africa as a continent of crises, conflicts and chaos (Mabe, 2007). In most cases, the 'uncivilised' (Duncan, 2014) workers were even blamed for their own deaths, while the police's reaction was noted as 'slightly exaggerated'. While the international community deplored this 'tragedy', sanction measures such as those taken during the apartheid era were not implemented.[3] In the meantime, the hazardous and miserable living and working conditions which the miners' strike sought to improve received little media coverage. The majority of the people in the immediate region where platinum – one of the world's most valuable metals – is mined live in corrugated iron shacks without access to running water, electricity or sewerage. The extraction of platinum requires the metal to be hammered, drilled and blasted out of the surrounding rock at a depth of up to 1,400 metres, and is considered to be one of the most dangerous jobs in the world. In 2016 alone, 27 people died in South African platinum mines and the number of fatalities within the platinum industry is increasing annually (Bergermann et al., 2017). However, far more mineworkers' lives are claimed by the occupational illness silicosis, a fatal lung disease. The air that is pumped underground via ventilation shafts is full of tiny dust particles, which cause chronic infections of the lung upon inhalation, leading to shrinkage of the lung and tissue hardening. According to a current study, 36 per cent of all mineworkers suffer from this condition due to insufficient ventilation of the mining shafts (Jephson, 2015). Outside the mines, the factories of the mine operators pollute the air: in addition to permanent particle pollution, the permitted (sulphur) dioxin emission values are regularly exceeded (Bahadur et al., 2016).

The public debate on the events leading up to the strike and the subsequent massacre of the Marikana mineworkers neglects the fact that, while European-based, transnationally operating corporations and their shareholders make high profits from the extraction, trade and processing of platinum, there has been no noticeable trickle-down effect for the mineworkers, despite the promises made by the pure doctrine of the 'free market'. Studies have shown that the real wages of South African workers, as well as their share of profits (which are primarily transmitted to tax havens), have been in steady decline since 1996 (Forslund, 2013a).

The media equally failed to mention the fact that BASF, the world's largest chemical company, is the main customer of the platinum mine in Marikana where the massacre took place. Founded in 1865 near the German city of Ludwigshafen as a producer of pigments and dyes, today BASF is a globally operating corporation with around 114,000 employees and over 570 business units in more than 80 countries. BASF is a product supplier to almost every branch of industry. The DAX-listed company's annual turnover is between 60 and 75 billion euro, of which 14 per cent is accounted for by BASF's role as an automotive supplier and its production of catalysts (BASF, 2016). For this industry, platinum and related precious metals – collectively referred to as platinum group metals (PGM) – are essential. With a value 60 times that of silver, the PGM, especially platinum and palladium, rank as the most valuable metals in the world after gold. BASF is the world's largest manufacturer of catalysts, making it the most powerful global player in the platinum business. In this position, the corporation makes annual purchases worth around 650 million euro from the mine operator Lonmin in Marikana.[4] This means that the mineworkers of Marikana produce an average of 2 million euro worth of platinum per day for BASF. Sourcing over 50 per cent of the mine's yearly production, BASF is Lonmin's main customer – the very mining company which is demonstrably co-responsible for the Marikana massacre, as well as for the miners' human rights-violating living conditions which have persisted in their current form for decades. In the following chapters of this book, Lonmin's complicity in these affairs will be portrayed and discussed in further detail against the backdrop of the still incomplete critical reappraisal of the massacre. The business relationship between BASF and Lonmin, spanning over 30 years, dates back to the apartheid era.

One supply chain, two realities

A very substantial part of BASF's corporate image relies on its business model which – according to the company's mission statement – combines 'economic success' with 'social responsibility'.⁵ As a founding member of the UN's Global Compact Initiative, BASF is committed to the principle that companies should respect and promote human rights in all areas of activity, as well as proactively prevent human rights violations. The German model company is equally committed to the UN Guiding Principles on Business and Human Rights, which define internationally recognised standards for companies' human rights due diligence obligations. Presenting itself as an international pioneer in 'voluntary supply chain responsibility', BASF has dedicated itself to fulfilling sustainability standards which 'exceed statutory requirements'.⁶ In this context, BASF not only promises to comply with fundamental principles of 'responsible care' such as human rights, occupational health standards, social sustainability and environmental protection, but also demands equal compliance from its suppliers as well. BASF's commitment to supply chain responsibility is, therefore, supposed to guarantee its clients that BASF's main suppliers such as Lonmin adhere to strict human rights and occupational health standards. The emphasis on 'social responsibility' is integral to the business model and trademark of BASF, increasing the company's market value – and thus its profits (Abelshauser, 2007). The events in Marikana, however, raise the question whether BASF's professed commitment to supply chain responsibility and human rights due diligence obligations is of any benefit to the most important subjects – the inhabitants of the platinum mining region. A thorough survey of the situation, as undertaken in this book, reaches the definite conclusion: no (Khulumani Support Group, 2015; Amnesty International, 2016; Bahadur et al., 2016). Six years after the massacre in Marikana, the situation still remains disgraceful: although the mine operators and police have been proven guilty, no reparations have been paid, and despite assurances to the contrary, the working and living conditions of mineworkers and their families have not improved.

How, then, is it possible that the people procuring one of the world's most valuable metals for a 'socially responsible' company such as BASF have been living in slums for decades? This question is not rhetorical in nature, but rather serves as an important starting point for this book. Accordingly, the authors of the essays collected here not only deal with the events and developments in Marikana, but also address the systematic suppression and structurally conditioned indifference of a neo-colonial raw material and economic policy and ask how this can be overcome or, at least to some extent, changed in a more equitable manner.

This book is the interim result and part of the transnational campaign Plough Back the Fruits (Bonase et al., 2016). The campaign's title was coined by the widows of the shot Marikana mineworkers and sums up one of their central demands: 'Give us back our rightful share of wealth and prosperity!' While the demand is directed towards the global North in general, BASF as a corporation sits at the very heart of this campaign. Since 2015, Plough Back the Fruits has been highlighting BASF's role and complicity in the Marikana massacre, as well as the mineworkers' living and working conditions. The campaign brings together two completely different realities not commonly associated, which in fact – as we will see– are deliberately separated from each other. On the one hand, we have an established, powerful German chemical corporation whose business model is to present itself as moral, sustainable and 'socially responsible'; on the other, we have the slums inhabited by the mineworkers, to whom a dignified life – a basic human right – seems unattainable. As different as these realities may seem, they are connected by a shared history. At the same time, they form the beginning and the end of a direct, and therefore very straightforward, supply chain.

Nonetheless, the collusion and multiple interrelations between these two physical realities addressed in this book do not constitute an isolated case. On the contrary, they describe the essential dynamics and symptoms of the prevalent global political economy. The BASF case study does more than simply illustrate the failure of 'voluntary supply chain responsibility' or the dangers of unbridled corporate power. Demonstrating the characteristics of neo-colonial raw materials policy, this case study also exemplifies the costs of an 'externalisation society' (Lessenich, 2016) and the accompanying 'imperial mode of living' (Brand and Wissen, 2017). Lastly, it is representative of the violent tendencies inherent in capitalist socialisation (Gerstenberger, 2017).

History of the present: On the 'platinum contact zone'[7]

The book brings current raw materials policy to the fore using the example of the platinum supply chain between Lonmin and BASF and thus between South Africa and Germany. It not only illustrates the violation of human rights by powerful corporations, but also addresses the underlying colonial continuities.

In post-apartheid South Africa, these continuities can be clearly observed. According to the Gini index, which measures the unequal distribution of income, the income gap in South Africa today is greater than ever before. The richest 8 per cent of the population is predominantly white, earning a higher income than the poorer 50 per cent of the population, who are almost exclusively black. This makes South Africa the global leader in terms of income inequality, while the mining industry benefits from this omnipresent cycle of poverty, unemployment and inequality (Alexander, 2010; Terreblanche, 2012; Saul and Bond, 2016). In the northern part of the country, migrant workers (about 8 per cent of miners are female) from the former homelands continue to work in the platinum, gold, diamond and coal mines for low wages and under extremely dangerous conditions. In order to comprehend the current discourses on supply chain responsibility and BASF's role in global raw material trading – in particular against the backdrop of South Africa's long-standing tradition of raw material exploitation – a historical approach is indispensable.

In their chapter, Barbara Müller, Simone Knapp, Jakob Krameritsch and Walter Sauer describe how countries of the global North and transnational corporations have not only contributed to the exploitation of migrant workers, but, as beneficiaries and thus part of the apartheid regime, also profited handsomely from it. Their essay focuses on Switzerland, Germany and Austria, whose historical role imposes an immediate responsibility to break with the continuities and adaptations of the colonially rooted apartheid regime. In an interview with Gavin Capps, an expert on platinum mining, it becomes clear just how strongly South Africa's apartheid past continues to shape the mining sector – and, with it, the country's entire political economy. Everywhere, we encounter the ramifications of colonial-racist legitimated exploitation in today's raw materials industry: some of these long-term effects have become exacerbated rather than overcome. Contemporary forms of economic exploitation, racism, classism and sexism perpetuate the social, cultural and economic marginalisation of black workers. This is exemplified by Asanda Benya and Judy Seidman in their portrayal of the different roles and positions assigned to women in mining. Benya and Seidman state that women are the 'shock absorbers of industry'; they are the invisible hands of the mining industry, securing high profits and acting as a lifeline in times of crisis.

The first set of chapters describes a type of contemporary 'platinum contact zone' (see front inside cover). This mind map lists the main actors in the field of platinum mining and trading with their differing positions of power and unequal distribution of capital. In addition, it cites laws, agreements, non-binding recommendations, initiatives and programmes that attempt to regulate relationships between the individual actors. Also mentioned are the socio-economic structures, often vastly superior in power, that influence and shape the actors' relationships and actions within the contact zone.

On this map, BASF appears as the central customer of South Africa's platinum production. The chapter by Maren Grimm and Jakob Krameritsch focuses on the corporation and its business activity in South Africa, which reaches back into the apartheid era. Also portrayed are the chemical company's past clashes with the campaign Plough Back the Fruits, which have predominantly taken place during its shareholder meetings. In his speech during BASF's 2017 shareholder meeting, Mzoxolo Magidiwana, one of the striking miners in 2012, documents his own personal story, as well as the dreadful living conditions in the peripheries of Lonmin's platinum mines. Mzoxolo Magidiwana was hit by nine police bullets; the fact that he survived verges on a miracle. In his speech, he asked BASF's CEO, Kurt Bock, whether wanting to live a life in dignity was too much to ask for. The reactions of the BASF board of executive directors during the shareholder meetings are examined by María do Mar Castro Varela. In her discourse analysis of a speech by BASF's CEO, she identifies strategies of postponement, concealment, trivialisation and distortion of the facts.

Voluntary supply chain responsibility: From suggestion to action

One of the campaign's reasons for the BASF case study is to critically scrutinise the concept of 'voluntary supply chain responsibility' as part of the company's business model and marketing strategy. The key problem introduced by Michael Reckordt is quickly outlined: the globalisation of the economy has not been accompanied by a globalisation of law. Falling into the category of soft law, existing UN and OECD Guiding Principles on supply chain responsibility serve as mere recommendations or standards that lack a legal binding character. Without an international criminal court to hold them accountable for their actions, transnational corporations can therefore largely operate with impunity. In addition, there is no coherent legal system to aid victims of human rights violations at the hands of corporations (Kramml et al., 2017). This means that, with a few national exceptions,[8] no legally binding regulations currently exist for the observance of human rights due diligences along the value chain. The German industry, including BASF, has blocked the introduction of such legally binding regulations on a national and European level. The commitment to voluntary – i.e. privatised and therefore not state-controlled – supply chain responsibility serves as an instrument to this end.

In the conversation with Dinah Rajak, it becomes apparent how companies such as BASF have helped to establish the Global Compact and similar initiatives for corporate responsibility, implementing their own voluntary measures that are beyond state control as a way of effectively forestalling legally binding regulations. Studies of voluntary supply chain responsibility in action show that this commitment primarily serves to polish the image of transnational companies (AK Rohstoffe, 2015), and does not provide one iota of help to people at the beginning of the supply chain, in raw material extraction sites or in textile factories. What could help these people are standards that are legally binding and independently monitored by independent state and local authorities, and that would result in lawsuits and sanctions in the event of non-compliance. With almost a third of allegations of human rights violations reported within the extractive sector – more than for any other economic sector – the need to hold transnational corporations finally accountable for human rights violations and breaches of economic and social rights seems particularly urgent for the raw materials sector (AK Rohstoffe, 2015). In this respect, too, the case study described here is exemplary for hundreds of similar cases.

The numerous state-led and transnational initiatives dedicated to introducing such hard laws differ greatly in their reach, scope and level of commitment. Given the tenacity with which they are developed – only to be met with resistance or watered down beyond recognition – one often gets the impression that their sole purpose is to suggest activity in this area, and to thus further delay appropriate solutions. Akhona Mehlo introduces these 'difficulties of the plain' (a term coined by Brecht) by focusing on the UN treaty on transnational corporations and human rights, while Sarah Lincoln addresses the German National Action Plan on Business and Human Rights. Both authors emphasise the importance of civil society participation in these processes, despite setbacks and frustrations. Carolijn Terwindt examines another measure taken by corporations in the context of supply chain responsibility which, despite first impressions, is in fact counterproductive: supplier audits. At least in their current, non-transparent form, these measures feign a reality which, to a somewhat dangerous extent, impedes rather than facilitates real improvements on the ground. To give one example, the supplier audits commissioned by the German clothing company KiK between 2007 and 2011 gave the Pakistani factory whose collapse in 2012 killed over 260 people a positive rating. Franziska Dübgen addresses the concept of 'responsibility' that underlies all these initiatives and debates from a socio-philosophical perspective and advocates its politicisation. She firmly rejects neoliberal discourses on the alleged power of the consumer, which shift responsibility downwards without changing power relations and structural injustices (Wicker, 2017). Dübgen makes it clear that responsibility is not a question of individual consumption, but a matter of political decisions based on power, privileges and interests.

Corporate power: Influencing the market and the state

The degree of corporate responsibility depends, then, on status, power and influence – which is exactly what transnational corporations in 21st century capitalism have at their disposal on a hitherto unprecedented scale. In fact, the concentration of power amassed by these corporations has reached such levels that the concept of a 'free market' opposed by a 'regulating state' – already disputable from an analytical perspective – must be expanded. The wealth, economic concentration and political power of transnational corporations have increased to such an extent that they tend to dominate both the markets and (international) politics. As their position of market dominance is accompanied by political influence, transnational corporations are capable of playing countries off against each other. These corporations are 'too big to fail', that is, they are systemically relevant to such a degree that they can effectively blackmail countries (or their respective governments) with threats of capital flight, as could be seen in the reactions to the 2008 financial crisis (such as bank bailouts or austerity policies). Other tactics include tax evasion techniques, relocation of profits to tax havens and driving countries into an often ruinous race for low tax rates. The impending threat of loss of jobs and withdrawal of taxable profits leads public policies to be aligned with the interests of these corporations. This is exemplified by the numerous initiatives adopted by various German ministries. The Marshall Plan with Africa (Federal Ministry of Economic Cooperation and Development), Compact with Africa (Federal Ministry of Finance) and the Pro!Africa initiative (Federal Ministry of Economics and Technology) all rely on private sector initiatives and are driven by politicians' search for new and lucrative investment opportunities, especially for German companies.

Christoph Trautvetter illustrates BASF's methods of tax evasion, highlighting their lobby work against the OECD and EU's planned reforms for achieving a more equitable, social and transparent international tax system. This modern form of corporate lobbying is no longer confined to generating positive PR for one's own cause; rather, it is about merging with politics. By now it has become common practice for people to move back and forth between political offices and positions within corporations; the 'revolving door effect' ensures a high degree of permeability (Attac, 2016). Originally, the lobby denoted the foyer area outside the hall where political decisions were taken; it was here that those who wished to influence these decisions, but did not themselves have access to the hall, would gather. However, today these same interest groups are directly involved in political decisions. They set standards, establish private regulatory systems, write laws, advise and reprimand ministers and heads of government,[9] delegate representatives to the ministries or – as in the case of members of BASF's board of executive directors – are official participants in G20 summits (Goffart, 2010; Crouch and Jakubzik, 2011).[10]

The chapter by Jan Pehrke examines this extended lobbyism practised by the German chemical industry and its consequences, using BASF as an example. However, the power exercised in this way is by no means democratically legitimised, but exclusively serves the profit interests of shareholders. The citizens themselves have no formal access to these companies, which is precisely why the concept of corporate social responsibility (CSR) can only be trusted to a limited extent. To rely on CSR to solve transnational problems would be tantamount to a declaration of bankruptcy of existing democratic institutions, as this would forfeit the objective of balancing public and economic interests (Kaleck and Saage-Maaß, 2016). Boniface Mabanza shows how the European Partnership Agreements with ACP countries (the group of African, Caribbean and Pacific countries) are dictated by corporate interests. With this, he places the central theme of this volume in the context of the EU states' interest-driven politics and the neo-colonial structural adjustment programmes of the WTO and the

World Bank. Patrick Bond examines the role of Germany in these organisations, thus also connecting the dots between PGM raw materials and the influential German automotive industry.

Invisibilisation and visibilisation: On the imperial mode of living and the externalisation society

From Marikana to Ludwigshafen, the case study of the platinum supply chain between Lonmin and BASF reveals a capitalist form of socialisation that has been conceived in terms of the 'imperial mode of living' and 'externalisation society'. Essentially, the concept of an 'imperial mode of living' argues that, since the days of colonialism, the resource- and emission-intensive production and consumption patterns in wealthy countries have been systematically based on, and indeed only made possible by, the sourcing of cheap resources and cheap labour in other regions of the world (Brand and Wissen, 2017).

At the many peripheries of the capitalist world economy, human labour exploitation, extraction of resources, release of toxins, storage of waste, devastation of natural territory, destruction of social spaces and the killing of people are bought at dumping prices – all so that the people in the centres of prosperity can sustain their imperial mode of life (Lessenich, 2016) This emission- and resource-intensive way of living has become normal in these centres of the world. The resulting routines and everyday practices remain largely unquestioned, and are now taken for granted across almost all social classes and milieus. Hence, with the majority of the population in these centres benefiting from this way of life, it concerns all of us – although to varying degrees.[11] The imperial mode of living is accompanied by global asymmetries of power, as its ecological and social costs are outsourced – in other words, externalised – to other people on this planet. According to Stephan Lessenich, the term 'externalisation society' rests on three fundamental pillars: exploitation, outsourcing and invisibilisation (Lessenich, 2016). Exploitation describes the one-sided appropriation of nature and labour, in which some benefit at the expense of others or of nature, for example by downgrading or undervaluing the work of others and paying little or no compensation (Biesecker and Winterfeld, 2014; Haidinger and Knittler, 2016:123).[12] Many forms of work are systematically outsourced, including dangerous or hazardous forms of production and – as in the case of BASF – environmental damage. This leads to the well-known paradox: in regions with a huge consumption of resources, environmental damage is very low, while in regions with very low consumption and a far lower ecological footprint environmental damage is often rampant. This becomes obvious when comparing the conditions in Marikana with those in Ludwigshafen. The case of BASF also shows that this type of outsourcing of risk also externalises social conflicts and the ensuing violence.

In order to sustain the imperial mode of living, it must appear legitimate to the majority of people. This means that the narrative of exploitation and outsourcing must be reinterpreted, repressed or rendered invisible. Any insight into the systematic cause of injustice, suffering and violence must not take hold in the collective consciousness. The mechanisms for achieving this type of invisibilisation are manifold.

Stefan Buchen examines one of these forms, raising the question why German journalists did not or could not link the Marikana massacre to the German economy in their reports. In this context, he also discusses why the business relationship between BASF and Lonmin was not discovered or discussed for such a long time. Rosemary Lombard examines dominant patterns of perception and their resulting narratives which systematically produce exclusions. On the basis of two stereoscopic photographs from the early twentieth century showing miners with machinery, she describes the 'symbolic annihilation' of and 'epistemic violence' against black miners, which – in a modified form – also become evident in the coverage of the Marikana massacre.

Corporate social responsibility (CSR) strategies constitute a part of this system of active suppression and (often tactical) ignorance. As Knud Andresen recently illustrated in VW's role in apartheid South Africa (Andresen, 2016), the beginnings of CSR derive from a situation in which corporations came under pressure and had to find ways to protect their business interests under morally and politically difficult conditions. Economist Dick Forslund comes to a similar conclusion in his study of Lonmin's sustainability reports:

> A tentative conclusion is that a mining operation can go on for as long as the company in charge of it displays public awareness of its failures, negotiates new agreements with the authorities, expresses respect for the laws and promises to correct failures in the coming years. This is what the corporate 'narrative' in the Sustainable Development Reports seeks to do in order to negotiate the political terrain. [...] No sanctions of any kind have ever been meted out against Lonmin (Forslund, 2013b).

In a 2015 interview on these reports, Forslund outlines how manipulative they truly are:

> The manner in which the reports are written is truly a high art. It really took me quite a while to realise that Lonmin hadn't built the 5,500 houses they had promised the workers. I spent five months reading these reports and it only dawned on me when proofreading my report that they hadn't built any houses

since 1999. That's nothing! Why didn't I see that? Because of the way they tell it. This fact was so carefully hidden away in the text between permanent promises and confessions that I overlooked it for a long time. [...] It disappeared in an avalanche of words (Forslund, 2015).[13]

This avalanche of words – and images, for that matter – conjures false realities which distort the perception of material and empirical truths and disappear behind Potemkin facades. The legend of Prince Potemkin does not necessarily stand for deception; it can also be interpreted as a secret consensus, in which Prince Potemkin knew that Empress Catherine II knew that the villages presented to her were only a facade, and vice versa. Thus, they wordlessly concluded an agreement that contained an 'as-if mode': if both parties accept the facades as reality, nobody can be prosecuted, and 'business as usual' can continue unabated.

However, it is not only a matter of the facades and their creators: it is also the receiving entities who, by placing their trust in them – whether intentionally or not – provide them with validity and stability. In this book, the Potemkin-like functional relationships are addressed at various points; they not only pervade the entire 'platinum contact zone', but are also vital for the maintenance of the prevailing political economy. As Stephan Lessenich emphasises, it is part of the work of emancipation to break up these Potemkinian loops of perception that obscure our view of the structural and inherent violence of capitalist socialisation.

The externalisation society's costs are as unevenly distributed in the global South as their benefits in the global North; in times of neo-liberal hegemony, this does not assist the forming of alliances for a more equitable world. In their chapters, Alexander Behr and Trevor Ngwane as well as Britta Becker and Boris Kanzleiter examine the challenges and possible solutions for new forms of transnational solidarity, as well as cross-border struggles against the externalisation society's causes and costs. Taking a closer look at the history of internationalist practice, Behr and Ngwane attempt to derive lessons for a new concept of solidarity between the North and South for the 21st century. In their essay on global social rights, Becker and Kanzleiter present an approach that goes beyond human rights discourses. As important, influential and valuable as the discourse on human rights has been, the concomitant Eurocentrism, depoliticisation and historical amnesia cannot be denied. The widespread ignorance displayed towards the ongoing struggles for human dignity in colonised societies serves as a particularly striking example (Mutua, 2001). The establishment of the concept of property and the emphasis on individual rights made possible by the Universal Declaration of Human Rights have given impetus to the capitalist form of economy (Klautke, 2008), and thus often legitimised the Western way of life (Samsa, 2006). Their enshrinement in national legislation continues to make these rights exclusively accessible to citizens of such states. Acknowledging and correcting these gaps, the approach manifested in global social rights, not only attempts to connect human rights with social and political rights, but furthermore calls for an unconditional and active appropriation of these rights. After all, it should be our common goal – as Silvia Federici invokes in the epigraph at the head of this chapter – to stand in defiance, to refuse a lifestyle which takes in its stride the suffering of others. Last but not least, in her speech held during Milo Rau's General Assembly, Marikana activist Thumeka Magwanqana demands a good life for all. We could not agree more.

Notes

1 Al Jazeera, Reuters and the two South African TV channels SABC and eNCA were on the ground during the events. For an analysis of the photographs taken, see the documentary film *Miners Shot Down* (Rehad Desai, RSA, 2014, 91 mins).
2 Historiographical concepts such as that of an 'entangled history' emphasise the importance of global cultural transfer processes beyond national units. See also Franziska Dübgen's relational model of 'political responsibility' in this volume.
3 See also the 2016 South Africa report by the UN Human Rights Commission and its demand for a prompt and effective reappraisal of the events, which the state-led commission failed to deliver. Available at: www.ohchr.org/EN/HRBodies/CHR/Pages/CommissionOnHumanRights.aspx.
4 According to figures requested by shareholders at BASF's annual meetings in 2015 and 2016, the transaction volume between Lonmin and BASF amounted to 450 million euro in 2014 and 650 million euro in 2015. The transaction volume for 2016 was not disclosed to shareholders by the BASF board of executive directors at the annual meeting on 12 May 2017. However, it was not expected to fall below that of the previous year.
5 See www.basf.com.
6 See www.basf.com/en/company/sustainability/management-and-instruments/topics.html.
7 The term 'contact zone' is derived from the term 'contact languages', which emerge when speakers of different languages interact with one another over longer periods of time. Examples include Fanakalo, a pidgin language spoken by migrant workers in the mining regions of South Africa. As a 'power-ridden scope of action' *(vermachteter Handlungsspielraum)*, the contact zone emphasises the dynamic, malleable character of hierarchies and the positions of power they entail. On the definition of the term, see Pratt (2010), Clifford (1997).
8 An exception is France, where a binding human rights due diligence (audit) obligation – albeit quite diluted – has been laid down by law. This shows the ambivalence of such 'voluntary commitments': on the one hand, they are used to prevent juridification in the sense of hard laws. On the other hand, the consistent reference to them can also become an instrument for gradually – and persistently – introducing such hard laws. See European Coalition for Corporate Justice, *French Corporate Duty of Vigilance Law*, www.corporatejustice.org.
9 Take, for example, BASF CEO Jürgen Hambrecht's vocal criticism of German Chancellor Merkel's official reception of the Dalai Lama in 2007. See Inacker (2017:24).
10 A G20 report from 2010 states that the managers – including BASF's CEO at the time, Jürgen Hambrecht – should 'work together with national finance ministers on the proposals to reform the banking sector'.
11 'The imperial mode of living is simultaneously necessity *and* promise, coercion *and* prerequisite of life and social participation. The relationship between coercion and enabling as well as the ability to avoid this coercion varies with the social position of individuals' (Brand and Wissen, 2017:56).
12 Feminist social and economic theory describes externalisation as a fundamental principle of capitalist economy that was already at work before the processes of globalisation, for example in the handling of care work. See, for example, Biesecker and Winterfeld (2014).
13 In this light, it is not surprising that in 2010 the Strategic Planning Society awarded Lonmin with the 'Lang Communications Award for Most Improved Narrative' in the competition for 'Strategic Value in Corporate Reporting'. During the award ceremony, the keynote speech emphasised the following: 'It is fundamentally important that good reporting gives investors and the public an understanding of what the business is trying to achieve, and that its business model and strategy is clear. The narrative plays a central part in achieving this.' See www.sps.org.uk

References

Abelshauser, W. (2007) *Die BASF. Eine Unternehmensgeschichte*, Münich

AK Rohstoffe (2015) *Verantwortung entlang der Lieferkette im Rohstoffsektor. Warum verbindliche menschenrechtliche Sorgfaltspflichten notwendig und machbar sind – Eine Auseinandersetzung mit Argumenten der deutschen Industrie*, Berlin

Alexander, P. (2010) Rebellion of the poor: South Africa's service delivery protests – a preliminary analysis, *Review of African Political Economy* 37, 123, pp. 25–40

Ambacher, J.E. (2010) *Südafrika. Die Grenzen der Befreiung*, Berlin

Amnesty International (2016) *Smoke and Mirrors: Lonmin's Failure to Address Housing Conditions at Marikana*, Johannesburg

Andresen, K. (2016) Moralische Ökonomie. Bundesdeutsche Automobilunternehmen und Apartheid, *Zeithistorische Forschungen/Studies in Contemporary History* 13, 2, www.zeithistorische-forschungen.de/2-2016/id=5354

Attac (2016) *Konzernmacht brechen! Von der Herrschaft des Kapitals zum Guten Leben für Alle*, Vienna

Bahadur, A., L. Kadel and S. Lincoln (2016) *Platinum for the World Market, Iron Shacks for Workers: Living and Working Conditions in Marikana Five Years after the Massacre*, Berlin and Johannesburg

BASF (2016) *BASF als innovationsstarker Automobilzulieferer ausgezeichnet*, www.basf.com/de/company/news-and-media/news-releases/2016/05/p-16-192.html, accessed 2 April 2018

Bergermann, M., A. Bahadur, L. Kadel and S. Lincoln (2017) *Das dunkle Geheimnis der Autoindustrie*, www.blendle.com/i/wirtschafts-woche/das-dunkle-geheimnis-der-autoindustrie/bnl-wirtschaftswoche-20171027-1c4036ec2e3?source=blendle-editorial&medium=twitter&campaign=DE-socialpicks-20171030, accessed 2 April 2018

Biesecker, A. and U.V. Winterveld (2014) Extern?: Weshalb und inwiefern moderne Gesellschaften Externalisierung brauchen und erzeugen, Working Paper 2014 of the DFG Research Group on Post-Growth Societies (DFG-KollegforscherInnengruppe Postwachstumsgesellschaft)

Bonase, N., M. Grimm, S. Knapp, J. Krameritsch, B. Mabanza and J. Seidman (2016) *Plough Back the Fruits: The Struggle for Justice and Restitution. The Bodymaps of the Widows of Marikana*, Hamburg

Brand, U. and M. Wissen (2017) *Imperiale Lebensweise. Zur Ausbeutung von Mensch und Natur im globalen Kapitalismus*, Münich

Clifford, J. (1997) *Routes: Travel and Translation in the Late Twentieth Century*, Cambridge, Massachusetts

Crouch, C. and F. Jakubzik (2011) *Das befremdliche Überleben des Neoliberalismus*, Berlin

Duncan, J. (2014) South African journalism and the Marikana massacre: A case study of an editorial failure, *Political Economy of Communication* 1, 2, www.polecom.org/index.php/polecom/article/view/22

Eggers, M.M. (ed.) (2009) *Mythen, Masken und Subjekte. Kritische Weißseinsforschung in Deutschland*, Münster

Federici, S. and M. Henninger (2012) *Aufstand aus der Küche. Reproduktionsarbeit im globalen Kapitalismus und die unvollendete feministische Revolution*, Münster

Forslund, D. (2013a) Mass unemployment and the low wage regime in South Africa, *New South African Review* 3, pp. 95–118

Forslund, D. (2013b) *Coping with Unsustainability*, Bench Marks Policy Gap 7 (Lonmin), www.bench-marks.org.za

Forslund, D. (2015) Interview, February, www.BASFLonmin.com

Gerstenberger, H. (2017) *Markt und Gewalt. Die Funktionsweise des historischen Kapitalismus*, Münster

Goffart, D. (2010) *Kritik am Gipfeltreffen: Von großen Plänen und heißer Luft*, www.handelsblatt.com/politik/international/kritik-am-gipfeltreffen-von-grossen-plaenen-und-heisser-luft/3472604.html, accessed 2 April 2018

Haidinger, B. and B. Knittler (2016) *Feministische Ökonomie. Eine Einführung*, Vienna

Inacker, M. (2017) Moral oder Profit. Bundeskanzlerin Merkel und Außenminister Steinmeier geraten in einen prinzipiellen Konflikt: Welche Stellung gebührt dem Markt und welche den Menschenrechten in der Außen- und Wirtschaftspolitik?, *WirtschaftsWoche*, 22 October

Jephson, G. (2015) Silicosis: The hidden legacy of gold mining in South Africa, in *Good Company: Conversations around Transparency and Accountability on South Africa's Extractive Sector*, Cape Town

Kaleck, W. and M. Saage-Maaß (2016) *Unternehmen vor Gericht. Globale Kämpfe für Menschenrechte*, Berlin

Kazeem, B. and J. Schaffer (2012) Talking back. bell hooks und Schwarze feministische Ermächtigung, in J. Reuter and A. Karentzos (eds.), *Schlüsselwerke der Postcolonial Studies*, pp. 177–188, Wiesbaden

Khulumani Support Group (2015) *'We Have to Talk, We Need Changes': Voices from Platinum Belt Mine Workers*, www.khulumani.net/truth-memory/item/1157-we-have-to-talk-we-need-changes-khulumani-s-report-of-the-conditions-of-migrant-mine-workers-on-the-platinum-belt.html, accessed 2 April 2018

Klautke, R. (ed.) (2008) *Globale soziale Rechte. Zur emanzipatorischen Aneignung universaler Menschenrechte*, Hamburg

Kramml, J., M. Kaufman, K. Küblböck and J. Planitzer (2017) *Mehr Menschenrechte in Rohstoff-Lieferketten. Sorgfaltspflichten – Handelspolitik – öffentliche Beschaffung*, Vienna

Lessenich, S. (2016) *Neben uns die Sintflut. Die Externalisierungsgesellschaft und ihr Preis*, Berlin

Mabe, J.E. (2007) *Was wissen Europäer kulturell von Afrika?*, Munich

Mutua, M. (2001) Savages, victims, and saviors: The metaphor of human rights, *Harvard International Law Journal* 42, 201

Pratt, M.L. (2010) *Imperial Eyes: Travel Writing and Transculturation*, London

Samsa, G. (2006) Hype oder kommunistisches Szenarion, *AK – analyse & kritik – Zeitung für linke Debatte und Praxis* 508

Saul, J. and P. Bond (2016) *South Africa: The Present as History – From Mrs Ples to Mandela and Marikana*, Johannesburg

Schaffartzik, A., A. Mayer, S. Gingerich, N. Eisenmenger, C. Loy and F. Krausmann (2014) The global metabolic transition: Regional patterns and trends of global material flows, 1950–2010, *Global Environmental Change* 26, pp. 87–97

Sontag, S. and R. Kaiser (2003) *Das Leiden anderer betrachten*, Munich

Terreblanche, S. (2012) *Lost in Transformation: South Africa's Search for a New Future since 1986*, Johannesburg.

Wicker, A. (2017) Conscious consumerism is a lie. Here's a better way to help save the world, www.qz.com/920561/conscious-consumerism-is-a-lie-heres-a-better-way-to-help-save-the-world/, accessed 2 April 2018

2. THE CONVERGENCE OF CORPORATE AND GOVERNMENT INTERESTS: THE UNFINISHED BUSINESS OF THE MARIKANA MASSACRE

Jakob Krameritsch and Maren Grimm
Translated by Simon Phillips

Lonmin has approximately 25,000 permanent employees and 8,000 contract and temporary workers based in Marikana, close to Johannesburg. On average they mine 26,000 tonnes of rock every day, resulting in the production of roughly 3,500 ounces of PGM (Platinum Group Metals).[1]

Marikana is located in the Bushveld Complex, which is home to about 95 per cent of the world's known PGM deposits.[2] In 2012, Lonmin, the world's third-largest platinum company, had an average daily turnover of 5 million euro.[3] In contrast, Lonmin's mineworkers received an average of 400 euro per month. This put them close to the poverty line.[4] However, on average, their wages also had to help provide for an additional eight people.[5]

On 10 August 2012, around 3,000 rock drill operators (RDOs) – workers who use hydraulic drills to hammer rock out of the ground – put down their tools in protest against the low pay and poor living conditions that they were facing. Moreover, they knew that RDOs in other platinum mines were paid better. At the same time, the RDOs in Marikana also withdrew their confidence from the National Union of Mineworkers (NUM), arguing that the union had been co-opted by the company a number of years previously, and that it represented the interests of the company more strongly than the interests and needs of the labour force. As a result, the workers began organising outside the union within independent worker committees.[6] Their goal was simple: to speak with Lonmin's management directly about salary increases. Six days later, 34 workers were shot dead by the police and more than 70 were injured, some of them seriously. How could this happen, and who bears the blame?

It should not be necessary to go into the details of what happened in Marikana here, as it has been covered several times elsewhere.[7] Instead, in this context, it is far more important to focus on the status quo in terms of understanding the massacre and, thus, the factors that led to it, who should be held accountable and to what extent. The causes of the massacre and the distribution of responsibility are contentious issues and have been ever since the massacre occurred. However, despite their complexity, it is possible both to name individual culprits and to point to the chain of events and the historical structures that contributed to the massacre.

Immediately after the massacre, the police, the government and the management of the mine set the tone of the debate. They unanimously claimed that the police had acted out of self-defence and had done nothing wrong; after all, police officers had been attacked by violent workers. The workers' opinions went unheard during this debate. Moreover, the media particularly ignored the workers' voices during the first few weeks, and it was during this time that the workers' actions were criminalised.[8] The claim that the police had acted in self-defence was still put forward during the commission of inquiry established by President Zuma shortly after the massacre. The commission was provided with a mandate to investigate the events that occurred between 10 and 16 August 2012, which resulted in the deaths of 44 people.

The first serious cracks in the argument of self-defence began to appear with the publication of research undertaken by committed journalists,[9] activists, researchers[10] and filmmakers,[11] who provided the strikers with a voice when reconstructing the events. The Farlam Commission, named after its chair, a retired judge, spent more than two and a half years investigating what happened at the mine. It was not until June 2015 that the commission finally published its results. Although the police had done everything they could to prop up their argument of self-defence, it fell apart during the course of the inquiry. At the very latest, their claims had been completely discredited by the time the report was published by the chair of the inquiry in October 2014.[12] The Farlam Commission concluded that the police had misappropriated evidence, falsified documents, colluded to produce false statements, refused to make statements, were guilty of perjury and had pressured and even tortured potentially incriminating witnesses.

The politicised and highly militarised actions of the police during the seven days beginning with the start of the strike until the massacre on 16 August 2012 bear all the hallmarks of a police state. Lonmin's approach certainly reflected the interests of industry and government, but it was the company that provided the police with direction, with the police executing the plan.

Various conflicts of interest also contributed to the massacre. On the one hand, instead of entering into talks with the workers' organisations, Lonmin was prepared to use almost any means to keep open the existing channels for wage negotiations with the miners' union. However, as mentioned above, the NUM had already been co-opted by the company. Furthermore, the NUM was concerned that a competitor – the Association of Mineworkers and Construction Union (AMCU) – might benefit from the situation and widen its membership base. Even the ruling party – the African National Congress (ANC) – wanted to prevent the NUM from losing ground, as the union played an important role in COSATU, the trade union federation, which, together with the ANC and the South African Communist Party, has formed the governing alliance since 1994. Ultimately, the ANC also feared that a rebel former party member, Julius Malema, might exploit the mood and found a rival political party.

Government officials and Lonmin's management were clearly more concerned about protecting capital than the interests of the labour force. The convergence of interests between Lonmin and the ruling party, which has been described as 'toxic collusion between state and capital',[13] had a strong impact on the actions of the police. Cyril Ramaphosa[14] is exemplary of this situation. In 2012, Ramaphosa held 9.1 per cent of Lonmin's shares via Shanduka, an investment company that he founded – he was also a member of the company's board. Using his influence within the ANC, Ramaphosa put pressure on the police and the Department of Mineral Resources to end the strike as quickly as possible and to do so by intensifying the deployment of the police – instead of negotiating with the strikers. Moreover, Ramaphosa criminalised the strike and called for resolute action to be taken against the workers.[15]

There is much to suggest that the police, who were armed with sharp ammunition, did not even act out of self-defence at the first 'scene' of the massacre – a large boulder that served as the worker's meeting place. The 328 bullets that 45 police officers fired in 11 seconds at the workers, which resulted in the murder of 17 workers, some seriously injured, were not fired at people who were attacking, but fleeing. The police killed a further 17 people at 'Scene 2', about 200 metres away. Today, no one denies that murders were committed in Marikana. Moreover, we now know that the police did not act in self-defence; they undertook an execution.[16] The police shot dead people at close range who had raised their hands and surrendered; they shot others from behind as they tried to flee.

Alongside the police, the officers on the scene and government officials, Lonmin is certainly the next main culprit. In fact, the company is responsible for the murder of the workers on a number of levels.

Lonmin's responsibility begins with a simple but profound fact: although the Social and Labour Plan legally obliged it to do so, Lonmin made no attempt to improve the living conditions of its workers or their community. Instead, false promises reigned for more than a decade: in 2006, Lonmin promised to build 5,500 new homes by 2011. However, no more than three houses were ever built because the company claimed that it could not afford to continue with the project. However, during this time the management paid out US$607 million in dividends, and a further US$160 million to a subsidiary based in Bermuda.[17] As Greg Marinovich emphasises, at a time when the platinum industry was booming, the company abandoned its workforce in Marikana:

> Just 20 per cent of the dividends paid out to Lonmin shareholders during the boom years of 2007 and 2008 would have paid for the entire cost of the 5,500 houses they had committed to build. It was during those good years that a soaring platinum price should have funded all of Lonmin's social responsibilities – workers' housing, water, contributing to local schools, infrastructure, etc. The company failed to meet these contractual commitments and the Department of Mineral Resources failed to force them to do so [...].[18]

Second, a further serious debt weighs on Lonmin's shoulders because the management refused to comply with one of the workers' central demands: to speak with them. Moreover, the company refused to do so despite the fact that it knew that it was paying its workers less than those of other platinum mining companies.[19] Although Lonmin initially sent out other signals and provided the workers with good reason to hope that they would indeed be invited to talks, ultimately the management refused to meet the workers. Moreover, it continued to do so even when the respected Bishop Jo Seoka, who also offered to mediate on the day of the massacre, pleaded with them to do so. Instead, the company urged the deployment of the country's highly militarised police force, and this significantly contributed to the bloodshed. Industry must have placed immense pressure on Lonmin. This pressure is clear from a report by the German Mineral Resources Agency (DERA), an information and consultancy platform for the extractive industry. A key study by DERA on South Africa briefly outlines the position and the interests of the extractive industry with regard to Marikana: non-tariff wage increases were viewed as constituting 'a serious precedent' and were to be avoided at all costs.[20] Lonmin's stubborn refusal to negotiate with the strikers can only be explained by the pressure placed on it by its business partners in terms of cost and the warnings it received from industry.

Third, Lonmin escalated the situation by forcing its workers to break their strike; it did so by threatening them with dismissal, even though the company knew that this could lead to clashes between the workers. In fact, the company's actions resulted in deadly clashes that cost four workers their lives even before the massacre in Marikana had taken place.

Fourth, Lonmin's security officers started the violence. On 10 August, the first day of the strike, Lonmin's private security shot at the unarmed workers in an attempt to break up a workers' meeting. The evidence leaders later unequivocally rejected Lonmin's excuses and stated for the record that the actions of the security officers were unjustifiable. In addition, two workers were injured the next day when the (still unarmed) strikers marched to the NUM's office. It was only after these two incidents, and as a reaction to the attacks and the threats they had faced, that some of the workers armed themselves with sticks and spears. During a confrontation with the police, three workers were killed (by the police) and two police officers were killed (by the strikers).

Fifth, Lonmin's management collaborated with the police to ensure that the strike was ended as soon as possible. The company even participated logistically and provided its infrastructure to the highly militarised police operation. Lonmin helped the police identify the leaders of the strike (the majority of whom were later killed or at least severely injured), and permitted the police to use its estate and safari grounds. Moreover, it orchestrated the pressure that was exerted by the politicians and the government ministries to criminalise the strike. This places Lonmin at the centre of the 'toxic collusion' between corporate and public interests which led to the massacre.

Despite pressing evidence that proves beyond all doubt that the police and Lonmin were responsible for the massacre, the Farlam Commission's report remains cautious and inconclusive: instead of clearly appointing blame and demanding real consequences, it simply recommends 'further investigation'.

The commission dragged on for two and a half years; unsurprisingly, its conclusions fell short of many people's expectations.[21] The list of its failures, omissions, gaps, errors, faults and mishaps is long.[22] Not a single member of the police was found guilty of murder, and none of the police officers who were shown on television opening fire on the strikers were even summoned as witnesses to testify before the commission. Finally, the commission's scope was limited by the government, and this made it impossible to carefully examine the responsibility of the state. Only two senior police commissioners were ever suspended from duty – on full pay.

The Farlam Commission's 'unfinished business' weighs heavy – particularly on the people who were affected by the massacre.[23] The voices of these people – the workers and their communities – were broadly lacking during the commission's hearings, and many of the demands made by the relatives of the victims were disregarded and have yet to be fulfilled. Neither the government nor Lonmin has ever paid reparations.[24] Lonmin merely promised the widows of murdered mineworkers that the company would cover the costs of the education of some of the children. In addition, the widows were also offered the possibility of replacing their dead husbands in the company. Due to a lack of other sources of income, they had to accept jobs that now separate them from their children and families. Many of the widows work in the mines – under the same terms and conditions as their husbands did before they were killed for going on strike against them. Ntombizolile Mosebetsane, whose husband was killed in the massacre, works as a cleaner in Lonmin's headquarters. She cleans the offices of the management who are co-responsible for the death of her husband.

The course taken by the commission and its findings make it quite clear that a single report with such a limited legal range could not adequately account for or address all of the specific causes, let alone the transnational connections and historical structures that led to the massacre. The reasons behind the massacre can be found on many levels. The commission also largely ignored the underlying socio-economic factors that hark back to colonial times and apartheid. However, these are all the more important when it comes to not only naming individual culprits, but helping to prevent similar events in the future. After all, the role and responsibility of Lonmin's customers – transnational corporations such as BASF – remained hidden.

The publication of the Farlam Report has done nothing to strengthen the work of groups that have been developing a more differentiated reappraisal of Marikana and struggling for justice ever since the massacre occurred; rather, the report marks the beginning of a new phase for these groups. This book should be understood as contributing towards this new phase of reappraisal.[25]

Notes and references

1. This makes Marikana the second-biggest platinum mine in the world. See, Lonmin plc, *Interim Report 2017* (Operating statistics), available online. In 2012, the year of the massacre, Lonmin had around 28,000 employees and 10,000 contract and temporary workers.
2. A Citigroup study conducted in April 2010 designated South Africa as the resource-richest country in the world and estimated the value of these resources at 2,500 billion euro. PGMs accounted for the lion's share of this value at around 2,300 billion euro, alongside gold, diamonds, titanium, coal, etc. For details, see Samantha Ashman, 'The South African economy: The mineral-energy-finance complex redubbed?', in Gilbert Khadiagala, Prishani Naidoo, Devan Pillay and Roger Southall, *New South African Review 5:Beyond Marikana* (Johannesburg, 2015), pp. 67–84; here p. 68. Data on the extent of the platinum deposits vary; the German Mineral Resources Agency quotes it as 95 per cent. See Deutsche Industrie- und Handelskammer, BGR, Deutsche Rohstoffagentur and Germany Trade & Invest (eds.), *South Africa: Möglichkeiten deutscher Unternehmen für ein Engagement im südafrikanischen Rohstoffsektor. Rohstoffvorkommen – Projekte – Investitionsbedingungen* (Bonn, 2013), p. 14. According to the United States Geological Survey (USGS), 133 tonnes of platinum were mined in South Africa in 2012; Russia, as the second-largest producer, exported 24.6 tonnes. USGS data and tools, www.usgs.gov/products/data-and-tools/overview.
3. See Greg Marinovich, *Murder at Small Koppie: The Real Story of the Marikana Massacre* (Johannesburg, 2016), p. 52.
4. See Zwelinzima Vavi, 'Minimum wage: Poverty report strengthens Cosatu's case', *Daily Maverick*, 18 February 2015, www.dailymaverick.co.za/opinionista/2015-02-18-minimum-wage-poverty-report-strengthens-cosatus-case/#.WvinB_5PqPY.
5. For information on this, see *Plough Back the Fruits: Voices from the Platinum Supply Chain*. Available at: basflonmin.com/home/de/movies.
6. See also the description of the massacre based on interviews with the workers in Peter Alexander, Thapelo Lekgowa, Botsang Mmope and Luke Sinwell, *Das Massaker von Marikana. Widerstand und Unterdrückung von ArbeiterInnen in Südafrika* (Vienna, 2013); Luke Sinwell and Siphiwe Mbatha, *The Spirit of Marikana: The Rise of Insurgent Trade Unionism in South Africa* (London, 2016).
7. See an earlier report: Alexander, Lekgowa, Mmope, and Sinwell, *Marikana*. This also provided the basis for the documentary by Rehad Desai (*Miners Shot Down*, RSA, 2014, 91 mins). More detailed reports were published later: Marinovich, *Murder*; Peter Alexander, 'Marikana Commission of Inquiry: From narratives towards history', *Journal of Southern African Studies* 42 (2016), pp. 815–839. The following text is also highly recommended: *Heads of the Argument of Evidence Leader* (the final report by the Heads of Evidence of the Marikana Commission of Inquiry), 27 October 2014, www.sahrc.org.za/home/21/files/marikana-report-1.pdf.
8. See Jane Duncan, 'South African journalism and the Marikana massacre: A case study of an editorial failure', *Political Economy of Communication* 1–2 (2013). A day after the biggest massacre of South African citizens since Sharpeville in 1960, the police minister, Nathi Mthethwa, stated in an address to the police officers who were in Marikana: 'I can assure you, as your Minister and on behalf of the government, the entire executive and the President and this country's top military personnel: We are all behind you. From my heart, as your Minister and on behalf of the government, I want to thank you.' Mthwethwa, who is now Minister of Culture, set out the approach of the government's ministries. The police were backed by the government and Lonmin, and the striking workers were kept at a distance; *Final Report of the Heads of Evidence*, p. 547.
9. See Greg Marinovich, 'The murder fields of Marikana: The cold murder fields of Marikana', *Daily Maverick*, 8 September 2012.
10. The first counter-narrative was the September National Imbizo, *Bloody Marikana: What the media didn't tell you!* (19 August 2012). The first detailed account was published by Peter Alexander, Theapelo Lekgowa, Bongani Mmope and Luke Sinwell, *Marikana: A View from the Mountain and a Case to Answer* (Johannesburg, 2012). See also Crispen Chinguno, 'Marikana and the post-apartheid workplace order', SWOP Working Paper, Johannesburg, 2013.
11. See Rehad Desai, *Miners Shot Down*, RSA, 2014, 91 mins.
12. See *Final Report of the Heads of Evidence*, p. 547.
13. *Final Report of the Heads of Evidence*, pp. 505ff. The quote is from Dali Mpofu, one of the solicitors who represented the miners who were killed or injured.

14 Cyril Ramaphosa, born in 1952, a lawyer who was arrested several times as an anti-apartheid activist, co-founded the NUM in 1982. Returning from exile in the UK and Sweden, Ramaphosa quickly rose up the ranks within the ANC and became its chief negotiator in the transitional talks with the National Party in the early 1990s. From 1996 onwards, Ramaphosa retired from politics and made a career as a private entrepreneur, manager and supervisory board member. He is considered to be one of the richest people in South Africa. From 2010, until his election as ANC vice president in December 2012, he owned shares in Lonmin. After Zuma's resignation, Ramaphosa, who had been elected chair of the ANC in December 2017, was elected president of South Africa on 15 February 2018.

15 For more details, see Peter Alexander, 'Cyril Ramaphosa's Marikana massacre "apology" is disingenuous and dishonest', *The Conversation*, 11 May 2017, www.theconversation.com/cyril-ramaphosas-marikana-massacre-apology-is-disingenuous-and-dishonest-77485.

16 Further evidence can be found in Vicky Abraham, 'Marikana massacre: Scene 2 officers speak out', *Mail&Guardian*, 11 February 2018, www.mg.co.za/article/2018-02-11-marikana-massacre-witnesses-to-slaughter-at-scene-2/.

17 See *Final Report of the Heads of Evidence*, p. 30; Dick Forslund, 'The Bermuda connection: Profit shifting, inequality and unaffordability at Lonmin 1999–2012', Johannesburg, 2015, www.aidc.org.za/download/Illicit-capital-flows/BermudaLonmin04low.pdf.

18 Marinovich, *Murder*, pp. 50f.

19 See Andrew Bowman and Gilad Isaacs, 'Demanding the impossible? Platinum mining profits and wage demands in context', Johannesburg, 2014, www.wits.ac.za/media/news-migration/files/Platinum%20Report%20.pdf.

20 Deutsche Industrie- und Handelskammer et al., *Südafrika*, pp. 47f.

21 See Jakob Krameritsch, 'The massacre underlines the wrongness of the situation', Sequences of interviews by Jakob Krameritsch with Primrose Sonti and Trevor Ngwane (about their work) in the wake of the Marikana massacre, in Suzana Milevska (ed.), *On Productive Shame, Reconciliation and Agency* (Berlin, 2014); see also Dumisa Ntsebeza, 'The Marikana Commission: Sacrifice of the great unwashed', Speech given on 20 August 2015 at the University of Cape Town. www.youtube.com/watch?v=Gg1nfwOO3yM.

22 See Kally Forrest, 'Marikana Commission: Unearthing the truth, or burying it?', SWOP Working Paper 5, 2015, www.raith.org.za/docs/KallyForrest_SWOP-Forrest-Report-FINAL.pdf.

23 This is also stated in the UN Human Rights Commission's report on South Africa, which demands a swift and specific review of the events. See the overview at: www.humanrights.ch/de/service/laenderinfos/suedafrika/.

24 The government has repeatedly announced that compensation is to be paid, but has yet to act on its promises. See for example, Govan Whittles, 'Cyril's atonement for Marikana: Compensation is nearly ready', *Mail&Guardian*, 20 February 2018. After fatal accidents, the immediate family has the right to receive a payment. The amount depends on the length of time their relative was employed by a corporation. Lonmin has largely met its obligations to pay these mostly quite low levels of payment to workers killed in the massacre.

25 Many groups are involved in this process, most notably those directly injured by the massacre. This includes the relatives of the people killed in August 2012, those who were injured by the police during the massacre and more than 270 workers who were wrongfully arrested or detained, some of whom were tortured. There are also local organisations such as the women's organisation Sikhala Sonke, the Wonderkop Land Claim Committee, independent workers' committees and not least the AMCU union. In their various struggles for justice in the aftermath of the massacre, they are supported by individual progressive South African lawyers' associations such as the Legal Resources Centre (LRC) and the Centre for Applied Legal Studies (CALS) as well as civil society organisations such as the Marikana Support Group or the Khulumani Support Group, as well as NGOs in South Africa and Europe such as the Bench Marks Foundation, AIDC (Alternative Information & Development Centre), KASA (Church Workplace Southern Africa), the Confederation of Critical Shareholders, Bread for the World, the Rosa-Luxemburg-Stiftung, KEESA (a debt relief and compensation campaign in southern Africa) and SOLIFONDS. The last-mentioned NGOs are Plough Back the Fruits' project partners.

◀ **pp. 54/55** Re-enactment of the Marikana massacre in a play of the women's organisation Sikhala Sonke, performed near the original location. One of the actresses, Ntombi Mthethwa (in the foreground), was seriously injured in a police raid one month after the massacre and has had to wear a support belt ever since.
◀ **pp. 56/57** Another scene from Sikhala Sonke's play. Left in the picture is chairwoman Thumeka Magwangqana.
◀ **pp. 58/59** BASF CEO, Kurt Bock, at a press confer-ence in February 2016, referring to the report of the state commission of inquiry and using the sentence shown to trivialise the responsibility of his platinum supplier, Lonmin, for the massacre in Marikana. Part of the ARD *Panorama* report 'Exploitation in Africa. What is BASF's responsibility?' aired on 28 April 2016. *Translation: The report says, Lonmin could have acted differently.*

Marikana, 16 August 2016: Three pictures from the commemoration of the fourth anniversary of the massacre
▲ AMCU union chairman, Joseph Mathunjwa, and Lonmin's CEO, Ben Magara, embrace each other on stage.
▲ Thousands of Lonmin's workers gather in front of the stage and on the hill that was the starting point of the massacre.
▶ Minute of silence at 'Scene 2' of the massacre. In the background: lawyer Dali Mpofu, Joseph Mathunjwa and Bishop Jo Seoka; in the foreground: Ntombizolile Mosebetsane, whose husband was murdered here.

3. 'ONLY THE STUPIDEST COUNTRIES STICK TO THE ECONOMIC BOYCOTT': GERMANY, SWITZERLAND AND AUSTRIA AS PROFITEERS AND PILLARS OF THE APARTHEID SYSTEM

Simone Knapp, Jakob Krameritsch, Barbara Müller and Walter Sauer
Translated by Sally McPhail

Let's start by taking a look back: in 1948, the National Party won the general elections in South Africa and immediately started to implement its programme of apartheid, which in many cases merely systematised the colonial legislation already in place. The foundational law was the 1950 Population Registration Act, which was aimed at classifying every person according to race as 'white', 'black', 'Indian' or 'coloured'. Hundreds of additional laws were passed that regulated everyday life for the groups thus constructed, and defined the systematic economic, social, cultural and political privileges of the white minority.

South Africa and apartheid from a global perspective

With the introduction in the 1960s of the policy of 'separate development', the apartheid regime sought to divide and separate the black population into 'national groups', which were allocated separate territories styled as 'homelands'. The ultimate intention was to remove all black people to their various homelands where they would exercise their rights of citizenship, leaving the white minority in control of the major part of the landmass and especially of the cities and economic heartlands of South Africa. Those black people seeking work in the cities would require a pass or permit to remain there; otherwise they and all the black unemployed would be removed forcibly to the impoverished homelands. Resettlement and deprivation of citizenship were a direct result of this policy.

The homelands thus served the apartheid regime as a reservoir of cheap labour. Poorly paid and poorly educated black workers were to provide labour and profits for the white minority, and were deprived of a fair share of the emerging wealth and improved infrastructure of the country. They found work in white households, on farms and plantations, in factories and not least in the mines, working under restrictive labour laws and inhumane conditions for extremely low wages. These elements of the apartheid capitalist system created ideal conditions for astronomical profits in the mining industry, which formed the economic backbone of the country. From an early stage, companies based in the US and Europe were heavily involved in South African industry.

Starting in the 1950s, the black majority responded to the oppression of the apartheid regime by staging protests, demonstrations, strikes and riots. These were savagely repressed. The Sharpeville massacre of 1960 was followed by the banning of the African National Congress (ANC) and the Pan Africanist Congress (PAC), while the Soweto student uprising of 1976 was put down by force. In the 1980s large-scale unrest in the townships and widespread strikes met with the declaration of a state of emergency. During this time, police powers were expanded, state terrorism was implemented in a systematic way, the media was even more strongly censored than before and around 40,000 opponents of the regime were imprisoned and detained without trial.

Even if the extent of police and state violence was enormous, the apartheid regime cannot be reduced to a repressive police state. Apartheid was a system that legitimised the systematic exploitation and suppression of the black majority, and strove by every means to advance the economic, political and cultural supremacy of the white minority.

How could such a regime become established in a world which had just survived the Second World War, and how was it able to sustain itself for over four decades? The spread of the 'imperial mode of living', the continuity of colonial racist ideology and the context of the Cold War were undoubtedly determining factors. The bipolar division of the world ensured that the Western powers lent significant economic, ideological and military support to the professedly anti-communist apartheid regime, despite international displays of outrage and the implementation of sanctions. In 1974 South Africa was prohibited from participating in the UN General Assembly, and in 1977 an arms embargo was imposed on the country. The UN General Assembly repeatedly called for measures such as boycotts and sanctions to isolate the regime. However, these embargoes and economic boycotts were just as repeatedly circumvented by individual countries, primarily the United Kingdom, France, (West) Germany and the US. Apartheid promised such countries unparalleled profits, in particular in the raw materials sector. As the demand for raw materials boomed in the 1960s and 1970s, apartheid South Africa with its rich resources of minerals became an ideal trading partner for the West.

During these decades, the imperial mode of living, which was the preserve of the upper class and parts of the middle class, became the internalised ideal and model of all classes in the global North (Brand and Wissen, 2017:85). This caused the demand for raw materials by the resource- and emission-intensive countries of the North to explode. Between 1960 and 1970 alone, the net imports of fossil energy sources to the Western industrialised countries tripled in number (Schaffartzik et al., 2014:7–97).

Circumventing multilateral sanctions was of vital importance for the apartheid regime. Apartheid was not limited to South Africa, but was a globally embedded regime which could only have survived, indeed even flourished, for as long as it did because of the international support it received. Its legitimisation and longevity can only be explained by looking at the close networks it developed with other countries and with companies operating on a transnational basis. The apartheid regime was actually dependent on its raw materials exports, which on average accounted for two-thirds of all incoming foreign currency. It would therefore have been fairly easy to use South Africa's dependency on this sector as a weapon against the apartheid regime, as was demanded by the South African freedom movements. However, the habitus of the imperial mode of living, the hegemonic political will of the West and the prospect of substantial profits caused individual countries and transnational companies to act in a different way.

Companies based in Germany, Austria and Switzerland invested in the apartheid state right to the end. Indeed, it is not by chance that these three German-speaking countries in central Europe have been selected as case studies for this volume. In Germany, BASF was founded more than 150 years ago and the company continues to have its headquarters there. Switzerland is a tax haven and the raw materials trade centre of Europe, while Austria serves as an example of how a comparatively small and insignificant country could nevertheless become a powerful force in the extended apartheid system.

GERMANY
'A bleak chapter in the history of the German economy'

While the Nuremberg Trials were taking place in Germany, in 1948 the newly elected South African government was implementing its race laws. Many Afrikaner nationalists had shown sympathy towards Nazism and had hoped for a German victory over the Allies during the Second World War. Afterwards some nationalists adopted German orphans – preferably 'pure German', Protestant children. 'Adopting a child from Hitler's master race was a status symbol for the Boer Nationalists' (ZDF History, 2010). After the war many of the old Nazi networks continued to exist in Germany, not only in politics and the justice system, but also in the major corporations. Beyond an economic convergence of interests, this also led to the development of a political and ideological consensus between German and Afrikaner actors. As Günter Verheugen has stressed, 'the fact that German managers went so willingly to South Africa was also because they found an economic and social order there which corresponded with their view of the world […] amongst other things, it was a goldmine because you could pay the black workers a pittance, because you didn't have to grapple with the trade unions regarding improved working conditions […]. A bleak chapter in the history of the German economy opens up here – and who today would be surprised to hear that this history includes the names of a number of those same companies which, during the period of National Socialism, made some handsome profits with the help of forced labourers' (Verheugen, 1986:94).

One of these companies was BASF, which was part of the notorious IG Farben, whose involvement in the Nazi death camps is well known. IG Farben produced Zyklon B, the gas which the Nazi regime used to send millions of people to their deaths between 1942 and 1944 in its concentration camps. In collaboration with the Schutzstaffel (SS), IG Farben established an additional camp in Auschwitz for the construction of a synthetic rubber factory. The SS ensured the availability and surveillance of the forced workers, and IG Farben provided for everything else. According to estimates, between 20,000 and 25,000 people died during the construction and operation of this factory (Wagner, 2000:187). Shortly after the war, BASF resumed its business relations with South Africa – long before the corporation developed an interest in platinum some 30 years ago (see the chapter by Maren Grimm and Jakob Krameritsch).

The alleged dependence on South Africa's raw materials

In 1987, the German NGO Werkstatt Ökonomie presented a detailed study of business relations between Germany and South Africa, with the aim of justifying sanctions against the latter. The study revealed: 'Without federal German deliveries of goods, loans, direct investments and expertise, the Republic of South Africa would not be in the position to maintain the apartheid system and advance its military–industrial [...] expansion' (Christen für Arbeit und Gerechtigkeit e.V., 1986:58).

Opponents of sanctions principally based their arguments on Germany's reported dependency on South African raw materials. However, as *Spiegel* editor Hans-Georg Nachtweh pointed out in 1986, this dependency was not as real as alleged. According to Nachtweh's analysis, it would have been possible and even unproblematic for the German economy to take part in the sanctions campaign without any economic losses, and the apartheid regime might therefore have been brought down at an earlier stage (Nachtweh, 1986). Ultimately, as experts agree, it was the economic situation which defeated apartheid. The costs incurred by maintaining racial segregation, militarisation and an isolationist policy were not economically viable in the long term, despite extremely low wages paid to black workers and despite major national raw materials deposits. Although South Africa provided 40 to 60 per cent of global exports of the 10 most important raw materials, sooner or later it would have been possible for the industrial countries to search for alternatives, even beyond the 'class enemy' of the Soviet Union. According to Nachtweh, 'the prices would [initially] increase; however, a sharp increase in price immediately leads other manufacturers to boost their production; it becomes worthwhile for them.'

Despite its own deposits, coal was a particularly important raw material for Germany because its importation was still economically worthwhile – not least because the lower wages paid for the South African coal created a competitive advantage for that country. In 1985, South Africa became the biggest coal supplier to Germany. However, this only amounted to 11.4 per cent of domestic consumption, and could have quite easily been replaced by domestically or externally sourced coal. Nonetheless, an embargo on coal would have had a serious impact on the apartheid regime. Even Werkstatt Ökonomie came to the conclusion that 'firstly looking at the structure of these imports, they are to a great extent superfluous to the Federal Republic; secondly, the dependence on raw materials from South Africa is smaller than is often claimed' (Christen für Arbeit und Gerechtigkeit weltweit e.V., 1986:77).

German companies in apartheid South Africa

A systematic analysis of the relations between German companies, banks and institutions and the apartheid regime has yet to be made. The Evangelical Church in Germany has attempted for its part to shine a light on its own entanglement with the South Africa regime; however, the proximity in time, the complexity of the issues and financial constraints have demonstrated how problematic this endeavour can be (Lessing et al., 2015).

In Germany and Switzerland, there was a joint campaign in the 1990s in favour of debt relief and reparations (KOSA, 2017),[1] which was principally concerned with banks and multinational companies based in both Germany and South Africa. The campaign supported a legal action by the South African victims' organisation Khulumani Support Group in the US under the Alien Tort Claims Act, in which companies, including Deutsche Bank, Dresdner Bank, Commerzbank, Daimler, Rheinmetall, Ford, IBM and General Motors, were accused of aiding and abetting serious human rights violations during the apartheid era. The case collapsed – not because it was unjustified, but because the court did not consider itself competent to try it. The true success of this legal claim and of the associated campaign lay, however, in the relatively large media response that it generated in its initial phase, and the fact that it uncovered for the first time the entanglement of politics and business in supporting the apartheid government.

In 2003, Birgit Morgenrath and Gottfried Wellmer published a book entitled *Deutsches Kapital am Kap*, a well-researched summary of the business practices of German companies during apartheid. Between 1986 and 1993, the years of UN-imposed economic sanctions against South Africa, to which Germany had given its assent, the authors estimate that the average value of commodity trading by German importers brought an annual profit of 1.2 billion euro (Morgenrath and Wellmer, 2003:13). During this time, German companies unashamedly filled the gap left by US and other countries' companies, which took the economic boycott more seriously. In our research BASF constantly crops up in this regard: the company acquired IBM's computer business when the latter pulled out of South Africa due to pressure from the US public, and consequently doubled its annual turnover. According to an article published in *Der Spiegel* (2 March 1987), 'the German multinational [BASF] increasingly enters the line of fire, because it rapidly earns easy money in South Africa. The managers of the Ludwigshafen-based group go about their business with the sensibility of an African bush fire: they take with them what they can get, even what others have left behind deliberately.'

Whenever the companies' managers were asked about the exploitative, inhuman apartheid system, they either stressed – as did German chancellor Willy Brandt – that business and politics should be separated, or they tended to adhere to the maxim of generating 'change through trade' (Andresen, 2016:231–253). In truth, however, their investments stabilised the apartheid regime. According to Morgenrath and Wellmer (2003:30), German capital and German goods flowed unimpeded into 'the sectors of the South African economy which formed the backbone of the regime', such as the energy supplier ESKOM, the SASOL fuel-from-coal giant and the armaments group

ARMSCOR – all of them South African public sector companies.

The brutal repression of the student uprising in Soweto in 1976 had little impact on bilateral trade between the two countries. Between 1977 and 1980, Morgenrath and Wellmer report that the value of German exports increased by a tremendous 78 per cent, from 1.2 billion euro to 2.3 billion euro. A statement by Daimler's spokesperson at the time serves as a good example of what German companies truly thought about UN resolutions against the apartheid regime, which had been passed with Germany's approval. In a 1981 article in *Der Spiegel*, the Daimler spokesman stated that 'there is too much discussion surrounding these matters. An "über-democracy" prevails there.'

During the course of the 1980s and 1990s, the campaign for debt relief and reparations increasingly disclosed links between German companies and the apartheid regime. These involved the protection of business transactions with German export credit guarantees, and the most generous interpretation of 'dual-use items' and their approval by the German authorities despite the obvious fact such goods and technologies would be used for military rather than civilian purposes in South Africa. Following the South African state's descent into bankruptcy in 1985, German banks participated in a questionable debt restructuring without making political reforms a condition of their intervention. Furthermore, no German company found it necessary after the end of apartheid to set up its own truth and reconciliation commission or to have its own past examined. When the Apartheid Debt and Reparations Campaign attempted to shine a light into the murkiness of the business relations between Germany and South Africa, the German federal government set itself strongly against the campaign when it brought actions before American courts, claiming that German national sovereignty was being called into question.

While US companies pulled out of South Africa after 1985, German companies set up subsidiaries in the country, and were therefore able to profit from the sanctions policies of others. This made it clear that they would also be the first on the scene after the democratic transition of 1994. Since 1994, German–South African bilateral trade has more than doubled.

SWITZERLAND
Bankers for the apartheid state

On many levels, a similar picture to that of Germany may be drawn for Switzerland. Various studies (Kreis, 2005; Künzli, 2005; Madörin, 2008; Bott, 2013) have documented the close and comprehensive relations between the apartheid state and the Swiss business elite, banking system, politicians and the army. What is lacking, however, is a systematic analysis, not least of the complex motives behind Switzerland's support of the apartheid regime. As Purtschert et al. (2012) have shown, one of the underlying reasons is that Switzerland seems to have no history of direct and active participation in colonial violence and rule. The prevailing image of Switzerland as merely a 'free rider' of colonialism is still very widespread. In particular, in the German-speaking area of Switzerland, Afrikaners could count on the sympathies of the elite, not least during the apartheid era. This was based on a distinct anglophobia, which had arisen during the Anglo-Boer War. For many years, South Africa was not only considered to be a bastion against the advance of communism, but also an outpost of white European civilisation.

It was in the 1960s that the struggle against apartheid, initiated by civil society groups, began in Switzerland. In essence it involved a cognitive process of decolonisation, which has to date found no equivalent form of expression. Following the Soweto uprising in 1976, political discussions about the role of Switzerland in the apartheid regime came to be conducted with a particular fervour. No other issue of foreign policy has produced as many parliamentary inquiries.

The same holds true for the churches, which were sharply polarised on this question: on the one hand, some displayed solidarity with the Dutch Reformed Church in South Africa, which supported the system of apartheid as being divinely ordained; and, on the other hand, some showed commitment to basic human rights and the struggle against racism. The declaration by the United Nations in 1976 that apartheid was a crime against humanity was perceived by a section of the Swiss public as a form of 'dictatorship of the majority'. (Even Swiss diplomats, who were criticised by African representatives because of their attitude to the apartheid state, used this metaphor in their reports.) Similar denunciatory attitudes towards the UN were reflected in many polls: even in 1986, 75.7 per cent of eligible voters rejected the idea of Switzerland joining the UN, citing the principle of neutrality. Only in 2002 did Switzerland finally join the United Nations after a fresh referendum.

Although left-wing parties demanded the condemnation of apartheid politics in numerous motions in Parliament and called upon Switzerland to join the international sanctions campaign against South Africa, these positions failed to attract a majority right up to the 1990s. The conservatively oriented government insisted on the separation of economics and politics as one of its principles and held on to the principle of 'integral neutrality', which allegedly stood in the way of combating apartheid policies. It was only because of pressure from the OPEC countries in the 1970s, especially Nigeria, and the power of the boycott movements in the US, Scandinavia and parts of Europe during the second half of the 1980s that the Swiss government issued a condemnation, at least verbally, of apartheid. This belated response comes as no surprise if one considers that half of the predominantly male Swiss parliamentarians were simultaneously members of boards of companies which were involved in business with South Africa (Koch, 1998).

Springboard for Swiss companies

After the National Party assumed power in 1948, South Africa became the springboard for the Swiss economy's rise in the world market. While the banks in particular knew how to turn the weakening of British interests in South Africa to their own advantage, many corporations based in Switzerland and operating internationally today had branches in South Africa – such as Novartis (previously Ciba-Geigy and Sandoz), Roche (previously Hoffmann-La Roche), LafargeHolcim (previously Holderbank/Schmidheiny and Portland), Nestlé, Schindler and Suchard. In 1988, there were 54 branches of Swiss companies in South Africa (Zollinger, 1997:52).

In 1968, the three Swiss major banks, SBG, SBV (today UBS) and SKA (today Credit Suisse), landed a major coup. Using a crisis at the centre of the gold trade in London, they persuaded South Africa to sell its gold production via the Zurich Gold Pool (Warwick-Ching, 1993). From then on, 75 to 80 per cent of South African gold was traded via Switzerland and processed for further sale in Swiss refineries. At the instigation of South Africa, the Swiss Statistical Office did away with the breakdown, according to country, of import statistics for gold. Swiss involvement in the gold trade was of crucial importance for the apartheid state's acquisition of foreign currency.

Following the uprising in Soweto in 1976, the Swiss share of South African banking business doubled, as many other countries terminated their business dealings with South Africa and joined the campaign for sanctions in protest. Gold and foreign loans were closely related: the precious metal was not only the most important way of bringing foreign currency into South Africa, but, according to Zollinger (1997), also served as surety for foreign loans. Towards the end of the apartheid era, forward contracts, or transaction contracts, which are paid for by future sales of gold at an agreed price, gained in importance. (When South Africa was no longer considered to be creditworthy from the mid-1980s onwards, foreign financial backers increasingly chose this path in order to minimise their risk.) Switzerland became an important hub for all these activities and developments.

The banks of the Swiss Confederation and the apartheid government were bound in an intimate relationship. As bankers of the apartheid state, the Swiss made a handsome profit from this business. In his comprehensive study, Hennie van Vuuren describes the extensive international business and trading networks of the apartheid state, based on political affinity, from which all involved parties profited (Van Vuuren, 2017). For its part, South Africa profited from the fact that it could rely on Switzerland during times of crisis. So it was no coincidence that it was the Swiss banker Fritz Leutwiler, former president of the Swiss National Bank and the Bank for International Settlements, who rescued South Africa from imminent disaster during its hour of need. In 1985, the country became insolvent and its 30 creditor banks were no longer prepared to guarantee further loans. Leutwiler negotiated and achieved a restructuring of the loans – at a time when international sanctions were biting, the South African state had imposed a state of emergency and, as a result, the repression of the black population had intensified. In his study of relations between Switzerland and South Africa, Kreis (2005) concludes that 'Switzerland in particular supported, strengthened and therefore facilitated the apartheid state with its hungry public-sector companies and its high government spending due to capital exports and the purchase of the South African gold export.'

It was not only the banks who aligned themselves with the needs of the South African state for the purpose of furthering their own interests. Even in the Swiss bureaucracy, creative measures were taken to move obstacles out of the way in order to do business with South Africa. The complicity of the Swiss administration and Swiss business was expressly criticised in a report by the National Research Programme: 'The core of the South Africa policy was the [Swiss] trade department, which, together with advocates of private enterprise, determined the path to be followed. [...] The policy consisted of largely preserving the leeway claimed by private enterprises, notwithstanding the political consequences.' The anti-apartheid activist and economist Mascha Madörin describes what this meant in the following way: 'It was fudged, played down and false information was given. Statistics were disappeared' (Madörin, 2008).

Switzerland's role in the raw materials trade

The collapse of the monopoly of the oil multinationals after the 1974 oil price crisis opened the door for dealers such as Marc Rich,[2] who set up business in Zug in 1974. Trade in cheap oil, which could be sold at a significantly higher price on the spot market, became highly lucrative for dealers like Rich. Trading with ostracised regimes such as Iran and South Africa was even more profitable. Despite a US trade embargo, Rich supplied the apartheid regime with oil. According to Rich's biographer, South Africa was his 'most important and most profitable business' (Ammann, 2010). Since this had to do with pure brokering – the crude oil traded by Marc Rich did not end up in Switzerland – the Swiss government did not consider itself liable to account for or prevent it. Until the end of apartheid, Marc Rich & Co. AG was able to rake in profits worth millions.

Rich's business dealings were also significant for the post-apartheid era, which has seen the Swiss town of Zug develop into a centre for global raw materials trading over the last 15 years. As the Erklärung von Bern (2011) shows, special loan instruments were created for the purpose of trading, which allowed a company such as Marc Rich

▶ Billboard of a security company in Kroondal, a small village between Rustenburg and Marikana (2017).

& Co. to gain generous credit limits for trade in raw materials, despite low equity capital. In 1993, Rich[3] was ousted from his company and his successors gave the business a new name – Glencore. This international raw materials corporation is still based in Zug today. Glencore was a major shareholder of Xstrata, which, at the time of the Marikana massacre in 2012, was the most significant individual shareholder in the Lonmin platinum mine (*Erklärung von Bern*, 2011:163).[4] Until 2016, BASF also sourced its raw materials purchases from Zug, including South African platinum.

Continuing decolonisation

At the end of apartheid in 1994, there was a lack of political will to critically appraise Swiss relations with the racist apartheid regime. People wanted to move on without dealing with unpleasant past issues. Besides, the new South African state did not make any demands of Switzerland. Whereas strong pressure from the US had ultimately forced Switzerland to answer for its role during the Second World War – in particular regarding its refugee policy and its handling of the 'dormant' assets of Jewish victims of Nazi persecution – in the case of apartheid, the country was largely able to escape prosecution.

This is the context in which the Apartheid Debt and Reparations Campaign movement KEESA (Kampagne für Entschuldung und Entschädigung im südlichen Afrika) should be seen. KEESA came into existence in 1998 as a coalition of different church and secular NGOs in Switzerland. It demanded that apartheid debts be cancelled and 'companies and banks, which profited from apartheid and supported them, make amends for the injustice committed and the damage caused' (KEESA, 2017). Today KEESA is part of the international Plough Back the Fruits campaign.

In the light of the revelations of the South African Truth and Reconciliation Commission (TRC), in May 2000 the Federal Council of Switzerland commissioned the Swiss National Fund to conduct a research programme on Switzerland–South Africa relations. However, the Swiss Parliament denied the researchers access to parliamentary sources. In 2003, when victims of apartheid filed civil compensation claims against companies which had profited from joint business activities with the South African regime, including Swiss banks and companies, the Federal Council imposed a partial block on access to the relevant files. This move, which lasted until June 2014 after the collapse of the apartheid lawsuits in the US, consequently torpedoed the research programme. In 2005, the Swiss National Fund presented its report, which contained many controversial findings. Around a hundred parliamentarians called on the Federal Council to pass a motion, which it refused to do. Not even a petition from South African human rights organisations, initiated by KEESA, could move the council.

AUSTRIA
A consistent course of 'proper' inconsistency

According to a 1979 foreign policy report by the Austrian government, 'proper relations exist between Austria and South Africa' (cited in Sauer and Zeschin, 1984:151). At a multilateral level, representatives of the Austrian government repeatedly supported resolutions and recommendations made by the UN against the apartheid regime, but on a bilateral level Austria did not practise what it preached, or if it did, it lacked conviction and the result was counterproductive and contrary to the resolutions and recommendations it had agreed to.

From the start of the 1970s, Austria's engagement with the apartheid system grew steadily – and vice versa. Trade relations were extended, more investments were made and, in comparison with international standards, an above-average number of bank loans were issued and arms agreements signed. State-owned companies such as Voest/Noricum and Länderbank AG were also – directly or indirectly – involved. As Sauer and Zeschin show, by invoking its 'neutrality' Austria frequently functioned as a hub for contacts and transfers of goods involving South Africa.

Transkei, raw materials trade, sport and culture

Austria also played a key role in the attempts of the Transkei homeland to gain international diplomatic recognition. Transkei was South Africa's largest homeland and in 1976 it gained so-called independence from South Africa. The UN, however, declared this to be invalid and called upon all countries to deny Transkei any form of recognition. As a result, Transkei attempted to circumvent its international isolation. To this end, Austria played an important role: three Austrian MPs were present at the 'independence' celebrations, having arrived without a valid mandate of representation from the federal government. Austria recognised Transkei passports and consequently enabled trade delegations from Transkei to negotiate and conclude business transactions with Austrian companies. The friendship association 'Transkei Trade Union and Information Office', established in Vienna, was the first of its kind in Europe and closely resembled a consulate. Austria became the hub for Transkei's foreign trade contacts. Vienna's role as UN headquarters made it the perfect location for such activities. Austria was also supportive of Transkei's schemes for rural development and supplied the homeland with Steyr-Daimler-Puch tractors at favourable rates. At the end of 1978, when asked which countries had afforded Transkei infrastructural support, the homeland government named two countries: Taiwan and Austria (Rogers, 1980:124).

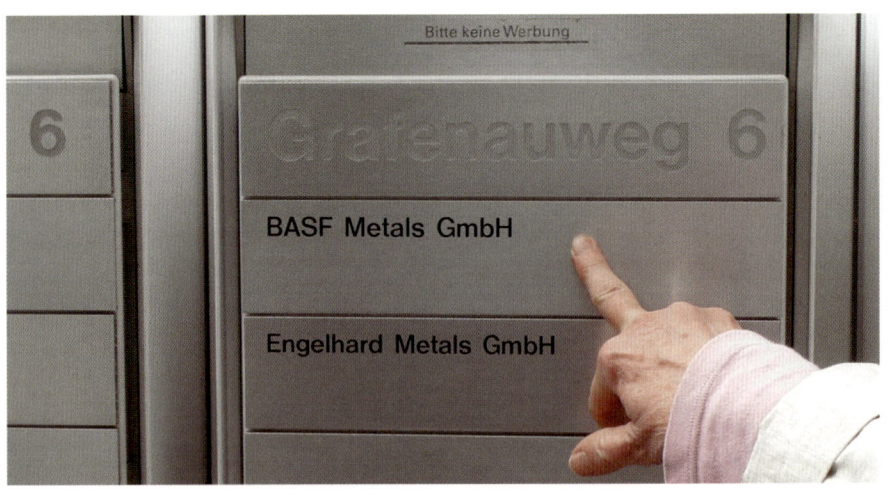

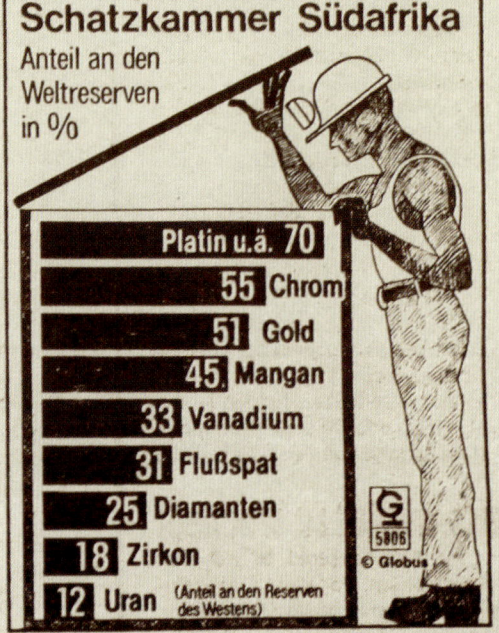

Südafrika ist neben der Sowjetunion die Schatzkammer der Welt, und weil der Westen eben nicht von der Sowjetunion abhängig sein möchte, wird er seine Bindungen an Südafrika nicht aufgeben. Warum sollten auch Edelmetalle vom Apartheidregime „unmoralischer" sein als vom Sowjetregime, das ja mit seiner eigenen Bevölkerung und jener in Afghanistan auch nicht zimperlich umgeht.

Schatzkammer Südafrika
Anteil an den Weltreserven in %

- Platin u.ä. 70
- 55 Chrom
- 51 Gold
- 45 Mangan
- 33 Vanadium
- 31 Flußspat
- 25 Diamanten
- 18 Zirkon
- 12 Uran (Anteil an den Reserven des Westens)

As regards South Africa itself, the raw materials trade was also big business for Austria: it imported coal, gold, chrome, manganese, asbestos, nickel, copper, platinum and uranium (for its nuclear power plant, which never went into operation) (Braun, 1984:82). In terms of the trade in gold, South Africa's most important export item, Austria could count itself as a world leader. On average, 60 per cent of Austrian gold imports came from South Africa during the 1970s and 1980s. With the exception of Luxembourg, Austria was the only country in Europe where the Krugerrand gold coin could be obtained free of VAT. The resulting profits for both Austrian financial institutions and the apartheid state, which produced these coins for the foreign currency market, were enormous. The proceeds of sales in Austria amounted to 5 billion schillings in 1983 alone, which represented more than 20 per cent of global sales (Sauer, 2008).

Furthermore, Austrian tourism in South Africa was expanded and cultural, sports and study exchange programmes were established. Those involved in these activities came from and worked for a variety of institutions: corporations, (nationalised) industry, the Federal Chamber of Commerce, diplomatic missions and consulates of both countries, travel agency organisations, migration recruitment offices and associations which were often managed by Austrian MPs, managers in high positions or influential journalists. The protagonists in this close-knit network linking Austria and South Africa were 'opinion leaders' at every level: MPs, diplomats, trade attachés, economic lobbyists, tourism professionals, teachers, scientists, sportspeople and even artists. Austrian performers such as the Vienna Boys' Choir, the Stierwascher-Volkstanzgruppe and Udo Jürgens were placed on the UN's blacklist of entertainers, actors and others who had performed in apartheid South Africa.

According to a survey held in 1986, 'in contrast with its size and economic capacity, Austria plays an above-average role in maintaining the apartheid system. It was specifically the scant international regard and the low level of public awareness of apartheid which allowed South Africa to use its Austrian contacts to breach its increasing isolation' (Sauer and Zeschin, 1984:10; Anti-Apartheid-Bewegung, 1988:25–30). It is to the credit of the Austrian anti-apartheid movement, founded in 1976 (Krims 1999:15),

◀ Mailbox of BASF Metals GmbH, which has meanwhile been liquidated, in the Swiss tax haven Zug.
◀ Article in the Austrian *Kronen Zeitung*, 5 July 1986.
Translation:
Treasury South Africa. Share of world reserves in %
Platinum a.o. 70/Chrome 55/Gold 51/Manganese 45/Vanadium 33/Fluorspar 31/Diamonds 25/Zircon 18/Uranium 12
Apart from the Soviet Union, South Africa is the treasury of the world, and because the West does not want to be dependent on the Soviet Union, it will not abandon its ties to South Africa.
Why should noble metals from the apartheid regime be "more immoral" than from the Soviet regime, which does not treat its own people and those in Afghanistan with modesty.

as well as representatives of the church and the Communist Party, that these entanglements were identified and became the subject of criticism and opposition.

As with Germany, the Austrian 'apartheid contact zone' (see the introduction to this book) was shaped by the interface of a post-Nazi society with the apartheid social order. Not only were Austrian companies' involvement in South Africa based on the high profit rates guaranteed by the apartheid state, but the country was also regarded by many Austrians as an anti-communist bastion and the 'vanguard of a white Europe at the Cape', a beacon of hope for white supremacy in Africa ('Africa, but then again not quite'). Austria's support for the regime was equally based on reasons of economic policy and strategic ideology. Right-wing Austrian parliamentarians described the racist regime as a 'viable model' (Sauer and Zeschin, 1984:10), and business representatives shook their heads in disbelief when criticism of apartheid was voiced: 'Only the stupidest countries stick to the economic boycott' (Sperner, 1980, cited in Sauer and Zeschin, 1984:88). In this respect, the Austrian anti-apartheid movement stressed that their work always pursued a dual goal: solidarity with the freedom movements in South Africa and engagement with racism and colonialism in their own country: 'information about apartheid and about the need for international sanctions […] cannot be separated from the struggle against racism and neo-fascism in Austria' (Sauer and Zeschin, 1984).

Conclusion

It is clear that Germany, Austria and Switzerland as well as the companies based there contributed enormously to maintaining apartheid in every respect. They supported the apartheid regime in terms of ideology, diplomacy, politics and economics and were therefore part of the system. The three countries were jointly responsible for the stability and long life of the apartheid regime. In all three, the Cold War, an unreconstructed colonial legacy and the continuity of elites from the Nazi era created the ideological and social-political conditions that underpinned their collaboration with the anti-communist apartheid regime. In particular, the imperial mode of living, which permeated all aspects of society in the global North, allowed the trade in raw materials with South Africa to grow exponentially. This generated huge profits for all three countries and for the companies based within them – at the expense and to the detriment of the majority black population in South Africa.

The interrelationship of economic and political factors was evident in the activities of individual actors. Apartheid was simultaneously supported by state and corporate actors, both economically and ideologically. Far from its being shunned, lobbying for the apartheid regime was carried out in many ways. Open affirmation of constitutionally based racism, the denial of tyranny, keeping what was happening far away as invisible as possible, resorting to relativism, turning a blind eye to repression as well as initial attempts to employ the rhetoric and strategies of corporate social responsibility (CSR) – all of these formed part of the repertoire used by German, Swiss and Austrian actors in order to continue their 'business as usual'. During the era of apartheid, major corporations were already shaping and exerting a significant influence on political opinion and decision-making processes.

To date, none of the three countries or their public sector or private enterprise actors have offered an apology for contributing to and supporting the apartheid regime – not to mention reparation payments for the millions of people disadvantaged by it. Such apologies and reparations have not only failed to materialise but attempts to obtain them have been opposed and stifled.

This is the historical background which must be taken into consideration when dealing with the problems of the post-apartheid era, be they 'supply chain responsibility', attempts at the legal regulation of human rights impact assessments, the lobbying of the chemicals sector or strategies for tax avoidance. The involvement of Germany, Austria and Switzerland in the stabilisation of tyrannies has remained unpunished to date. Their participation remains 'unpaid for', both in the symbolic and material sense. What is more, they provide fertile ground for successors to follow suit. As Pierre Bourdieu argues, 'the truth of the interaction is never entirely contained in [itself]' (Bourdieu, 2009:181). This lack of penalties and sanctions forms the basis of current practice, which means that today's actors can afford to pay less attention to preventing the continuation of exploitative and repressive practices in current developments. Yet impunity only serves as an incentive for further crimes.

Notes

1 In addition to KOSA, the successor organisation of the anti-apartheid movement in Germany, KASA, Medico International, SODI and KEESA from Switzerland were also substantially involved.
2 Marc Rich had been an employee of the raw materials company Philipp Brothers, which was founded in 1901, and became manager of their Madrid branch before he moved to Zug, where he set up his own business in 1974. In 1983, he was charged with tax offences in the US. In addition, there were lawsuits due to 'trading with the enemy Iran'.
3 Only a few months before the indictment in the US, Rich had relocated to Switzerland, where he felt more secure, as tax evasion in Switzerland does not represent a criminal offence. He was pardoned by Bill Clinton on his last day in office on 20 January 2001.
4 In 2011, after Glencore, Nestlé, Novartis, Roche and ABB, Xstrata was the sixth-largest listed Swiss company.

References

Ammann, D. (2010) *King of Oil. Marc Rich – Vom mächtigsten Rohstoffhändler der Welt zum Gejagten der USA*, Zurich
Andresen, K. (2016) Moralische Ökonomie. Bundesdeutsche Automobilunternehmen und Apartheid, *Zeithistorische Forschungen* 2, pp. 231–253
Anti-Apartheid-Bewegung in Österreich and Koordinierungsstelle der Bischofskonferenz für internationale Entwicklung und Mission (1988) *Südafrika – Apartheid*, Wien
Bott, S. (2013) La Suisse et l'Afrique du Sud, 1945–1990. Marché de l'or, finance et commerce durant l'apartheid, *Schweizer Beiträge zur internationalen Geschichte* 11, Zurich
Bourdieu, P. (2009) *Entwurf einer Theorie der Praxis*, Frankfurt, www.monoskop.org/images/7/71/Pierre_Bourdieu_Outline_of_a_Theory_of_Practice_Cambridge_Studies_in_Social_and_Cultural_Anthropology_1977.pdf
Brand, U. and M. Wissen (2017) *Imperiale Lebensweise. Zur Ausbeutung von Mensch und Natur im globalen Kapitalismus*, Munich
Braun, G. (1984) Die Kohlen müssen stimmen. Österreichs Rohstoffimporte aus Südafrika, in W. Sauer and T. Zeschin (eds.), *Die Apartheid-Connection. Österreichs Bedeutung für Südafrika*, Vienna
Christen für Arbeit und Gerechtigkeit weltweit e.V. (1986) *Die deutsche Wirtschaft und Südafrika: Zur Notwendigkeit von Wirtschaftssanktionen*, Heidelberg
Erklärung von Bern (2011) *Rohstoff. Das gefährlichste Geschäft der Schweiz*, Zurich
KEESA (2017) www.apartheid-reparations.ch/
Koch, E. (1998) Im gelobten Land, *Tages-Anzeiger Magazin* 7, pp. 24–35
KOSA (2017) www.info.kosa.org/thema_entschaedigung.html
Kreis, G. (2005) *Die Schweiz und Südafrika 1948–1994*, Bern
Krims, A. (1999) Kleine Geschichte der Anti-Apartheid-Bewegung in Österreich, in Walter Sauer (ed.), *Südafrika fünf Jahre nach der Apartheid. Politische und soziale Transformation während der Regierungszeit von Nelson Mandela*, Wien
Künzli, J. (2005) *Zwischen Recht und Politik. Der rechtliche Handlungsspielraum der schweizerischen Südafrikapolitik (1976–1994)*, Zurich
Lessing, H. et al. (eds.) (2015) *Umstrittene Beziehungen. Protestantismus zwischen dem südlichen Afrika und Deutschland von den 1930er Jahren bis in die Apartheidzeit*, Wiesbaden
Madörin, M. (2008) *Helfer der Apartheid oder "Verlässliche Freunde". Wie die Schweizer Banken das Apartheid-Regime stützten*, Zurich
Morgenrath, B. and G. Wellmer (2003) *Deutsches Kapital am Kap. Kollaboration mit dem Apartheidregime*, Hamburg
Nachtweh, H. (1986) Wir sind die Herren, das Land ist unser, *Der Spiegel*, 3 March, www.spiegel.de/spiegel/print/d-13516884.html
Purtschert, P. et al. (eds.) (2012) *Postkoloniale Schweiz. Formen und Folgen eines Kolonialismus ohne Kolonien*, Bielefeld
Rogers, B. (1980) *Divide and Rule: South Africa's Bantustans*, London
Ross, R. (2008) *A Concise History of South Africa*, Cape Town
Sauer, W. (2008) Austria and South Africa during apartheid, in South African Democracy Education Trust (ed.), *The Road to Democracy in South Africa*, vol. 3, Johannesburg
Sauer, W. and T. Zeschin (eds.) (1984) *Die Apartheid-Connection. Österreichs Bedeutung für Südafrika*, Vienna

Schaffartzik, A. et al. (2014) The global metabolic transition: Regional patterns and trends of global material flows, 1950–2010, *Global Environmental Change* 5, pp. 7–97

Van Vuuren, H. (2017) *Apartheid Guns and Money: A Tale of Profit*, Jacana, Johannesburg

Verheugen, G. (1986) *Apartheid und die deutschen Interessen am Kap*, Cologne

Wagner, B. C. (2000) *IG Auschwitz. Zwangsarbeit und Vernichtung von Häftlingen des Lagers Monowitz 1941–1945*, Munich

Warwick-Ching, T. (1993) *The International Gold Trade*, Cambridge, www.books.google.de/books?isbn=1845699173

ZDF History (2010) Weiß bleiben in einem schwarzen Land. Warum deutsche Waisenkinder nach Südafrika geholt wurden, www.zdf.de/dokumentation/zdf-history/weiss-bleiben-in-einem-schwarzen-land-100.html

Zollinger, L. (1997) Die Wirtschaftsbeziehungen zwischen der Schweiz und der Republik Südafrika 1961–1994, unpublished MS, Bern

▲ Ad in the broadsheet *Süddeutsche Zeitung*, 27 November 1986.
Translation: PLATINUM NOW! The investment tip of the week: Invest now in a Christmas gift for your wife.
▶ Lonmin information board at its property boundary.

4. LONMIN IN CONTEXT: THE POLITICAL ECONOMY OF THE SOUTH AFRICAN PLATINUM INDUSTRY

An interview with Gavin Capps

Jakob Krameritsch Mining is a symbol of racialised exploitation in times of colonial rule and particularly in the apartheid era. In the context of the development of the mining industry many of the most decisive features of the apartheid regime were installed, like the 'migrant labour system'. Could you outline the milestones of this development?

Gavin Capps After the diamond strikes in 1867, South Africa's importance for British imperialism increased and was further heightened with the discovery of vast gold deposits in the Witwatersrand basin in 1886. Johannesburg rapidly emerged as the centre of the new gold industry, whose frenetic growth gave the economy its modern shape, at the levels of capital, labour and the state.

While the Witwatersrand goldfields were the largest hitherto discovered, the ore itself was low grade and deep underground and so difficult and expensive to mine. Profitable extraction thus came to depend on a combination of large-scale investment (to develop sufficient economies of scale) and vast supplies of cheap wage labour (to maximise the rate of exploitation). The first of these conditions was met through the rapid concentration of mine ownership (including coal mines) into the hands of six major producers whose interests were coordinated through the Chamber of Mines. These mining houses benefited from massive state support in key inputs – most notably energy, but also transport – to form what Ben Fine and Zav Rustomjee (1996) dubbed the 'minerals-energy complex' (MEC), which would revolve around close ties between the private and public sectors and generate a distinctive accumulation dynamic that profoundly shaped South Africa's industrialisation during the 20th century.

For its part, gold's 'labour problem' was progressively resolved in the critical period between 1890 (when deep-level mining began) and 1920 through the construction of an increasingly expansive and regulated system of (male) African migrant labour. This sourced black workers from across South Africa (mostly the Eastern Cape) and its neighbouring territories (above all, Mozambique and Lesotho) and, at the end of their contracts, returned them to rural homes where agriculture supported (or 'subsidised') their low wages and the reproduction of their labour power. At the mines, these labour migrants were subjected to harsh cost and work disciplines through the compound system and a stark division of labour in which semi-servile black work gangs executed the tasks set by a rigid hierarchy of white miners, supervisors and management. Meanwhile, in the rural areas, it was largely the subsistence labour of women that reproduced this distinctive worker-peasantry, both partially tied to and separated from the land.

Finally, the 'mineral revolution' set in motion a major set of changes at the level of the state. There were two major elements to this. First, British imperialism attempted to curtail and then completely destroy the independent power of the Afrikaner settler republics in order to gain control of the whole region. This culminated in the so-called Anglo-Boer War of 1899–1902, out of which was constructed a new, unified state (1910) firmly focused on the needs of the mining industry. Secondly, the remaining political independence of the African kingdoms within the region was decisively smashed, while a combination of accelerating land dispossession, coercive taxation and other discriminatory measures destroyed independent peasant agriculture and created new cash needs, leaving Africans with no choice but to enter wage employment at the mines and in white commercial agriculture and secondary industry.

JK Another key feature connected to mining and the migrant labour system was the Land Acts of 1913 and 1936 and the spatial division of South Africa between black and white in the segregation era (1910–1939).

GC Yes, the Land Acts eventually designated 87 per cent of the country for exclusive white occupation and use. This is largely where the most valuable minerals were located, where industrialisation took off and where the new urban centres developed. On the periphery of that, in the remaining 13 per cent, were the black rural areas, the so-called 'native reserves', which were desperately overcrowded and deeply impoverished and, as I have mentioned, where migrant labour was both produced and dumped when it was no longer needed. This also meant that there was a stark dualism, or 'bifurcation' in Mamdani's term (1996), within the South African state. 'White' South Africa, as it increasingly becomes known, was characterised by Western-style private property regimes, full citizenship rights and all the other trappings of bourgeois democracy (though exclusively for 'whites'). However, in 'black' South Africa, the rural reserves remained under 'communal' tenure and the local control of chiefs, constituting Africans as rightless subjects. And this spatio-racial divide would become really important in the platinum story.

JK And apartheid built up on this …

GC The apartheid state, which came into existence in 1948, intensified the logic of the migrant labour system: increasing control over the movement of labour, installing new laws and means of oppressing black workers and strengthening the conditions of their super-exploitation. It also deepened the distinction between white South Africa and the black rural reserves, designating the latter as quasi-independent states or 'homelands'. Part of the apartheid project was also to promote Afrikaner capital, which had historically been based in agriculture and finance. Now the state began to create the conditions for its integration with 'English' mining capital, creating larger and more complex conglomerate structures, which in turn interlocked with the giant parastatal companies at the heart of the MEC.

JK From a certain perspective, apartheid was not limited to South Africa, but the regime was heavily dependent on transnational enterprises not based in South Africa.

GC Yes, that's right. The key moment here is the Sharpeville massacre in 1960, when Africans protesting against the imposition of the passes designed to control their movements were gunned down by the police. One of the effects of the Sharpeville massacre was to send a message to the rest of the world that South Africa was going to stand on the neck of black workers and guarantee the conditions for massive profit-making. And indeed, after Sharpeville, there was a dramatic rise in foreign direct investment into South Africa, above all from the United States and Britain but also from many other major capitalist states, including Germany. So, for capital, this becomes apartheid's 'golden age'.

JK Let's shift now to the platinum industry and its origins and specifics.

GC Platinum was discovered in the 1920s, by which time the gold industry was already developed. However, these reserves would soon prove to be the largest in the world. Over 88 per cent of known platinum resources are concentrated in the northern part of South Africa in a vast, bowl-shaped geological formation called the Bushveld Complex. Yet, unlike gold, the uses for platinum were at this point very restricted and the industry only really began to take off in the 1960s and the 1970s as new applications were found. Critically, the Bushveld Complex itself primarily outcropped not in 'white' South Africa but in two of the fictively independent homeland states: Bophuthatswana (in what is now the North West and Gauteng Provinces) and Lebowa (now part of Limpopo). As such, the areas which had historically been designated as the areas of black labour supply would now become the centres of the new platinum industry, signalling the beginning of a shift in the spatial organisation of the mining sector as a whole.

JK What were the effects of the development of the platinum industry at the levels of capital, labour and the state?

GC The take-off of the platinum mining industry in the 1960s and 1970s exemplified a wider process of diversification within and out of the MEC core as the apartheid-era conglomerates began to move beyond the South African staples of gold, diamonds and coal (while still continuing to invest heavily in them) into 'new' minerals such as chrome and vanadium. This was reflected in the ownership structure of the platinum industry, which was dominated by three major companies: first, Rustenburg Platinum Mines, the number one producer and a subsidiary of the giant South African Anglo American Corporation; second, Impala Platinum, which was integrated into the Afrikaner mining house Gencor; and, third, Lonmin, which somewhat went against this pattern as the subsidiary of the British multinational Lonrho. Nevertheless, Lonrho itself was founded in 1909 as the London and Rhodesian Mining Company and thus had a southern African colonial origin in what is now Zimbabwe. Lonrho subsequently expanded its mining operations through Africa and, from the 1960s, moved into areas as diverse as newspapers, hotels, distribution and textiles to create a sprawling global empire under the leadership of Tiny Rowland (cf. Van Vuuren, 2017). This gave it an international reach that the South African conglomerates did not have, but it was no less embedded (and implicated) in the political economy of apartheid for that.

A crucial feature of the South African platinum industry from its inception was that all the producers faced a common problem: although the bulk of the world's reserves were concentrated in the country, there was very limited and sporadic demand for the mineral globally. The big change came when new vehicle emissions legislation – the result of successful campaigning by the environmentalists – began to be implemented, first in California in the 1970s and subsequently throughout the West and now most of the world. This drove the use of catalytic converters in vehicle emissions systems, which use platinum as a non-substitutable element, leading to a steady growth in demand and thus the conditions for the newer South African producers – Impala and Lonmin – to enter a market which had been historically dominated by Anglo's Rustenburg Platinum. However, here it's also important to distinguish between the different platinum group metals – platinum, palladium, ruthenium, rhodium, osmium, iridium – which are mined together but in different ratios (depending on the geographical location of the reserves) and which have different applications. Thus while platinum, which is largely sourced from South Africa, is used in catalytic converters for diesel engines, palladium is more commonly used in emissions systems for petrol engines, favouring the smaller Russian industry, which exploits palladium-rich reserves. The massive promotion of the light diesel market in the United Kingdom and European Union during the 1990s – itself a (questionable) response to environmental pressure to reduce CO2 emissions – would drive an unprecedented boom in global platinum demand that transformed the South African industry. This we'll come back to. But the main points here are that, first, the relative success of the environmental movement in the global North would paradoxically lead to the expansion of platinum production in the South and, second, that this is where companies that are involved in the fabrication of autocatalysts, like BASF, come into the picture.

Historically, fabricators and end users in the motor industry have acquired their platinum through forward-selling contracts with individual producers rather than through the open market. These guarantee the supply of a specified amount of platinum over a fixed time period – usually around five years – and within an agreed price range. The effect has been to lock the major producers and consumers – such as Impala, General Motors, Lonmin and BASF – into tight and enduring relationships along the supply chain, which also tend to act as a barrier to entry to other mining companies attempting to enter the platinum market. The monopolistic character of the South African platinum industry has been further intensified by the technical challenges of extracting the PGMs from the rock that has been mined. This entails a very complex, time-consuming and capital-intensive set of chemical operations with the effect that processing has been historically dominated by the big three producers, further strengthening their vertical integration. But by far the most important element of all has been their historical control of the resource base.

JK Is this where the question of who owns the land and the mineral rights comes into the picture?

GC That's right. As mentioned earlier, one of the most distinctive features of the platinum industry under apartheid was that its major reserves fell within the borders of two 'homelands': on the one side was Bophuthatswana, where the western limb of the platinum bowl outcrops. This is the region centred on Rustenburg and where

Marikana is situated. The other was Lebowa, where the eastern and northern limbs were located.

Now, a critical feature of mineral law throughout South Africa as a whole (including the homelands) was that surface rights and mineral rights were treated as distinct forms of property, which could be separated from one another (Capps, 2012a). Ordinarily, a mining company would therefore not only have to negotiate a surface lease with the landowner and pay rent but also negotiate a minerals lease with the minerals owner – who could either be the same or a different person – and pay them a royalty for the exploitation of those resources. During the colonial era, for example, exploration companies bought up the mineral rights to vast tracts of land, which could then either be sold on or leased out to mining interests independently of the surface owners. And this is exactly how Lonrho started out, which is why it had 'Land and Exploration Company' in its title.

However, there was also a crucial difference in the way that this property regime was structured in 'white' and 'black' South Africa. In the former, both land and mineral owners (farmers, exploration companies, etc.) had very strong private property rights in law, which would guarantee them a good return if they leased out their assets to mining companies. And this in turn meant that mining companies operating in 'white' South Africa would have to yield a substantial part of their profits to these third parties in the form of royalties and rents. Generally, however, they were able to get around this problem by buying up the rights themselves, as was particularly the case in the gold industry. But in the 'homeland' areas it was different. The intense racial discrimination of the apartheid era meant that individual black people had very limited property rights, and generally it was the homeland governments that exercised control over the land and minerals within their borders. As such, mining companies were able to deal with the homeland states directly, and any rents or royalties – which were invariably lower than in 'white' South Africa – were paid to them. The effect was that it was far easier and cheaper to gain access to mineral resources in the homelands at the expense of the ordinary people living on the ground.

Precisely because of the unique geopolitical location of its reserves, this homeland property regime was of particular benefit to the platinum industry in two key ways. First, it enabled the major producers to acquire virtually all the rights to the world's largest platinum reserve, with Anglo's Rustenburg Platinum Mines taking the lion's share through deals with the homeland governments in Lebowa and (to a lesser extent) Bophuthatswana. And secondly, this not only meant that potential rivals would find it very hard to gain access to these resources and hence enter the industry, but also that the major producers could exercise an usual degree of control over the rate of global platinum supply by unilaterally exploiting or mothballing their vast reserves in response to changes in the world price. As such, the homeland property regime played a vital role both in securing their monopolistic position and in developing an accumulation strategy that could cope with the extreme booms and slumps that had historically beset the platinum industry.

JK How did Lonmin fit in with this pattern?

GC It's important to note that there was an important variation of the homeland property regime in those parts of the Rustenburg region that were incorporated into Bophuthatswana and hence were in Lonmin's area of operation around Marikana. During the late nineteenth and early twentieth centuries, black people in what was then the Western Transvaal had begun to group together to 'buy back' the land of which they had been dispossessed by white settlers since the latter first arrived on the scene in 1837. Because for much of this time it was illegal for black people to enter the property market, they purchased it via white missionaries, who formally registered the land to their mission stations. Interestingly, Lutheran missionaries from Germany played a prominent role here. Later this land was re-registered to local tribal authorities within whose jurisdictions it fell while a change in law permitted chiefs themselves to enter the land market on behalf of their subjects. However, all this was tightly regulated by the state, which also exercised significant powers of 'trusteeship' over this tribally registered land. The effects were twofold.

First, because much of this land was purchased with mineral rights attached and formally registered to them, tribal authorities were legally entitled to negotiate leases with prospectors and mining companies and to receive any rents or royalties generated by its exploitation. Second, however, since the state was also officially designated as the trustee of this land, government officials would have to ratify these deals, while the royalties would be paid into special 'trust funds' (later termed D-, or Development, Accounts) administered by the state on behalf of the tribes concerned. The intervention of state trustees in lease negotiations in these tribal areas often meant that deals favoured the (white) mining companies rather than the (black) landowners while also creating the conditions for the abuse of the mineral revenues that accrued in the tribal trust funds on the part of corrupt government officials. In 1977, these powers of state trusteeship over tribal land and mineral revenues were transferred from the apartheid government to the new regime in Bophuthatswana when it was granted its fictive independence and so became an important feature of the homeland property regime in the Rustenburg region.

This is all particularly relevant to the Lonmin case since the bulk of its mining area is made up of land that was historically registered in this way to the local tribal authority, the Bapo Ba Mogale. As Stanley Malindi and I have shown in a recent working paper, the Bapo got a very raw deal with the original mineral lease which was negotiated with Lonmin during the late 1960s, and it would take over 30 years before they actually saw a full royalty payment from the mining multinational. There has also been systematic looting of these mineral revenues by government officials and struggles have erupted over the ownership of this land between smaller groups in the area and the Bapo chieftaincy. But perhaps these are issues that we can come back to.

JK How did mining in a homeland area affect the migrant labour system?

GC The mining companies that were now operating within the borders of Bophuthatswana, above all Impala and Lonmin, largely continued to source their mineworkers from the traditional labour-sending areas elsewhere in South and southern Africa, partly because of their existing experience and skills, and partly because locals at this time tended to shun underground work as too dangerous and poorly paid compared with employment opportunities elsewhere. This had two key implications. First, the inherent flexibility of the migrant labour system meant that workers could easily be laid off whenever production was shut down in response to unfavourable market conditions. And so it became an important element of the producer's accumulation strategy since the migrant system allowed the social costs of the industry's periodic economic crises to be 'externalised' to labour-sending areas far from the actual mining operations. Second, however, it also meant that the rural areas 'hosting' these operations were now themselves 'receiving' as well as 'sending' migrant labour. At this time, everything was done to keep the 'incoming' mine migrants apart from the local population by isolating them in giant hostels that looked like military barracks. If they ever tried to rent or build accommodation in the local villages, they were driven out by chiefs, and initially there was generally popular suspicion and fear of them. However, over time, political activists on both sides were able to reach out and build connections, and in one particular instance in Bafokeng (which neighbours the Bapo tribal area) mineworkers and villagers briefly came together in a common struggle against the homeland regime. But things would shift again with the end of apartheid in 1994, creating new social relationships and tensions between locals and mine migrants.

JK So let's look at the patterns of change and continuity after 1994.

GC The major changes in the platinum industry after 1994 reflected the problematic fact that South Africa had won its liberation at the very moment that the forces of neoliberal globalisation were really gathering momentum across the world. The giant conglomerates that had been built up under apartheid began to restructure their operations by selling off their least profitable assets and focusing on those areas where they would be most internationally competitive. In the platinum sector, this 'un-bundling/rebundling' process was led by Anglo American, which got rid of its 'underperforming' gold and base metal holdings and pulled its different platinum interests together into a new company – Anglo Platinum (Amplats) – of which it remained the majority shareholder. Soon after, the giant Gencor conglomerate was broken up and Impala reconstituted as a stand-alone corporation, while Lonmin itself was created out of the amalgamation of Lonrho's Western and Eastern Platinum mines as the remainder of the Lonrho group was dismantled. At the same time, the major South African companies effectively 'globalised' themselves by listing on the world's major stock exchanges and relocating their headquarters overseas. The restructured platinum corporations – or their parent companies – would thus increasingly be held by international investors and, as with so much of the post-apartheid economy, subject to the pressures and disciplines of 'financialisation'. As such, all production decisions in the platinum sector were increasingly subordinated to the single imperative of maximising 'value' – that is, profits – for a new and more aggressive breed of global shareholder who viewed platinum as no more than one of a number of potential assets that could be bought or sold, depending on the short-term rate of return (Bowman, 2016).

Ironically, it was the incoming ANC government that had permitted the South African conglomerates to divest as part of the 'negotiated compromise' between the forces of national liberation and big business that underpinned the democratic transition. But the effect would be to dramatically shift the historical relationship between the state and capital in favour of the latter in the post-apartheid dispensation, a process exemplified by the platinum boom itself. As I mentioned earlier, the global platinum price began to rise dramatically from the end of the 1990s in response to surging demand from the autocatalyst industry – driven in particular by the burgeoning light diesel market in Europe – and also the white metal jewellery market, especially in India and China. Virtually overnight, this transformed platinum from a relatively small and marginal element of the South African mining industry to its most dynamic and fastest-growing component. Between 1994 and 2009, platinum output grew by a staggering 67 per cent, while production in the gold industry continued its long-term decline at an almost identical rate of 63 per cent. And by 2010 over 24,000 more workers were employed in platinum than gold, while platinum sales were generating higher returns than any other local mineral commodity. The profits were enormous. In 2001, Amplats became the first-ever South African company that earned US$1 billion solely from domestic operations, and its annual profit rate increased by 87 per cent from 1996. And all this, of course, coincided precisely with the industry's globalisation. Yet, while this made platinum the favourite of the international stock exchanges it also meant that the bulk of these profits now flowed out of the country into the hands of investors and speculators rather than being ploughed back into the domestic economy. Thus, in effect, the more industry expanded, the less South Africa would get to share in the platinum bonanza, as Andrew Bowman (2016) has demonstrated.

The changes at the level of labour were no less paradoxical. From the mid-1980s, the legislative cornerstones of the old migrant labour system had been progressively eroded and reformed. But it would be even more dramatically reconfigured after 1994 in two key ways. First, the mining houses were compelled to upgrade the old single-sex hostels – which had been such potent expressions of apartheid oppression – into family units so mineworkers were no longer divided from their wives and children, and they could all live together. But hostel upgrading was expensive and slow, and so the mining companies began to offer their employees a small Living Out Allowance (LOA) on top of their salaries to rent or buy accommodation in the vicinity. However, because mine wages were so low, and it was virtually impossible for them to raise the bank loans necessary to buy a house, most mineworkers would simply use the LOA to boost their salaries and build themselves a tin shack. And this is one of the key reasons why we saw the dramatic growth of impoverished 'shacklands' on the platinum belt at the exact moment the industry was going through its record phase of productive expansion and profit-making. Over time, migrant workers have become more permanently settled in these informal residential areas, sometimes starting a second family while retaining a rural base in their areas of origin. But the effect has been to increase the pressures of social reproduction as wages have failed to keep pace with increased living costs, particularly in the absence of basic public services in the informal settlements. And inevitably these pressures are particularly borne by the women who both replenish the labour power of mineworkers on a daily basis around the mines and raise the next generation in remote rural areas. It is little wonder, then, that the emblematic demand of the great platinum mineworker strikes of 2012 and 2014 was for a 'living wage' of R12,500.

The other major change at the level of labour has been an accelerating shift towards short-term contract workers on the mines. Contract labour first began to be used for basic, low-skilled surface operations, but it is now increasingly being utilised in 'core' functions underground as well. Recruited from 'labour brokers', this growing category of the mine workforce replicates one of the key logics of the migrant labour system in the platinum industry: it is both cheap to employ and can easily be laid off when market conditions are unfavourable, certainly in comparison with the more permanent workers who now have greater formal protection and rights in terms of post-apartheid labour law. Exploitable and expendable labour therefore remains at the base of the platinum industry, but its conditions of procurement and reproduction have changed.

JK If these were the changes at the levels of capital and labour, what about the homeland mineral property regime on which the industry had historically rested?

GC Here we must note more ironies. Although the homelands had ceased to exist with the creation of a new, unitary South African state in 1994, all the mineral leases and deals from the apartheid period remained in force. This meant that the major producers were particularly well positioned to take advantage of the upsurge in global platinum demand, selectively bringing the best resources on stream from their vast portfolios of unexploited rights. However, the industry's very success at retaining control of the national endowment would also make it the primary target of the ANC's new minerals and mining policy. Legislated as the Minerals and Petroleum Resources Development Act (MPRDA) in 2002, this had three key components which I'll outline in turn (Capps, 2012b).

First, the government would effectively nationalise all mineral resources in South Africa by abolishing mineral rights as a private form of property and replacing them with a centrally administered licence to prospect and mine. Given its deepening neoliberal macroeconomic policy stance, it may at first seem surprising that the ANC government would be prepared to nationalise any kind of economic property. However, when seen from the perspective of capital as a whole, this was merely a rationalisation measure since it would save mining companies the trouble and expense of having to negotiate individual deals with a plethora of private mineral owners, while breaking the white corporation's historical control of the resource base, thus opening it up for new foreign and domestic investment. Indeed, while this move was vehemently opposed by the established platinum producers, the ANC was able to point out that it was merely acting in line with the World Bank's mining policy guidelines for Africa.

Second, the MPRDA would enable the government to transform the *racial* structure of mine ownership, both through the preferential allocation of these new mining and prospecting licences to black-owned companies and by requiring historically white mining corporations to meet a minimum black shareholding target in order to retain their right to mine. Eventually set at 26 per cent of a company's equity, this Black Economic Empowerment (BEE) component would become the main means through which a new black capitalist class was promoted in the mining industry, even if, in keeping with broader trends of financialisation, this largely still tends to be at the level of share ownership rather than effective control at the level of production, and it is mainly leading figures in and around the ruling party who benefited. Moreover, the MPRDA also attached a 'use it or lose it' principle to the new mine licences to force the established producers to either utilise their remaining mineral resources or risk having them reallocated to a new black mining company or another investor who was in partnership with one.

Finally, the MPRDA contained measures to promote the socio-economic development of the rural areas 'hosting' mining operations. It would now also be a condition of the new mining licences that every company had an approved Social Labour Plan (SLP) that specified how it would contribute to the 'upliftment' of local communities, for example by building houses or schools or providing equipment and training, alongside other kinds of 'corporate social responsibility' investments. Moreover, while under the new mine licensing regime all mining companies would have to pay a standardised royalty to the state (another form of rationalisation), rural communities that had previously been in receipt of royalties would be able to retain them so long as they were used for local development. At the same time, mining companies would be 'encouraged' to convert these 'community royalties' into direct equity stakes, thus avoiding double royalty payments and transforming the mine-hosting communities themselves into BEE partners.

JK How did these different elements of the MPRDA come together in the case of Lonmin?

GC Really, they came together in three main ways (Capps and Malindi, 2017). First, like all the other established platinum producers, Lonmin was forced to go out and find black partners in order to meet the 26 per cent BEE requirement and stay in business. Its initial solution was to form an entirely new 'empowerment' company called Incwala Resources, which would hold an 18 per cent stake in Lonmin. Incwala's shares were first offered to a group of black investors who were close to the presidency of Thabo Mbeki, and mainly financed by private bank loans. However, although the deal was initially lauded as a masterstroke by the mining press, it soon ran into trouble when the platinum price collapsed in 2008 and the investors could not service their debts. Under pressure to keep Incwala afloat, Lonmin then loaned Cyril Ramaphosa's Shanduka Resources (now part of the Pembanani Group) R2.5 billion of its own money to buy the original black investors out. As a former general secretary of the National Union of Mineworkers and ANC luminary, Ramaphosa was appointed by the Lonmin board as a non-executive director in the hope that he would bring the company political influence and cover. And indeed, as is now apparent from his infamous emails, this was exactly the role he played in the Marikana events. However, as Lonmin's profits continued to fall, Shanduka itself would prove unwilling or unable to service its massive debt, and the transaction has led Lonmin to lose money hand over fist.

Second, Lonmin has also fallen far short of its own SLP commitments. During the Commission of Inquiry into the Marikana Massacre, it was revealed that Lonmin had reneged on a pledge to build 5,500 houses for mineworkers and local villagers around its mining complex, a responsibility that lay directly with none other than Cyril Ramaphosa as chair of its 'transformation committee'. This R665 million commitment formed part of its 2006 SLP, yet, by 2012, only three show homes had been constructed at a time when Lonmin was paying Shanduka 'advance dividends' to help service its own loan (Forslund, 2013; Hamann, 2014). This not only meant that Lonmin was technically in breach of its legally binding obligations (Chamberlain, 2015). It could also be taken as evidence that it had cynically prioritised its main BEE partner over socio-economic development of its operational area, calculating – and not without good reason – that if the state were to enforce any aspect of its mine licence requirements, it would be in respect of the former and not the latter.

Finally, there are the ways in which the MPRDA shifted the terms of Lonmin's economic relationship with the Bapo Ba Mogale traditional authority whose territory forms the greater part of its mining area around Marikana. As was noted earlier, the original mineral lease very much worked in the favour of Lonmin, and the situation was only made worse by deep political divisions in the Bapo chieftaincy itself. Nevertheless, from an early point one of these factions began to push for the existing royalty to be converted into a direct equity stake in line with MPRDA, but Lonmin repeatedly prioritised black investors with political connections, not least Ramaphosa. Worse, it transpired that during the 2000s Lonmin had underpaid the royalties that were due to the community in terms of the lease agreement while elements in the provincial government and tribal authority had looted over R600 million in mining revenues from the Bapo's trust account. Still some way short of its 26 per cent BEE target, Lonmin management changed tack and in 2014 reached an agreement with the dominant faction in the Bapo chieftaincy (which also now had the backing of the ANC-led provincial government) that the existing royalty would be converted into a direct equity stake in the company, valued at R564 million, along with a number of other benefits. However, no sooner was it done than ordinary community members came forward arguing that the deal was flawed and that the new Bapo leadership was corrupt. Meanwhile, struggles have erupted over its historical control of mineralised land while political violence in the area has intensified.

Here, it's also worth mentioning that one of the other reasons that the informal settlements where the workers themselves live are so deeply impoverished is that they are often located on tribally registered land. A particularly prominent example is the Nkaneng settlement, which is adjacent to the koppies where the massacre took place. According to the Madibeng Local Municipality, there have been numerous efforts to upgrade Nkaneng and deliver proper services like water, electricity and roads. However, although the funds have been made available through various schemes at both the national and provincial level, these efforts have been blocked by the Bapo traditional authority, which is the registered owner of Wonderkop, the farm on which Nkaneng is situated. For its part, the Bapo authority argues that the mineworkers and their families are illegal 'squatters' who have no respect for local customs and should be accommodated elsewhere. Meanwhile, unemployed Bapo youth are regularly mobilised in protests over mine jobs, which they say should first go to 'locals' rather than 'foreigners'. This then points to the ways in which platinum's unique geopolitical location and the legacies of the migrant labour system are combining in a situation of increasing social desperation, which rather than being alleviated by the 'transformatory' measures of the MPRDA is being intensified by them.

JK As a last point, may we shift to the reasons for the bust in the platinum industry in 2008, and what this means for its future prospects?

GC One of the greatest casualties of the 2008 world financial crisis was the car industry. Major manufacturers disappeared overnight while huge state bail-outs were necessary to prevent the whole industry from going under, particularly in the United States. As the leading source of platinum demand collapsed, so did the global price, yet all the major producers had made long-term investment decisions on the basis that the market would continue to grow, and it soon became apparent that the industry was now locked in a crisis of overproduction. Meanwhile, input costs had steadily risen over the preceding years and corporate debts increased. As profits plummeted, the platinum producers came under massive shareholder pressure. But the MPRDA had eroded the big three's ability to control the rate of supply, both by enabling new players to enter the industry and because the 'use it or lose it' principle made it harder to mothball mines until market conditions improved. Worse still, there has been a massive growth in recycled platinum from the catalytic converters of older cars that are now being scrapped.

All of these problems remain, and analysts currently estimate that over 70 per cent of the platinum sector is failing to turn a profit at present. Of the major producers, Lonmin has been worst hit, particularly as a result of poor management decisions over the years. According to its latest results, Lonmin is in such deep financial crisis that it is currently unable to repay its debts despite multiple bail-outs and the support of the South African Public Investment Corporation, which now holds almost a third of its stock. With its share price at an all-time low, Lonmin has now become the target of a takeover bid by a major new player in the platinum industry, Sibanye-Stillwater. Sibanye began life as GFI mining (which was spun out of Gold Fields South Africa) but has more recently been acquiring bargain-basement platinum assets: first, Anglo Platinum's ageing Rustenburg Platinum Mines, then the newer entrants Aquarius and Stillwater, which were wiped out by the platinum slump. At the time of this interview, Sibanye's bid for Lonmin has yet to be approved by the South African government and the competition authorities in the United Kingdom, but, if successful, this will make it the world's second-largest platinum producer, knocking Impala into third place. However, while this may rescue Lonmin's beleaguered shareholders and stop the mine from going under, analysts warn that the main attraction for Sibanye is Lonmin's impressive mineral-processing facilities, control of which will cement its place as an independent producer. Consequently, thousands of underground jobs are at risk at Lonmin, while at this point it is also not clear what the takeover will mean for the local rural community and its own equity stake.

As for the future of the industry as a whole, it's impossible to predict and I can only point to some factors to consider. The light diesel vehicle market is continuing to shrink in Europe and the United States, particularly in the wake of the Volkswagen scandal. This is hitting the South African producers particularly hard because, as we previously discussed, platinum is used in diesel autocatalysts and the South African ore tends to be platinum-rich. Conversely, a new round of growth in global petrol engine sales has pushed up the palladium price to the benefit of the Russian producers. And while there are many other uses for platinum, especially in the white metal jewellery market and a range of industrial applications, this has not yet proven sufficient to offset the combined effects of the decline in the diesel market and the erosion of control over supply. So, things are looking pretty grim for the South African producers at present, and it is probable that more firms will go under and mergers and acquisitions will increase.

The most obvious way out of this predicament, at least in the short term, is the imposition of tighter vehicle emission legislation in existing diesel markets – particularly in the global South – which would require catalytic converters with higher platinum loadings. Some analysts believe South Africa should be lobbying hard for stricter emission controls in emerging car markets and setting an example by enforcing them in its own. But there has been little sign of this happening so far. The longer-term hope for the industry, somewhat ironically, is a shift away from carbon-based energy altogether through the uptake of new hydrogen fuel cell (HFC) technologies. HFCs generate electricity by combining hydrogen and oxygen, with platinum as the catalyst. The major motor manufacturers have for some years been experimenting with HFCs as an alternative to battery-powered cars, while there is also strong interest in the possibilities for HFCs in public transport systems, both road and rail. If any of these took off, it could completely transform the platinum industry in the way that catalytic converters did from the 1970s. But opinion is currently divided on whether the technology will be viable on a mass scale given that HFCs currently require high – and hence expensive – platinum loadings and an entirely new hydrogen infrastructure – encompassing manufacturing, transportation and fuelling – would have to be put in place. Still, given its enormous potential, the South African state could be playing a leading role in developing a new carbon-free economy centred on HFCs through a coordinated industrial strategy that began with its enormous platinum reserves and ended with its substantial energy and car industries, under worker and community control. But for now, the industry remains locked in crisis and is unable to escape the pathologies of the market.

References

Bowman, A. (2016) Dilemmas of distribution: Financialisation, boom and bust in the post-apartheid platinum industry, SWOP Working Paper, Johannesburg

Capps, G. (2012a) Victim of its own success? The platinum mining industry and the apartheid mineral property system in South Africa's political transition, *Review of African Political Economy* 39, 131, pp. 63-84

Capps, G. (2012b) A bourgeois reform with social justice? The contradictions of the mineral development bill and black economic empowerment in the South African platinum mining industry, *Review of African Political Economy* 39, 132, pp. 315-333

Capps, G. and S. Malindi (2017) Dealing with the tribe: The politics of the Bapo/Lonmin royalty-to-equity conversion, SWOP Working Paper 8, Johannesburg

Chamberlain, L. (2015) Lonmin has broken law by dodging housing obligations, *Business Day*, 1 July

Fine, B. and Z. Rustomjee (1996) *From Minerals-Energy Complex to Industrialization*, Westview Press, London

Forslund, D. (2013) Coping with unsustainability, Bench Marks Policy Gap series, 7, www.bench-marks.org.za/

Hamann, R. (2014) Lonmin's mining charter compliance and the social conditions around mines near Marikana, Senior Researcher Phase 2, Marikana Commission of Inquiry

Mamdani, M. (1996) *Citizen and Subject: Contemporary Africa and the Legacy of Late Colonialism*, Princeton University Press, Princeton

Van Vuuren, H. (2017) *Apartheid Guns and Money: A Tale of Profit*, Jacana, Johannesburg

Three monuments in Johannesburg
▶ Commemorating the importance of miners in the history and development of the country, the statue of Andile Msongelwa (2013) is a gift from the Chamber of Mines and a number of trade unions.
▶ The statue of the settler George Harrison designed by Tinie Pritchard in 1987. Harrison is said to be the first person to discover gold in 1886. A work commissioned by the city of Johannesburg for its 100th anniversary.

▶ The Miners' Monument by David McGregor (1964) shows an underground team of miners from 1936, consisting of two black workers and a white foreman. It is a donation from the Mining Association of the former provinces of Transvaal and Oranje Free State to the City of Johannesburg.

5. THERE IS NO CHANGE IN MARIKANA: THE PERSPECTIVE OF WOMEN

Asanda Benya and Judy Seidman

There is no change in Marikana. […] The people are living in shacks that are leaking, there is no sanitation, no running water, no electricity. And there are no roads. Where is the better life for all?
– Thumeka Magwangqana at the General Assembly, Berlin, 4 November 2017. [1]

When women living in the shadow of platinum mines today say that there is no change in their lives, we must question the narrative that South Africa's mining sector has moved from apartheid into an era of democracy and human decency. This chapter explores the lives of women affected by platinum mining in South Africa, stories that have been ignored and silenced in understanding the mining industry today.

We examine the different ways that women's lives are shaped by mining: women in labour sending areas, who historically formed the invisible backbone of South Africa's mines; women who have migrated from traditional homes to live near the mines; women who were born and raised in areas where the mines are found; and women who have recently started working in the mines. These are not distinct categories. Women's lives are fluid, changing as the industry and society itself change. Our study focuses on Lonmin, with its bloody history of the 2012 Marikana massacre. The story women tell here is not a one-off event or disaster but of embedded and ongoing strategies used by platinum companies, supported by transnational companies, to maximise profits, profits which flow from the lives and work done by women as much as from the labour of men. We ask: what has changed or not changed around women's roles in the platinum mines since the 1990s? What has been done to improve women's lives? How do these changes impact on the behaviours of both women and men? How does this affect the lives of women today?

Backdrop: Apartheid, social reproduction and migrant labour

The mines, and cheap migrant labour to the mines, formed the soil in which South Africa's ingrained racism and apartheid flourished. From the 1870s, South African mines relied on the labour of low-paid black migrant men who came from distant rural areas to work underground, living in single-sex hostels, while women remained in far removed rural areas, today called labour sending areas (LSAs), previously named native reserves, Bantustans and homelands. Scholars have described how these racialised and gendered workforce structures 'externalised' the cost of reproductive labour for the black working class from the mine companies to the LSAs. Wages paid to (black, male) mineworkers were insufficient to support families nor did wages pay for community infrastructure, schools and health facilities to sustain the supply of mine labour. Instead, women in LSAs carried the costs of supporting families that provided labour to the mines, bringing up children who would later work in the mines and caring for returning sick mineworkers and the elderly. Wolpe summarised this 'externalisation of reproductive labour costs' in 1972:

> The extended family in the reserves is able to, and does, fulfil 'social security' functions necessary for the reproduction of the migrant workforce. By caring for the very young and very old, the sick, the migrant labourer in periods of 'rest', by educating the young, etc., the reserve families relieve the capitalist sector and its state from the need to expend resources on these necessary functions (Wolpe, 1995:67).

Scholars have done relatively little research on how gender discrimination and oppression emerged from, and reinforced, this structure of mine labour. Apartheid's pass system forced men to come alone to the mines while families – women, children, those too old to work – were left in (or removed to) 'tribal areas'. Apartheid laws, backed by a battery of gendered behaviour, patriarchy and state violence, forced women to remain in the homelands. A typical woman's story said:

> My husband was working in the mines. I married him in 1968, he was already a mineworker. [...] We had no food to put on the table. He would stay there the whole year and come back with that little money. [In 1988...] he came back and spent a month with us, then went to hospital from breathing problems, then he passed away. They called me into TEBA and gave me R2,000 for the funeral (Seidman and Bonase, 2015:54).

Cash sent home by the mineworker was never enough. Family members left in the LSAs – especially women – supplemented inadequate remittances with subsistence farming and other non-cash survival mechanisms, mostly 'traditional' women's work of building homes, gathering wood for fuel, carrying water. Women held together families (often extended families) while their men were away. After 1948, apartheid solidified this: where you lived and worked, how you survived, was defined by race, by 'tribe' and by gender. In sum, cheap black labour to the mines was extensively subsidised by African households. Thus black women's labour underpinned profits made from South African mines.

What happened in post-apartheid society?

Studies today show how South Africa's platinum mines have perpetuated, adapted and reinvented key aspects of the apartheid mine labour system. Older mineworkers speak of an unbroken continuum of migrant labour and underdevelopment. Younger mineworkers say: 'We are the youth of this democracy. But we came here to find these same conditions where our forefathers, our fathers were working, it has not changed: the same dust, the same air, polluted air, the tools and everything, the same that have killed our fathers' (Seidman and Bonase, 2015:3).

The end of apartheid did not end entrenched poverty and underdevelopment in LSAs. Rather, the mines adapted to fit new legal and political frameworks, leaving structural faults intact. The post-apartheid state took several steps aimed at ending migrant labour. It removed apartheid laws relegating women and families to the LSAs, and it ended single-sex hostels at the mines.

Government also ended regulations that barred women from mine work. The 1911 Mines and Works Act had categorically stated that 'no person shall employ underground on any mine a boy apparently under the age of sixteen years or any female' (Alexander, 2007:214). The Minerals Act of 1991 also banned women from working underground (Simango, 2006:15). But later laws replaced these: the Mine Health and Safety Act (1996), the Mineral and Petroleum Resources Development Act (MPRDA of 2002) and the Broad-Based Socio-Economic Empowerment Charter (Mining Charter of 2002).

Today, in theory, mine companies implement these laws. Yet, in practice, men work in the mines while women stay 'at home' in LSAs. Numerous factors drive this: historical patterns of employment and work; structural underdevelopment in LSAs; and the failure to build viable communities near the mines. Gender discrimination remains key to all of these.

Employment patterns entrench migrant labour

In South Africa today, (black, male) miners still do not earn a living wage that supports the miner and his dependants. Research in 2008 showed that permanently employed workers across the Platinum Belt, including Lonmin's Marikana mine, took home R3,000 (200 euro) a month while contract workers took home less (Webster et al., 2008). By 2012 workers reported earning between R4,000 and R6,000 (270–400 Euro) (Benya, 2012a). The 2012 strike of rock drill operators at Marikana, followed by strikes across the Platinum Belt in 2014, demanded a monthly wage of R12,500 (800 euro), double the take-home pay of many rock drill operators.

Low wages mean that families cannot survive on what the mineworker sends home. This in turn determines the course of women's lives and work in mining communities and LSAs. In the last 20 years, laws covering mine recruitment and employment were extensively rewritten. New laws require mines to hire workers on permanent contracts and to hire locally where possible. Platinum mines must by law provide statistics to government agencies to prove compliance with these laws (Benya, 2015c:70). But the new regulations leave a large grey area between 'permanent' employment, defined-term contracts (employment for specific jobs for a set time) and subcontracted work (where other companies subcontract to do work for the mine).

Rather than hiring permanent employees, mine companies bend regulations by using labour brokers and subcontracting work. Mines engage labour brokers to hire workers, the broker signs a contract with the worker and then sells his labour to the mine. With subcontractors, mines contract a smaller company to do a specific job and the subcontractor then hires workers to do the work. The mining industry estimates that 29 per cent of all mineworkers are subcontracted. In 2012, Anglo Platinum

(Amplats), Lonmin and Impala Platinum (Implats) reported that between 7 and 30 per cent of workers were subcontracted (Forrest, 2013). But independent researchers report that on some platinum mines as much as 60 per cent of the workforce is subcontracted: 'The use of these subcontracting workers has been highest in the platinum sector [...]. For example, in 2005, 54,667 of a total of 96,734 employees in the platinum group metals were outsourced [...]' (cited in Gwatidzo and Benhura, 2013:14).

Contract workers are usually hired to work in more hazardous areas of mines. When mines compile statistics for compliance reports that monitor the Labour Relations Act, the Health and Safety Act and the Mining Charter, they often leave out workers employed through labour brokers and subcontractors. This was more the case for Health and Safety statistics. In 2007, for example, the *Financial Mail* reported that the Chamber of Mines (an employer organisation) was selectively reporting accidents and fatalities, only when an accident has more than four deaths, presumably excluding those affecting subcontracted workers. They reported that between 2000 and 2005 the Chamber only reported 90 deaths in 15 incidents while the Department of Mineral Resources recorded 1,584 fatalities and 26,893 accidents (*Financial Mail*, 10 August 2007).

Platinum mines boast that they pay employees far more than workers in other fields. But workers hired by labour brokers and subcontractors do not work for the mine. Even where permanent employees and subcontracted miners work on the same team, subcontractors may offer different conditions, pay and work structures to those given to permanent employees. Subcontracted workers can earn less than half of what a permanent employee earns for the same job. While all platinum miners work overtime (often up to 12 hours a day), permanent employees receive standard overtime pay and benefits; contracted labour get less overtime and benefits or none at all. Contract workers often work under less safe conditions than full-time mine employees.[2] Contract labour often has no union protection or job security. One labour broker admitted, 'We have no union members and we don't bargain wages.' Subcontractors and labour brokers also undermine post-apartheid efforts to end migrant labour. The Mining Charter requires mines to hire local residents, but labour brokers hire mineworkers coming from far off at the local recruiting office near the mine:

> Labour brokers prefer experienced retrenched mineworkers as they come with skills, such as rock drilling, and tend to be less educated whilst requiring little or no training. Many of these workers had previously been recruited by TEBA for the gold mines but now return to register with brokers. In order to get employment they present themselves as locals thus allowing mines to comply with the Mining Charter and simultaneously avoid the levy on the recruitment of foreign labour (Forrest, 2013).

Further, although new mining legislation encourages mines to employ women as well as locals, the preference for migrant workers means that brokers also overlook women for mine jobs.

Underdevelopment in labour sending areas

A known cause of underdevelopment in the LSAs is that workers too ill or unfit or old to work are sent back home to become a burden on their families. Mine companies today boast of improved health measures for workers in prevention, treatment, and disability pay. But companies still find ways to shift the burden of ill health, disability and death onto mineworkers' families (especially onto women) and onto the (inadequate) public health system in LSAs.

Companies by law provide regular medical check-ups and treatment for employees at the mines. Yet workers complain that a check-up once a year picks up serious illness only after it has spread. The worker who is diagnosed with serious illness is hospitalised, but if he does not recover he is sent home. Injury or occupational disease ends the worker's income, then he returns home to add financial strain to the family and daily burdens of care work performed by women. Ex-workers and families fail to access pensions, disability and death benefits, further feeding underdevelopment in LSAs. Families have no choice but to send another younger, healthy member to the mines, reinforcing the cycle of impoverishment and underdevelopment at their home areas (Seidman and Bonase, 2015).

In the LSAs, underfunded public health clinics rarely have resources to treat these illnesses. Moreover, mine health facilities do not diagnose or treat miner's family members, even when the family member has a mine-linked illness like TB or HIV. Women therefore carry the burden of care for ill mineworkers without compensation or support from the mines. Some women forgo their own jobs and deplete limited household resources to care for men who are injured at the mine or whose lungs have been ravished by mine dust. When the ex-mineworker dies, the family is poorer through lack of income and may be sick from contagious mine-related disease.

At the mines

> We cannot bring our families here – there is nothing for them here, this is no way to live. (Seidman and Bonase, 2015:35)

The post-apartheid democratic dispensation presumed that mineworkers would bring their families to live near the mines. The mines agreed to convert single-men hostels into family living units or pay workers a 'living-out allowance' to find housing for their families near the mines. Today the platinum mines give about a third of mineworkers a 'living-out allowance' of around R1,800 (120 euro) per month. But mineworkers say this amount does not pay for suitable accommodation, food and transport for a single person living near the mine, far less for a family.

Further, there are no decent family houses available, nor infrastructure to support viable communities, near the mines. Mineworkers spend 'living-out allowances' to rent illegal and un-serviced shacks in informal settlements that are rife with health risks, crime and environmental degradation, without their families (Bench Marks Foundation, 2011:42).

In 2013, the Bench Marks Foundations noted:

> The overwhelming majority of Lonmin's 28,230 established employees stay in informal settlements or in township shacks. As for the additional 8,300 contract workers, for which accommodation Lonmin takes no responsibility, their residence in informal settlements is almost given by definition. According to a very well-placed source, Lonmin estimates that it provides acceptable accommodation for about 5,000 out of over 28,000 established employees.

Evidence at the Farlam Commission of Inquiry showed that Lonmin consistently failed to meet legal commitments made in social responsibility agreements with the government to provide housing for workers. Between 2007 and 2010, Lonmin promised to build 5,500 houses for workers and convert 92 hostels to family units but only built three show houses and converted five hostel blocks. By 2012, Lonmin had built no more houses, although it had converted 108 hostel blocks (Bapo Ba Mogale, 2014).[3] As well as no decent housing near the mines, there is little or no infrastructure for homes: roads, sewerage, sanitation, water, electricity, schools or clinics. 'We do not have good roads. We would like the mine come here and help these people build better roads, so we can go to work. But also this water: we drink it because it is all we have. It can make you sick, see, it is brown from that tap. But we do drink it' (Seidman and Bonase, 2015:43).

Neither mining companies nor local government take responsibility for mineworker settlements. Under South African law, mine companies own mineral rights but not the surface of the land. Since mine companies do not own the surface, they are unwilling to provide infrastructure for communities that build on it (even where communities consist of mine employees). Local authorities also refuse to construct infrastructure for new settlements where the mines own underground rights since, as the mines expand, blasting and digging destroys the new construction. Company management claims that workers prefer to live like this: 'Many employees have opted not to invest their resources in formal housing and have chosen to live in informal housing. This has precipitated the emergence of a backroom informal economy, which brings with it a host of negative socioeconomic issues, not least of which is a rapidly growing community without basic services and infrastructure' (Lonmin, 2014).

The mineworkers themselves tell a different story:

> Who wants to live in a shack? […I]t's cold in the winter, it is hot in the summer. This is not a good condition where a person can stay. This is our home because we spend a lot of our time here. We don't get enough money to build proper homes where we are coming from either. The money we get here is not even enough for us to stay in these shacks where we are living, for our basic needs here (Seidman and Bonase, 2015:38).

One result of this is very few wives and children from far-off rural areas join the workers at the mines. These women remain in the LSA; they still subsidise the miner's wage by subsistence farming and traditional women's work, they still provide social reproductive labour, and they remain ignored and unseen in this new democratic dispensation.

The 'two households' myth

Mine management attribute both migrant labour and the gendered structure of work at the mines to the workers' traditional, patriarchal culture. Companies assert that mineworkers prefer to maintain a wife 'at home' in the LSAs, then move in with a second woman living near the mine (portrayed as a girlfriend or *nyatsi*, or perhaps a polygamous second wife). Management argue that supporting two households drives mineworkers' demands for higher wages. One paper written in 2013 states:

> The migrant labour system led to the development of 'second families' in which migrant workers establish local households with second wives or girlfriends in the shanties around the mines. This has been encouraged by the abolition of the single sex hostels and paid for by 'living-out allowances'– a cash allowance to 'live out', that is to exit the migrant hostel system […]. This socio-economic condition of mineworkers supporting a second family on or near the mine while at the same time needing to visit his rural home has led to demands for higher wages (Gwatidzo and Benhura, 2013).

Mineworkers reject this with anger: 'This is an insult to us and our families. We love our wives, we would like to see them coming and staying with them, the amount of money we are earning does not allow for that. Who would bring their loved ones to live under these conditions where there is no water, no electricity, no schooling facilities for the children?' (Seidman and Bonase, 2015:62).

This myth has disastrous consequences for women who live near the mines. Women who remain in LSAs are labelled legitimate wives; women who live near the mines are stigmatised as 'town women', prostitutes or girlfriends who cannot be seen as workers' helpmates or family and thus get no benefits from the employer. In reality, women's lives are fluid in this changing environment: a woman from the LSAs may move to the mines as a mineworker herself or as a worker's wife, while a woman living near the mine may develop a long-term relationship and have a family with a migrant worker.

Destroying local communities in mining areas

We also find a third 'category' of women: women defined as 'local' (or even 'indigenous') whose ancestors lived in areas where the mines are located today. Since the 1960s, platinum mining has caused massive disruption and destruction of nearby established 'traditional' or 'tribal' communities. Today, 20 years into a democratic South Africa, these communities face relocation to make way for mine development. One research group in Bojanalo in 2015 demanded that government end forced relocation without negotiation with residents and provide adequate alternative residence for those dislocated (Seidman and Bonase, 2015:65).

Gavin Capp points out (see the interview in this book) that platinum mining developed in the 1960s mostly in or near areas designated as homelands. Where commercial farmers owned the land (i.e. land owned by white farmers), platinum companies bought mineral rights from farm owners and black farm labourers were summarily expelled. Where mineral deposits occurred on land falling under so-called 'tribal authorities' (designated Bantustans or homelands), the companies dealt with the apartheid minister of native affairs on behalf of chiefs. Post-1994, the government confirmed that traditional authorities continue to govern 'communal lands'; mines now deal directly with these 'tribal authorities'.

More recently, platinum mines have provided shares in the mine company to the tribal authority's investment arm instead of paying royalties to the tribal authorities for use of mineral rights. These direct equity arrangements are likely to further remove the community from the tribal authority's decisions around use of communal land.

Local communities displaced by mine operations often start shack settlements on land no authority has claimed. Immigrant mineworkers then rent rooms and shacks there, straining infrastructure (water supplies, roads, sanitation and schools). Overcrowding, pollution and overuse of scarce resources lead to destruction of the land itself. The dislocation of communities through deals between mines and tribal authorities has led people to challenge whether tribal authorities represent the local population. Displaced communities point out that these chiefs were often confirmed in power by settler and colonial powers and then by the apartheid state (Seidman and Bonase, 2015:41).[4]

More questions arise when tribal authorities are viewed through a gendered lens. When colonial and apartheid authorities appointed tribal authorities, they also entrenched patriarchy.[5] Under these tribal authorities women had no rights over land where the women lived and farmed. Women could not rule, except as regents for male children. Women could not speak for themselves in the tribal political space. When the post-apartheid South African government confirmed the powers of tribal authorities, they confirmed what has been called 'toxic hyper-patriarchy' (Suttner, 2017). Gender activists argue this has no place in South Africa's democratic constitution.[6]

Arrangements between mines and tribal authorities also provide for corporate social responsibility programmes that promote employment and economic welfare for local communities affected by the mines. These include Social Labour Plans (SLPs) legally required by the Mining Charter and MPRDA. But local communities displaced by the mines rarely benefit from SLPs. They receive no alternative homes or employment. Land and water are polluted. Mines fail to provide decent houses for their own workers; they do not provide replacement houses for those moved off their land.

Lonmin has repeatedly failed to implement SLPs. In 2014 Lonmin agreed to spend over R201 million (13.5 million euro) on SLP projects to provide 'for 126,000 people living in the greater Lonmin community' (Kotze, 2017; Krause, 2015). In September 2017, community members took to the streets over lack of service delivery as projects failed to materialise (IOL, 2017).

Women have no say in deals between mines and tribal authorities, but the impact of these decisions on women's lives is stark. The mine controls scarce water resources, and exhausts and pollutes existing ground water while local residents (in practice, women) are barred from accessing water and land they previously used for daily survival.[7]

Women displaced from traditional communities who move into informal settlements often lose what little status they had. If and when these women develop relationships and have children with immigrant workers, they give up any position in the clan. As a result, neither these women nor their children benefit from mine social responsibility projects set up by tribal authorities in the clan's name.

Gender segregation in the workforce

In the last two decades, government has legislated to include women in mining, in the Mine Health and Safety Act (1996), the MPRDA (2002) and the Broad-Based Socio-Economic Empowerment Charter (the Mining Charter of 2002). The Mining Charter sets a 10 per cent target for women mineworkers and ties this target to the renewal of mine operating licences. Currently, in the country's platinum mines 11.5 per cent of the workforce is female (Botha and Cronjé, 2015:10-37; Botha, 2013; Chamber of Mines, 2017:27).

But while mines now allow women to work underground, their inclusion remains tenuous. Nominally, women work 'as equals' in the mines but in reality women's daily experiences at work, especially underground, are marked by exclusion. Women remain on the fringes of the mining labour market. One of the reasons for their peripheral status has to do with the 10 per cent quota set by the Mining Charter. At best mines have viewed the 10 per cent target as a maximum percentage for hiring women, an end goal; at worst it is treated as tokenism.

Men in mining and those in power at times remark that men are employed because they are competent to do mine work, but women are incompetent tokens of transformation. Some say that 'women's bodies are weak and cannot do mine work' or that 'doing mine work will render them sterile' or 'their bodies will collapse if they continuously physically exert them' as mine work demands. Adding to these pseudo-scientific reasons rooted in protectionist discourse, some say that 'women are only included because the government *insists* on including them' (Benya, 2012c; Benya, 2008).

As a result of these beliefs that men in the mines still hold, some occupations such as rock drilling remain exclusively reserved for men, even though women have been in mining for more than 13 years. Men, both in management and at training centres, insist that women's bodies are not suitable for holding and continuously operating drilling machines (Benya, 2012b).

Instead of viewing women as legitimate mineworkers who add value to teams and the mines, women are seen as an inconvenience or non-core helpers brought in to appease the government. Their bodies are viewed as illegitimate and weak for mining, and relegated to the margins. At the training centre, women are not allowed to take classes that are considered masculine or perceived to require strength. In cases where some 'compulsory' practical session requires physical exertion, male instructors insist that women observe instead of partake in practical training. Instructors suggest that women act as assistants, holding down the rope, passing material or carrying equipment, while men do the actual physical work. These gendered differences at the practical sessions mean that by the end of the training most men, even those who struggled significantly at the beginning, perform better than most women. As a consequence of these gender ideologies and the protectionist discourse which reinforce female fragility, the mine workforce remains segregated by gender, with most women in entry-level and low-paying jobs (Benya, 2017:509-522).

When women are assigned to core mining jobs such as winch or locomotive operation, their team members usually informally reallocate the work. While a woman might be hired as a winch operator, in reality she is reallocated to tasks such as bringing material, painting walls, fixing pipes, cleaning drains or fetching water for her team. Other women work as *pikininis* (also known as assistants) for their shift supervisors, carrying bags and doing administrative work and sometimes personal tasks for them. The *pikinini* is an occupation that has no formal status; in recent years it has been increasingly done by women.

Reallocation of jobs and tasks means that women are alienated from their work and isolated from their teams. In other words, the gender segregation of the mining workforce continues unabated, albeit within the mines, invisible from the public's and the government's view: literally and figuratively 'underground'. Since women are often far removed from their teams they hardly learn skills on the job and hardly build strong friendships with their co-workers, important elements that strengthen solidarity in the dangerous underground world. The isolation from teams and alienation from work mean there is hardly any transfer of skills to women.

These informal job reallocations come at a heavy price. Not only do women not learn mining skills, but they also take home substantially less than their male colleagues. By not doing core mining activities they are not paid production bonuses earned by male co-workers who do core mine work. Thus, work reallocation reinforces the idea that women cannot do mine work and deprives them of extra production income that male workers get. The 'tokenistic and objectifying inclusion' of women in mining is 'as disempowering as complete exclusion' (Crenshaw, 1993).

In addition, studies confirm that sexual harassment and violence against women working at Lonmin and other platinum mines are 'common and pervasive'. 'Sexual harassment was reported to have occurred in the cages that transport employees to mining areas, as well as during transit, and in ablution facilities. Individual women who were working on their own had also reported instances of harassment' (McKay, 2017). After the rape and murder of mineworker Pinky Mosiane while working underground at Anglo Plats' Khomanani mine in 2012, the Department of Mineral Resources issued a directive saying that women workers should not be made to work in isolation underground; however, cases of rape and murder underground continue (IndustriAll Union, 2017).

After reaching the 10 per cent quota for women, mines do very little to attract and retain more women and nothing at all to transform mining culture to build inclusivity and gender equity. Instead, mines continue to mobilise masculinity to achieve production targets, to the exclusion of women who refuse to embrace masculinity and 'masculine' ways of working and being at work.

There is also a race dimension to employing women. Underground jobs are filled by black women; white women are only found above ground. White women who form part of the above-ground workforce mainly hold positions with administrative powers (Pretorius, 2016). These positions pay more and have better benefits: when a woman who works in these jobs is sick she can go to a doctor of her choice rather than the mine hospital. As well as holding positions of power, white women also have social capital, sometimes through their husbands who worked as supervisors or support managers in the mines. Other vestiges of the apartheid workplace order continue in the post-apartheid era: white women are seen as fragile and not capable of manual work, while black women are viewed as 'labouring bodies' (Benya, 2016). Black women are scraping the bottom of the mining barrel. They enter the workforce as second-class citizens and a good source of cheap labour.

In all of this, unions are complicit with mine management. Unions refuse to recognise that workplace struggles are not gender-neutral; workplace struggles also must be viewed through a gender-sensitive lens. The union 'boys' club' tends to focus on so-called 'real workplace' (masculine) issues and then signs agreements with employers that fortify women's subjugation.

Take for instance housing and accommodation policy. This policy, designed long before women entered the mines, was renegotiated and tweaked when women entered the mines to include a clause that women should not be housed in single-sex hostels. Mining officials say this was added because mines and unions did not want to 'separate women from their families', thereby destabilising families. Union officials argue that they 'did not want to reproduce the apartheid migrant labour system'. This policy reproduces old ideologies about women being *first* obligated to their families and not the workplace sphere, embedding gender stereotypes of women as both ultimate homemakers and outsiders in mining (Benya, 2013). It reinforces the gendered attitudes that lead to women's removal from certain teams and their exclusion from 'masculine' occupations.

The continued gender-segregated workforce at mines is a consequence of the 'masculine design' of mines, not an unavoidable natural phenomenon. While post-apartheid legislation allows women to work in the mines, their inclusion remains uncertain and the mechanisms used continue to emphasise female domesticity. Numerical changes have been accompanied by very little transformation of gender relations, biases and gender order. Women remain outsiders, systematically and strategically marginalised by the masculine mining order and occupational mining culture.

Women living near the mines

Very few of the 11.5 per cent of women mineworkers come from communities where the mines are located. In today's tweaked migrant labour system, few mines around the Platinum Belt hire local women, preferring male workers who have worked in mining before. Even women working on the mines are likely to come from traditional LSAs. Thus, women who hope to find jobs in mines operating near their villages are disappointed.

In a country with an unemployment rate of 26.6 per cent where over 30 million people (out of 55.9 million) live below the poverty line, with 58.6 per cent females living in poverty compared to 54.9 per cent males, hiring males over females condemns women to continued poverty and reproduces gender inequality in mining towns. This in turn reinforces the stereotyping and categorisation of women in mining communities (Benya, 2015c).

Women from mining communities report that if they want jobs in the mines they have to bribe officials. One woman remarked, 'Jobs are for sale, if you don't have money you don't get a job.' Getting a job in the mines costs between R1,800 and R3,000 (120–200 euro) with those hired by labour brokers paying the higher prices (Benya, 2015a:277). Also, bribing mine or union officials for a job is not only financial but in kind. A *masiza* (human resource officer) and a number of women report that sometimes to get a job, 'women have to sleep with the men from the mines'.

Women from communities around the mines (whether born locally or immigrant) who do not work in the mines do not qualify for benefits and services provided to mineworkers. Even as women in rural areas still struggle to support families of mineworkers without water, roads or good schools, women who live near the mines also perform unrecognised and underpaid labour to support mineworkers. In informal settlements around the Platinum Belt women wake up early every day to collect bathing and drinking water and cook food so that mineworkers can get ready to go to work. Water taps are often kilometres away from miners' housing in informal settlements; women go out to search, queue for water and return home before workers can prepare for their morning shifts. If women are late fetching water the worker is late for work and the mine's daily production suffers (Benya, 2015a:287). Since the mine's morning shift starts at 5 a.m., these women cannot sleep in.

This work defines women's days and depletes women's energies. 'Women's work' for male mineworkers is defined by the mines and contributes to productivity at the mines. Yet women do this hard work without pay for their labour or recognition from the mines.

The mines go further, labelling these women as prostitutes and girlfriends of mineworkers, an outcome of the 'two households' myth. This stereotype from apartheid days states that women living in mining communities survive through illegal, precarious means, selling liquor and sex. These 'loose' and 'undesirable' women are seen as posing a threat to the productivity, health and morality of male mineworkers.

This causes massive damage to women who live near the mines. The mine companies refuse to provide town women and their children with access to services or benefits, which are supposed to go to mineworker families. Mine clinics often refuse to treat town women when they are sick or in emergencies. Shortly after the Marikana massacre, when four women were shot and injured by the state police while going to a meeting to support the strikers, the mine clinic refused to treat the wounded women (Benya, 2015a:284).

But like their sisters in the LSAs, town women play an integral role in the social reproduction of labour at the mines. Their hard labour on a daily basis underpins profits of the platinum industry, but these women are also treated as an inconvenience, invisible and unpaid. These women confront a daily reality where mines dig precious minerals from rock literally below their homes but refuse to build decent houses and paved roads for their use.

The local government authorities add a range of excuses to the reasons the mines give for failing to support communities near the mines. They justify refusing to provide basic services such as sanitation or clinics or clean water because the community residents do not belong to the right tribal group, they vote for the 'wrong party' (not the ANC but the Economic Freedom Fighters) or they are unemployed (often adding that these women are sex workers and girlfriends).

The companies' stigmatising and disadvantaging of 'town women' stirs up divisions between these women and country wives, as well as dividing both these groups from women who are still part of the traditional community. Emphasising 'differences' between these groups of women, and refusing to provide services to them based on this stereotyping, systematically reinforces ethnic tensions between groups of women and throughout mining communities (Benya, 2015b).

Lonmin as case study: After the massacre

One of the most striking examples of how gender exploitation continues in post-apartheid platinum mining comes in the treatment of women after Lonmin's Marikana massacre in 2012. After the massacre, Lonmin and government would only recognise the claims of wives and family who had been registered with mine authorities as beneficiaries. This excluded women whom the company called 'town women' and 'second households' in Marikana, forcing a gap between grieving communities and isolating family members from LSAs who came to Marikana after the massacre.

When women living in informal settlements in Marikana organised themselves under Sikhala Sonke to protest against the massacre and Lonmin's treatment of mine communities, Lonmin further demonised these women. Lonmin's rejection has become more strident since Sikhala Sonke brought a case of neglect and lack of accountability by Lonmin before the compliance adviser of the International Finance Corporation, the World Bank investment body overseeing social responsibility for private sector transnationals in developing countries (see the chapter by Patrick Bond).

For the women from LSAs that Lonmin sees as 'legitimate' widows, Lonmin still denies responsibility for the massacre and refuses to pay compensation. Then, just before the Farlam Commission announced its results, Lonmin offered limited assistance to the families of those killed (Seidman and Bonase, 2015:76).

Lonmin management proposed that the widows themselves or another family member should get a job working at Lonmin to replace the income of the killed breadwinner. Over the last 15 years mines have offered jobs to family members of workers who died at the mines (most often through mine accidents) to 'assist' the family for the loss of income. Replacing the deceased mineworker by a family member, often their own children, highlights the biological reproductive work that women do for the mines. When the mines extended job offers to the widows, they further boasted that this would address the gender injustices of previous years.

The widows of the massacre see this not as a remedy but as further entrenching the exploitation of the family in the LSAs – now on offer to women as well as men. This 'solution' neither allows them to take control of their lives nor addresses inherited gender inequalities. Rather, the jobs widows were offered at the mine entrenched existing power relationships between management, mineworkers and their families, and indeed cemented the migrant labour system in its new shape. The widows themselves argue that this 'solution' causes more damage, pushing them into living situations that they would not choose if they had any other way to support their families.

Since the massacre these women desperately need incomes. Asked what they wished for the future, the widows said they wanted to get money and skills so that they could stay in their home areas and earn a living (most often by running a small business). Several hoped to finish building the house that they and their husbands had planned. The widows saw Lonmin's offer of work as a 'quick fix' that would provide a cheap solution for Lonmin instead of paying compensation for killing their husbands.

Lonmin further offered to provide education for the children of mineworkers killed in the massacre (but only children of those registered as wives in the company books). The company offered to send children over the age of five to boarding schools. This would give the children a better education than that available in their home areas while enabling their mothers to work in the mines without having to bring their children with them to their new jobs.

The widows realise that Lonmin's offer to send their children to boarding school fails to respond to the demand that the mines should take responsibility for educating all children of mineworkers, alive and dead, in LSAs and mine communities. But when the widows asked Lonmin to upgrade schools in LSAs rather than take their children away to school, the company responded that this would be far too expensive as the orphaned children come from many different areas.

Lonmin CEO Ben Magara boasts about this, pointing out: 'While we can never replace their loved ones, we have offered employment opportunities to their families and every child of school going age is a beneficiary of the 1608 Education Trust. This is in addition to the statutory payouts from pension and life funds (RDM News Wire, 2015).

The widows commented at the BASF shareholders' meeting in 2016:

Lonmin tells me that this job is a kind offer so that I can earn the money that my husband worked for in their mines, so that I can feed my children. But for me, going to work at Lonmin was a hard choice because I had no other way to feed my children. They do not even pay me today the living wage of R12,500 that our husbands died for, three years ago. Today they take my hard work, and pay me this small amount, and say I should be grateful to them. This is not compensation, it is more exploitation, and revictimisation: from slave to slavery.

Lonmin is proud that they have sent my children, and the children of some of the other widows, to boarding school. We say that education for our children is something we want and need, but it is not easy that our children must be away from us. We, the widows say, 'They killed our husbands. They have taken our children away to boarding school. We cannot stay with our families, when we are working in Marikana. Our houses are closed now. We do not have homes any more.'

Since 2016, 32 women in this group work at Lonmin, 22 employed as surface workers and 10 as mineworkers underground. (Where a woman goes to work depends upon her physical fitness.) The widows say they took jobs in the mines in desperation, to support families and children. This is not the reparation that they sought. Moreover, offering mine jobs to these widows further divides workers along gender, urban-rural, and ethnic lines.

When the widows started work in Marikana, the women discovered that Lonmin had retrenched newly hired (male) workers to 'open up' jobs for the women. These retrenched workers stood outside the mine gates, hoping for work, openly hostile to the widows who took their jobs. One widow commented: 'Our husbands did not fight and die so that we could take another worker's job. They wanted a better life for all workers, not this' (Seidman and Bonase, 2015:33).

In 2016, presenting their case and Lonmin's treatment at BASF's annual general meeting in Mannheim, BASF refused to support their demands (see the chapter by Maren Grimm and Jakob Krameritsch).

Towards justice for women in South Africa's platinum mines

Thus, while the apartheid laws have been repealed and new laws aim to redress past gender imbalances, on the ground very little has changed. Despite the shifting character of the industry in post-apartheid society, the platinum mines still treat the hard labour done by women as invisible, marginalised and unpaid. The mines still systematically externalise social reproduction labour costs to groups of women and reap the profits. Mines are still primarily male spaces, recycling myths that reinforce ethnic and gender hierarchies. The continuity of gender disparities between apartheid and post-apartheid platinum mining are glaring, adapting gender inequality and oppression to new shapes and colours but leaving the fundamental exploitation in place.

In effect, women continue to be the invisible pillars of mining, the hidden shock absorbers of the mining industry. The mines maintain established exploitative gendered work structures because they bring in profits. And no one, in South Africa or globally, seems ready to hold the mining industry to account for this. Until such a time that these issues are systematically recognised and until we demand that companies pay back the fruits of women's labour, we can expect that the marginalisation of women, and the impoverishment of our society, will continue.

But we also see that the cracks are widening. Even now women are rising. Resistance is inevitable if the system does not adopt fairer and less exploitative ways of extracting the minerals. As we saw in Marikana in 2012, people are demanding change. There is no turning back.

Asijiki!!!

Notes

1. See http://international-institute.de/en/general-assembly-generalversammlung-assemblee-generale-2/
2. When deaths on South African mines increased by 27 per cent in the first three months of 2011, researchers blamed the poor safety and health record of subcontractors. See *www.iol.co.za/business.../rising- sa-mine-deaths-need-urgent-attention-1055349.*
3. See also www.mail.businesstimesafrica.net/index.php/engineering/item/1445-south-africa-four-years-after-marikana-massacre,-british-mining-company-fails-to-improve-squalid-housing-conditions-for-workers.
4. Some also question whether 'tribal authorities' qualify as 'indigenous peoples' in the international framework adopted by the UN. Although the Bapo Ba Mogale website claims it first formed a political structure in a previous century, mine companies and transnationals such as BASF claim that chiefs represent 'indigenous' populations. Bojanala residents recently challenged tribal authorities in court, claiming that the Boer Republic in the 1880s forced their families to give up privately owned land to Bafokeng chiefs. Not all people born and raised in Bojanala are Tswana clan members. Migrant workers came to work on white-owned farms; some remained there. As traditional chiefs do not recognise these people as clan members, they have no rights in the clan.
5. There is ongoing debate about whether patriarchy was inherent in precolonial societies or brought in by the colonialist authorities. A literature review can be found at politicaleconomicandsocialissues.blogspot.com/2007/09/african-women-under-pre-colonial.html.
6. The ANC December 2017 conference passed a resolution to curb the powers of tribal authorities over land (www.heraldlive.co.za/news/2017/12/22/chiefs-bite-back-land-move/). It remains unclear how this will be taken forward in government.
7. Newspapers carry stories about violent community protests over water shortages in the Madibeng area (near Lonmin's Marikana) from 2014 (www.mg.co.za/article/2014-01-21-brits-residents-to-march-over-continued-water-shortages) and near Brits from 2015 (www.mg.co.za/article/2015-03-19-more-to-brits-protests-than-meets-the-eye).

References

Alexander, P. (2007) Women and coal mining in India and South Africa, 1900–1940, *African Studies* 66, 2–3

Bapo Ba Mogale (2014) Submissions of the Bapo Ba Mogale community to the Marikana Commission of Inquiry, 3 November 2014, www.marikanacomm.org.za/docs/201411-HoA-BapoBaMogale.pdf, accessed 5 July 2015

Bench Marks Foundation (2011) *Rustenburg Community Report 2011*, www.bench-marks.org.za/publications/rustenburg_community_report_2011.pdf, accessed 5 July 2015

Bench Marks Foundation (2013) *Coping with Unsustainability*, Policy Gap 7 (Lonmin 2003-2012), October

Benya, A. (2008) Research diary, September

Benya, A. (2012a) Interviews with mineworkers in Rustenburg, Research diary, April

Benya, A. (2012b) Interviews with mineworkers and middle mine managers in May–October 2012.

Benya, A. (2012c) Interviews with mineworkers, Rustenburg, April, June, July, September and October

Benya, A (2013) Gendered labour: A challenge to labour as a democratizing force, *Rethinking Development and Inequality* 2 (Special Issue)

Benya, A. (2015a) Marikana: The absence of justice, dignity, and freedom?, *Human Rights in Minefields, Extractive Economies, Environmental Conflicts, and Social Justice in the Global South*, 1, Dejusticia Series, Bogota, Colombia

Benya, A. (2015b) The invisible hands: Women in Marikana, *Review of African Political Economy* 42, dx.doi.org/10.10 80/03056244.2015.1087394

Benya, A. (2015c) Women, subcontracted workers and precarity in South African platinum mines: A gender analysis, *Labour, Capital and Society* 48, 1&2

Benya, A. (2016) Women in mining, PhD thesis, University of the Witwatersrand, http://wiredspace.wits.ac.za/handle/10539/22425

Benya, A. (2017) Going underground in South African platinum mines to explore women miners' experiences, *Gender & Development* 25, 3, pp. 509-522

Botha, D. (2013) Women in mining: A conceptual framework for gender issues in the South African mining sector, PhD thesis, University of Pretoria

Botha, D. and F. Cronjé (2015) Women in mining: A conceptual framework for gender issues in the South African mining sector, *South African Journal of Labour Relations* 39, 1, pp. 10-37

Buhlungu, S. and A. Bezuidenhout (2008) Union solidarity under stress, *Labour Studies Journal* 33, 3, pp. 262-287

Chamber of Mines (2017) *Mine SA 2016 Facts and Figures Pocketbook*, Johannesburg

Crenshaw, K. (1993) Beyond racism and misogyny: Black feminism and 2 Live Crew, in M. Matsuda, C.R. Lawrence, R. Delgado and K.W. Crenshaw (eds.), *Words That Wound: Critical Race Theory, Assaultive Speech, and the First Amendment*, Boulder, CO

Forrest, K. (2013) Migrant labour: Discarded but not discontinued, *Wits Journalism*, 1 October 2013, www.journalism.co.za/blog/migrant-labour-discarded-but-not-discontinued, accessed 5 July 2015

Gwatidzo, T. and M. Benhura (2013) Mining sector wages in South Africa, LAMP Working Paper 1, Labour Market Intelligence Partnership

Kotze, C. (2017) Lonmin hands over social projects worth R18.8m, *Mining Review*, 6 November, www.miningreview.com/news/LONMIN-hands-social-projects-worth-r18-8m/

Krause, R.D. (2015) Actors in the social and labour plan system, in *Good Company?*, Social and Labour Plans Report, Centre for Applied Legal Studies (CALS), Wits University

IndustriAll Union (2017) Murder exposes rampant sexism in South African mines, 12 December, www.industriall-union.org/murder-exposes-rampant-sexism-in-south-african-mines

IOL (2017) Marikana 2.0: History repeats itself as Lonmin fights with community, 11 May, www.iol.co.za/business-report/companies/marikana-20-history-repeats-itself-as-LONMIN-fights-with-community-9064255

Lonmin (2014) *Rebuilding Bridges*, Sustainable Development Report 2014, Human Settlements, sd-report.LONMIN.com/2014/reporting-according-to-our-material-focus-areas/1-employee-relations/human-settlements/, accessed 5 July 2015

McKay, D. (2017) Lonmin says sexual harassment of women 'common and pervasive', *Miningmx*, 2 November, www.miningmx.com/news/platinum/30861-lonmin-reports-sexual-harassment-women-common-pervasive/

Pretorius, C. (2016) An exploration of the experiences of white women workers in the coal mining industry of South Africa, Master's dissertation, University of Pretoria

RDM News Wire (2015) Release of Marikana report a 'vital step in the healing process', 26 June 2015, www.sowetanlive.co.za/news/2015/06/26/release-of-marikana-report-a-vital-step-in-the-healing-process, accessed 26 June 2015

Seidman, J. and N. Bonase (2015) *We Have to Talk, We Need Changes: Voices from Platinum Belt Mine Workers*, Khulumani Support Group, Johannesburg

Simango, K.B. (2006) An investigation of the factors contributing to failure of heat tolerance screening by women at Impala Platinum, MA dissertation, Da Vinci Institute for Technology Management, South Africa

Suttner, R. (2017) Cyril Ramaphosa's presidency: An opportunity for clean-up and new beginning, *Daily Maverick*, 9 January, www.dailymaverick.co.za/article/2018-01-09-op-ed-cyril-ramaphosas-presidency-an-opportunity-for-clean-up-and-new-beginning/#.WITGGIQ-fq0

Webster, E., A. Benya, X. Dilata, K. Joynt, T. Ngoepe and M. Tsoeu (2008) Making visible the invisible: Confronting South Africa's decent work deficit, SWOP Working Paper, Wits University

Wolpe, H. (1995) Capitalism and cheap labour power in South Africa, in W. Beinart and S. Dubow (eds.), *Segregation and Apartheid in Twentieth Century South Africa*, London

▶ **pp. 124/125** After a meeting of Sikhala Sonke in the informal settlement of Wonderkop, Marikana.

▶ **pp. 126/127** Drinking water being transported in the village of Ncgobo in the Eastern Cape, South Africa's largest labour sending area.

▶ **pp. 128/129** Asanda Benya (left) and Nnaniki Mosito at the Phokeng mine near Rustenburg after a day of work, where they were employed as winch operators.

6. CONFRONTATIONS WITH BASF: ADDITIONS TO THE COMPANY HISTORY AND THE PLOUGH BACK THE FRUITS CAMPAIGN

Maren Grimm and Jakob Krameritsch
Translated by Nivene Rafaat and David Beckett

You could have heard a pin drop as the approximately 6,000 shareholders listened to Bishop Jo Seoka's speech at BASF's Annual Meeting on 30 April 2015 in the Rosengarten in Mannheim.

Because none of what Seoka was addressing had even been mentioned in the media or by BASF itself. The connection between BASF, Lonmin and the Marikana massacre was new to the majority of people present. Seoka, bishop of Pretoria and a confidant of the workers of Marikana, asked simple questions: 'What is your reaction facing the news, that one of your most important platinum suppliers is co-responsible for murder, violation of human rights and inhuman living conditions of its workers?' (Seoka, 2015).

The company's management was prepared for the visit, as the Association of Critical Shareholders,[1] whose shares gave Jo Seoka access to the shareholders' meeting, had announced the visit of the bishop four weeks in advance and had also submitted a motion against giving formal approval to the board of directors (see counter proposal pp. 12, 13). More surprising was that the relationship between BASF and Lonmin, almost three years after the massacre in South Africa and more than 30 years after the start of business relations, had after all now become public. Although the massacre was reported in the German media in 2012 and supply chain responsibility was certainly discussed in other contexts, German journalists had not traced the route of the South African platinum any further (see the chapter by Stefan Buchen).

The reaction of Kurt Bock, chair of BASF's board of directors from 2011 to May 2018, to Jo Seoka's speech was not surprising at first. He assured the bishop and all those present of BASF's sympathy for the 'tragic events' and then referred to the final report of the South African Commission of Inquiry, which had not yet been published. But then he made it clear that BASF regarded Marikana as a domestic problem for South Africa, as Bernd Freytag reported in an article for the *Frankfurter Allgemeine Zeitung* (6 May 2015): 'These things have to be sorted out in your country first.' Bock tried to keep BASF's room for manoeuvre to a rhetorical minimum. He admitted that Lonmin has been a 'trusted' partner of BASF for decades, but 'it's hard for them to judge from the distance'. At present, he argued, his company could not do anything. Therefore, no contribution could be made to the required compensation fund. They did not have the power to act or sufficient knowledge of the situation in South Africa, as Jakob Krameritsch reported in *Afrika Süd* (May/June 2015).

The power and size of the company, the way the company presented itself as valuing social and ecological responsibility and, last but not least, its decades-long presence in South Africa – all of this was disregarded by Bock.

What follows illustrates the discrepancy between the way the transnational company presents itself and the reality, and also supplements the narrative of the company with lesser-known aspects. The second half of the chapter illustrates the confrontations so far surrounding the Marikana 'case' at BASF shareholders' meetings from 2015 to 2017.

The global corporation from the Palatinate

The chemical industry in Germany is responsible for almost half a million jobs and 185 billion euro in revenues, making it the third-largest sector after the automotive and mechanical engineering industries. About a quarter of the products manufactured go directly to end-consumers, 75 per cent go to processing industries such as plastics processing and the automotive, packaging and construction industries. Additionally, the chemical industry is also an important customer for other sectors: in addition to the mineral oil industry and the electricity, gas and machinery industries, this also includes the waste disposal, transport and legal, tax and management consulting sectors.[2]

This brief outline shows the importance of the chemical industry for the German economy alone. Until 2017, BASF had been the world's leading company in this sector for over a decade – in short, the largest chemical company in the world.[3]

Since 1865, BASF has had its headquarters in Ludwigshafen am Rhein, Germany, where it still operates the world's largest integrated chemical complex with around 110 production sites and 200 different plants. It employs approximately 33,000 people and, according to the BASF website, 2,800 kilometres of above-ground pipelines have been laid. This BASF site alone consumes about 1 per cent of Germany's total power requirements, according to the 25 February 2014 edition of *ARD Mittagsmagazin*. The company employs around 115,000 people worldwide across 353 locations in over 80 countries.[4] The company's products are largely invisible to ordinary consumers, but are just about everywhere: in clothing, in PlayStation consoles, in the dashboard of the car and in everything that can now be made of plastic; in vitamin tablets, cosmetics, in lacquers and paints, in the fizz of our lemonade, in baby diapers, sneaker soles, animal feed, packaging materials and, not least, vehicle catalysts. BASF is a supplier for almost every industry: it produces dyes, textiles, materials, components, food, pharmaceuticals and pesticides for the agricultural, automotive, electrical, chemical and construction industries, and is also involved in the exploration and production side of the gas and oil industry.

The bigger picture

Anyone who visited BASF's German website at the beginning of 2018 would have come across this image: in the foreground, a man in overalls carrying a lavishly filled box of various vegetables. He is bathed in the warm light of the setting sun. A set of three vegetable icons catches the eye, adorning both his overalls and the vegetable box. The concrete structure of a long bridge can be seen in the background, slightly blurred, spanning a wide waterway and in harmony with the colour of the overalls and the wooden box.[5]

One click takes you to a video: the vegetable supplier again, loading more crates from his van, children with a hand-painted picture and a model of the bridge, a woman playing the harp on the bridge, a man and his dog driving over the bridge in a car, a fisherman in front of the bridge. 'Bridges connect. And we make sure they hold.'

This is an advertisement for the construction chemicals division of BASF. However, it is very likely that BASF products are used not only in the bridge, but also in the paint, plastic parts and the catalyst of the van that delivers the vegetables, perhaps also in the carbon fibres of the fishing rod and the dyes of the crayons or the strings of the harp. And what about the eye-catching vegetable box? Is the world market leader also responsible for food residues, monocultures and unforeseeable effects of genetic engineering projects, all associated with increasing dependence on a few transnational corporations? In view of the following news, the vegetable supplier may not have ended up in the picture composition by chance.

In March 2018, EU Competition Commissioner Margrethe Vestager announced the EU Commission's approval of a mega-merger in the agricultural chemicals industry: Bayer may acquire US seed manufacturer Monsanto. The market leader for genetically modified seeds, which are known to be particularly spray resistant and treatment-intensive, was to merge with Bayer, the market leader in plant chemistry. To reduce the risk of cartelisation, however, the acquisition is subject to conditions, including the divestiture of Bayer's soy, cotton and oilseed rape portfolio and the associated agricultural chemicals segments. These business units will be acquired by BASF. The remedy package includes research platforms for plant biotechnology, licences for digital applications in agriculture – and also a few vegetable varieties (Grefe, 2018).

In any case, the bishop from South Africa was right when he expressed his conviction that BASF would certainly want to maintain its good image, which it had worked so hard for. This reputation is the result of decades of hard work, as we shall see.

BASF's image

The 2002 company biography (Abelshauser, 2003) commissioned by BASF was edited by the economic historian Werner Abelshauser,[6] who had already proven himself as a specialist for sensitive subjects with his company biography of the Essen-based steel giant Krupp. Under the keyword 'South Africa' he registers a single, short entry. The context focuses on regional sales in connection with events of global political significance. It states that 'operating in a global market almost inevitably entailed minor upsets'. One of these 'upsets' shown on page 100, alongside the Boxer Uprising in China and presidential elections in the United States, is the Anglo-Boer War in South Africa. This suggests that South Africa has long played a role in BASF's business activities,[7] but nothing more can be learned about it.

The following is listed on BASF's current website under the section 'Chronology of BASF history in Africa'.[8] 'BASF products were first sold in South Africa in the nineteenth century.' We go on to learn that BASF products were sold by the South African sales company Taeuber & Corssen. The next entry in the timeline is the establishment of the Johannesburg head office in 1966. Otherwise little more can be gleaned. From 2006, the entries become more numerous: 'BASF South Africa celebrates 40-year existence in South Africa.' The same year, BASF took over a number of South African competitor companies and branches: CHC Elastogran, the automotive refinishing technology company ART, and South African branches of US competitor Johnson, as well as the synthetic resin products division and part of Degussa's construction chemicals division. Among the acquisitions in 2006 was the automotive supplier, speciality chemicals group and precious metal trader Engelhard, the world's largest manufacturer of automotive catalysts, which also has a long history in South Africa.

Gauteng,[9] Hollywood, Ludwigshafen

The founder of Engelhard, Charles Engelhard Senior, emigrated in 1896 from Germany to the United States, where he specialised in the industrial application of precious metals and the associated manufacturing processes. Precious metals, more precisely gold and platinum, also brought him to South Africa, where he founded the Engelhard Precious Metals Corporation in 1949, one year after the National Party came to power with their apartheid programme. His son, Charles Engelhard Junior, who took over the company after his father's death in 1950, knew how to circumvent the gold export bans that existed in the 1950s. He had the South African gold cast into statues, which he then legally exported as works of art. This laid the foundation of the Engelhard empire. The James Bond author Ian Fleming, who knew Engelhard personally, was inspired by him to create the character of Goldfinger.[10] In the film (Hamilton, 1964: minute 109), he is introduced as follows: 'Big operator, worldwide interests. All seem reputable. Owns one of the finest US stud farms.' A British intelligence expert describes the core of his business model in a later scene: 'Gold, gentlemen, which can be melted down and recast, is all but untraceable, which makes it, unlike diamonds, ideal for smuggling, attracting the biggest and most ingenious criminals'(Hamilton, 1964: minute 20). The characteristics of commodity trading during the early apartheid era can therefore also be found in this form in pop cultural references.

But Engelhard Junior was not just a businessman on the border of legality who knew how to exploit loopholes in the law for his profit and thus set an example for the tax avoidance tactics of today (see the chapter by Christoph Trautvetter). He was also a thoroughly modern figure: a political lobbyist.[11] Engelhard is considered the engine of the South Africa Foundation, an association of businessmen founded in 1955 who worked to portray apartheid in a positive light in the United States – but also worldwide – and to block or delay embargoes against the regime. The South Africa Foundation was described by a South African business magazine as the 'most effective foreign lobbyist in Washington' for apartheid – from its foundation up until the Reagan era

(Nixon, 2015:96). Engelhard was a close adviser of presidents Kennedy and Johnson, and in this role he played down the Sharpeville massacre and repeatedly convinced them not to refrain from further investments in apartheid South Africa. The acquisition of Engelhard in 2006 made BASF the world's largest player in the catalysts business and was also the beginning of its relationship with Lonmin as its main customer.[12]

Technologies for a state of emergency

In 1950, towards the end of the IG Farben era,[13] the South African state-owned enterprise South African Synthetic Oil Limited (SASOL) acquired the rights to a process to produce synthetic fuel and other petrochemical substances from coal. BASF had been the first to file a patent application for this process, which had been developed in the 1920s, and expanded by the IG Farben group for large-scale industrial use. During the Second World War, when Nazi Germany was cut off from oil imports, this enabled the country to produce synthetic petrol on a large scale.

In particular, the large deposits of hard coal but, perhaps even more so, the threat of isolation made this synthesis process attractive to the apartheid regime. With the help of German industry, SASOL was established from 1950 onwards. The company was privatised in 1979, but continued to maintain close relations with the government as a strategically important company. BASF still maintains good business relations and international joint ventures with SASOL until today.

Good business climate with the apartheid regime

In 1975 the business journalist Jürgen Räuschel published his book *Die BASF. Zur Anatomie eines multinationalen Konzerns* (BASF: The Anatomy of a Multinational Corporation) in which he took a critical look at the company. In it he provides a chronological list of the acquisitions and takeovers of shares by BASF since its foundation in 1952. The portfolio includes, among other things, coal and copper mines, mineral oil refineries, paint factories, fertiliser and special plastics manufacturers, potash mines and also the majority holding in a Turkish bank. During these decades, BASF expanded worldwide, in Antwerp and Addis Ababa, Bangkok and Barcelona, from Austria via India to Australia, from Brazil to Canada – and grew into a company that operates globally. Räuschel also records the opening of BASF South Africa Ltd in Johannesburg in 1966, but he has no more to say about the company's involvement in South Africa.

The global automotive industry certainly played an important role for BASF as a major customer for, among other things, coatings, plastics and – from the 1980s at the latest – catalysts. In South Africa, the three major German automobile manufacturers, Volkswagen, BMW and Daimler-Benz, had their own local production facilities from the late 1960s, indicating that BASF was involved in business here too. It can also be assumed that agricultural products were important for sales in an agricultural country like South Africa. The only other entry on BASF's website during the time of the apartheid government confirms this: the announcement that animal feed production in South Africa began in 1987. Overall, the export world champion Germany did good business in South Africa and in 1981 its sales there were equal to those it made in neighbouring Denmark (*Der Spiegel*, 14 December 1981).

During the years of apartheid, *Der Spiegel* regularly published opinion pieces about South Africa. Although the brutal suppression of the 1976 Soweto student uprising marked the beginning of one of the most violent phases of the apartheid regime, BASF was left untouched, and the company remained calm, as the 26 February 1979 issue of *Der Spiegel* reported. BASF South Africa CEO Rolf Rauschenbach called on the 400 West German companies in South Africa not to be troubled by the disturbances ('Wir Schwarze werden als erste leiden' (Us black people will suffer first)). Most of the large German companies were undeterred by the international campaigns, sanctions or UN embargoes that followed the Soweto Uprising and remained in the country even during the last, bloody decade until the end of the apartheid regime.

Although Germany officially joined the UN economic sanctions against South Africa in 1983, BASF and Hitachi, its Japanese partner at the time, took over the sale of computers to South African government authorities after US-based IBM bowed to growing public pressure against the apartheid regime and withdrew from business (see the chapter by Simone Knapp). The decision caused an international stir after the *New York Times* reported on it in 1986, and civil rights activist Jesse Jackson and several US trade unions criticised Hitachi's and BASF's behaviour. Anti-apartheid activists threatened BASF by claiming that this would have a negative impact on BASF's US business. The Japanese computer systems had been sold by BASF to the Persetel agency, which had been supplying the South African state, police and secret services with weapons, weapon parts and computer technology since the beginning of sanctions (*Der Spiegel*, 2 March 1987). Although BASF publicly declared that it had not violated any embargo rules, it admitted to having sold the computer systems because, it claimed, others would have done it anyway if they hadn't. At the beginning of May 1987, the Green Party in the German parliament demanded clarification on Germany's participation in computer sales to South Africa and submitted a parliamentary question to the federal government,[14] since the Foreign Ministry would have had to approve the export.[15] The answer, on the authority of Hans-Dietrich Genscher (Free Democratic Party), then foreign minister, came six months later and defended BASF, as there was allegedly no evidence of irregularities.

German government circles also had a direct and leading role in arms deals with the apartheid regime. This was apparent in the scandal surrounding German military submarines that Franz-Josef Strauß had 'promised'[16] his friend Pieter Wilhelm Botha, South Africa's president. In 1986 it became known that HDW of Kiel, the largest German shipyard, had helped the South African military to expand their submarine fleet, which violated the arms embargo that had been in place since 1963. An inquiry committee of the German parliament, which sat for several years, did not finally clarify who exactly had been involved in the matter on the part of the German government or how deep the involvement had been. It was not until 2016 that the minutes of meetings were made public, from which it is clear that Helmut Kohl had even discussed the business personally with President Botha during the latter's state visit to Bonn in June 1984 (Van Vuuren, 2017). The fact that BASF sells coatings for submarines to HDW can be found on BASF's website.[17] In this book, Jan Pehrke writes about the good relations that the long-time chancellor, a native of Ludwigshafen, maintained with BASF throughout his life.

The 'hardline faction'

On 18 December 1989, an article entitled 'Chemieindustrie: Geschäft ist Geschäft' (Chemical industry: Business is business) was published in *Der Spiegel* on the occasion of a forthcoming change in BASF's board of executive directors. This provided a broad overview – from the classic problem areas of the chemical industry to the morality of BASF's corporate leaders and the mood among the German population. Every fifth respondent to a survey conducted by the Düsseldorf Institute for Applied Marketing Sciences stated that BASF was particularly irresponsible, immoral and unethical. Other chemical companies used BASF as a negative yardstick against which to measure their own actions. When Hoechst decided to use a more effective method for wastewater treatment, the company's hardliners expressed concerns and referred to BASF. They would only do what the law required and no more. Elsewhere the outgoing CEO, Hans Albers, was quoted as saying: 'The tendency to political overreaction in the field of environmental legislation strangles research.' The article also explained that the future chair, Jürgen Strube, had been involved in the computer business with apartheid South Africa. Furthermore, BASF had long been reselling a pesticide that had been banned in Germany to South America. And members of the staff of a US subsidiary who requested information about the toxicity of certain products during a trade dispute were locked out without further ado.[18] Finally, BASF was responsible for 14 'water-related pollutant discharges' into the Rhine in 1989 alone. All in all, it was a sobering assessment by the magazine.

Flight forward – moral turning point

From the beginning of the 1980s, BASF – like the entire chemical industry – was confronted with increasing popular environmental awareness, the Green Party in the Bundestag and stricter environmental legislation and controls. With the collapse of the Eastern Bloc[19] and the end of the Cold War, images of the enemy shifted, ethical parameters changed and – not least – new markets opened up as a result. Kurt Bock, who has been chair of the board for many years, wrote his doctoral thesis, entitled 'Corporate success and organisation', in 1985 on how companies can react to external challenges, adapt their organisational structure and secure their competitiveness. This is certainly a subject that has always interested business economists. However, the challenges facing transnational corporations from the 1970s onwards concerned not only ecological but also increasingly human rights issues that directly affect the relations between economy and morality. Recent research has focused on the extent to which public disputes over political and economic relations between Western Europe and South Africa during apartheid played an essential role in these adjustment processes (Andresen, 2016). Companies that were successful in the apartheid state and therefore came under political pressure often argued at the time that it was only through their presence that they could exert a positive influence by allowing black trade unions in their companies or by setting up their own training and qualification programmes for black workers. Only in this way could they contribute to improving social conditions, while sanctions, boycotts and disinvestment would hit the black population first and hardest. The extent to which these positions were a strategy to avoid major losses will not be discussed in detail here. Of particular importance and interest is that this argument offered itself as a blueprint for reconciling seemingly irreconcilable positions. A model was developed that allowed companies to act as moral players, absorbed criticism from outside and at the same time enabled business interests to be protected under difficult conditions. Apartheid was therefore also the birthplace and training ground of modern corporate social responsibility (CSR) politics.

The fact that the chemical industry in particular was predestined to develop solutions for problems that it had helped to cause not only pacified the critics, it was also increasingly interesting from an economic point of view. According to *Der Spiegel* on 8 February 1993, BASF planned to use a first large-scale plant costing around 100 million marks at their site in Ludwigshafen in order to detoxify the approximately 175,000 metric tons of waste gases produced there every year. The municipal waste incineration plant in Ludwigshafen was also to be equipped with the system. In 1990, Jürgen Strube became the new chair of BASF, the first not to be a chemist. Almost 20 years later, Sybille Zehle looked back in *Manager-Magazin* (21 August 2009): 'Thanks to Jürgen Strube, BASF is a pioneer: from the chemical company's 'Verbund' strategy to its ethical orientation.' As Dinah Rajak also describes in this book, it was particularly those corporations that were regarded as ignorant of human rights or responsible for ecological misconduct that then became pioneers of the new policy of corporate social responsibility in the 1990s. In this light, the Engelhard acquisition also fitted well into BASF's new portfolio. Since the 2000s, Engelhard has also specialised primarily in environmental technologies, chemical catalysts and precious metals trading.[20] From today's perspective, the companies' strategies have been successful. In many cases, they have succeeded in taking on the arguments of their critics and maintaining a great deal of room for manoeuvre through CSR strategies. So far, voluntary initiatives have largely prevented companies from being overly regulated and monitored by national or international legislation. What is more, the fundamental incompatibility of continued economic growth and social and ecological sustainability in capitalism initially seems to have been invalidated.

Core competence: Sustainability

For BASF, the inspiration and part of the solution may have been its own 'Verbund' system. As early as the 1960s, BASF set itself a 'new technological paradigm' (Abelshauser, 2003:493). To this day, the company produces a wide range of chemicals in its own value chain, from the basic product to the highly refined special product, whereby the accumulated energy and waste products are also recycled. The Verbund system – as part of its new image – was more than adequate to mediate between the company's own profit interests and the ecological and ethical reorientation that the public was demanding. Until today, it has been a unique selling point for BASF – at that time the company decided not to follow the trend towards specialisation, but to offer a broad range of basic products for further processing as well as to go into refining itself and develop special applications in line with customers' demands. This was considered sustainable, at the time for reasons that certainly had little to do with ecological aspects. Today this is what BASF's website says: 'In addition, the by-products of one plant can be used as the starting materials of another. In this system, chemical processes consume less energy, produce higher product yields and conserve resources. In that way, we save on raw materials and energy, minimise emissions, cut logistics costs and exploit synergies.'[21] And as Thorsten Pinkepank, head of CSR, also explains in the BASF *Sustainable Development Report* (February 2014): 'For us, sustainability is both a responsibility and a business opportunity. In this way, we contribute to solutions for sustainable development.'

Sustainability has become one of the most contentious terms, and has unfortunately meant a less sustainable balance sheet especially for those who are concerned not only about share price and dividends. That is why, for example, the name of the audit initiative, which was founded in 2011 by some of the globally operating chemical companies, is TfS – Together for Sustainability.[22] Carolijn Terwindt describes in this book the companies for which TfS has so far proved to be sustainable. Similarly, BASF never gets tired of referring to its founding membership of the UN Global Compact in 2000, in which companies undertake to comply with minimum social and environmental standards wherever they operate and along their supply chains (see the chapter by Akhona Mehlo).

Even though BASF is right to claim that it conducts innovative research and development, the company's product range continues to be highly specialised in fossil fuels. Even if the Wintershall[23] subsidiary will soon merge with DEA, and in this way initiating BASF's exit from a hundred-year history of oil and gas production, Kurt Bock, the outgoing chair, recently stated in *Automobilwoche* (24 March 2018): 'But to believe today that e-mobility will replace the combustion engine in the next ten years would be absolutely naive.' BASF is also well positioned for the future of agriculture – chemically supported monocultures that will be managed digitally in the future. Even with the best CSR department, these contradictions will not disappear in the long term. And so, BASF is also high up on the list of climate polluters: sixth in the world rankings (*taz*, 12 September 2017).

In the legal sense, BASF may think it is on the safe side, but for moral reasons the company can no longer continue to refuse the outstretched hand of the bishop from South Africa.

KEY MOMENTS IN THE PLOUGH BACK THE FRUITS CAMPAIGN
2015: Bishop Jo Seoka focuses on cooperation, which BASF rejects

Bishop Seoka's speech at the 2015 BASF shareholder meeting, which took place three years after the Marikana massacre, marked the first time that the company was called upon to accept responsibility for the terrible living and working conditions that existed at the start of BASF's supply chain. This initial confrontation with BASF challenged the corporation to follow their self-imposed ethical principles with action and to help put in place sustainable measures that would improve the situation at Lonmin, its long-term business partner. The bishop's speech was focused less on accusations and more on forming a constructive partnership with the most powerful stakeholder in the platinum sector. He did this by directly appealing to the company's integrity.

After speaking at length about the massacre and the living conditions faced by workers, he explained why BASF had an interest in seeing improvements at the site. 'Now, the news from South Africa is obviously a high reputation risk for BASF. I think we all agree, that it is not affordable for BASF to face such escalation of violence strongly connected to one of your supplier [sic] just to remain silent. It cannot be sustainable for BASF not to help to improve the inhuman working and living conditions of the people who dig its platinum out of the rocks.' He called upon BASF to provide reparation payments to the victims of the massacre, as well as to contribute tangibly and structurally to substantial improvements at the mining site: 'I think this is the time to act and talk less' (Seoka, 2015).

Seoka's speech was followed by lengthy applause. Those attending the meeting were moved, taken aback – some even shocked. The speech left a lasting impression, and Marikana was one of the themes that dominated a shareholder meeting originally meant to focus on BASF's 150th anniversary. Many of the speakers who followed made reference to Seoka's remarks; most of them were ashamed, but some were also furious at BASF's silence and lack of action.[24]

In his response, Kurt Bock highlighted the company's lack of sufficient power to act and lack of knowledge about the conditions at the Lonmin site. In no way did Bock's strained narrative correlate with the image the firm wanted to present on its 150th anniversary. During celebrations to mark its milestone year, BASF showcased itself as a modern, flexible company and a global player. Multilingualism, knowledge of the world and 'intercultural competency' are key factors in everything the corporation does. The firm also visually pushed their globality to the fore. The 'We create chemistry' campaign, which was developed especially for the anniversary year, almost exclusively featured photos that depicted race and gender diversity within the company. BASF's own website claims that its employees are active in 'almost every country in the world'.[25] Bock's assertion that the company had limited influence and limited power to act as well as a lack of knowledge about the area due to their apparent 'geographical distance' thus glaringly clashes with BASF's own corporate image.

More worryingly, these claims blatantly contradict the facts. BASF was able to become the world's leading chemical company not least because, throughout its history, it has shown itself to be unscrupulous about translating corporate power into political influence. As the chapter by Jan Pehrke illustrates, BASF's lobbying efforts have today made it part of a corporate, financial and political elite with unprecedented global reach and influence.[26] That alone removes all credibility from its claim to be a corporation with limited influence.[27] Moreover, as we have seen, BASF has extensive knowledge of South Africa, has been working with Lonmin for more than 30 years and, since its takeover of Engelhard in 2006, is the main purchaser of Lonmin's platinum. Annual business dealings total roughly 650 million euro. A corporation that transfers approximately 2 million euro per day to one of its most crucial suppliers knows precisely what conditions are like at the site – anything else would contradict BASF's own principles, apart from being grossly economically negligent.[28] After all, strikes, industrial accidents and other incidents could lead to a loss of production and thus gaps in the supply chain, forcing BASF to act. Moreover, the terrible living conditions faced by workers are plain for all to see: the slums surround both the mines and Lonmin's company premises. There is only one way to avoid seeing such conditions and that is to deliberately look away – to be actively ignorant – as Dumisa Ntsebeza, an advocate acting on behalf of the murdered mineworkers, described the behaviour of BASF: 'They must have been blind not to have seen the squalor where the mineworkers from Lonmin were working. It's like an ostrich putting its head in the sand and pretending that something he should have seen is not there simply because its head is in the sand' (Buchen, 2016: minute 9).

Of course, this ignorance and lack of action also ultimately contradict BASF's commitment to supply chain responsibility, to which it agreed as one of the founding members of the UN Global Compact in 2000. In this respect, BASF's inaction goes beyond the Marikana massacre and stretches back more than a decade – not to mention the profits the corporation pocketed under the apartheid regime in South Africa.

Furthermore, BASF continues to act in contravention of the UN Guiding Principles for Business and Human Rights, to which the company proudly claims to adhere. Over several decades, BASF has neglected its duty to 'identify, prevent and mitigate' human rights violations.[29] This corporation, which in its mission statement claims to combine 'economic success' with 'social responsibility', has instead been focusing solely on its profit margins – as it has done several times in the past. On multiple occasions BASF has been found guilty of manipulating prices in contravention of competition law, such as in 1999 when the corporation, together with Hoffmann-La Roche, had to pay what was at the time a record-breaking fine (a total of US$725 million) for conspiring to raise and fix vitamin prices.[30] In 2011 BASF reached an out-of-court settlement after being accused of manipulating the prices of certain chemicals (Abelshauser, 2003:633).

Then, in 2014, BASF was taken to court by US jewellery manufacturer Modern Settings, which alleged the chemical giant had fixed the price of platinum.[31] The complaint was dismissed by a US court in 2017, not because the claims were unsubstantiated but because the court claimed the dispute lay outside its jurisdiction. Whatever the outcome of this case, there is no denying BASF's clear fixation on low market prices. That is why it is hardly surprising that BASF is not focusing its attention on human and labour rights at Lonmin. BASF has neither checked its human rights and labour law standards nor has it taken steps to prevent or redress human rights violations as stipulated in the UN Guiding Principles. There is therefore no doubt that BASF bears some responsibility for, and is complicit in, the inhumane living and working conditions that persist at Marikana. For decades, the corporation has taken no action to rectify these shameful abuses. Not only has BASF stood by idly and watched, it has profited from Lonmin's inhumane practices, which have helped keep down the price of platinum (e.g. by not paying statutory social benefit payments or by giving striking mineworkers the cold shoulder). This has not only been the case 'just' since the Marikana massacre; this has been true for decades (Bahadur et al., 2016:33). That is why BASF is 'non-legally complicit' in the numerous transgressions of its supplier, even under the UN's conservatively formulated Guiding Principles. Independent of any legally actionable responsibility, BASF is still obligated to promptly rectify its failures, to acknowledge its 'complicity', to issue an apology and to offer restitution payments. BASF – at least indirectly – bears non-legal responsibility for the Marikana massacre. It was the inhumane living conditions and Lonmin's empty promises that led to the strike and, ultimately, to the massacre. BASF, however, was happy to turn a blind eye to it all.

'Is BASF therefore one of those companies that rake in a profit at the expense of other people's suffering whilst simultaneously claiming to be a socially responsible enterprise?' asks Koketso Moeti in the *Mail&Guardian* ('Almost five years after the massacre, the battle for Marikana justice continues'). In the media, BASF was criticised for its lack of action and its long silence concerning Marikana, which was only broken thanks to the interventions at the 2015 shareholder meeting.[32]

Seoka's speech not only caused a stir in the media, but also among groups and NGOs with similar causes in German-speaking countries, as well as in England and South Africa. Several social movements and civil society organisations across the world are fighting for legally binding due diligence along the entire supply chain and are doing so within a range of industries and using several specific cases. The case addressed by Bishop Seoka had previously gone unnoticed. The example also perfectly illustrated the problematic nature of voluntary supply chain responsibility: in this case, the chain in question did not involve a convoluted mesh of suppliers – there was an easy-to-follow, direct link. What is also striking is the stark discrepancy between BASF's Potemkin village and reality; between the way a flagship German company portrays itself and the truth that lies at the start of its supply chain.

2016: BASF suggests action and ignores the 'widows of Marikana'

In the years since 2012, countless scandals have plagued the story of the Marikana massacre and efforts to come to terms with the event. The way Lonmin treated the 'widows of Marikana' is certainly one of the most shameful. The 'widows of Marikana' – the family members of those killed during the massacre – have yet to receive any reparation payments, either from the South African state or from Lonmin, despite the latter's partial culpability for the massacre. Lonmin offered the widows the chance to work in the mines in place of their late husbands. Not only was the death of their spouses a trauma in itself, but for many the loss of income meant their very livelihood was at stake. Some of the widows also had no secure access to food; they were close to falling into absolute poverty. Faced with few options, they felt they had no choice but to take the company up on this 'offer'. Many of them now work underground under the same terrible conditions that their husbands went on strike to change and that ultimately cost them their lives. Some work as cleaners, cleaning the offices of those managers who bear some responsibility for the deaths of their husbands. Lonmin boasts of keeping the 'widows in employment'. On several occasions, the widows themselves have criticised the desperate circumstances they find themselves in, but their complaints have fallen on deaf ears (see the chapter by Asanda Benya and Judy Seidman).

Those left behind were, for the most part, ignored by the state and left to fend for themselves in the face of a precarious, potentially life-threatening future. Even as witnesses, they initially struggled to have their voices heard. During the first months of the government's investigative commission, they were not given the right to testify. The family member of a murdered mineworker pithily summed up the situation: 'We are treated like stones' (Khulumani Support Group, 2015:3).

The Khulumani Support Group gave the victims' families a platform to meet and to share experiences, thus supporting the formation of a group that increasingly began speaking with a single voice. One medium of this collective struggle for justice is the widows' so-called 'bodymaps', which were exhibited in Vienna in 2016 as part of a speakers' tour.[33] These bodymaps are based on sketches of the widows' bodies. Visual representations of the widows' lives are then added to and around the body: the massacre often features; there are also frequent references to the basic challenges the women face and their worries about the futures of their now fatherless children. The bodymaps are accounts of the massacre from a group that has been directly affected. These images also address the expectations of and demands on those responsible for the massacre; they criticise the corporations' and the state's policies. These works thus also serve to document the impacts of neo-colonial raw materials policies.

During a joint workshop, an image was created that brings together two stories, each of which concludes with Lonmin and platinum mining: the story of BASF, a story of wealth and commercial success, and the story of the widows, a story of death, exploitation and, ultimately, humiliation. The image features the widows' demands made to Lonmin and BASF. In this respect, it also provides the two women who had travelled to the BASF shareholder meeting on 29 April 2016 with a mandate to represent the group.

The situation was slightly different from the AGM that took place the previous year. Shortly after the 2015 meeting, the Marikana commission released its report, which confirmed what was already evident and what Seoka had outlined in his speech: that

Lonmin was partially to blame for the massacre and that it had failed to improve the workers' living conditions. BASF could no longer claim it was waiting for the outcome of an ongoing process and play for time: the pressure was mounting.

So what does a corporation do when it publicly comes under pressure because evidence has shown that gross human rights violations have been taking place along its supply chain for decades? It carries out an audit among its suppliers. Here BASF is no exception. Like so many others, this corporation fell back on this widespread neoliberal instrument which usually pretends to offer transparency and to rectify the problem while actually helping to reinforce the status quo. At the 2016 shareholder meeting, these two realities collided: the world of audit results and the reality faced by the widows. It quickly became apparent that the two were irreconcilable.

The widows spoke first. Ntombizolile Mosebetsane and Agnes Makopano Thelejane explained that they had come to Mannheim 'to speak to [BASF] directly, to tell you of what is happening at the far end of your platinum supply'. 'You, BASF, are saying that now it is all better. But we say to you, all is not well with us. Lonmin has not repaired the harm they have done. They have not paid reparation. What Lonmin has claimed they are doing to assist us, has caused more harm and division amongst us.'[34]

Mosebetsane, who works at Lonmin as a cleaner, described the situation as follows: 'I [...] am now working at Lonmin cleaning their yard, working [...] for the very company that made sure my husband died. I am learning no skills doing this work, that will make my life better. Today they take my hard work, and pay me this small amount, and say I should be grateful to them. This is not compensation, it is more exploitation, and revictimisation: from slave to slavery.'

Agnes Makopano Thelejane's husband, Thabiso Thelejane, had worked in the mines for over 40 years. In 2012 he was just a few months away from retirement. He was effectively executed by police at what came to be called Scene Two[35] of the massacre. As he was a contract worker at Marikana and not directly employed by Lonmin, the company feels it has no obligation to him or his family.[36]

Thelejane said: 'I [...] am one of those who have been excluded. Lonmin did pay for us to bury our loved ones, after Lonmin and the police killed them. But when I went to Lonmin and asked them for reparation, they said they had already paid for the funeral, they do not owe me anything more. I ask myself, did I ask Lonmin to kill my husband?'

At the end of their speeches, the two widows pressed the company for action and demanded support. They requested 'relief payments' such as those that had been provided by German textile group KiK to the victims of the Rana Plaza factory collapse. They said that BASF should be willing to at least do as much as KiK:

We ask you, BASF, to establish a trust fund of eight million euro, to help improve our desperate situations.[37] [...] So we now ask, what will you do to ensure that Lonmin will deal with the ongoing and unresolved problems that caused workers to strike, over three years ago: paying less than a living wage, failing to provide acceptable living conditions at the workplace, failing to negotiate with the workers' chosen representatives? In your recent statements, these issues are not addressed. And until these questions are answered, there can be no resolution. We say: Plough back the fruits.

In her chapter, María do Mar Castro Varela provides a detailed examination of Kurt Bock's response to the speeches given by the two widows in 2016. Here we will thus only highlight three elements. Firstly, Kurt Bock persistently evaded the widows' accounts, questions and demands. As a group, the widows were not included as part of the dialogue process by the corporation's functionaries; they refused to speak to them and to consider their requests.[38] The only person to be addressed was the delegation's sole male representative, Bishop Seoka. Not only was this an insult to the widows; for a company that has only one token woman on its board of executive directors, it is as telling as it is shameful.[39]

No less shameful was the way in which Kurt Bock played down and trivialised Lonmin's complicity in the massacre – the second element in the analysis – dedicating just one sentence to the case. 'It was established in the final report released by the investigative commission that Lonmin, that our supplier whom we have been working with for 30 years, did not do everything in its power to prevent these incidents, this tragedy' (Buchen, 2016). This response completely ignores the fact that Lonmin undoubtedly must shoulder some of the blame for the largest massacre to take place in post-apartheid South Africa and that the company had the power to prevent it from taking place.

Thirdly, Bock went on to pontificate about the audits BASF has commissioned. Carolijn Terwindt's chapter in this book analyses non-transparent, privatised audits with all their cynicism, flaws and, ultimately, their devastating impacts. All of Terwindt's points of criticism also apply to the audit that BASF conducted at Lonmin. The catalogue of questions was kept secret, the whole audit process was entirely non-transparent, the results were not published – the list of criticisms is long.

Bock's remarks concerning the audit speak for themselves. He notes that 'no critical observations were made regarding the company's management, its respect of human rights or the working conditions at Lonmin, and neither were any other violations established'.[40] The only area where room for improvement was noted was in the company's fire safety systems. Business could thus continue as usual – it was as though nothing had happened, and the fact that something was already amiss was completely ignored. Kurt Bock's message to the 2016 shareholder meeting was that in the past, the present and the future, Lonmin had met and would continue to meet BASF's high standards with the corporation's support. Bock also stressed: 'We play our role by being a good partner to Lonmin, an experienced partner; by ensuring that Lonmin can continue to meet our requirements moving forward.'[41]

2017: BASF threatens the South African delegation

After the widows' speeches, BASF began to attract greater media scrutiny. The corporation subsequently tried to show itself to be taking decisive action – not least by commissioning an audit – and also began mentioning a 'dialogue initiative' it claimed to have started in South Africa. According to a special section of the BASF website dedicated to Marikana,[42] the aim of this 'multi-stakeholder dialogue' is 'that the platinum mine operators develop a common approach to improve the living and working conditions of all the people throughout the platinum mining belt in a long-term and sustainable manner and thus ensure a permanently responsible supply chain of raw materials for their customers'.[43] As promising as this may sound, the result of this initiative has been limited to just one joint meeting and the formulation of this goal. The project lies dormant and BASF is only pursuing it with little to no enthusiasm. A 'follow-up audit' carried out at Lonmin in 2017 'yielded a positive result in several areas' but identified some need for improvement: 'Lonmin should take steps to better understand how the mining operation affects local communities and which measures can be derived from this.' The irony at play here is two-fold: firstly, such measures are already prescribed by law in the Social and Labour Plan (see interview with Capps and the chapter by Patrick Bond); secondly, Lonmin is one of the world's most scrutinised companies, at least since the Marikana massacre. Numerous studies have been dedicated to this issue, be it court-ordered investigations,[44] or studies conducted by independent NGOs (Bahadur et al., 2016; Amnesty International, 2016; Khulumani Support Group, 2015) or by academic institutions (e.g. Capps and Malindi, 2017). There is certainly no shortage of expertise, knowledge or ideas. Rather, what is needed is for the company to fulfil its ecological and social duties towards the local communities. However, both the studies mentioned here and the people of Marikana have come to the same conclusion: no action is being taken; there are no improvements.

In January 2017 Bishop Seoka travelled to Lonmin's annual shareholder meeting in London together with Kritischen AktionärInnen Deutschlands and the London Mining Network. Their aim was to show Lonmin that even in Europe, people had not forgotten who was mainly to blame for the massacre. During the meeting, which was considerably smaller than that of BASF, Lonmin CEO Ben Magara made promises to the delegation that were not even partly met.[45]

Seoka was then accompanied to the BASF shareholder meeting that took place on 12 May 2017 by Joseph Mathunjwa, head of the AMCU, the largest union in South Africa's Platinum Belt, and Mzoxolo Magidiwana, a mineworker who had been severely injured during the Marikana massacre.

In his speech, AMCU president Mathunjwa called upon BASF to follow their many promises with concrete action: 'For years AMCU has formulated a number of specific demands related to working and living conditions of the mineworkers. BASF–Lonmin has a long and close business relationship. […] Through your relationship to Lonmin, we believe that [you can] support the implementation of our demands' (Mathunjwa, 2017). Bishop Seoka also made clear that this was not a case of charity but a matter of justice: 'We are not here as beggars but for justice. This is about human dignity and your integrity and credibility! What we request is a clear indication of your willingness and commitment to contribute to a sustainable development programme in the affected areas' (Seoka, 2017).

In his speech, which is printed in full after this chapter, Mzoxolo Magidiwana describes the living conditions in Marikana:

> […] the majority of the people that work at Lonmin live in tin shacks that are infested with rats. There is no running water in the households, just one tap for a lot of families, not all the areas have electricity and toilets are shared ones and just dug in the ground with no chemical treatment of the waste. Under these conditions a life of dignity is not possible. It is my understanding that BASF is buying platinum from Lonmin for millions of euros per month, I therefore believe that what we, the workers, are asking for is not unreasonable. We know that the management of Lonmin and BASF are making huge profits; we know that we dig out one of the most precious metals on earth – we just want to live in dignity – I cannot see that this wish is unreasonable. I ask you, the CEO of BASF, Kurt Bock, to answer me: is this too much to ask? (Magidiwana, 2017)

Kurt Bock's response provoked audible discontent among those present: he justified the dreadful living conditions that have persisted for decades by stating that Lonmin did not have 'sufficient financial means'. He made this statement in full knowledge of the fact that the sum of money that changes hands between Lonmin and BASF in just a single week (roughly 14 million euro) would suffice to drastically improve the situation.

However, Bock triggered even greater incredulity and criticism, as reported in the *Mannheimer Morgen* (27 May 2017), when, visibly irritated, he made an open threat to the delegation from South Africa: 'We could purchase from another supplier. We don't have to work with them. But if we don't work with them, there will quite literally be over 10,000 people out on the street. Is that really what you want?'

Of course, this is not (nor has it ever been) the wish of the South African delegation. Bock knows that full well. Right from the start, the delegation was pushing BASF to use its power, as the world's largest chemical producer, to effect change and not to just simply turn its back on the situation. That would be the opposite of the responsible action that BASF so vocally claims to be taking. It amounts to nothing more than 'devil-may-care' politics. In Bock's rhetorical question – 'Is that really what you want?' – it is not hard to read the implicit threat: perhaps you ought to be careful about continuing to criticise BASF so vocally, or the consequences for the people in Marikana could be disastrous. This threat is ultimately a clear departure from the UN Guiding Principles for Business and Human Rights; if BASF wishes to pursue a scorched-earth policy – and do so deliberately and wilfully, as such a statement suggests – then the corporation would be violating the exact same standards that it purports to value so highly.

Moreover, portraying the situation as one that consists of merely two options – business as usual or an end to the business partnership – is not only trite, it is simply not true. BASF, the world's biggest stakeholder in the platinum sector, has a multitude of tools at its disposal to help bring about tangible improvements: it could pay reasonable prices (Bergermann et al., 2017), help fund the necessary investments or draw up official, contractually fixed and verifiable arrangements with its main platinum suppliers, with adherence to human and labour rights, as well as environmental standards, playing a crucial role.

Bock openly signalled to the South African delegation that he would rather they did not make an appearance next year. But he is set to be disappointed. Bishop Jo Seoka stressed: 'And as long as we don't get a convincing answer, we won't be tired to come here' (Seoka, 2017).

Notes

1. Seoka's appearance at the 2015 Shareholder Meeting was organised by the authors of this article, by KASA (Kirchliche Arbeitsstelle Südliches Afrika) and Dachverband der Kritischen Aktionäre and Aktionärinnen Deutschland. The Rosa Luxemburg Foundation, Brot für die Welt, KEESA (Kampagne für Entschuldung und Entschädigung Südliches Afrika), SOLIFONDS, the Bench Marks Foundation and the Khulumani Support Group in South Africa as well as the London Mining Network and War on Want joined the network. Many other groups expressed their solidarity and offered support. For more information on this, see basflonmin.com/home/de/partner.
2. See Annual Report of the German Chemical Industry Association VCI, Chemical Industry 2017.
3. In 2018 the merged US companies DuPont and Dow Chemical are expected to take over this position.
4. See www.basf.com.
5. See www.basf.com/de/we-create-chemistry/urban-living/construction-innovation.html.
6. In 2011 Abelshauser was appointed to the History Commission of the Federal Ministry of Economics and Energy, the Independent Commission for Accounting for the Past of the BMWi.
7. Exports to Africa are not shown in detail; BASF produced about a third of the world's demand for synthetic dyes at the time.
8. See www.basf.com/za/en/company/about-us/History.html.
9. 'Gauteng' is Sotho for 'Place of Gold'. The city of Johannesburg is located there.
10. **In 2004, Engelhard generated sales of around 4 billion euro** (Kühnlenz, 2006).
11. Engelhard is therefore also on a par with the infamous Tiny Rowland, head of Lonrho, later Lonmin. Rowland (1917–1998), who lived in Germany in the 1930s and probably also spent some time in the Hitler Youth, was often treated with contempt even in the British conservative, bourgeois camp, since he united the two evil characteristics at the time in himself: the negative effects of past colonial megalomania and its future relation, the unbridled greed for profit (Van Vuuren, 2017:372).
12. At the annual meeting in 2015 Kurt Bock said that BASF has been doing business with Lonmin for over 30 years.
13. IG Farben went into liquidation and was broken up into individual companies in 1952, but not removed from the German commercial register until 1991.
14. First term of office of Helmut Kohl in a coalition between the CDU and FDP.
15. Art. 26, German Basic Law, para. 2: Weapons intended for warfare may only be manufactured, transported and placed on the market with the approval of the Federal Government.
16. At the time he was the Bavarian minister-president and former federal minister (including minister of defence) with excellent contacts with industry, involved in various corruption scandals.
17. In 2011, BASF Coatings published an article ('Taking a dive with RELIUS paints') on its homepage promoting the 'more than 30-year cooperation' with HDW–Thyssen Krupp in the coating of submarines.
18. This conflict lasted for half a decade (Moody, 2014:236). One lesson from working with trade unions and environmental activists there was that careful research into the financial and legal vulnerability of the company played an important role in the labour dispute. For more on this, see also Estabrook (2007) and Minchin (2003).
19. Disposing of toxic waste by selling it to the GDR for foreign currency had not become any easier after the fall of the Wall. Plans by BASF to store pollutants in abandoned mines in the former GDR failed. For more on this see the article in *Der Spiegel* of 8 August 1993, 'Kali-Bergbau: Müll nach Bischofferode' (Potash mining: Rubbish to Bischofferode).
20. In 2004, Engelhard generated sales of around 4 billion euro (Kühnlenz, 2006).
21. See www.basf.com.
22. See tfs-initiative.com.
23. For information on the massive adverse effects on people and the environment in Wintershall's Argentine gas fields, see Germanwatch and Misereor (2017:78).
24. 'It is beyond belief that in the 21st century people are still living and working under such inhumane conditions. It is a disgrace that BASF has been directly involved in such production practices for so many years. That the company has withheld this from the public and, what is more, refused to actively play a responsible role in improving these conditions is absolutely outrageous.' This comment was made by one shareholder in response to Seoka's speech. See *BASF-Vorstand weicht den Vorwürfen des Bischofs*, press release from the Kritischen AktionärInnen (Association of Critical Shareholders in Germany), 1 May 2015.

25 See *BASF: About Us: Strategy and Organization*, www.basf.com/en/company/about-us/strategy-and-organization.html.
26 The speakers at the BASF 150th anniversary celebrations included German Chancellor Angela Merkel and Malu Dreyer, deputy leader of the Social Democratic Party and minister-president of Rhineland-Palatinate. See also Attac (2016:68).
27 Incidentally, this position is also diametrically opposed to the mission statement and ethos of the Protestant Business Leaders Working Group, whose board of trustees Bock sits on. See www.aeu-online.de/selbstverstaendnis.html.
28 Bock also said that he was very aware of the circumstances in South Africa's mining industry, but he offered no response as to why BASF had taken no action concerning 'social responsibility' over a period spanning more than a decade.
29 UN Guiding Principles, Human Rights Due Diligence.
30 At the time, it was the largest fine to be issued by the US Department of Justice. See Department of Justice, Antitrust Division: Hoffman-La Roche and BASF Agree to Pay Record Criminal Fines for Participating in International Vitamin Cartel, 20 May 1999.
31 The complaint is available online, reference number 1:14-cv-09391-GHW The Platinum and Palladium Antitrust Litigation, US District Court, Southern District of New York.
32 A selection of media reports from 2015–2017 are available at basflonmin.com/home/de/presse.
33 The KASA – Kirchliche Arbeitsstelle Südliches Afrika (Ecumenical Service on Southern Africa) – exhibited reproductions of the images in Germany in 2014. In April 2016 the original images were displayed at the House of the Austrian Trade Union Federation in Vienna. It marked the start of a speakers' tour, which moved from Vienna to Berlin, Zurich, Zug, Speyer and Frankfurt before finishing at the BASF shareholder meeting in Mannheim. The agenda featured public podium discussions, meetings with German members of parliament and representatives of the church as well as rallies in the Swiss tax haven of Zug. The South African delegation included Bishop Jo Seoka, Nomarussia Bonase and Judy Seidman from the Khulumani Support Group as well as two of the widows of Marikana, Ntombizolile Mosebetsane and Agnes Makopano Thelejane. The complete exhibition catalogue can be found at Bonase et al. (2016).
34 Speech by Ntombizolile Mosebetsane and Agnes Makopano Thelejane at the BASF shareholder meeting, 29 April 2016.
35 On 16 August 2012, 17 striking mineworkers were shot to death at the foot of a koppie. A short while later, 17 other strikers were murdered in an area roughly 200 metres away. These two locations are named 'Scene One' and 'Scene Two' in the commission's report.
36 Lonmin's refusal to take action contradicts the investigative commission's final report, which establishes that Lonmin must also bear responsibility for its murdered subcontractors. See final report of the Marikana Commission of Inquiry, p. 479.
37 This sum, equivalent to roughly 0.01 per cent of BASF's current turnover, would require just under one euro cent to be deducted from the 2.90 euro dividend issued per share.
38 BASF's brief, unannounced visit to Ntombizolile Mosebetsane after the shareholder meeting does not redeem this behaviour but ought to be seen within the same context, i.e. as a lack of respect.
39 This behaviour can be read within the context of BASF's reactionary gender politics. A representative of the Deutschen Juristinnenbundes (German Association of Female Lawyers) who pleads with the company at the BASF shareholder meetings to increase its share of female executives and managers is regularly booed and ridiculed. BASF's board of executive directors defends its unambitious goals with the classic argument put forth by male bastions of power, i.e. that what matters is competency, not fulfilling quotas. See Newsletter Number 2/2017 of the Plough Back the Fruits campaign, available at basflonmin.com/home/de/deutsch-newsletter.
40 See *Controlling Standards: Evaluation and Auditing of Lonmin*. The BASF report is available online on the special Lonmin/Marikana section of the BASF website: *Sustainability in Procurement: Marikana: What Is BASF's Commitment?*
41 Plough Back the Fruits: Minutes of the BASF shareholder meeting, 29 April 2016, p. 4 (in the possession of the publishers of this collection of essays). See also basflonmin.com.
42 See *Sustainability in Procurement: Marikana: What Is BASF's Commitment?*, www.basf.com/en/company/about-us/suppliers-and-partners/sustainability-in-procurement.html.
43 Ibid.
44 Heads of the Argument of Evidence Leader (final report of the Marikana investigative commission), 27

October 2014.
45 This happened again in March 2018 during the Marikana Solidarity Week, which was partly organised by the War On Want. Alongside Seoka, Andries Nkome, the attorney representing the miners, and Thumeka Magwangqana were in attendance. Brian Beamish, non-executive chair of Lonmin, once again refused to issue a formal apology for the company's role in the massacre. For more information, see the websites of the relevant organisations.

References

Abelshauser, W. (ed) (2003) *BASF. Eine Unternehmensgeschichte* (BASF: A History of a Company), Munich

Amnesty International (2016) *Smoke and Mirrors: Lonmin's Failure to Address Housing Conditions at Marikana*, Johannesburg

Andresen, K. (2016) *Moral Economy: Federal German Automobile Cmpanies and Apartheid*, Hamburg

Attac (ed.) (2016), *Konzernmacht brechen. Von der Herrschaft des Kapitals zum Guten Leben für alle*, Vienna

Bahadur, A., L. Kadel and S. Lincoln (2016) *Platinum for the World Market, Iron Shacks for Workers: Living and Working Conditions, Marikana Five Years after the Massacre*, Brot für die Welt, Berlin, and Bench Marks Foundation, Johannesburg

Bergermann, M., S. Book, A. Busch, L. Deuber and M. Seiwert (2017) Das dunkle Geheimnis der Autoindustrie (The dark secret of the auto industry), *WirtschaftsWoche* 45

Bonase, N., J. Seidman, S. Knapp, B. Mabanza, M. Grimm and J. Krameritsch (2016) *Plough Back the Fruits: The Struggle for Justice and Restitution. The Bodymaps of the Widows of Marikana*, Hamburg

Buchen, S. (2016) *Ausbeutung in Afrika. Welche Verantwortung hat BASF?* (Exploitation in Africa, What is BASF's responsibility), Panorama, NDR, 28 April 2016

Capps, G. and S. Malindi (2017) Dealing with the tribe: The politics of the Bapo/Lonmin royalty-to-equity conversion, SWOP Working Paper, Johannesburg

Estabrook, T. (2007) *Labor-Environmental Coalitions: Lessons from a Louisiana Petrochemical Region*, Amityville

Germanwatch and Misereor (ed.) (2017) *Global Energy Economy and Human Rights: German Companies and Politics under Close Scrutiny*, Aachen and Berlin

Grefe, C. (2018) Bayer-Monsanto: Monokulturen in den Köpfen (Bayer-Monsanto: monocultures in the heads), *Die Zeit*, 21 March 2018

Hamilton, G. (1964) *Goldfinger* [film]

Khulumani Support Group (ed.) (2013) *Justice, Redress and Restitution: Voices of Widows of the Marikana Massacre*, Johannesburg

Khulumani Support Group (2015) *We Have to Talk, We Need Changes – Voices from Platinum Belt Mine Workers*, Johannesburg

Kühnlenz, A. (2006) Firmenporträt Engelhard. Vom Gold zu Katalysatoren (Company portrait of Engelhard: From gold to catalysts), *WirtschaftsWoche*

Magidiwana, M. (2017) Speech at the BASF AGM, 12 May 2017, Mannheim

Mathunjwa, J. (2017) Speech at the BASF AGM, 12 May 2017, Mannheim

Minchin, T. (2003) *Forging a Common Bond: Labor and Environmental Activism during the BASF Lockout*, Gainesville

Moody, K. (2014) What's the matter with workers?, in *Solidarity: Essays on working class organization in the United States*, Chicago

Nixon, R. (2015) *Selling Apartheid: South Africa's Global Propaganda War*, Johannesburg

Räuschel, J. (1975) *BASF: Zur Anatomie eines multinationalen Konzerns* (BASF: The Anatomy of a Multinational Corporation), Cologne

Seoka, J. (2015) Working together: Changing extractive industry to a sustainable development agency, Speech at the Annual Shareholder Meeting of BASF 2015, 30 April 2015, Mannheim

Seoka, J. (2017) Speech at the BASF AGM, 12 May 2017, Mannheim

Van Vuuren, H. (2017) *Apartheid Guns and Money: A Tale of Profit*, Jacana, Johannesburg

▶ Matchbox advertising (around 1985–90)
Translation: Dominant. A tape more is never too much.

▲ Mobile Emissions Catalysts Division of BASF South Africa (Pty) Ltd., Struandale near Port Elizabeth, 2016. Port Elizabeth is the centre of the automotive industry in South Africa.

'Plough Back the Fruits: The Struggle for Justice and Restitution. The Bodymaps of the Widows of Marikana' exhibition, Vienna 2017.
▼ Views of the exhibition
▶ Nomarussia Bonase (Khulumani Support Group) explains the body map of Agnes Makopane Thelejane at the opening of the exhibition.

▲ Widows of Marikana: Plough Back the Fruits. Oil pastels and food colouring on paper, 150 x 280 cm, February 2016.

7. ARE WE REQUESTING TOO MUCH?
SPEECH AT THE BASF AGM, MANNHEIM, GERMANY, 12 MAY 2017

Mzoxolo Magidiwana

I am Mzoxolo Magidiwana. I am 29 years old. I started working at Lonmin in 2011. I am one of the workers who participated in the strike in 2012, where 34 mineworkers were massacred. I was hit with nine bullets, with two going through my body and seven were removed in the hospital. That's why they called me 'dead man walking'. It's a miracle how I survived. I spent six months in the Intensive Care Unit; thereafter I went to rehabilitation to learn to walk again.

In 2012, we were on strike for living wages and better working and living conditions at Lonmin. We expected Lonmin, our employer, to come to talk to us. Instead Lonmin called the police on us, who then shot and killed our fellow comrades. I believe that this matter could have been resolved by Lonmin coming to us to tell us that Lonmin was unable to meet our demands or even to retrench some of us, but not to cause that we be killed, as if we were just animals. Even when Bishop Jo Seoka and Joseph Mathunjwa, the president of AMCU, came to speak to us, our request to them was to ask the Lonmin management to come and talk to us. Bishop Jo Seoka and Joseph Mathunjwa of AMCU tried to convince the management to talk to us, but Lonmin refused. Instead, heavily armed police came already with ambulances and hearses, implying they knew exactly what they were going to do. Government and Lonmin had planned to end the strike at all costs, including loss of life: shoot to kill. Therefore the hearses were there to take the dead, ambulances for the injured, and police vans for those who were detained and faced criminal charges.

I am one of those 200 people against whom criminal charges were laid. I'm also one of 20 people against whom further criminal charges were laid, and I am still facing those charges, as I am speaking today. Of the 20, three passed away, 17 of us remained and we are charged for shooting one person to death. What I don't understand is how 17 people can hold one gun to shoot a person.

What hurts me most is that I am a victim of the police brutality, and yet I face criminal charges for something I didn't do. I am a victim but I am treated like a perpetrator and nobody has been charged for shooting and killing us. I am here to tell people what happened in 2012 and what we still wish for.

Having given you this background, let me speak on the current conditions. Since the massacre, nothing much has changed. We still have not achieved the living wage that we were demanding. Our working and living conditions have not improved that much. There has not been any compensation for us as victims: the deceased, the widows, the orphans and the injured and even those who were tortured by the police wanting statements regarding the massacre. As things stand today, nobody in government or Lonmin has been charged for the massacre. Even as we speak today, the majority of the people that work at Lonmin live in shacks that are infested with rats. There is no running water in the households, just one tap for a lot of families, not all the areas have electricity and toilets are shared ones and just dug in the ground with no chemical treatment of the waste. Under these conditions a life of dignity is not possible.

It is my understanding that BASF is buying platinum from Lonmin for millions of euro per month, I therefore believe that what we, the workers, are asking for is not unreasonable. We know that the management of Lonmin and BASF are making huge profits; we know that we dig out one of the most precious metals on earth. We just want to live in dignity – I cannot see that this wish is unreasonable.

I ask you, the CEO of BASF, Kurt Bock, to answer me: is this too much to ask?

Also, the working conditions have not improved much. People still die underground because of the pressure put on them by Lonmin to the benefit of its customers, which include BASF, in a situation where workers have not even achieved the living wages they were striking for in 2012.

What I wish to happen is that BASF puts some pressure on Lonmin to resolve its unfinished business with its workers. If that were to happen, it would make us workers appreciate and therefore make us be at peace with what happened, even though we may not be able to bring back those who have died; it will also bring peace and reconciliation for those who were injured. It could make Lonmin create peace and for the workers to work in peace and with love. And bring some closure to what happened in 2012.

I do hope that BASF will play a major role in resolving our issues with Lonmin. What I am expressing is the pain I feel. Me as a worker living in those conditions, as a worker for Lonmin and therefore also you, BASF. Look at me, I struggle walking. I liked to play football, I cannot do this anymore, I am under heavy medication for chronic pain. All of this at age 29. I do not know what the future holds for me, considering the injuries that I have suffered. Even though I am left like this, I am still better than the widows who have had to come and work in a place where the blood of their loved ones was shed, where their loved ones perished. As I leave, I would like to know what BASF commits to in making our lives better as workers in Lonmin.

I thank you for the opportunity to address you.

BASF shareholder meeting at the *Congress Center Rosengarten* in Mannheim. The speakers are being projected onto a screen behind the stage where the board is seated.

▸ Mzoxolo Magidiwana, a survivor of the massacre, 2017.
▸ Ntombizolile Mosebetsane (left on the screen) and Agnes Makopane Thelejane speak for the Widows of Marikana; Simone Knapp of KASA (Kirchliche Arbeitsstelle Südliches Afrika) delivers her speech in German, 2016.
▸ BASF CEO Kurt Bock, 2016.

8. THE THEATRE OF IRRESPONSIBILITY: CYNICISM AND PROFITABILITY

María do Mar Castro Varela
Translated by Nivene Rafaat

For those who show little interest in analysing the post-colonial capitalist state of the world (Castro Varela and Dhawan, 2015), it is almost impossible to grasp why people who mine one of the planet's most expensive precious metals under the harshest conditions have to live in such poverty (Gerstenberger, 2017). On the African continent, however, this tends to be the rule rather than the exception. It would be wrong to speak of the end of colonial influence; while it may be true that local power structures are no longer under the direct rule of European nations, an imperial balance of power remains in place.

Post-apartheid South Africa is a case in point. German, Swiss and Austrian companies who were able to rake in jaw-dropping profits during the apartheid years – not in spite of but thanks to the regime – continue to do so (see the chapter by Simone Knapp, Jakob Krameritsch, Barbara Müller and Walter Sauer). Meanwhile, black workers in South Africa have seen little or no change: 'A hewer [mineworker] earns roughly 340 euros in their first year working for one of the largest mining companies. He must travel kilometres deep underground to extract platinum at temperatures of around 45 degrees. Six days a week, nine hours at a time. This form of labour makes many workers ill; tuberculosis is rife. Hewers in some tunnels have to work with heavy pneumatic drills that are old and worn out' (Faigle, 2014).

This is evidence that the post-apartheid and postcolonial age certainly does not mark a 'rupture' with what has gone before. Rather, these are times in which it should no longer be justifiable for Europe to evade its responsibilities regarding the terrible systems of violence that exist in the global South. But on the face of it, the continent's inaction seems to be legitimate. For a long time – too long – Europe was able to shirk its responsibility for the barbarity that once sprang from within its borders.[1] It is as though violent conflicts taking place far away from Europe's shores have absolutely no link to the societal conditions that exist in the here and now; as though there was no link between the massacres that repeatedly befall countries in the global South and the imperial acts of violence committed both today and in the past: the transatlantic slave trade, which enriched Europe tremendously (and not only those nations that were directly involved in colonialism); the introduction of a plantation economy, which brought about the demise of countless colonised peoples; the most brutal exploitation of natural resources (spices, cotton, precious metals, cacao, tea and coffee); the disempowerment and abasement of former rulers; genocide and rape; epistemicide, or the intentional destruction of knowledge (Santos, 2014); and the introduction of the colonisers' native tongues as national languages while thousands of native languages were erased, together with knowledge, ethical perspectives and philosophical beliefs – the list goes on. Colonialism is a history of violence that has left a lasting mark not only on colonised countries but in those nations that were either directly or indirectly involved in colonialism. In addition, epistemic, political and economic power structures were established that not only allowed exploitation to continue but also helped render the violence invisible. Exploitation would not have been possible without such an effective masking technique.

In the summer of 2012, police shot dead 34 striking mineworkers in Marikana who were fighting for better wages and better living and working conditions. 'Many of them died from shots to the back, some were run over by armoured police vehicles. Many of them could have survived if the paramedics had been allowed to reach the site of the massacre immediately, and not one hour later' (Alexander et al., 2013:7). All too quickly, incidents such as these are met with cynical comments such as 'Well, that's just how it is down there!' from the majority of Europeans (see the chapter by Stefan Buchen). Many consider African nations to be little more than 'failed states': a symptom of the African population's inability to establish democratic practices. The idea of democracy, which originated in Europe, appears to be incompatible with the 'true nature' of those in the global South. Whenever politics turns into brutal violence, corruption becomes visible or governments are ousted, the age-old preconceived notion that former colonised nations are incapable of governing themselves is rolled out (see interview with Dinah Rajak and the chapter by Boniface Mabanza). Official indices that are used to measure a nation's 'stability' deem almost every African state to be either 'failed' or 'fragile'. South Africa is considered 'borderline' or 'critical'.[2] Here it is irrelevant whether, and according to which criteria, this statement is true. The critique of these indices is multifaceted and offers a range of opportunities for debate (Nay, 2013:326–341).

In this chapter, however, I shall examine how a discourse on 'Africa', which depicts the continent as a symbol of failure and barbarity, creates a disastrous discursive silence – one which emanates from the violence triggered by the West and which, as a consequence, seems to be mostly irrelevant. The language surrounding the 'failure' of African states is clearly interspersed with the racist imagery that continues to shape the European vision of Africa. As Achille Mbembe pointedly explains: 'African politics and economics have been condemned to the sign of a lack, while the discourse of political science and development economics has become that of a quest for the causes of the lack' (2001:8).

In order to illustrate this point, in the following sections I will explore a specific form of language that relies on this (non-)perception. It is a language that attempts to steal itself away from responsibility; a language that reassures those who should actually be lying awake at night for covering up a multitude of crimes while simultaneously profiting from them. If African politics and economics are, as Mbembe describes, the sign of a lack, then we should ask ourselves how we can stabilise this sign. We might ask ourselves how it is possible that the tremendous unrest enveloping Europe seems to have merely been triggered by Africans fleeing to the continent, seeking refuge from conflict and misery. Why do we in Europe know so little about the political and economic goings-on of the global South? And why is it that the majority of Europeans claim to know precisely what developments are taking place within Africa's political and economic landscape? Is it a lack of interest, irresponsibility or an actively engendered silence that keeps Europe in a state of ignorance?

This chapter does not intend to find answers to these questions. Rather, the aim is to take the lack of moral outrage as a starting point and impetus for a discourse analysis. The focus on the hegemonic postcolonial–European discourse of power and domination will be informed by an analysis of a specific remark: the response of Kurt

Bock, BASF's chief executive, to the speeches given by Bishop Jo Seoka, Ntombizolile Mosebetsane and Agnes Makopano Thelejane, along with Markus Dufner, Boniface Mabanza, Maren Grimm and Jakob Krameritsch, at BASF's 2016 shareholder meeting will be subjected to a discourse analysis. This study will reveal the company's discursive strategies that can be subsumed under the heading 'stealing away from responsibility'.

Ethics and responsibility

The 'international division of labour' underpins the current globalised system. The aim of international trade deals is to regulate the links subsequently created between national economies. This form of labour division is, however, also based on Western countries moving arduous and dirty tasks to former colonies to reduce production costs. Such outsourcing is a defining feature of the externalisation society. However, not only does this entail the outsourcing of production sites; in many cases, perpetuating the structures of exploitation that were established during colonial rule and apartheid is a fundamental part of this system (see the chapter by Boniface Mabanza). The case of Lonmin and BASF in the South African platinum mining industry illustrates this perfectly. Here there is an urgent need for ethical examination. How are these systems of exploitation justified? And who is profiting from them?

In his 2007 work *Infinitely Demanding*, British philosopher Simon Critchley writes of an 'ethics of commitment'. He claims that philosophy starts with disappointment and not, as so often suggested, with a question or a reflection. Critchley goes on to explain that it is this disappointment that gives rise to the crucial questions, drawing a key distinction between two key disappointments – that of religion and that of politics. It is the latter we are interested in here, for it is this very disappointment that is notably connected to such wonderful and narcissistic concepts as the idea of human rights (Castro Varela and Dhawan, 2014). For although we have hope in abundance, the truth is that we live in a violent and unjust world: 'a world defined by the horror of war, a world where, as Dostoevsky says, blood is being spilt in the merriest way, as if it were champagne' (Critchley, 2007:3).

This disappointment can give rise to a multitude of outcomes: from frustration and lethargy to boundless political engagement. If we transpose this idea onto the situation of postcoloniality, we could argue that the disappointment that followed the euphoria of decolonisation should actually have led to a continuous calling into question of the global political balance of power – a questioning that requires an active and stimulating politics of memory. Within this context, we must imagine Critchley's ethics of commitment as political engagement and constant remembering. In Critchley's eyes, an ethics of commitment is an endlessly provocative form of ethics as this is the only ethical basis on which to oppose the current immorality. This immorality is imbued with a moralism that continually succeeds in bringing up the subject of Africa's apparent 'lack' which Europe seems almost incapable of remedying. Whatever Europe does, Africa's 'lack' remains. Yet Europe and the West are portrayed as saviours, as Makau Mutua (2001:205) brilliantly and impressively establishes in his critique of the West's human rights policy: the uncivilised torment their victims and the West must once again come to the rescue. As Mutua observes, this image remains ingrained in an '"othering" process that imagines the creation of inferior clones, in effect dumb copies of the original'.

To be able to create and stabilise this imagined picture, it is essential that the West portray itself as the conveyor and defender of human rights, even when it is blatantly obvious that all it actually cares about is economic benefits (Spivak, 2004). In defiance of Kant's analyses, ethics and the market are in an irreconcilable state of tension. The situation is simply not as the (neo)liberals would have us believe, i.e. that the market enables freedom and individual fulfilment. Even eternal peace, as formulated by Kant in his essay *Perpetual Peace* (1796), cannot be realised through a globalised economy.

Rather, the situation is the opposite: while European politicians argue over which state is the most humane, the living conditions in the global South are becoming increasingly 'unliveable'. Competition and the war over resources, the merciless exploitation of workers in textile factories as well as the arms exports from the West to warring nations in the South are well-known facts that practically never bring about any change to global politics. Increasingly it seems as though the human rights discourse is simply a smokescreen that instead of tempering the world's social injustices often creates a framework in which they can take place.

Kurt Bock rightly points out that, in terms of the interest of companies, 'what is at stake is also commercial success, *which is extremely important;* without commercial success, nothing else can work' (Plough Back the Fruits, 2016:4) emphasis added by author). Here the obvious question is: what else would stop working? At shareholder meetings, a range of different people, both those individuals affected and their supporters, try to raise awareness of the degrading working and living conditions in the Lonmin mines. They ask questions; they demand accountability. The BASF representatives, on the other hand, talk about 'commercial success', which is undoubtedly verifiable, as well as the 'valid concern that companies should also be aware of what their customers are doing with their products' (Plough Back the Fruits, 2016:1). It is breath-taking how the issue of fairness is twisted here. Of course, the corporation acknowledges that their suppliers cannot simply violate ethical regulations, but the customers (at least those in the West) come first.

The resource at the heart of all this is platinum, a precious metal. According to Wikipedia, it is a 'malleable, ductile [...] precious, silverish-white transition metal' that can be used to make jewellery (it is worth much more than gold) but is mostly found in automotive catalysts. It is ironic that a metal extracted under the harshest and dirtiest conditions is frequently used to keep European emissions down and thus helps keep *our* air clean. In this context, it is also interesting to examine the description on the BASF website: 'The metals purchased from Lonmin – platinum, palladium and rhodium – are primarily used in the production of BASF's mobile emissions catalysts. These catalysts enable automakers to comply with increasingly stringent global emissions regulations by eliminating pollutants from engine exhaust before they enter the atmosphere' (BASF, 2017). One could thus come to the conclusion that the regulations are the reason why these metals are being mined under such disgraceful conditions: an interesting linguistic tactic in the overall attempt by BASF to absolve themselves from responsibility.

The theatre of irresponsibility

Let us now explore the minutes of a shareholder meeting that offers a textbook example of 'postcolonial non-dialogue'. A dialogue is an exchange in which statements and responses are given by two equal partners. Ideally, this conversation takes place without emotion and in a controlled manner – with all participants having the same opportunities to put forward their own arguments and views. This fully reflects Jürgen Habermas's idea of a perfect speech act (1981), which assumes not only equal opportunities in terms of the quality of interpretation and argumentation but that no one party dominates the discourse. But this raises the question: is this nothing more than an absurd fantasy?

However, one other issue is more important than finding out whether such an 'ideal speech act' is even conceivable: we must establish how such an enlightened idea is exploited to continue to legitimise violence. Time and again in the face of international conflicts, we hear calls for dialogue, which is why I would like to focus on a slightly different term: that of non-*dialogue*. A non-dialogue occurs when those in possession of power appear to conduct a dialogue but simply use it for the purpose of showing that no wrongdoing has taken place. Dialogue thus becomes a weapon that serves to reinforce injustice and power structures: it becomes a non-dialogue. Perhaps the idea of an 'ideal speech act' could only come from a modern European philosopher who remains silent on the 'expansionist aggressive nature of European Modernity, the problematic elements of [his] thinking or the focus [of his] reflections' (Serequeberhan, 2015:67).

The shareholder meeting that took place on 29 April 2016 was pervaded by an almost unbearable cynicism. It was akin to the pitch-perfect performance of a theatre of irresponsibility, expertly deploying the weapon of non-dialogue. These types of meetings are controlled, ritualistic and staged. They often leave behind a bitter taste and, when it comes to the victims, a feeling of powerlessness rather than agency. At this BASF shareholder meeting, there was regret concerning the massacre; at the same time, the critical questions were either disqualified or deferred, or the company's responsibility roundly denied. At hardly any point was the impression given that a violent conflict was under way that had already needlessly cost lives. Matter-of-factly, coolly – i.e. rationally – the focus was instead turned to the subject of how strong the relationship with Lonmin was and how good and vital business relationships were in general. As soon as the opening statements began, it became clear which line of argument would be taken. It started with an act of irreverence: 'Yes, thank you, Mr Hambrecht, and my thanks also to Bishop Seoka and also to the two widows for travelling all the way to Ludwigshafen today. It is vital that you also give us an insight into the circumstances and conditions in your home country' (Plough Back the Fruits, 2016:4). Mr Hambrecht and Bishop Seoka are thanked by name. As a figure of authority and a representative of the Anglican Church, the bishop is accorded a certain level of respect; the two women are simply addressed as 'widows', thus denying them any form of agency. They are simply there to mourn the loss of their husbands. They are not expected to raise arguments, offer resistance or challenge the exploitative system.

The second sentence sets the tone for the statements to follow – it is as though the BASF representatives had no clue about the political situation in the country; as if they did not know how brutally the mineworkers were being exploited, even after the end of apartheid. At the same time, a clear distinction is being made: it is up to the South Africans to explain what is happening in *their* country. The fact that the conditions under which they have to live and work are also linked to globalised interdependence is undermined right from the start. There is a 'there' and a 'here'. What happens 'there' seems to have little to do with what is being negotiated and implemented 'here'. Here a civilising discourse is being continued, one which situates all forms of barbarism firmly in the global South – while the West can only do what it can to keep all these phenomena in check. There are thus repeated references to laws, controls and regulations which BASF has introduced and which it claims to adhere to as a matter of course, while the challenging circumstances in South Africa are frequently mentioned. 'I'm not sure', Kurt Bock commented at a press conference held in February 2016, 'that we can really offer advice on how these things, these industrial disputes, can be structured in a way that is more civilised and ultimately more peaceful, and thus avoid the truly regrettable loss of human life' (Buchen, 2016).

A somewhat confusing statement, to say the least. The passive form is used to transform an active crime into an inevitability. Here the colonial distinction between the 'civilised' and the 'savages' is being echoed in a downright perfidious manner; the message is that in South Africa, conflicts over better pay invariably go hand in hand with the 'loss of human life'. This company, active throughout the globe and not only the world's largest chemical producer but the mine's main customer (to the tune of 650 million euro per annum), generally portrays itself as being potent and virile. However, in this instance, the same corporation claims it has only limited influence over the circumstances under which the individuals who secure the company's vast profits work and live. A far more likely story is that both the poor working conditions and the violent conflicts are tolerated – perhaps partly because workers in South Africa do not count; they are just numbers in the company's books.

BASF's strategies are revealed as tactics that serve to delay, cover up, play down and twist the facts. For example, it was established that an investigation into the events in Marikana was only initiated years later – largely thanks to Seoka's intervention at the 2015 shareholder meeting. Company management justified this by stating that they had to first examine the government report, which was only released after a three-year delay.

> We discussed this issue here last year and decided that we were unable to respond substantively for the simple reason that the South African government's own report on the massacre – as is, I believe, the most appropriate term – had yet to be released. The government may have had access to it but the dossier had yet to be published. The massacre took place in 2012; it [the report] was then finally released in July 2015 (Plough Back the Fruits, 2016:1).

Despite considerable protest, the company did not use the intervening months and years to conduct its own assessments. Responsibility was placed squarely on the shoulders of the South African government. BASF consistently painted a picture of irresponsible government bodies that were antagonistically frustrating their supposedly humane approach. Word by word, line by line, an independent narrative was constructed that portrayed any line of critical questioning regarding the actions of unions, the police and the company as being outside reality. 'This question has already been asked: what our definition of sustainability is, i.e. that which you connect with pre-emptive obedience and neoliberal ideas. The line of argument is interesting, but I do not believe that [it] reflects reality' (Plough Back the Fruits, 2016:4).

For the speaker, the mere mention of neoliberalism and pre-emptive obedience makes this discourse feel as though it comes from another world. This form of critique is not one to which BASF representatives wish to respond. It is not their reality, which places the market above everything else as a matter of course. BASF is forthright in stating that economic efficiency is the company's top priority; both the environment and 'social issues' are further down the list. Everything else is accepted as 'regrettable'. 'And we also know that the living conditions in South Africa are not always ideal,' explains Kurt Bock, thus insinuating that the company has nothing to do with the living conditions in question. It is a classic approach, making more palatable the bitter disappointment that comes with realising that what Europe doles out is not humanity but barbarity (Dhawan, 2016). It is bewildering, not least because Kurt Bock is also a member of the board of trustees for the Protestant Business Leaders Working Group, whose mission statement contains the following paragraph: 'Against this backdrop, it must be considered an egregious display of inadequacy should a business leader absentmindedly resort to stating that there is "no alternative" to a given situation. Arguing the case for an apparent lack of alternatives may be convenient, but it is also unscientific and undemocratic' (AEU, 2017).

Non-performativity of international ethical regulations

The phenomenon is widely known: Europeans buy products featuring the 'fair trade' label because they assume that they have been produced under equitable conditions in the global South. By paying a little more at the till, they can put their minds at ease. However, it has long been recognised that by no means all of these products are made in a way that most of us would consider fair.[3] Such labels are not dissimilar to agreements signed by companies to encourage diversity or to promote non-discriminatory practices or sustainable production. Often, they are not even worth the paper on which they are printed. Within the context of diversity policies at British universities, Sara Ahmed used the term 'non-performativity': she stated that although official measures and documents existed in abundance, these had had almost no impact on the everyday discrimination experienced by, for example, students of colour. In *On Being Included*, Ahmed (2012:114) explains that the acknowledged shortfalls that appear in such documents effectively free the institution from taking action to address these shortcomings. The documents allow the institutions to profess to being good, but, in so doing, they are no longer obliged to follow this with appropriate steps. These mechanisms can also be applied at the international level.

On repeated occasions during the shareholder meeting, other 'voices of authority' were called upon to offer some form of backing. For example, the Ten Principles of the UN Global Compact were cited. This agreement between the United Nations and businesses supposedly aims to create a more ecological and social form of globalisation. The companies commit to ensuring that human rights are observed, that employees have the opportunity to unionise and that discrimination is eliminated. The question thus arises: how could the massacre have occurred if a multinational company such as BASF had signed this compact? And did this happen because the mine owners, platinum suppliers to BASF, had brutally suppressed the more than justifiable protests of its workers? As so often, these events even call into question the work of the United Nations. Companies voluntarily sign up to the rules outlined in the Global Compact (UNGC) and, unsurprisingly, there are no sanctions if regulations are not – or only partially – adhered to. If they have signed the document, however, companies can use it as a claim to moral authority, as was the case at the stakeholder meeting.

> The UNGC primarily serves as a forum for learning and dialogue, within which CSR 'best practices', i.e. good examples that should be replicated, are identified and implemented by other companies. All the companies within the UNGC are obliged to annually disclose their corporate engagement by publishing reports on the Global Compact homepage (Communication of Progress – COP). The purpose is to provide written evidence of progress being made regarding the implementation of the Ten Compact Principles as well as regarding activities to encourage sustainable development. These reports must fulfil certain criteria; however, the contents are not checked and penalising options are largely absent (BPB, 2017).

Signed documents, given legitimacy thanks to the authority of the United Nations, are frequently used to undermine justice. They can also be used to enable a non-dialogue. This goes far beyond Ahmed's postulated 'non-performativity'. Not only does it not amount to a performativity of anti-discrimination and thus fairness; but unjust scenarios are further legitimised.

The 'little brother': Solidarity in exploitation

> The police were then ordered to leave no worker alive.
> – Betty Lomasontfo Gadlela (Bonase et al., 2016:52)

Over and over, BASF asserts that '*sehr, sehr viel*' (so, so much) has been done. Here the mantra-like repetition of the intensifier 'so' appears to be an attempt to make the statement (that something has been done) clearer and more explicit. What is also apparent is that in the minutes taken at the shareholder meeting, a solidarity discourse is invoked in which those who are perpetuating the (post)colonial structures of suppression and exploitation appear to stand in solidarity with one another:

> Why then don't we publish [our audits with Lonmin]? That was the question. We're not publishing them, firstly, because that is an issue between Lonmin and BASF, and Lonmin has shown itself to be very open to approaching the recommendations in a very, very constructive manner, as well as to accepting

further audits. They could say no and refuse to let us in – but the opposite was true. Lonmin are very open (Plough Back the Fruits, 2016:3).

Here, solidarity above all means that the companies are working together to cover up the brutal exploitation that is taking place. This solidarity is, however, misleading. In this passage, South African mine operator Lonmin is addressed as the junior partner who is behaving like the 'big brother'. 'They could say no and refuse to let us in,' says Kurt Bock, omitting the fact that Lonmin is dependent upon its European buyers. Both sides profit from this business partnership, but it is clear that BASF is the one pulling the strings. A form of solidarity is thus hinted at that makes it seem immoral to threaten action. 'In concrete terms, this means that, as far as we are concerned, Lonmin shall remain one of our trusted partners, especially in light of its new management, and we feel it is our job to continue to work together with the company and to work together to continue to improve the situation' (Plough Back the Fruits, 2016:3).

As is usually the case in such business contexts, Bock makes no reference to the fulfilment of criteria and agreements, but instead mentions the importance of not leaving your partner in the lurch. The report released by the Marikana investigative commission unequivocally confirmed that Lonmin was partly to blame for the massacre, highlighting its failure to improve the living conditions of its employees: 'The fact that we feel Lonmin is open to continuing to evolve is a good enough reason for us to continue to work with them' (Plough Back the Fruits, 2016:3). The corporation once again speaks of how Lonmin is 'open' – suggesting that what was at stake was not a business partnership but an actual relationship. The rather disparaging 'with them' simultaneously flags trustworthiness and distance: it linguistically creates a distinct hierarchy. Even subsequently, Lonmin is still portrayed as the 'poor little brother' whom we should not be too harsh with. 'We play our role by being a good partner to Lonmin, an experienced partner; by ensuring that Lonmin can continue to meet our requirements moving forward' (4). Here we see the deployment of another strategy to circumvent the company's own responsibility: at no point does BASF address its direct responsibility, but it consistently comes to the defence of all those who were directly involved in the massacre, effectively as justification of the fact that the cooperation, which generates such gigantic profits, can be unequivocally continued – even if human rights abuses are taking place.

By contrast, Agnes Makopano Thelejane offers clarity in her statement:

I, Thelejane, am one of those who has been excluded. Lonmin did pay for us to bury our loved ones, after Lonmin and the police killed them. But when I went to Lonmin and asked them for reparation; they said they had already paid for the funeral, they do not owe me anything more. I ask myself, did I ask Lonmin to kill my husband? (Thelejane, 2016)

Conclusion

> To grieve, and to make grief itself into a resource for politics, is not to be resigned to inaction, but it may be understood as the slow process by which we develop a point of identification with suffering itself.
> – Judith Butler (2004:30)

The minutes of the shareholder meeting once again make clear that a social transformation cannot rely solely on human rights activism if this falls victim to the simple hope that what mattered was demonstrating to these exploitative companies the suffering they were causing – they are clearly aware of this already. A post-Marikana analysis illustrates that more fundamental questions are at stake: 'Who counts as human? Whose lives count as lives? And, finally, *what makes for a grievable life?*' (Butler, 2004:20)

A postcolonial perspective on the theatre of irresponsibility staged at the BASF shareholder meeting clearly demonstrates that not only must asking questions remain an element of critical practice, but that we must also collectively and generally push forward a process of decolonisation that makes it impossible for Europe to forget its guilt (Castro Varela, 2015). In *The Wretched of the Earth*, Frantz Fanon (1981:267) called for a 'new humanism': 'For Europe, for ourselves, and for humanity, comrades, we must turn over a new leaf, we must work out new concepts, and try to set afoot a new man.' Perhaps it is time to look once more at forgotten anti-colonial writings and set ourselves on a path to forging a new humanism.

Notes

1. An example that is both well-known and frustrating is the long-standing struggle of the Herero and Nama peoples to obtain an official apology from Germany, and reparations from the German government and German companies for a genocide that took place during colonial rule (see also www.genocide-namibia.net).
2. See the 2017 Fragile State Index available at www.fundforpeace.org/fsi/data/. The DERA, the German Mineral Resources Agency, which links the German government to the raw materials processing industry, uses this index. See also Herwig Marbler and Peter von Hartlieb-Wallthor, *Rohstoffe Subsahara. 31 Länder, Stand 2016/2017*, Commissioned by the Energie Agentur North Rhine-Westphalia and the DERA. Here South Africa is given an 'Economic Freedom Score' of 62.3.
3. See also an article that appeared in *ZEIT* on 5 November 2014. 'The consumer advice centre in Hamburg tested 32 fair trade products – and half of them either failed or were deemed "not transparent" [...] Fair trade products are a huge market that is gradually becoming ubiquitous in our society. In 2013 brands bearing the most well-known label, "fair trade", sold to the tune of over half a billion euros – a figure that is 23 per cent higher than the previous year. In Germany the products are sold in 42,000 supermarkets, cafés and restaurants.'

References

AEU (2017) www.aeu-online.de/selbstverstaendnis.html
Ahmed, S. (2012) *On Being Included: Racism and Diversity in Institutional Life*, Durham
Alexander, P., T. Lekgowa, B. Mmope, L. Sinwell and B. Xezwi (2013) *Das Massaker von Marikana. Widerstand und Unterdrückung von ArbeiterInnen in Südafrika*, Vienna.
BASF (2017) www.basf.com/de/company/about-us/suppliers-and-partners/sustainability-in-procurement/ensuring-sustainability-in-the-supply-chain.html
Bonase, N. et al. (eds.) (2016) *Plough Back the Fruits: The Struggle for Justice and Restitution. The Bodymaps of the Widows of Marikana*, Hamburg
BPB (German Federal Agency for Civic Education) (2017) *UN Global Compact*, www.bpb.de/nachschlagen/zahlen-und-fakten/globalisierung/52823/un-global-compact
Buchen, S. (2016) Ausbeutung in Afrika. Welche Verantwortung hat BASF?, *Panorama*, NDR, 28 April 2016
Butler, J. (2004) *Precarious Life: The Powers of Mourning and Violence*, London
Castro Varela, M.d.M. (2015) Europa. Ein Gespenst geht um, in Gert Hoff (ed.), *Europa Entgrenzungen*, pp. 49–82, Innsbruck and Vienna
Castro Varela, M.d.M. and N. Dhawan (2014) Human Rights and its Discontents. Postkoloniale Interventionen in die Menschenrechtspolitik, in Julia König and Sabine Seichter (eds.), *Menschenrechte. Demokratie. Geschichte. Transdisziplinäre Herausforderungen an die Pädagogik*, pp. 145–162, Weinheim and Basel
Castro Varela, M.d.M. and N. Dhawan (2015) *Postkoloniale Theorie. Eine kritische Einführung*, 2nd edn, Bielefeld
Critchley, S. (2007) *Infinitely Demanding: Ethics of Commitment, Politics of Resistance*, New York and London
Dhawan, N. (2016) Doch wieder! Die Selbst-Barbarisierung Europas, in María do Mar Castro Varela and Paul Mecheril (eds.), *Die Dämonisierung der Anderen. Rassismuskritik der Gegenwart*, pp. 73–84, Bielefeld
Faigle, P. (2014) Ihr Leben für unser Platin, *ZEIT magazine*, 7 July 2014
Fanon, F. (1981) *The Wretched of the Earth*, Frankfurt
Gerstenberger, H. (2017) *Markt und Gewalt. Die Funktionsweise des historischen Kapitalismus*, Münster
Mbembe, A. (2001) *On the Postcolony*, Berkeley
Mutua, M. (2001) Savages, victims, and saviors: The metaphor of human rights, *Harvard International Law Journal* 1, pp. 201–245
Nay, O. (2013) Fragile and failed states: Critical perspectives on conceptual hybrids, *International Political Science Review* 3, pp. 326–341
Plough Back the Fruits (2016) Minutes of the BASF shareholder meeting, 29 April
Santos, B.d.S. (2014) *Epistemologies of the South: Justice against Epistemicide*, New York
Serequeberhan, T. (2015) Die Philosophie und das postkoloniale Afrika: Historizität und Denken, in Franziska Dübgen and Stefan Skupien (eds.), *Afrikanische politische Philosophie. Postkoloniale Positionen*, pp. 55–84, Frankfurt

Spivak, G.C. (2004) Righting wrongs, *South Atlantic Quarterly* 103, 2/3, pp. 523–581
Thelejane, A.M. (2016) Speech at the BASF shareholder meeting, 29 April 2016

▶ **pp. 180/181** A large number of studies, campaigns and initiatives now deal with raw materials policy, supply chain responsibility and human rights.

9. HARD ROCKS – SOFT RULES:
HUMAN RIGHTS VIOLATIONS, THE DESTRUCTION OF NATURE AND THE ROLE OF THE STATE AND CORPORATIONS IN INTERNATIONAL MINING

Michael Reckordt
Translated by Lyam Bittar

'What's the definition of a mine? A hole in the ground with a liar on top.'

Writing around a century ago, Mark Twain, the author of this observation, homed in on two crucial problems: the mining industry's violation of rights and its failure to honour the promises it makes. Both issues continue to scar the history of one of the world's oldest industrial sectors, and the Marikana massacre against striking miners is no exception. Human rights violations in mining are documented on a regular basis – almost a third of all allegations about violations in industry are linked to the extractive sector (AK Rohstoffe, 2015a:8).

Monitoring from different perspectives

From a historical perspective, the United Nations Environment Programme (UNEP) estimates that 40 per cent of all global conflicts in the past 60 years were related to activities surrounding the extraction of natural resources (UNEP, 2009). In 2016 alone, as the Heidelberg Institute for International Conflict Research (HIIK, 2017:21) reports, 98 conflicts revolved around water, metals and minerals, or arable land. Of these conflicts 67 per cent involved violence, with nine of them resulting in wars. The institute points out that resource-related conflicts tend to be more violent. But conflicts are not limited to those between states. As a number of studies show, civil society initiatives are being restrained with increasing force, with people being intimidated, threatened or murdered (Forum Menschenrechte et al., 2016). According to the British NGO Global Witness, in 2016 200 activists across 24 countries were murdered as a result of their work, compared to 186 in 2015. Many of them had stood up against the exploitation of natural resources. The number of victims from indigenous communities is also increasing. Activists from Brazil (49 documented victims), Colombia (37), the Philippines (28), India (16), Nicaragua (11) and the Democratic Republic of the Congo (10) were particularly affected (Global Witness, 2016). These numbers underline the fact that environmental activists are at risk across the world.

The Max Planck Foundation has also looked into human rights risks in mining, and published the results in a 150-page study commissioned by the Federal Institute for Geosciences and Natural Resources (Max Planck Foundation, 2016). The report's analysis of the various risks posed by the different stages of mining – from licensing and exploration, to mine construction, operation and extraction, to closure and abandonment – identifies a range of rights violations. Among the examples it gives are cases of violations and environmental destruction that have occurred in South Africa.

Locally affected groups, international civil society, critical journalists and politicians have also helped over the past years to document protests and violence. The Environmental Justice Atlas, an open digital resource maintained and coordinated by scientists and activists to map violations of environmental regulations and human rights, is one such project (Ejolt, 2017).

In most cases there are direct or indirect ties which link those resource-producing countries to the most resource-dependent countries of the global North, be it through financing, project development, supply chains, logistical and operational support, or the export of machines, equipment and knowledge. Global networks of critical voices from local and international civil society have therefore come to play an increasingly important role. Monitoring, documentation and access to information are often helpful, even crucial, for the success of local protests. This, at least, is the strong impression given by the tense debates around the voluntary or obligatory disclosure of information and of working conditions in the mining sector.

Conflict minerals and the struggle for binding due diligence obligations

In recent years, the media and political discourse have focused mainly on conflict resources. These resources help finance illegally armed groups, including rebels or military units that no longer recognise state authority. Various political regulatory frameworks, including the US Dodd-Frank Act, EU regulation on conflict minerals and OECD standards, define gold, tin, tantalum (or coltan) and tungsten as conflict minerals. The extraction of these four minerals finances illegally armed groups, especially in countries such as the Democratic Republic of the Congo, Colombia and Myanmar.

Civil society organisations, including the German NGO network AK Rohstoffe (Working Group on Raw Materials), have criticised this narrow focus on four minerals, as any resource can potentially be extracted and traded to finance illegally armed groups (AK Rohstoffe, 2013). But it is not enough to stress the structural shortcomings of these laws and regulations. We also have to bear in mind that this focus on conflict financing foregrounds only one particular aspect. Even if this aspect is often linked to massive human rights violations, and cutting off the perpetrators' financial sources does lead to a reduction in the number of human rights violations, the laws and regulations on conflict minerals still fall short of addressing most resource-related human rights violations. This is because it is often extraction per se that leads to conflicts and protests, which in turn trigger human rights violations involving local populations. Copper and gold exploitation in the Grasberg Mine in Western Papua, Indonesia, for instance, has exacerbated a conflict that has effectively destabilised and militarised the entire province.

Over the past years, reports have regularly – and thoroughly – documented the killings of journalists, trade unionists, or members of indigenous communities (Reckordt, 2011:101; Urgewald, 2013:15; Aktionsbündnis Menschenrechte Philippinen, 2017:30). The murder of 34 striking miners in Marikana is also part of this troubling development (Khulumani Support Group et al., 2016). In addition, there are regular reports highlighting the intimidation of civil society members. They are often exposed to threats (Human Rights Watch, 2014) or 'strategic lawsuits against public participation' (Slapp), which often create a climate in which people resort to murder. The Amadiba Crisis Committee in the north-east of South Africa's Eastern Cape has been opposing plans to exploit titanium-bearing sands along the coast for over

10 years. The plans entail the construction of a highway that would cut through conservation areas and farmland. The protests have led to a temporary moratorium and prompted the Australian mining company MRC to partly pull out of the project, but two of the crisis committee's spokespersons have already been murdered, and other activists have been threatened (Pearce, 2017).

Many local communities find themselves affected in similar ways, not just by mining projects but also by excessive logging, plantations and monocultures, to the extent that they face losing their livelihoods and access to drinking water (FIAN, 2008; Misereor, 2013). Mining companies often refuse to deliver on earlier promises to provide adequate housing, improve living standards, create jobs for the local population, or comply with environmental protection measures. Exacerbated by the misinformation they provide on the impact of their mining operations, their behaviour often leads to protests among workers and local communities. Natural resource exploitation is often also a major cause of rights violations, with company representatives, security forces, and state police and military units among the perpetrators. Many environmental risks – water, land and air emissions, for instance – often have direct repercussions on the health and food supply of neighbouring communities. This overview, though brief, is sufficient to highlight how on various levels and with varying intensity human rights activists, local communities and those who report critically on such incidents are risking their lives and their well-being.

El Salvador bans mining

In many countries civil society actors are now calling on authorities to halt individual mining projects or even the entire sector. In March 2017 El Salvador voted to ban metal mining altogether. The decision was pushed by a campaign led by NGOs and the church highlighting the risks of mining and the damage that has been documented throughout the country (Wimberger, 2017). In the Philippines, former activist Gina Lopez was appointed minister of the environment in the summer of 2016. In this role she quickly addressed the issue of mining licences and looked into environmental offences as well as social conflicts. She then advised Parliament to close down dozens of mines, and went on to revoke further mining licences (Reckordt, 2017a). For years, Philippine NGOs such as Alyansa Tigil Mina (Alliance Against Mining) and the Legal Rights and Natural Resources Center / Kasama sa Kalikasan (Friends of the Earth Philippines) have been demanding legislation that will strengthen the rights of locally affected groups and put a stronger focus on social rights and environmental conservation (Reckordt, 2012). Yet after just one year in office, in the face of massive criticism from mining companies and industry-friendly politicians, Ms Lopez was forced to step down. Nevertheless, her work attracted extensive media coverage, and has done much to raise the awareness of mining as a high-risk sector.

Since 2002, there have been referendums on mining in six countries across Latin America, among them Colombia. In the communities of Piedras, Ibagué and Cajamarca, three local referendums were held between July 2013 and March 2017, the results of which all spoke clearly against plans to construct and operate the La Colosa gold mine (Dietz, 2017).

Colombia, the Philippines and El Salvador are just three of the many countries whose populations are growing increasingly critical of mining projects. In many places, local alliances regularly succeed in building global networks and making their voices heard outside their region. The campaign against gold mining in Rosia Montana, Romania, is a good example (PowerShift et al., 2017a). By resorting to various forms of protest, and staging some of its actions in front of embassies in other European countries, the campaign attracted international attention that ultimately proved central to the Romanian government's withdrawal of support for the project.

At the same time, it should be noted that it is not only across the global South that opposition against mining projects has been gaining momentum. Protests in the US and Europe have been growing stronger, too, especially against projects involving fossil fuels. These include civil disobedience actions such as the occupation of coal mines in Lusatia or the Rhineland in Germany organised by the activist network Ende Gelände, or international protests against the extractive industry's global infrastructure projects, from the protests in Standing Rock, North Dakota, US, against the construction of an oil pipeline through indigenous territory, to the intermittent actions against Rotterdam's coal-loading port. The protests against gold mining in Greece or Romania, and against fracking in Great Britain, Germany and Poland, are also part of this trend.

Untangling the many transparency initiatives

Local and international civil society faces two major challenges: a high degree of lack of transparency and a lack of binding legislation forcing businesses to protect human rights. The Extractive Industries Transparency Initiative (EITI) seeks to help combat the first of these. The EITI was founded in 2002, after civil society PWYP (Publish What You Pay) networks called for the full disclosure of payment flows from companies and states in order to expose corruption. Fifty-two countries are currently part of the initiative, disclosing their revenues from licensing, levies and taxes from mining companies, while the companies operating in those countries in turn disclose the amounts they pay to the state (EITI, 2017). By comparing these figures, actors can identify possible cases of corruption and also assess whether societies actually profit from the way their natural resources are being managed. Moreover, the EITI is one of the first initiatives in which governments, companies and civil society organisations negotiate as partners and are required to reach a consensus. Especially in authoritarian regimes, this initiative is often one of the few ways for civil society organisations to access the political arena. The EITI Standard is updated and improved at regular intervals, and in the future will include the disclosure of ownership information and individual contracts. Both would be important steps in improving the way in which the sector is monitored.

Yet South Africa, for instance, is not an EITI member. Germany has applied for membership and submitted its first report in the autumn of 2017. But for the time being, the document will not afford a look into the country's involvement in overseas mining and its payments to foreign governments – despite the fact that there are three German companies involved in extracting chrome in South Africa: Lanxess, Cronimet and the ELG Haniel GmbH (as a shareholder of Hernic Ferrochrome). Other aspects, too, make Germany's first EITI report less innovative than initially promised by Uwe Beckmeyer, the former state secretary for the Ministry of Finance, when he stressed that Germany could 'serve as an international model' (BMWi, 2015; Forum Umwelt & Entwicklung, 2017).

Instead, South Africa has joined the Open Government Partnership (OGP) and has committed itself to transparency (Open Government Partnership, 2017). The Open Budget Initiative, which promotes transparent public budgets, manages the Open Budget Index, a ranking system that reflects the amount of information made accessible to the public. This ranks South Africa third behind New Zealand and Sweden (Open Budget Index, 2015). But unlike the EITI, the OGP is not sector-specific, and it also does not make demands on companies. This means that in South Africa what is absent is precisely the mechanism that allows actors to compare payment flows against current company and government reports. Yet the South African government sees no need to join the EITI since it believes its efforts are creating sufficient transparency, a study has found. Moreover, government representatives criticise the double standards shown by many European countries which are not EITI members themselves but which expect African states to join (Compaoré, 2013).

Yet transparency of payment flows alone does not ensure fairer taxation. Many corporations use transfer pricing and other methods to avoid taxes, which lowers the revenues of resource-rich countries (SOMO 2015; Christoph Trautvetter's chapter).

In addition, international trade policy unilaterally affords corporations a great deal of power. While multinational corporations can draw on Bilateral Investment Treaties (BIT) or Investment Protection Agreements to sue states and claim compensation for democratic decisions on, for instance, tightening environmental regulations or improving social standards, they continue to have no obligations imposed on them.

Most of the larger mining companies are transnational corporations: not only can they create and take advantage of new tax-saving models by relocating business activities, but they can also avoid national legislation (Reckordt, 2017a).

The Canadian mining company Gabriel Resources, for instance, sued Romania after 15 years of local opposition and protest had swayed the government to grant Roşia Montană cultural heritage status. The claim covers lost profits as well as expenses, most of which have been spent on public relation campaigns in the Romanian media.

Absence of international social standards

For the mining sector, only a limited number of social standards are internationally binding. Two of these were drawn up by the International Labour Organisation (ILO). The first is the Convention Concerning Indigenous and Tribal Peoples in Independent Countries (ILO 169). ILO 169 recognises 'the aspirations of ... (indigenous) peoples to exercise control over their own institutions, ways of life and economic development and to maintain and develop their identities, languages and religions, within the framework of the States in which they live' (ILO, 1989). South Africa has not ratified this convention, nor have the majority of states in the global North where extractive companies are either based or natural resources are processed, among them Great Britain, Germany, Australia, Canada and the US. South Africa has, however, ratified the second of these, the Safety and Health in Mines Convention (ILO 176), as have other countries such as Germany and the US (ILO, 1995). But a report released by Bread for the World and the Bench Marks Foundation in 2017 shows that South Africa is not meeting its obligations. Among other things, both organisations criticise the lack of safety measures and the health risks faced by miners in Marikana (Brot für die Welt and Bench Marks Foundation, 2017). According to ILO 176, Lonmin, the company operating the mine, is actually legally obliged to 'take all necessary measures to eliminate or minimize the risks to safety and health in mines under their control' (ILO, 1995).

Corporations forestall legislation – with voluntary initiatives

In their current versions, both the UN Guiding Principles on Business and Human Rights and the OECD Guidelines for Multinational Enterprises now call on companies to take greater responsibility for the impact of their economic activities – all the way down to the supply-chain level. This includes companies operating in the extractive sector, whether in prospecting, exploitation, trade or financing, as well as the resource-processing industries. According to UN Guiding Principle no. 15, due diligence demands that enterprises develop processes that help them 'identify, prevent, mitigate and account for how they address their impacts on human rights' in the context of their own activities and relationships (DGCN, 2014). The OECD Guidelines stipulate that businesses sourcing materials from conflict areas should implement a multi-step system in order to identify and concretely address risks in their supply chains (OECD, 2011).

Both policies, however, share a crucial failing: they are voluntary and legally non-binding. Despite the many negative experiences that have been documented across all continents, laws making companies in the extractive sector liable for the protection of human rights all along their supply chains are still few and far between. In the US, listed companies are obliged to report any use of conflict resources (the official US definition comprises gold, tantalum, tungsten and tin) and set out the measures they implement to ensure due diligence is carried out along their supply chain. The aforementioned Dodd-Frank Act may be formally limited to monitoring resources coming from the Democratic Republic of the Congo and its nine neighbours, but as supply chains are part of its focus, the Act has also forced resource-processing companies based in Germany, China and elsewhere to disclose relevant information (Küblböck and Grohs, 2017).

Similar legislation was adopted in Europe in June 2017. After facing massive resistance from the industry and a number of member states, the European Commission, the European Parliament and the European Council were ultimately able to agree on a regulation that will oblige importers as well as refiners and smelters in Europe to carry out due diligence in importing these four resources (PowerShift et al., 2017b).

This legally binding framework obliging companies to carry out due diligence along their value chain could, in the future help to identify and prevent human rights violations early on. This will require a political will that is responsive to the challenges currently affecting the exploitation of and trade in natural resources and that gives prominence to human rights and environmental issues. The debate to define the necessary steps has only just begun and is likely to face fierce opposition from both industrial and political actors. Already, companies such as BASF are attempting to water down or altogether avoid legislation by drawing up their own voluntary initiatives. At an event hosted by Econsense in November 2016, BASF and the Federation of German Industries (BDI) together announced plans to found an initiative called Made in Germany – The Responsibility of German Businesses in Global Competition (Econsense, 2016). BASF had previously co-founded the platform Together for Sustainability, which promotes sustainability in the chemical industry's supply chains, and is also a founding member of the voluntary initiative UN Global Compact (BASF, 2017; Akhona Mehlos's chapter). All these initiatives have the same thrust: they are aimed at forestalling, and thus effectively preventing – or at least delaying – the adoption of much-needed legislation. The discussions about the Berlin Declaration, which seeks to promote sustainable supply chains on a voluntary basis, have also been driven by a similar agenda (Book and Haerder, 2017).

No-go zones

There are further initiatives and standards that encompass social and environmental aspects. However, they all leave unresolved one central challenge: they contain loopholes. These loopholes are not related primarily to the social or environmental issues that they address; they are functional. They arise from an absence of legally binding standards and comprehensive, generally accepted implementation guidelines (Rüttinger et al., 2016). The situation is aggravated by the fact that there are no internationally defined no-go zones. No-go zones are areas where mining is banned for social, environmental or other reasons. The International Council on Mining and Metals (ICMM), an association of large mining companies, declared it would exclude World Heritage Sites from the entire spectrum of its exploration and exploitation activities as early as 2003 (Turner, 2012), but this regulation is only observed by a small number of mining companies. It is neither accompanied by similar initiatives along the value chain, nor does the industry seem willing to extend its scope. But as the debate on deep-sea mining serves to show, it is beyond question that the sector needs many more no-go zones (Reckordt, 2017b).

The way forward

Embracing social and environmental standards cannot be the only solution, however. The global North will also have to cut down on its heavy consumption of natural resources. Discussions about what means and approaches are needed to achieve this are still in their early stages (AK Rohstoffe, 2016). Apart from calls to phase out fossil fuels, there is a lack of ideas about how to reduce the consumption of metallic resources in a realistic or constructive manner. Instead, we already seem to be heading in the opposite direction. Given the thrust of current economic policy discourses and their focus on electric mobility (Brunnengräber and Haas, 2017; Blume et al., 2011), green growth (Fatheuer et al., 2015), or the digital economy and industry 4.0 (Groneweg et al., 2017), we are already well on the way to shifting global resource flows from fossil to metallic and mineral, which will only create new path dependencies. Nevertheless, the vast range of issues – repairing rather than throwing away, recycling quotas, self-sufficiency, etc. – and the sheer multitude of discourses – ranging from improved resource and material efficiency to debates on de-growth and governmental interventions in the form of regulations and tax policies – make up a wealth of ideas that can contribute to the overall target of minimising consumption.

Civil society organisations in Germany and Europe thus face a number of different challenges. Firstly, they will need to establish channels that facilitate cooperation and dialogue with actors from the global South and from mining regions. Besides fostering international exchange and mutual learning, they will also have to identify fields in which to take joint action. At the same time, awareness at the political level of the challenges related to resource extraction is still lacking. Many political and economic decision-makers are still unfamiliar with concepts such as human rights due diligence or supply chain responsibility. In order to give these concepts legislative form, the issue of companies' misconduct needs to remain in the public eye and there needs to be a broader discussion aimed at re-evaluating those practices that are currently legal. BASF's and Lonmin's conduct in the context of Marikana, where, five years on, families of murdered miners have still not been compensated for their loss, makes the urgency of such discussions all too clear.

References

AK Rohstoffe (2013) *Positionspapier des AK Rohstoffe für eine umfassende EU-Initiative zur Vermeidung von Konflikten beim Rohstoffabbau!*, www.power-shift.de/wordpress/wp-content/uploads/2014/04/20131223-PositionspapierKonfliktrohstoffe-final.pdf

AK Rohstoffe (2015a) *Verantwortung entlang der Lieferkette im Rohstoffsektor!*, www.alternative-rohstoffwoche.de/wp-content/uploads/2015/07/verantwortung-entlang-der-lieferkette_webversion.pdf

AK Rohstoffe (2015b) *Menschenrechtsaktivist im Tschad zu zwei Jahren Haft verurteilt*, www.alternative-rohstoffwoche.de/menschenrechtsaktivist-im-tschad-zu-zwei-jahren-haft-verurteilt/

AK Rohstoffe (2016) *Für eine demokratische und global gerechte Rohstoffpolitik*, www.power-shift.de/wordpress/wp-content/uploads/2016/08/AK_Rohstoffe_demokratische_und_global_gerechte_rohstoffpolitik.pdf

Aktionsbündnis Menschenrechte Philippinen (2017) *Human Rights Report Philippines*, www.asienhaus.de/archiv/user_upload/AMP_-_Human_Rights_Report_Philippines_2017_final.pdf

Alternative Mining Indaba (2017) *Declaration of the 8th Alternative Mining Indaba – 'Making Natural Resources Work for the People: Domestication of the African Mining Vision: From Vision to Reality*, www.altminingindaba.co.za/wp-content/uploads/2017/02/2017-AMI-Declaration-.pdf

Asia-Europe People's Forum (2016) *Ulaanbaatar Final Declaration*, www.aepf.info/images/AEPF11_Ulaanbaatar_Final_Declaration_and_Action_Plans.pdf

BASF (2017) *Initiative der Chemieindustrie 'Together for Sustainability'* (TfS), www.basf.com/de/company/about-us/suppliers-and-partners/sustainability-in-procurement/together-for-sustainability.html

Blume, J., G. Nika and W. Pomrehn (2011) *Oben hui, unten pfui? – Rohstoffe für die 'grüne' Wirtschaft: Bedarfe – Probleme – Handlungsoptionen für Wirtschaft, Politik & Zivilgesellschaf*, www.power-shift.de/wordpress/wp-content/uploads/2011/08/PowerShift-ForumUE-StudieRohstoffe-Gr%C3%BCneWirtschaft-2011web_klein.pdf

BMWi (2015) *Staatssekretär Beckmeyer ernennt Multi-Stakeholder-Gruppe für deutsche EITI-Kandidatur*, Press release, 20 April 2015, www.bmwi.de/Redaktion/DE/Pressemitteilungen/2015/20150420-staatssekretaer-beckmeyer-ernennt-multi-stakeholder-gruppe-fuer-deutsche-eiti-kandidatur.html

Book, S. and N. Haerder (2017) 'Berliner Erklärung' Unternehmen blockieren Mindeststandards für Soziales und Umwelt bei Zulieferern, *WirtschaftsWoche*, 18 August 2017, www.wiwo.de/unternehmen/industrie/berliner-erklaerung-unternehmen-blockieren-mindeststandards-fuer-soziales-und-umwelt-bei-zulieferern/20201898.html

Brot für die Welt (2015) *Tschad: Menschenrechtler Djéralar Miankéol ist frei*, www.info.brot-fuer-die-welt.de/blog/tschad-menschenrechtler-djeralar-miankeol-ist-frei

Brot für die Welt and Bench Marks Foundation (2017) *Platinum for the World Market, Iron Shacks for the Workers: Living and Working Conditions in Marikana Five Years after the Massacre*, www.info.brot-fuer-die-welt.de/sites/default/files/blog-downloads/platinum_for_the_world.final_.pdf

Brunnengräber, A. and T. Haas (2017) Die falschen Verheißungen der E-Mobilität, *Blätter für deutsche und internationale Politik* 6

Compaoré, W.R.N. (2013) *Towards Understanding South Africa's Differing Attitudes to the Extractive Industries Transparency Initiative and the Open Governance Partnership*, https://eiti.org/document/towards-understanding-south-africas-differing-attitudes-to-eiti-ogp

DGCN (2014) *Leitprinzipien für Wirtschaft und Menschenrechte. Umsetzung des Rahmens der Vereinten Nationen 'Schutz, Achtung und Abhilfe'*, Berlin

Dietz, K. (2017) *Working Paper No. 4 – Direkte Demokratie in Konflikten um Bergbau in Lateinamerika: das Goldminenprojekt La Colosa in Kolumbien*, www.land-conflicts.fu-berlin.de/publikationen/working-papers/Working-Paper-No-4/index.html

Econsense (2016) *Impulse für Nachhaltigkeit*, www.globalcompact.de/wAssets/docs/Flyer-Veranstaltungen/071116_Berliner_Forum_FINAL.pdf

EITI (2017) *The Global Standard for the Good Governance of Oil, Gas and Mineral Resources*, www.eiti.org/sites/default/files/documents/eiti_factsheet_en.pdf

Ejolt (2017) *Environmental Justice Atlas*, www.ejatlas.org/

Fatheuer, T., L. Fuhr and B. Unmüßig (2015) *Kritik der Grünen Ökonomie*, Oekom Verlag, Munich

FIAN (2008) *Ghana im Goldrausch. Menschenrechte, Landwirtschaft und Wälder in Gefahr*, www.fian.de/fileadmin/user_upload/dokumente/shop/Bergbau/fian_ghana-doku2008_web.pdf

Forum Menschenrechte et al. (2016) *Zivilgesellschaftliches Engagement weltweit in Gefahr. Für gerechte Entwicklung, Umweltschutz, Demokratie, Menschenrechte und Frieden*, www.boell.de/sites/default/files/uploads/2016/12/zivilgesellschaftliches_engagement_weltweit_in_gefahr-forderungspapier_final_digital.pdf

Forum Umwelt & Entwicklung (2017) *Erster deutscher EITI-Bericht veröffentlicht. Zivilgesellschaft begrüßt mehr Transparenz im Rohstoffsektor, fordert aber ambitionierteres Vorgehen*, Press release, 6 September 2017, www.forumue.de/pm-erster-deutscher-eiti-bericht-veroeffentlicht-zivilgesellschaft-begruesst-mehr-transparenz-im-rohstoffsektor-fordert-aber-ambitionierteres-vorgehen/

Global Witness (2016) *Defenders of the Earth: Global Killings of Land and Environmental Defenders in 2016*, www.globalwitness.org/en/campaigns/environmental-activists/defenders-earth/

Groneweg, M., H. Pilgrim and M. Reckordt (2017) *Ressourcenfluch 4.0. Die sozialen und ökologischen Auswirkungen von Industrie 4.0 auf den Rohstoffsektor*, www.power-shift.de/ressourcenfluch-4-0/

HIIK (Heidelberg Institute for International Conflict Research) (2017) *Conflict Barometer 2016: Disputes, Non-Violent Crises, Violent Crises, Limited Wars, Wars*, No. 25, www.hiik.de/de/konfliktbarometer

Human Rights Watch (2014) *Azerbaijan: Transparency Group Should Suspend Membership – Stifling Pressure on Activists Violates Commitments*, 14 August 2014, www.hrw.org/news/2014/08/14/azerbaijan-transparency-group-should-suspend-membership

ILO (1989) *Übereinkommen 169 – Übereinkommen über eingeborene und in Stämmen lebende Völker in unabhängigen Ländern*, www.ilo.org/dyn/normlex/en/f?p=NORMLEXPUB:12100:0::NO::P12100_ILO_CODE:C169

ILO (1995) *Übereinkommen 176 – Übereinkommen über den Arbeitsschutz in Bergwerken*, http://www.ilo.org/dyn/normlex/en/f?p=NORMLEXPUB:12100:0::NO:12100:P12100_ILO_CODE:C176

Irin News (2017) How advocacy gave Trump ammunition on conflict-free minerals, www.irinnews.org/investigations/2017/04/06/how-advocacy-gave-trump-ammunition-conflict-free-minerals

Khulumani Support Group, KASA and Academy of Fine Arts, Vienna (2016) *Plough Back the Fruits: The Struggle for Justice and Restitution – The Bodymaps of the Widows of Marikana*, www.rosalux.de/fileadmin/rls_uploads/pdfs/Veranstaltungen/2016/katalog_final_dig.pdf

Küblböck, K. and H. Grohs (2017) *Konfliktmineralien: Auswirkungen der bisherigen Regulierungsinitiativen und Schlussfolgerungen für die Implementierung der EU-Verordnung*, www.oefse.at/fileadmin/content/Downloads/Publikationen/Studien/5_Konfliktmineralien_Studie_Kueblboeck_Grohs_Jaenner2017.pdf

Max Planck Foundation (2016) *Human Rights Risks in Mining: A Baseline Study*, www.bmz.de/rue/includes/downloads/BGR_MPFPR__2016__Human_Rights_Risks_in_Mining.pdf

Misereor (2013) *Menschenrechtliche Probleme im peruanischen Rohstoffsektor und die deutsche Mitverantwortung*, www.misereor.de/fileadmin/publikationen/studie-rohstoffe-menschenrechte-in-peru.pdf

OECD (2011) *OECD-Leitsätze für multinationale Unternehmen*, www.oecd.org/corporate/mne/48808708.pdf

Open Budget Index (2015) *The Open Budget Index 2015*, www.internationalbudget.org/wp-content/uploads/OBS2015-OBI-Rankings-English.pdf

Open Government Partnership (2017) *South Africa*, www.opengovpartnership.org/countries/south-africa

Pearce, F. (2017) *Murder in Pondoland: How a Proposed Mine Brought Conflict to South Africa*, www.theguardian.com/environment/2017/mar/27/murder-pondoland-how-proposed-mine-brought-conflict-south-africa-activist-sikhosiphi-rhadebe

PowerShift et al. (2017a) *Goldgrube Konzernlage*, www.power-shift.de/wordpress/wp-content/uploads/2017/04/Rosia-Montana_Studie_DE.pdf

PowerShift et al. (2017b) *Pressemitteilung: EU: Konfliktmineralien-Verordnung tritt in Kraft. Breites Bündnis der Zivilgesellschaft fordert Nachbesserungen*, www.power-shift.de/pressemitteilung-eu-konfliktmineralien-verordnung-tritt-in-kraft-breites-buendnis-der-zivilgesellschaft-fordert-nachbesserungen/

Reckordt, M. (2011) Gold, Guns and Goons – Menschenrechtsverletzungen und Gewalt im Kontext von Bergbau, in L. Breininger and M. Reckordt, *Die Auswirkungen von Bergbau in den Philippinen*, Philippinenbüro e.V., Essen

Reckordt, M. (2012) *Wie Rohstoffe in Südost-/ Ostasien zur Entwicklung beitragen könn(t)en. Das alternative Bergbau-Gesetz der Philippinen*, www.asienhaus.de/old/public/archiv/bergbau-nr1_philippinen.pdf

Reckordt, M. (2016) *Rohstoffreichtum in der Mongolei*, www.power-shift.de/rohstoffreiche-mongolei/

Reckordt, M. (2017a) Wenn Konzerne klagen können, *IZ3W*, 358, January/February 2017, www.iz3w.org/zeitschrift/ausgaben/358_dschihadismus/schiedsgerichte

Reckordt, M. (2017b) 20.000 Tonnen unter dem Meer. Tiefseebergbau und seine Risiken für Mensch und Natur, in *Großbaustelle Nachhaltigkeit. Deutschland und die globale Nachhaltigkeitsagenda 2017*, www.2030report.de

Rüttinger, L., L. Griestop and C. Scholl (2016) *Umwelt- und Sozialstandards bei der Metallgewinnung. Ergebnisse der Analyse von 42 Standards und Handlungsansätzen*, www.umweltbundesamt.de/umweltfragen-umsoress

SOMO (2015) *Fool's Gold: How Canadian mining company Eldorado Gold destroys the Greek environment and dodges tax through Dutch mailbox companies*, www.somo.nl/fools-gold-eldorado-gold/

Turner, S.D. (2012) *World Heritage Sites and the Extractive Industries*, whc.unesco.org/document/140635

UNEP (2009) *From Conflict to Peacebuilding: The Role of Natural Resources and the Environment*, Nairobi

Urgewald (2013) *Bitter Coal. Ein Dossier über Deutschlands Steinkohleimporte*, www.urgewald.org/sites/default/files/bittercoal_mai.broschure_web.pdf

Wimberger, C. (2017) Sieg über Bergbauindustrie in El Salvador. Das Parlament verabschiedet ein gesetzliches Bergbauverbot, *Lateinamerika Nachrichten* 514, April 2017, www.ci-romero.de/rohstoffe_stopmadmining/

Human Rights Violations to the Benefit of German Corporations
Oxfam Deutschland e.V.[1]

Country	Sector	Branch	NGO / Sources	Involved German companies
Argentina	Mining	Natural gas	OPSur, Germanwatch	Wintershall (subsidiary company of BASF)
Argentina	Mining	Lithium	SÜDWIND	German network operators selling mobile devices
Bahrain	Technology	Surveillance technology	ECCHR, Bahrain Center for Human Rights (BCHR), Bahrainwatch, Privacy International, Reporters Without Boarders	Trovicor, Gamma Group, FinFisher Labs (German subsidiary of the Gamma Group)
Bangladesh	Consumption goods	Clothes	Clean Clothes Campaign, SOMO, FEMNET, Christian Initiative Romero (CIR), INKOTA-network	KiK, Adler Modemärkte, NKD, Guldenpfennig, Kanz – Kids Fashion, TÜV Rheinland (Rana Plaza), Lidl, Karl Rieker, C&A, KiK (Tazreen)
Brazil	Agriculture	Oranges	Christian Initiative Romero (CIR), ver.di	Edeka, Rewe, Lidl, Kaufland, Aldi
Brazil	Infrastructure	Resevoir/dam	GegenStrömung, infoe, Pro Regenwald	Voith Hydro (Joint Venture von Siemens und Voith), Mercedes-Benz, Munich Re, Allianz
Brazil	Industry	Steelmill	FDCL, Cooperation Brazil (KoBra), Medico International, Association of Ethical Shareholders Germany	ThyssenKrupp
Chile	Agriculture	Avocadoes	Danwatch	Lidl, Aldi
China	Consumption goods	Electronics	Germanwatch, Swedwatch, Finnwatch, Danwatch, Südwind (Österreich), SOMO, WEED, Electronics Watch, Good Electronics	German electronic markets, network operators selling mobile devices
China	Infrastructure	Resevoir/dam	GegenStrömung, infoe	Voith Hydro (joint venture of Siemens and Voith)
China	Consumption goods	Shoes	INKOTA-network	Adidas, Puma
Colombia	Agriculture	Bananas	Oxfam, SÜDWIND, Misereor	Edeka, Rewe, Lidl, Aldi
Colombia	Mining	Coal	urgewald, FIAN, PowerShift, Misereor, Kolko	RWE, E.ON, EnBW (über Drummond), Vattenfall and STEAG
Colombia	Infrastructure	Resevoir/dam	GegenStrömung, Misereor	Siemens, Allianz, Munich Re, Hannover Re
Colombia	Mining	Tungsten	Bloomberg, PowerShift	BMW, VW, Porsche, Siemens
Costa Rica	Agriculture	Pineapples	Oxfam	Edeka, Rewe, Lidl, Aldi
Democratic Republic of Congo	Mining	Cobalt	SÜDWIND	German network operators selling mobile devices
Democratic Republic of Congo	Mining	Tantalum (Ore, Coltan)	SÜDWIND	German network operators selling mobile devices
Democratic Republic of Congo	Agriculture	Timber	ECCHR, Global Witness	Danzer Group
Ecuador	Agriculture	Bananas	Oxfam	Edeka, Rewe, Lidl, Aldi
El Salvador	Agriculture	Plant breeding (poinsettia)	Christian Initiative Romero (CIR)	Dümmen
Ethiopia	Technology	Surveillance technology	Privacy International, netzpolitik.org	Trovicor (former Siemens Intelligence Solutions), Elaman, Gamma Group
Ethiopia	Agriculture	Roses	Society for Threatened Peoples (STP)	German supermarket chains
Ghana	Agriculture	Cacao	SÜDWIND, INKOTA-network	German chocolate manufacturers
Honduras	Agriculture	Honeydew melons	Christian Initiative Romero (CIR)	Rewe, Edeka, (Kaiser's Tengelmann)

1 For a full, commented list, see: www.oxfam.de/unsere-arbeit/themen/menschenrechtsverletzungen-fuer-profite

Country	Sector	Branch	NGO / Sources	Involved German companies
Honduras	Infrastructure	Resevoir/dam	FDCL, GegenStrömung, SOMO, urgewald	Voith Hydro (joint venture of Siemens and Voith, withdrawal from the project announced)
Honduras	Agriculture	Palm oil	FIDH, FIAN	DEG (withdrawal 2011)
India	Agriculture/ Trade	Fruits and vegetables	Oxfam	Metro Group
Ivory Coast	Agriculture	Cacao	INKOTA-network, SÜDWIND, Südwind (Österreich)	German chocolate manufacturers
Malaysia	Mining	Rare earth conditioning	Öko-Institute	Siemens, BASF
Mexico	Infrastructure	Wind farm	Association of Ethical Shareholders, Ökumenisches Büro München, Robin Wood	Siemens
Mexico	Industry	Car tyres	Germanwatch, FIAN	Continental
Morocco	Agriculture	Beans	Christian Initiative Romero (CIR)	Edeka, Aldi Nord, Rewe, (Kaiser's Tengelmann)
Mozambique	Mining	Coking coal for steel production	Christian Initiative Romero (CIR), SumOfUs, Danwatch	ThyssenKrupp
Myanmar	Consumption goods	Clothes	SOMO	C&A, Deuter
Pakistan	Consumption goods	Clothes	Clean clothes campaign, INKOTA-network, Medico International, FEMNET, SOMO	KiK
Panama	Infrastructure	Resevoir/dam	FIAN, Rettet den Regenwald, urgewald	DEG
Peru	Agriculture	Mangoes	Oxfam	Edeka, Rewe, Aldi, Lidl
Peru	Infrastructure	Wind farm	Germanwatch	RWE
Peru	Mining	Copper	Misereor	Aurubis
Philippines	Mining	Nickel	PowerShift, philippinenbüro	ThyssenKrupp, ArcelorMittal, Salzgitter
Philippines	Mining	Gold	SÜDWIND	German network operators selling mobile devices, Schmuckhersteller
South Africa	Agriculture	Wine and grapes	Oxfam, Kirchliche Arbeitsstelle Südliches Afrika (KASA)	German supermarket chains
South Africa	Mining	Coal	Misereor, urgewald	Hitachi Power Europe, Bilfinger Berger, Rheinmetall Defence Electronics, KfW IPEX Bank, Siemens, Steag Energy Services (coal plants), German coal importers
South Africa	Mining	Platinum	KASA, Bread for the World, Association of Ethical Shareholders, KASA, RLS, KEESA, SOLIFONDS, PowerShift a.o	BASF
South Africa	Industry	Amor, automotive industry	ECCHR, Medico International, KOSA, KASA, Center for Constitutional Rights, Khulumani Support Group	Daimler, Rheinmetall
Sudan	Infrastructure	Resevoir/dam	ECCHR, GegenStrömung	Lahmeyer
Turkey	Infrastructure	Resevoir/dam	GegenStrömung	Züblin, Euler Hermes
Uganda	Agriculture	Coffee	FIAN	Neumann Coffee Group
Uzbekistan	Agriculture	Cotton	ECCHR, INKOTA-network	Otto Stadtlander, Commerzbank, Deutsche Bank
Western Sahara	Infrastructure	Wind farm	Medico International	Siemens
Zambia	Agriculture	Farmland	FIAN	Amatheon Agri, DEG
Zambia	Mining	Copper	SÜDWIND	German network operators selling mobile devices, jewellery manufacturers

10. HORIZONS OF RESPONSIBILITY

Franziska Dübgen
Translated by Lyam Bittar

In a digitalised world characterised by transnational biographies, global economic relations and worldwide migration, the lives we lead are increasingly entangled with those of a vast number of other people. The fates of people living in other nations, with different histories and different languages, are in a complex way interwoven with our own: our own biographies, our own desires, the goods we consume, and the individual ways in which we act. This means that we can no longer ground responsibility solely in the existence of shared state institutions, shared identities or local conventions.

The assumption that there exist homogeneous entities that are politically, culturally or economically indivisible has proven a fiction serving merely to externalise the responsibilities that we all bear in the face of transnational dependencies, our exposure to global environmental threats, economic structures of exploitation and international conflicts. Often, though, socio-political discourse and our moral intuition lag behind these empirical everyday circumstances.

Thorough definitions of responsibility will therefore have to move beyond measuring only the everyday, visible effects of our actions. In a global society, what takes place outside our immediate domain has also become part of the actions we need to assume responsibility for. While in a juridical sense we can be held responsible only for those actions that can be ascribed to us as agents, a social philosophy perspective sees things in a more complex light, especially when we consider events that are caused because people are structurally involved in them without being liable for them as individuals. This raises the question whether privileges, interests and profits constitute additional parameters besides the causative principle that we should use to reflect on responsibility in the context of global asymmetries of power. This chapter will argue that responsibility needs to be understood against the background of structural injustice, especially in cases in which the institutions involved are powerful transnational agents such as corporations. It will also look at what it actually can and should mean to take on responsibility in this context. We will begin by reflecting on the concepts essential to any discussion on global responsibility – freedom as a foundation for taking responsible action and the question of the responsible subject.

The condition of responsibility: Freedom unconstrained by domination

To begin with, being responsible for something in a philosophical sense means being morally conscious of who we are and what we do. Responsible agents will base their actions on moral grounds. This basic condition is linked to a second: an agent must have freedom of choice. A free subject is generally understood as having, in all situations, the means to act differently. If I am coerced into carrying out a certain action or I act under constraint, we cannot speak here of a 'free' action for which I would consider myself or others responsible. Even if a person exposed to grave material deprivation is forced to choose from a number of options, all of which she would rather avoid, she is free only in a limited sense. We are only fully free when we carry out actions that we can actually decide to perform, i.e. if we are free in a 'positive' sense.[1] In social realities heavily infused by power, freedom needs to be adequately reflected upon in the light of the background conditions informing individual decisions. In these contexts, the condition enabling us to take responsibility is the capacity to act in a positive sense, which means being able to choose between alternatives without exposing, as a result of making that choice, my own life or the lives of those closest to me to grave consequences. In this sense, a person working for an extremely low wage and under bad working conditions to secure his or her survival does not enjoy any degree of positive freedom in terms of career choices. While this person may decide to end that employment relationship, or protest against her working conditions, she can do so only if she is prepared to face severe consequences. For in doing so, she chooses between two evils: to survive without a wage, or to continue supporting a system that promotes her and others' exploitation. The situation is different for persons who have different career options to choose from, for they have access to actual options, which makes them agents that can and should be held responsible.

The concepts of shared and role-specific responsibility

Aside from this, there is also the issue of defining responsible agents. Are corporations agents that we can hold responsible? This question has triggered a controversial debate in philosophy (May and Hoffman, 1991; Neuhäuser, 2011). In terms of the law, we can speak of the responsibility of legal persons; in Germany, Austria, and South Africa, corporations are considered legal persons, which makes them accountable, although not criminally liable. But if we speak of responsibility in a moral or political sense, if we expect from them a 'response' when they are called upon to care and take responsibility, then it is not corporations that we appeal to, but in fact its employees, its management and the individuals earning the profits that a corporation's activities generate. Legally, a corporation might be a 'person', but in actual fact it is dependent on the people who advance its systemic interests, define its targets and help generate its profits. Corporations are constructions that depend on our belief in them and in the actions that we perform on their behalf. A corporation itself does not have a moral consciousness. It does not base its actions on moral grounds, and in this strict sense it cannot be considered 'responsible' either. Understanding corporations in this way – as moral agents – would give rise to two problems. Firstly, this perspective would cause us to blame and shame an abstract entity instead of targeting the persons holding relevant positions, i.e. managers and profiteers. Secondly, it could encourage us to imagine corporations as beings who 'act' and pursue 'intentions' rather than as legal fictions, which would in turn ascribe to corporations interests and claims to which people could submit themselves. This means that a corporation's 'actions' are the result of the influence of various parties, but it is people who are ultimately the agents of these actions.

It therefore seems logical and productive to assume that persons standing in an institutionalised relationship with a corporation can be thought of, by virtue of their professional function, as morally responsible for both that corporation and the actions carried out on its behalf. This concept is called role responsibility; it defines the responsibilities held by a person on the basis of a specific social role (Cooper, 1991:41). Usually, however, people adopt a number of social roles. I can be part of a company's top management, a mother to three children and also a member of a civil society organisation. The loyalty I feel towards my company – which because of its systemic interests within the capitalist relations of production, incentivises me to align my actions with its logic of profit maximisation – may clash with my responsibility as a member of civil society to base my actions on ethical standards (Neuhäuser, 2011:165; Kaleck and Saage-Maaß, 2016:43). This means there are cases in which different roles come into conflict with each other. Nevertheless, my function as a promoter of my company's systemic targets will not relieve me of my role as a citizen: a person's social existence is never fully absorbed by one single role. In this sense, role responsibility is not understood as the simple adoption of a specific role, but rather as a bid to take responsibility for the actions that I carry out in that specific social role.

Furthermore, an individual in a company will rarely be able to make fully independent decisions. Most cases here fall within the scope of what is called 'shared responsibility', a concept that considers individuals co-responsible for the decisions they are involved in (May, 1992). A company's employees are thus subject to differing degrees of responsibility, which are contingent upon the power, privileges and influence they hold. We will look at these various degrees of responsibility in detail in a later section. For the time being, we will have to lay out why we bear responsibility in the first place and, if so, to whom.

Global approaches to grounding responsibility

Modern philosophy distinguishes roughly between at least three different ways of justifying responsibility that account for why we are responsible for one another in the first place. Each entails a different assessment regarding the degree and the addressees of responsibility.

The first approach holds that defining the foundations of justice always requires a context that also marks out the limits of responsibility. This model includes both national (Miller, 1995) and communitarian approaches (MacIntyre, 1988). The former assumes that we need shared political institutions to be able to define mutual obligations of justice, whereas the latter holds that it is a community and its culturally incorporated norms that serve as our basis for establishing relationships of responsibility for each other. These historically contingent norms cannot be applied beyond their respective contexts, however. Therefore, according to this approach, we cannot argue why relationships of responsibility should be extended to include people who are members of other political systems or other cultures.

Unfortunately, though, defining the scope of responsibility only in terms of context fails to take into account the reality of transnational relations and interdependencies from a social philosophy perspective (Fraser 2009:52). This methodological nationalism – read provincialism – faces the difficulty of explaining why we owe members of other societies less in terms of basic rights and claims than the people we live with side by side, an assumption that openly undermines the idea of equal dignity to which we are all entitled by virtue of being human. From an egalitarian perspective, therefore, the provincialism betrayed by social philosophy seems highly questionable and will therefore not be discussed further in this chapter.

The second approach holds that we also bear responsibility for people who are not our neighbours and not members of our own society, who neither speak our language nor share the same religion. I want to call this approach 'humanist'. It includes both ethical and political models that fundamentally consider each and every one of us responsible for all of humanity. Cosmopolitan theories of justice argue in favour of principles of justice that treat all humans alike. The conception of responsibility resulting from this view excludes no one; it operates beyond the categories of class, religion, sex or political ideology. It is therefore a universalist approach which holds that responsibility is grounded in our shared humanity and the dignity associated with that humanity.

The third approach, in turn, which I will label 'political', builds on a closer definition of responsibility, even if it assumes that all people have the same claims to justice. According to this model, the scope of responsibility extends primarily to those with whom we are in some way connected – through a shared history, an interconnected world economy, or global political institutions. This model of responsibility is a relational model of responsibility, and it addresses relations of structural injustice.

In what follows, I will reconstruct a humanist model of grounding responsibility and highlight some of its weaknesses. I will then sketch a political grounding model that promises to solve the challenges that arise in the context of communitarian and humanist justification models of responsibility.

Face-to-face: Responsibility as a response to vulnerability

Shortly after the Second World War, Emmanuel Lévinas developed a humanist conception of responsibility closely oriented towards the needs and the vulnerability of a specific other. For Lévinas, the face is the physical expression of human vulnerability – naked, disarming, vulnerable, defenceless (Finkielkraut, 1997). The very moment a human sets eye on a vulnerable other, he becomes responsible. He is forced to respond (*répondre*) because encountering the other has made him responsible (*responsable*). Lévinas considers this relationship asymmetrical: responsibility increases with the degree by which it is claimed. The structure of responsibility, he says, is therefore anarchical and beyond the logical (Lévinas, 1998). According to Lévinas, responsibility cannot be weighed up. The need of the other is the only – and the crucial – criterion in defining the extent of responsibility. It may well be that the other cannot return what he or she receives. But for Lévinas, morality is not grounded in cold calculations and benefits, but in neediness and sensitivity. Responsibility is thus principally infinite and cannot pragmatically be limited in any way from an ethical perspective: 'The face of the Other calls me out of narcissism towards something finally more important' (Butler, 2004:138).

The subjective inner murmur described by Lévinas acts as the individual's moral conscience, which ought to speak out against the partially inhumane impact of politics and the economy. Every institutional action failing to recognise this neediness in each human falls within the scope of wrong that Lévinas calls on us to oppose.

The positive aspect of this conception of responsibility is that it moves beyond moral philosophy's provincialism by linking responsibility to our humanity, which is determined neither by passports, nor the colour of our skin, nor a person's sex. And yet this humanist conception of responsibility leaves open which forms of precarious life we should turn to and whether this responsibility depends on our experience of a specific other's suffering. Responsibility conceived as infinite does not rely on our reasons and motivations for taking action, nor does it provide guidance as to whom or what we should engage. In a way, this renders it contingent: if we are responsible for all human beings alike, it means we are responsible for no one in particular. We thus need to reflexively question our ethical impulse in order to ascertain whether our own actions are reasonable and appropriate. The humanist conception therefore provides little normative orientation regarding what we ought to become involved with in order to fulfil our responsibility.

Delimiting responsibility: Cosmopolitanism and 'love of the most distant'

The step I want to take next involves consciously widening the limits of the discourse on responsibility beyond the borders of the nation-state. Such models of responsibility are often called 'cosmopolitan'. The existentialist and Kantian philosopher Hans Jonas argues for such a universalist conception of responsibility; his model aims to provide us with orientation in a technology-focused and increasingly unequal global society.

He criticises ethical thinking's narrow focus on those who seem close, on our neighbours, and insists that in addition to neighbourly love we ought to practise 'love of the most distant'. While psychologically this focus on those who seem close is easily explained, Jonas reminds us that responsibility as a moral imperative encompasses all animate beings – including the distant other. In addition, he distinguishes between a responsibility based on the causal attribution of past actions, on the one hand, and a responsibility based on what is to be done, on the other (Jonas, 1985:90–95). The former retrospectively refers to the consequences of an action that has caused harm, injury or damage. This harm or injury may not have been caused intentionally (which is why we speak of legal liability in such cases). The situation is different, however, if the motive for acting itself establishes guilt. The first case is usually followed by claims for compensation (without a moralising undertone), the second by claims for adequate retribution. For Jonas, this exclusive focus on the past is formalistic and ethically unsatisfying, which is why he argues that our attention to past injustice needs to be extended to endorse a positive, future-oriented sense of responsibility, one that encourages 'the forward determination of what is to be done'. This other responsibility is rooted in the power to act, and it necessitates itself: 'The dependent in its immanent right becomes commanding, the power in its transitive causality becomes committed' (92). Here, the degree of responsibility correlates with status: Jonas considers vertical responsibility towards weaker individuals (for instance, the responsibility of an employer towards his workers) to be stronger than horizontal responsibility towards one's peers (94). In this sense, it is vulnerability and dependency that determine the extent of our responsibility towards even the remotest other. Here, Jonas links cosmopolitan with relational arguments, to which I want to turn in detail in the next section.

Exploitation, interaction and structural responsibility

Actions do not take place in a vacuum. They are embedded in complex processes of interaction and varying degrees of agency. Like Jonas, Iris Marion Young also considers responsibility as not merely a matter that affects only those close to me. In a globalised world it extends to include the remotest other, whose lifeworld I am not familiar with and whose face, to echo Lévinas, will always remain unknown to me. In her view, a political model of responsibility therefore has to be sensitive, above all, to domination. She establishes her basis for the justification of responsibility by pointing out the complex relations of transnational cooperation which are framed by various forms of structural injustice, and calls her conception a 'social connection model' (Young, 2011:95–122). To illustrate her point, she sketches the poor working conditions in the sweatshop industry (125), although of course working conditions in mines, in the extractive industry or in agriculture could be analysed in a similar vein. Economic cooperation has forged new social processes that in turn have created transnational links between workers, management and consumers – a connectedness that establishes relations of responsibility. Young opens up her understanding of 'responsibility' to accommodate more than purely causal relations. In most cases, after all, tracing cause and effect is a challenging proposition; instead, we increasingly find ourselves confronting events that are not just loosely connected, but are in fact entangled in so many complex ways that individual agents can always find an excuse for not being responsible, in the sense of the causative principle, for an incident.

Her argument therefore takes a different approach. She considers responsible all those who are involved in reproducing social structures, and thus in shaping the background conditions of transnational production. This aspect sets Young's model apart from the liability model we are familiar with from juridical contexts. Its holistic perspective on the social dimensions of relations of exploitation makes hers a decidedly political model. And, like Jonas's conception of responsibility, it too is focused on the future. Taking responsibility as a social agent in this sense involves not only lessening the immediate effects of a relation of exploitation. Rather, it also involves contributing to reshaping social relations in such a way as to dissolve the causes of injustice. This perspective does not isolate individual agents or their actions (who are perhaps only relatively small cogs in a larger wheel of production), but includes all those involved in the reproduction of social processes that in turn determine individual actions. One possible objection to such an interactive grounding responsibility is that it will eventually have to identify all people as affected in one way or another, which will unseam its concept of connectedness. This 'butterfly effect' makes it difficult to distinguish at an analytical level who is to be held responsible for what (Fraser 2009:64).

To avoid this conceptual inflation, Young introduces a number of parameters. Our responsibility varies, firstly, with the degree of power that we as agents have in effectively influencing a process; secondly, it varies with the position of privilege emerging from the particular form of structural injustice to which a group is exposed; it varies, thirdly, as a result of our own personal interest in undermining and transforming these unjust relations;[2] and, finally, it is subject to our collective ability resulting from our participation in a political movement aimed at ending injustice (Young, 2013:184–186). Taking as a basis a person's particular position that he or she holds in relation to these parameters, we can determine his or her degree of responsibility to end a wrong, or at least to protest against it.

Decision-makers in companies have the power to improve the conditions governing the production processes in their sector by taking action collectively. Furthermore, they profit from existing relations of exploitation, which increases their moral responsibility towards the victims of unjust relations. Even if they cannot – or cannot yet – be held criminally liable for inhumane working conditions along their supply chains (which are at least partly opaque, one should add), they nevertheless do carry responsibility for the workers' well-being in a political sense since they are involved in structural processes and derive benefits from this involvement – for instance, economic profit, which can take the form of high wages, dividend pay-outs to shareholders or access to symbolic capital. An exacting political conception of responsibility will therefore consider events in their overall social context and call on those who are responsible to back collective processes and to fight the background conditions of exploitation and humiliation instead of withdrawing to focus on the immediate consequences of their actions only.

The background conditions constituting an event include, among other things, a situation's historical becoming, its 'having-become', which for instance may refer to the persisting influence of former colonial structures on the economy and politics, or of racist demarcations resulting from the transatlantic slave trade. In the context of a post-apartheid society, these conditions also comprise the unequal distribution of property and the means of production, as well as the specific vulnerability of migrant workers from conflict zones or impoverished rural areas who have no real choice regarding the conditions under which they take up work. Responsibility in a historically informed sense thus insists on analysing existing political and economic inequalities as the background conditions of specific events, and, in doing so, it must also take into account their coming-into-being and determine how far the current distribution of wealth is a result of precisely these persisting relations (Oruka, 2000).

How to respond? The postcolonial ambivalences of a politics of solidarity

We therefore need to define how we can act responsibly at a global level. Whereas obligations often specify in detail the things that need to be done, responsibility initially leaves open how it expects to be fulfilled (Feinberg, 1966:141). Collective action arising from a (co-)responsibility for social wrongs across the world and aimed at dissolving their causes can be described as 'solidarity' that fights for just practices and institutions. But how can we practise such solidarity, especially given the structural asymmetries of power? In a global context, solidarity cannot rest primarily on a shared history or similar status if its intention is to overcome established demarcations, i.e. existing structures. Instead, it has to be 'reflexive' (Dean, 1996; Dübgen, 2014:262–268). Reflexive solidarity does not build on a shared identity to which we are expected to subscribe. It also does not build on a sentiment of belonging to a specific group. Rather, it is founded on the shared reflection upon the conditions under which we live; it bridges existing differences without erasing them. This makes the 'we' at the heart of such a solidarity-based community a discursive web that is open to constant modification and critically questions its own exclusions. The form that solidarity-based actions assume is shaped by the political aims with which activists identify. This solidarity is different from models that stress the affective component of solidarity and accordingly build on existing conventions and emotions.

Solidarity-based actions targeting transnational structures of exploitation require communication to cross established borders and boundaries so we can learn about the demands of those others with whom we want to forge an alliance. We otherwise risk imposing our own views, needs and conceptions of the good life on other people, and thereby overlook the fact that responsibility has to be conceived as a dialogic process. Meeting our responsibility in the face of existing power relations in a postcolonial world therefore requires a strong degree of critical self-reflexivity, sensitivity to differences in status that shape discourse and an awareness of the different communicative and habitual conventions that vary from context to context. These difficulties increase the more the conditions framing the life of those others with whom we want to forge an alliance diverge from our own.

The Indian postcolonial critic Gayatri Spivak has drawn up a conception of 'postcolonial responsibility' that addresses precisely this communicative challenge and is intended as a crucial contribution to a model of political responsibility. She analyses how people structurally located in the global North can take responsibility for persons who are excluded from the global economic and cultural flow of information and who are without access to money and goods. Drawing on the Italian Marxist Antonio Gramsci, she refers to these persons as the 'subaltern'. The subaltern is so far removed from the reality of First World activists and intellectuals that the latter often fail to register their speaking or, when they do, fail to comprehend them. In the majority of cases, therefore, our commitment has the effect of patronising, even silencing, those whom we set out to help.

To critically analyse relationships of responsibility, Spivak distinguishes two conceptions of responsibility. One seeks a radical alterity in order to answer an authentic call for help – a call which it is structurally incapable of hearing because of its radical alterity. Attempts to translate between these individual lifeworlds fail because of this radical difference. The intellectual therefore projectively imagines the subaltern's call, from which she derives an obligation to generously help the poor (Spivak and Shaikh, 2007:179). Spivak therefore embraces a second, different approach, according to which 'something else wills me' (180) – a state of heteronomy, in which we need to keep in mind that we as agents are always structurally embedded. At the same time she warns, quoting Jacques Derrida: 'No responsibility could ever be taken without equivocation and without contradiction' (Spivak, 1994:19). This means that there is always space for our assumption of responsibility to sway in directions that those involved may initially not have predicted. She formalises this ethical relationship as follows: 'It is all action that is undertaken in response to a call (or something that seems to us to resemble a call) that cannot be grasped as such' (22).

The process of taking on responsibility is always exposed to the danger of being contaminated, appropriated and distorted. The required heteronomy of engaging with the language of the other, the marginalised and weaker person, is not supposed to culminate in self-abandonment, but rather in an extreme form of self-reflexivity that turns to the other in empathy while at the same time subjecting his or her statements to critical scrutiny. The 'organic intellectual' (named after Gramsci) is called upon to make use of her capacity to articulate herself by trying to tune into the other's silence inscribed within a hegemonic narrative, a task that Spivak refers to as 'measuring silences' (Spivak, 1988:286). Identifying who in a conversation has not been given a voice requires more than a mere exchange of arguments. It entails sharpening one's awareness of the other's weaknesses and vulnerability. If at a structural level subalternity means being excluded from the hegemonic episteme – if it means being radically cut off from the possibility of upward social mobility – then the subaltern cannot also participate in a dialogue on fairer structures. For Spivak, the responsibility of intellectuals and political and civil society activists towards the 'distant other' thus lies in their using their intellectual capacities and their knowledge (for instance, of human rights) as tools for emancipatory practices. In this way, they can put themselves at the service of translating the subaltern's demands and interests into a language that has a voice in the hegemonic discourse of global institutions and political agents.

The function of organic intellectuals is to integrate the subaltern into the hegemonic episteme, not by representing the interests of the subaltern, but by committing themselves to a political struggle aimed at emancipating the subaltern to articulate her interests such that she will be heard. At this point, the organic intellectual loses control over events as they unfold. In this respect, responsibility (following Spivak) is always a reciprocal process, which does not imply that all sides are expected to contribute in equal measure. Rather, it is a process of epistemic approximation and translation that steps across structural differences and conventional boundaries.

Reflected through the prism of postcolonialism, then, solidarity would be about building communicative relationships that increase our sensitivity and acceptance of other, different, diverging perspectives, relationships that encourage us to listen actively – to an idiom, a way of speaking that is not our own, but is attached to social realities that we are at the same time close to and unfamiliar with: unfamiliar, because we may not know how to interpret them the first time we hear them, and because in everyday life we often fail to connect with others; yet close, because in this world there are, after all, so many processes that constantly bring us together.

Postscript: Neoliberal subversions of responsibility

Over the past years, as the neoliberal world view has begun to highlight the notion of responsibility, political discourse has started to read responsibility as self-responsibility. We have become responsible not only for managing our pension schemes, but also for maintaining our health, keeping our professional skills and qualifications up to date, and, not least, caring for the people in our social environment when the welfare state stops providing the assistance they need. The 'I' is increasingly overburdened with carrying responsibility for itself and for its own happiness (Vogelmann, 2014). As individuals we are caught up in constant, narcissistic self-reflection, subjecting to scrutiny our consumer habits, our needs, our (pathological) fears, our failures. Neoliberalism's list of headwords includes not solidarity, not equality and not dignity, but responsibility. In this sense one could claim that responsibility in itself is not political, and that the discourse on responsibility is rather a reflex of neoliberal thought. This would make the discourse on responsibility a depoliticised discourse for the human monad thrown back on itself.

We therefore need to analyse critically the cases in which taking on responsibility functions as a legitimising strategy that helps sustain a public image without pushing for substantial change. 'Corporate social responsibility' (CSR) may function as one such vehicle of neoliberalism. Wolfgang Kaleck and Miriam Saage-Maaß have doubts about the concept. They argue that while individual CSR initiatives do set out packed with good intentions, the best they do is help alleviate misery; they hardly ever bring about structural change (2016:43). Individual, public acts of taking responsibility might even serve to cement existing structures of exploitation when they seek to profit from a moral economy of justification and stage their agents as generous 'donors' (Rayak, 2016).

Such a neoliberal appropriation of the concept perverts its emancipatory character. To push that contradiction even further, I would like to conclude by calling for a repoliticisation of the depoliticised discourse on responsibility. A political conception of responsibility will not seek responsibility in the I alone – it will set out to identify structures in the world that produce and perpetuate degrading, insulting and exploitative relationships that harm the I and all being-in-the-world. It will seek holistic responses to structural challenges. To end and to begin with, responsibility is a question of justice.

Notes

1. Isaiah Berlin distinguishes between negative freedom, by which he means freedom from coercion, and positive freedom, which is the ability to do something (2005:166–201). His liberal approach considers negative freedom decisive, whereas this chapter argues that we ought to always assess individual actions against a society's background conditions.
2. Young maintains that the victims of injustice are those most interested in eliminating its social causes, which is why she assigns to them a co-responsibility for eliminating these causes. She argues that victims often have in-depth knowledge of the processes of their exploitation. I consider her argument questionable because it burdens those who are already exposed to precarious living conditions with eliminating harm and injustice. Nevertheless, and precisely because of their specific insights into their own situation, we owe them solidarity for their struggle for justice, *in so far as* they stand up for their rights and fight for social change. This, however, must not be formulated as a moral imperative.

References

Berlin, I. (2005) *Liberty: Incorporating Four Essays on Liberty*, Oxford University Press, Oxford
Butler, J. (2004) *Precarious Life: The Powers of Mourning and Violence*, Verso, London
Cooper, D.E. (1991) Collective responsibility, in L. May and S. Hoffman (eds.), *Collective Responsibility: Five Decades in Theoretical and Applied Ethics*, Rowman and Littlefield, Savage, Maryland, pp. 35–46
Dean, J. (1996) *Solidarity of Strangers: Feminism after Identity Politics*, University of California Press, Berkeley
Dübgen, F. (2014) *Was ist gerecht? Kennzeichen einer transnationalen solidarischen Politik*, Campus, Frankfurt
Feinberg, J. (1996) Duties, rights, and claims, *American Philosophical Quarterly* 3, 2 (April), pp. 137–144
Fraser, N. (2009) *Scales of Justice: Reimagining Political Space in a Globalizing World*, Polity Press, Cambridge
Finkielkraut, A. (1997) *L'Humanité perdue: Essai sur le XXe siècle*, Seuil, Paris
Jonas, H. (1985) *The Imperative of Responsibility: In Search of an Ethics for the Technological Age*, University of Chicago Press, Chicago
Kaleck, W. and M. Saage-Maaß (2016) *Unternehmen vor Gericht. Globale Kämpfe für Menschenrechte*, Wagenbach, Berlin
Lévinas, E. (1998) *Otherwise than Being: Or, Beyond Essence*, Duquesne, Pittsburgh
MacIntyre, A. (1988) *Whose Justice? Which Rationality?*, University of Notre Dame Press, Notre Dame
May, L. (1992) *Sharing Responsibility*, University of Chicago Press, Chicago
May, L. and S. Hoffman (eds.) (1991) *Collective Responsibility: Five Decades in Theoretical and Applied Ethics*, Rowman and Littlefield, Savage, Maryland
Miller, D. (1995) *On Nationality*, Clarendon Press, Oxford
Mohanty, C. (2003) *Feminism without Borders: Decolonizing Theory, Practicing Solidarity*, Duke University Press, Bloomington
Neuhäuser, C. (2011) *Unternehmen als moralische Akteure*, Suhrkamp, Berlin
Oruka, H. O. (2000) Philosophie der Entwicklungshilfe. Eine Frage des Rechts auf ein menschliches Minimum, in polylog. *Zeitschrift für interkulturelles Philosophieren* 6, pp. 6–16.
Rayak, D. (2016) Hope and betrayal on the Platinum Belt: Responsibility, violence and corporate power in South Africa', *Journal of Southern African Studies* 42, 5, pp. 929–946
Spivak, G. C. (1988) Can the subaltern speak?, in C. Nelson and L. Grossberg (eds.), *Marxism and the Interpretation of Culture*, Illinois University Press, Chicago, pp. 271–313
Spivak, G. C. (1994) Responsibility, *Boundary 2*, 21, 3, pp. 19–64
Spivak, G. C. and N. Shaikh (2007) Gayatri Chakravorty Spivak, in S. Nermeen (ed.), *The Present as History: Critical Perspectives on Global Power*, Columbia University Press, New York
Velasquez, M. G. (1991) Why corporations are not responsible, in Larry May and Stacey Hoffman (eds.), *Collective Responsibility: Five Decades in Theoretical and Applied Ethics*, Rowman and Littlefield, Savage, Maryland, pp. 111–131
Vogelmann, F. (2014) *Im Bann der Verantwortung*, Campus, Frankfurt
Young, I. M. (2013) *Responsibility for Justice*, Oxford University Press, Oxford

▶ This article by South African journalist and activist Koketso Moeti was published in *The Daily Vox* on the occasion of the BASF shareholder meeting on 29 April 2016 (Mannheim).

Justice for Marikana? Four Reasons South Africa should care about the upcoming BASF shareholders' meeting

Koketso Moeti, 26 April 2016

Lonmin is the multinational mining company where a strike for a living wage led to the death of 44 people, 34 of whom were brutally gunned down in a single day by SAPS. On the 29th April 2016, BASF, a principal customer of Lonmin will be hosting their annual shareholders' meeting. Apart from the usual attendees, a South African delegation which includes two of the women made widows by the Marikana massacre will be present, calling for justice for Marikana. Koketso Moeti lists four reasons why we should care about this meeting.

1. Lonmin clearly won't take responsibility on its own The Farlam Commission report found that Lonmin did not sufficiently try to engage with workers on ending the strike or protect its employees. The report also recommended that Lonmin »be investigated for knowing the risks but failing to protect employees«. Apart from this, Lonmin was found to be complicit in the poor conditions in which mineworkers lived, those conditions that led to the Marikana massacre. Another damning report by the Alternative Information and Development Centre (AIDC) shows that the company could afford the living wages demanded by the mineworkers. It also found that Lonmin was involved in profit shifting and abuse of the transfer price mechanism. It's important that customers and investors in Lonmin actively support the call for justice.

2. BASF prides itself on being a founding member of the United Nations Global Compact The Global Compact is »a call to companies to align strategies and operations with universal principles on human rights, labour, environment and anti-corruption, and take actions that advance societal goals«. BASF continues to brag about this, yet is the principal customer of a company that reneged on its duties as far as its workers are concerned, leading to deadly consequences. Surely as an entity that claims to be concerned with human rights, BASF should take responsibility in ensuring that these rights are upheld throughout its supply chain?

3. Justice for Marikana is about more than Marikana Marikana is a microcosm of South African society and the lead up to the massacre had features of the everyday exploitation of black workers, poverty, inhumane living and working conditions. It's also about the ruthless profit-maximising ways that the extractive sector has always operated in South Africa, and justice for Marikana would be a symbolic victory for many others working tirelessly to hold corporates to account.

4. We can't allow »business as usual« Almost four years later, many of the families affected are struggling to make ends meet after the brutal murder of their loved ones, many of whom were breadwinners in their respective households. The injured miners, some of who are no longer able to work and have medical requirements, are also yet to be compensated. Apart from that, very little has changed for this community, after such a tragic spotlight was put on the conditions in which they work and live. Not to address these conditions would be to allow for those slain to have died in vain.

11. THE LIMITS OF VOLUNTARY INITIATIVES: HOW BUSINESS STANDS IN THE WAY OF BINDING HUMAN RIGHTS STANDARDS

Sarah Lincoln
Translated by Cornelia Gritzner

For decades, human rights, development and environmental organisations have been calling on national governments, the United Nations (UN) and other political institutions to compel companies to respect the environment and human rights in their global business operations. Numerous scandals, such as the destruction of the Niger Delta by Shell or more recently the collapse of a textile factory in Bangladesh, have caused international outrage. Yet, binding global human rights and environmental standards for companies are still lacking. While the economy has become increasingly globalised and investor rights are protected through binding trade agreements and are being enforced before international courts of arbitration, the protection of human rights is lagging behind. Victims of human rights violations have often no means to hold the relevant companies accountable (ECCHR et al., 2017).[1]

Voluntary initiatives: Well-protected against legal regulations

The UN has made numerous proposals for regulation of the global economy: the Code of Conduct for Transnational Corporations in the 1970s, and the draft of the UN Norms on the Responsibilities of Transnational Corporations and Other Business Enterprises with Regard to Human Rights in 2003, for example. The negotiations on the UN Binding Treaty on Business and Human Rights started the third round in October 2017 (see the chapter by Akhona Mehlo). All these initiatives have failed so far, due to the resistance of industry associations and the unrestrained faith in the market. In addition, companies are working hard to make people believe that they fulfil their responsibilities within the framework of voluntary initiatives.

Since the turn of the millennium, almost every large company has adopted a corporate social responsibility (CSR) strategy portraying themselves as sustainable and socially oriented. This allegedly self-regulatory approach fits into the neoliberal discourse of the past decades (see interview with Dinah Rajak): of liberalisation and privatisation instead of state regulation (Brot für die Welt et al., 2014). Founded by the UN in 2000 as a voluntary self-regulation instrument, the UN Global Compact is a good example of this approach. Global Compact member companies commit themselves to specific standards, but this commitment is voluntary and there is no monitoring of implementation. The Guiding Principles on Business and Human Rights adopted by the UN Human Rights Council in 2011 are another consensus-based, voluntary approach that was developed by Harvard professor John Ruggie. The guiding principles specify requirements for states and companies that do not, however, go beyond soft law, i.e. their implementation is voluntary and no enforcement mechanisms are in place.

The National Action Plan for Business and Human Rights

National governments are required to implement the UN guiding principles, which means they must establish framework conditions in their countries to strengthen corporate responsibility and improve legal protection for those affected. The German federal government adopted a National Action Plan (NAP) to implement the UN Guiding Principles on Business and Human Rights on 21 December 2016, following a two-year consultation process (Federal Government, 2016). The NAP is generally limited to voluntary recommendations for German companies. All of them 'should' implement human rights diligence processes to prevent human rights violations in their supply chains. This will be verified by monitoring a sample of large companies. If companies ignore these requirements, however, they will not face any consequences. Neither will they be excluded from public tenders nor do they have to fear actions brought by those affected.

This result is more than disappointing in the opinion of NGOs and trade unions (Amnesty International et al., 2017). A glance at the process shows how economic interests prevailed in the debate. The German Foreign Ministry led the development of the NAP, while a steering committee – comprising five further ministries and one representative from each of the German Trade Union Confederation (DGB), the umbrella organisation for development and humanitarian aid NGOs in Germany (VENRO), the Human Rights Forum (Forum Menschenrechte), the German Association of Chambers of Industry and Commerce (DIHK), German Employers' Associations (BDA) and the Federation of German Industries (BDI) – supervised the process. The steering committee was established to ensure that demands of different interest groups were taken into account. It organised 11 hearings where different interest groups could discuss gaps and solutions with regard to supply chain responsibility, legal protection, reporting obligations and other topics (Foreign Office, 2017).

While trade unions and NGOs provided numerous case studies, surveys and cross-country comparisons to show the urgent need for action, industry associations had little to contribute. They limited themselves to iterating their negative stance: German companies already respect human rights and voluntary commitments were sufficient. They claimed that binding requirements would be an excessive burden on German companies in global competition. No efforts were made to address civil society demands or even consider possible solutions throughout the development process. From the perspective of industry associations, additional efforts were not necessary, as it became clear throughout the process that corporate and governmental interests coincided to a significant degree. Employees of the Federal Ministry of Economics, for example, stated on many occasions that they regarded themselves as representatives of corporate interests; they spoke out publicly against any form of binding regulation on a regular basis. The steering committee was originally intended to be involved in the drafting, but the federal government finally prepared and negotiated the plan behind closed doors. The steering committee was no longer involved in 2016 and was not given any opportunity to comment on the draft NAP before it was adopted.

Nevertheless, the private sector maintained a strong influence on the negotiation process. At the beginning of the process, for example, a Siemens employee was seconded to the foreign ministry and contributed directly to the NAP process. The German Foreign Ministry seemed to regard this form of 'loan' from the business sector as the normal course of business and mentioned it only in passing much later in the negotiations. The business lobby actively intervened by sending numerous letters to the involved ministries during internal negotiations emphasising their position against binding rules. As a result of this intervention by business lobbies, the draft NAP was watered down twice during the negotiations, and finally no binding rules were adopted. In the summer of 2016, the German Ministry of Finance (BMF), during an 'extended inter-ministerial round of voting', eliminated many progressive elements from the draft, such as imposing obligations on state-owned enterprises. The intervention of the BMF was preceded by a detailed letter with proposed amendments prepared by the Confederation of German Employers' Associations (BDA). Deutsche Bahn AG expressly requested that the intended obligations of state-owned enterprises to engage in due diligence be eliminated. Only after NGOs filed an action against the BMF with reference to the Freedom of Information Act were they allowed to inspect the files. The fact that Steffen Kampeter, CEO of the BDA (German Employers' Association) since July 2016, was parliamentary secretary of state at the BMF until the summer of 2015 and had close contacts there was probably helpful for the BDA.

The myth about voluntary corporate responsibility

The NAP builds on support and dialogue, instead of state regulation. The number of consulting and training offers for enterprises is growing, and trade unions and NGOs are encouraged to jointly develop industry-specific instructions and best practices (Federal Government, 2016:20). This means further dialogue and roundtables according to the logic of the NAP. This approach suggests that German companies are committed and willing to accept their responsibility and merely lack guidance. However, it is hardly surprising that all analyses conclude that voluntary corporate responsibility is failing. A study commissioned by the EU Commission analysed the effects of voluntary CSR measures in 17 countries in 2013. Emphasis was laid on the environment and working standards. The study shows that CSR activities have very little effect. Most activities were carried out in sectors that are highly regulated, such as the use of chemicals or safety at work. The study included recommendations to the EU Commission stressing that greater regulation was desirable and effective (CSR Impact, 2013). A brief look at the Dodd-Frank Act in the US on conflict minerals confirms this. It had been known for many years that the proceeds of mining in the Democratic Republic of Congo have been used to finance the conflict. Still, nothing was done until a law requiring disclosure rules for corporations was adopted in 2010. This gave rise to a series of transparency initiatives and certifications aimed at improved transparency in the minerals trade in the east of the Congo (Heydenreich, 2016:9–10).

Behind the scenes of BASF

While most of the large German corporations today state that they ensure labour and human rights are respected in their supply chains, these programmes often only scratch the surface. Many companies shift the responsibility to suppliers through contractual clauses, while ignoring that they significantly influence the operations of suppliers in terms of pricing and delivery. Other companies refer to their self-organised social audits in production plants or mines, well aware that little can be concluded from their results. A good example is the supply chain management of BASF with regard to the platinum mine in Marikana. According to the federal government's National Action Plan, BASF and other corporations are requested to comply with the UN Guiding Principles on Business and Human Rights, which means that they are committed to identifying human rights violations in their supply chains and – in the case of BASF – to using its influence on its business partner Lonmin to improve the local situation.

BASF declares that it links economic success to environmental and social responsibility, which is why the company was industry leader in the area of corporate responsibility, founding member of the UN Global Compact and co-founder of the Together for Sustainability (TfS) initiative of the chemical industry. Six multinational chemical companies founded the TfS in 2011 to develop and implement a global audit programme for the industry. However, it was only in 2015 that BASF responded to the situation in Marikana and carried out an audit at Lonmin with Together for Sustainability after massive public pressure. Although there is hardly any other mine that is under such scrutiny as Lonmin, and the still precarious working and living conditions in Marikana are fully documented, the first audit report identified only weaknesses in fire protection standards and not in the areas of human rights or working conditions. Neither the majority union at Marikana, AMCU, nor relevant NGOs were involved in the audit or even consulted. Due to persistent criticism, BASF commissioned a second audit in 2017 promising to focus on the working and living conditions of people in Marikana this time. However, this audit again failed to involve relevant local stakeholders, such as NGOs, trade unions and affected people. Neither audit report was published, since the reports are – according to BASF – the intellectual property of TfS and thus its copyright was protected. Even after numerous attempts at dialogue, including Brot für die Welt, phone calls and numerous correspondence with the CSR department, it is hard to identify what BASF is actually doing to improve the situation in Marikana.

On its website, BASF reports on the launch of a sector initiative in South Africa in December 2016 to improve the situation in the Platinum Belt. However, the announcement lacks the names of participants and planned activities, and no action has been taken within the framework of this initiative since the first meeting in December. The people in Marikana have not seen any improvement, even five years after the massacre of striking workers. Working at the mine is hard and dangerous. Many workers die every year in the narrow shafts. The wages are too low to feed their families. Mineworkers live in corrugated iron shacks without electricity, running water or sewage disposal systems. BASF has, however, extended its long-term contracts with Lonmin in 2016 – again without binding agreements regarding the fulfilment of social duties (Brot für die Welt, 2017).

BASF is not an isolated case: So far, surveys conducted with the thirty DAX members[2] show that only a few of them have carried out systematic risk analyses or effective measures to prevent human rights violations (Germanwatch and Misereor, 2014).

Roundtable discussions

The German federal government is planning multi-stakeholder initiatives between trade unions, NGOs, companies and their associations to agree on sector-specific requirements. That this can be very difficult and frustrating has been demonstrated in the case of the Partnership for Sustainable Textiles. This partnership is a project of the German Federal Ministry for Economic Cooperation (BMZ) and brings German textile companies, trade unions and NGOs together to reach specific agreements on improved living and environmental conditions, from cotton cultivation to textile factories. Almost four years after its foundation, the alliance succeeded for the first time in November 2017 in agreeing on the need for binding targets for each member, such as the obligation to carry out risk analyses, waiving the possibility of sanctions, except for a possible exclusion (Partnership for Sustainable Textiles, 2017). Since its foundation, some companies have already left the partnership, such as Ernsting's Family and Real, without making this information known to the public.

One cannot say yet whether the textile partnership will bring any improvements for workers along the supply chain. In the light of an assessment of similar agreements, however, it is highly doubtful whether such initiatives provide sufficient incentives for companies to change their business practices. For example, Brot für die Welt demonstrates significant weaknesses in its comprehensive evaluation of the multi-stakeholder initiative (MSI) Roundtable on Sustainable Palm Oil – with regard to the substantive scope of the criteria as well as to monitoring (Brot für die Welt and VEM, 2014). The Royal Society for the Protection of Birds (RSPB) prepared a more comprehensive overview in 2015 when it evaluated 161 self-regulation approaches from all walks of life, including the reduction of greenhouse gases in Canada, the aggressive marketing of drugs in Sweden and the protection of albatrosses in New Zealand. In 80 per cent of the cases voluntary agreements failed because the targets that had been set were not achieved or only a small number of companies participated in the initiatives (RSPB, 2015:10). According to this analysis, minimum requirements include clearly defined and verifiable objectives, an independent review and transparent reporting. Unsurprisingly, the study concludes that companies are only willing to change their business practice if this move brings financial benefits. Voluntary initiatives therefore only work if there are clear incentives, such as tax reductions, or if they are tied to statuary regulations (RSPB, 2015:12ff, 39ff).

Global struggles for stronger regulation

Instead of having regulatory issues negotiated in multi-stakeholder partnerships, the German federal government should focus on its principal mission, which is creating binding regulations for the observance of human rights. France has set a good example: it adopted a new law in February 2017 that requires French companies, including their subsidiaries and main partners, to prevent human rights risks.

Some progress can be observed at the international level too. Many governments of the global South are no longer willing to accept that transnational corporations have only rights and no duties. On the initiative of Ecuador and South Africa, the UN Human Rights Council voted in 2014 in favour of intergovernmental negotiations on an international treaty to regulate transnational corporations. Three meetings of the intergovernmental working group have taken place in Geneva since 2015. At the last meeting in October 2017, 101 states took part and discussed possible elements of the future treaty. More than a thousand NGOs worldwide support this so-called UN treaty process. However, many industrial countries, including the EU and Germany, are not particularly enthusiastic about the project. They maintain their focus on voluntary corporate responsibility while industry associations strongly mobilise against the project. In order to overcome this opposition by powerful states and business and successfully establish binding rules for business, civil society needs to scale up their mobilisation efforts. Above all, civil society organisations must take care that they do not get lost in 'particitainment' and business dialogue. They need to strengthen international networks and link more effectively national and international global efforts towards binding rules.

Notes

1 Operational and regulatory obstacles often make it impossible to go to court, both in the countries where the damage is incurred and in the home countries of the corporations.
2 The 30 companies form the leading index of the German stock exchange (DAX).

References

Amnesty International, Brot für die Welt, Germanwatch and Misereor (2017) *No Courage to Commit: Comments on the German Government's National Action Plan on Business and Human Rights*

Brot für die Welt (2017) *Platinum for the World Market, Iron Shacks for the Workers: Living and Working Conditions in Marikana Five Years after the Massacre*, Berlin

Brot für die Welt, Global Policy Forum and Misereor (2014) *Corporate Influence on the Business and Human Rights Agenda of the United Nations*, Aachen

Brot für die Welt and VEM (2014) *Sustainable Palm Oil: Aspiration or Reality? The Potential and Limitations of the Roundtable on Sustainable Palm Oil (RSPO)*

CSR Impact (2013) *Impact Project. Executive Summary: Headline Findings, Insights and Recommendations for Policy Makers, Business and Stakeholders*

ECCHR, Brot für die Welt and Misereor (2017) *Holding Corporations to Account for their Failure to Exercise Human Rights Due Diligence: Experiences in Transnational Litigation*, Berlin

Federal Government (2016) *National Action Plan for Business and Human Rights*

Foreign Office (2017) *Entwicklung des Aktionsplans unter Einbindung von Politik, Wirtschaft und Zivilgesellschaft*, 23 November

Germanwatch and Misereor (2014) *Global Business and Human Rights, Putting Germany to the Test*

Heydenreich, C. (2016) Kein Blut mehr am Handy? Die Politik muss die Weichen stellen für einen verantwortlichen Rohstoffbezug, in Brot für die Welt and Germanwatch, *Holding Companies Accountable: Lessons from Transnational Human Rights Litigation*, Weltsichten-Dossier 4/2016

Partnership for Sustainable Textiles (2017) *Partnership for Sustainable Textiles Enters a New Phase in 2018: Binding Targets for All Members and Greater Internationalisation*

RSPB (Royal Society for the Protection of Birds) (2015) *Using Regulation as a Last Resort? Assessing the Performance of Voluntary Approaches*, Sandy, Bedfordshire

◄ Call for global standards for the respect of human rights by companies at a demonstration against the TTIP agreement organised by German environmental groups, charities and opposition parties in Berlin on October 10, 2015.

◄ First round of negotiations on the UN Treaty on Human Rights and Business Enterprises in Geneva, 2015.

▲ Activist in front of the UN building in Geneva during the renegotiation of the UN Treaty on Human Rights and Business Enterprises, March 2017.

12. THE UN TREATY ON BUSINESS AND HUMAN RIGHTS:
SOUTH AFRICA'S ROLE

Akhona Mehlo

In June 2014, a resolution was adopted by the Human Rights Council (HRC) following an initiative by Ecuador and South Africa to press for a binding instrument relating to transnational corporations (TNCs) and human rights (UNGA, 2014). Many hoped that an HRC initiative would contribute to respect for and protection of human rights and end impunity for human rights violations by transnational corporations (TNCs), particularly in the global South.

This chapter discusses the United Nations treaty process with special focus on South Africa's supporting role.

The information on the role played by the South African state is predominantly sourced from the Department of International Relations and Cooperation (DIRCO), the driving force behind the South African delegation. The wind behind the initiative's sails has been provided by civil society and various institutions and the range of expertise they have lent to this process. This chapter briefly discusses South Africa's involvement and ends with the different contributions made by some of the civil society organisations supporting the initiative.

Background

Owing to the gaps and imbalances in the international legal order that undermine human rights, the then UN Subcommission on the Promotion and Protection of Human Rights, which served as a research body for the former Commission on Human Rights (CHR), produced a report on the corporate sector, entitled 'The Responsibilities of Transnational Corporations and Other Business Enterprises with Respect to Human Rights' (UN, 2003). This report followed numerous others in which TNCs were implicated in abuses such as child labour, discrimination, unsafe working conditions, repression of trade unions and collective bargaining, limitations on technology transfer, low wages and environmental destruction (Weissbrodt and Kruger, 2003).

When presented before the CHR in 2005 for a decision and way forward, the report became the subject of much debate. South Africa and Ecuador, with the support of a few other countries, called for action on the report by the CHR. South Africa was concerned about the effects of globalisation on the continent as well as the fact that many developing countries do not have legislative frameworks or that, where they exist, they are relatively very weak, presenting an avenue that can be exploited by TNCs. The report spoke specifically to grave and serious violations of human rights by the corporate sector (Weissbrodt and Kruger, 2003).

A compromise was reached which called for a mandate to be created for a special representative of the secretary general (SRSG). John Ruggie[1] was appointed as the SRSG and developed the United Nations Guiding Principles on Business and Human Rights (UNGPs), which are both voluntary and non-binding. They are essentially a tool for implementing the Protect, Respect and Remedy Framework underlying international human rights standards, allowing TNCs to monitor themselves and determine their own sanctions.[2] The Guiding Principles include three basic assumptions: the duty of the state to protect human rights; corporate responsibility to respect human rights; and access to remedy or redress for victims of business-related human rights abuses. The biggest criticism levelled by South Africa against the UN Guiding Principles is that they are not legally binding nor form part of international human rights law, as they have never been adopted by the General Assembly of the United Nations. They did not follow the usual course of multilateral negotiation by states in an intergovernmental process, which is how treaty law evolves, as Ruggie was primarily responsible for the content.

During his mandate, one of Ruggie's first visits was to South Africa, where he attended a conference organised by Mary Robinson on an Ethical Globalization Initiative. After the conference he met the South African delegation, who concurred that a binding instrument was controversial and that an all-encompassing approach would be more acceptable. This was to be dealt with in two phases, beginning with one of soft law and eventually culminating in hard law.

The hard law would be in the form of a binding treaty concluded between states governed by international law, and possibly enforced through an international tribunal and effective mechanisms of sanctions, to prevent TNCs hiding behind investment protection agreements and the legal personality of their subsidiaries. To its proponents, the UN treaty consists of internationally binding rules to end the impunity of TNCs and would place people's rights at the centre, before corporate profits (Ortiz, 2017). This would be in contrast to relying solely on the UN Guiding Principles, which approach human rights from a business perspective, advocate 'corporate social responsibility', and provide for voluntary measures though they have so far failed to hold corporations to account. Moreover, once states had signed the treaty they would, in terms of article 27 of the Vienna Convention,[3] be precluded from invoking the provisions of their domestic law as justification for their failure to perform a treaty obligation.

While some regard Ruggie's views as a volte-face and in opposition to the treaty, he believes that they are cautionary and seek to avoid 'going down a road that would end in largely symbolic gestures, of little practical use to real people in real places, and with high potential for generating serious backlash against any form of further international legalisation in this domain' or resulting in 'another instance of the classic dysfunction of doing the same thing over and over again and expecting a different result' (Ruggie, 2014).

It appears, however, that Ruggie has moved away from his initial view and that his support for a binding treaty has waned considerably now that the Guiding Principles are complete. The South African delegation was surprised by his about-turn as well as by his recommendation that he be replaced as SRSG by a working group instead of an expert representing the African or Asian human rights system for which many were calling. There was also concern about the soundness of the recommendation that a group of experts carry out the mandate, while Ruggie himself had served for two three-year terms on his own.

South Africa is not alone in expressing concern that the process which Ruggie oversaw was derailed from its original intent. Patricia Feeney, the executive director of the UK-based NGO Rights and Accountability in Development and director of the Centre for the Study of Governance and Transparency at Kellogg College, University of Oxford, has also expressed 'an abiding suspicion that the corporate world was persuaded to give strong endorsement to the Guiding Principles only in return for a promise that there would be no move towards binding regulation' (Feeney, 2013).

Cause for further misgiving was given by the establishment of an annual UN Forum on Business and Human Rights[4] with the support of the EU. Some view this as a platform at which TNCs embellish their image by presenting themselves as saving the world and uplifting the marginalised around the world but which fails to realise a true dialogue between stakeholders or address instances of business-related human rights abuses raised by rights holders (Van Huijstee, 2012). Feeney (2013) and others are of the view that the first forum lacked a focus on human rights, was dominated by industry voices or their agents purporting to be 'experts' in the field of business and human rights and allowed only one plenary session on the victims of corporate abuse. The UN Forum for Business and Human Rights is, in this view, being used to punt the UN Guiding Principles and promote a managerial response to corporate-related human rights violations, reducing them to a communications issue (Feeney, 2013). The forum's objective, which could potentially complement the treaty initiative, is at odds with the UN treaty approach.

These are not the only initiatives that may present challenges to the treaty process, however. Another arose when the Committee on Economic, Social and Cultural Rights (CESCR) drafted the general comment on state obligations under the International Covenant on Economic, Social and Cultural Rights in the context of business activities.[5] While general comments are usually welcomed with open arms, this initiative was cause for concern to the South African delegation, because the instrument would be based on the UN Guiding Principles. South Africa believed this might expose the CESCR general comment to the same shortfalls which continue to plague the UN Guiding Principles, i.e. in respect of implementation as well as the lack of proper means to ensure access to remedy (Treaty Alliance, 2016).

Despite Ruggie's misgivings about a binding instrument, the process of intergovernmental negotiations and discussion on a regulatory framework for transnational corporations and other business enterprises regarding human rights continued within the United Nations.

The treaty process

On 26 June 2014 the HRC adopted Resolution 26/9 in order 'to establish an open-ended intergovernmental working group on transnational corporations and other business enterprises with respect to human rights, whose mandate shall be to elaborate an international legally binding instrument to regulate, in international human rights law, the activities of transnational corporations and other business enterprises' (UNGA, 2014). It was decided that the first session of the working group would have an initial constructive exchange; would solicit the advice of independent experts; and would inform the various delegations about the main issues of the future instrument in order to lay the groundwork for the second session of the working group (CETIM, 2015). At the third session, negotiations would begin on the content of the instrument on the basis of a proposal prepared by the chair-rapporteur of the working group.

The first session of the working group took place from 6 to 10 July 2015 and was attended by governments, international governmental organisations, the Council of Europe, the International Labour Organization, the United Nations Conference on Trade and Development, national human rights institutions and accredited non-governmental organisations (ICJ, 2016). The working group presented its report to the Council at its 31st session.

During the first session the EU made objections to the adoption of the work programme, reiterating its conditions for participation, which were viewed by some as an attempt to block the session and derail the entire process. The objections were mainly in regard to (a) the appointment of a 'neutral chair'; (b) expanding the scope of the instrument from being applicable not only to TNCs but to domestic companies as well; and (c) having the corporate sector form part of the meetings of the working group (CETIM, 2015).

The demand for a 'neutral chair' appeared inexplicable to many participants because the usual practice is that the chair of a working group is held by a representative of one of the countries that first presented the relevant resolution to the HRC, which in this case was Ecuador or South Africa. All intergovernmental working groups are chaired by an ambassador, someone whose government has an interest in the matter and appreciates what is at stake, but in this case the EU demanded a neutral chair. This call was seen as a cover for the EU to install its own preferred candidate, John Ruggie, who critics believed was firmly under the EU's control and under the influence of TNCs. The EU also took the opportunity to secure the commitment of all to enforcing the Ruggie principles and requested an additional panel on the implementation of the UN Guiding Principles despite the fact that this did not fall within the working group's mandate (CETIM, 2015).

The EU's demand that the work programme refer explicitly to all businesses and not only to TNCs was the subject of heated discussion at the time of the adoption of the resolution. Indeed, it was the deciding factor in getting many countries that had initially been against the treaty to come on board. The resolution adopted by the HRC provided that the instrument would cover TNCs and other enterprises but clarified in a footnote that 'other enterprises' referred only to those whose activities have a transnational character. Because the EU was so determined to impose its position, the session was suspended for several hours to find a compromise and an additional panel on the Guiding Principles was added although no change to the text concerning the scope of the instrument was made (CETIM, 2015).

Aside from the Western countries, the intergovernmental working group involved major emerging countries or developmental states such as Brazil, China, India, Russia and South Africa, which took the lead. Other countries from Latin America, Africa and Asia were present but mainly to hear the experts and ascertain the various positions of other states. There was also a strong civil society presence, representing social movements. Victims and communities affected in the global South also attended in numbers (CETIM, 2015).

The second session of the open-ended intergovernmental working group took place from 24 to 28 October 2016, after which it presented its report at the HRC's 34th session from 27 February to 24 March 2017. It was characterised by wide participation by states and civil society groups. In contrast to the first session, the EU and some of its member states were present for the entire session and the programme of work was adopted unchallenged. The EU reiterated its position on expanding the treaty's application to include domestic businesses and ensuring that discussions be rooted in and complement the UN Guiding Principles (ECCJ, 2016a). As a whole, the session involved robust engagement, culminating in disagreement between Russia and the EU with South Africa on the chair's mandate in preparing the 2017 session. A compromise was reached in which it was agreed that the focus of the next meeting would be on preparing elements for the draft of the legally binding instrument for substantive negotiation (ECCJ, 2016b).

SOUTH AFRICA'S ROLE IN THE TREATY PROCESS
Role played internationally

As has already been mentioned, the current treaty process was revived thanks to an initiative by Ecuador and South Africa, which demanded that the HRC take action on the basis of a report furnished by the Subcommission. With Ecuador chairing the process, South Africa provided the political support needed to sustain the process against the backdrop of what some have termed disruptive and intimidation tactics on the part of the EU (CETIM, 2015). The collaboration between the two states has, however, not been as robust as it could be, considering that at the time of writing they had not even issued a joint statement. Given the small size of the South African delegation and the limited financial resources of both delegations, the two states may have to reassess their current approach of working mostly independently except in the context of the working group, where they endeavour to maintain a united front. Matters are not entirely unpropitious, however. South Africa and Ecuador need to nurture and capitalise on the support of powerful countries which joined and even sponsored the creation of the resolution. In the past two years, the two countries have engaged with the UN system, including all the regions. They consulted with the then president of the General Assembly, Sam Kutesa, who gave the process the full support of his office. They also spoke to the chairperson of the Non-Aligned Movement, a political formation of the countries of the South.

Regional advocacy

Although it has managed to involve individual African countries, South Africa has had little engagement on the matter with the SADC, leaving much to be done given that a lot of these countries are not represented at the UN in Geneva within this specific sector. To rectify this, South Africa sought to arrange a meeting at the AU Summit in June or July 2017 where African leaders could meet the Ecuadorian ambassador and other key stakeholders so as to engage them in the treaty process and allay their fears that support for the treaty might result in divestment. This meeting was then postponed to January 2018. Such an event is crucial given that the competing initiative, the UN Forum on Business and Human Rights, which is promoting voluntary mechanisms, seems to be far ahead in terms of popularisation and creating public awareness of the Guiding Principles. Moreover, the forum has been more successful in engaging political and corporate supporters globally.

It is at the AU Summit that South Africa also hopes to discuss with African states the Malabo Protocol, which the AU adopted and which involves issues of corporate criminal liability, human rights violations and the exploitation of African minerals without benefit for the continent, issues that resonate with the work done towards a treaty process.[6] One of the matters that will hopefully be discussed at the Summit is the irony of the EU cautioning African states against the adverse consequences of insisting on a treaty which provides for decent wages, criminalises child labour, prohibits exploitation and protects the environment, when the EU member states expect nothing less in their own jurisdictions

South Africa also reiterated that international law is always the law of last resort. If companies promote and protect human rights in the course of their operations, the provisions in the treaty may never be invoked against them. They will only apply where there are violations and there is no domestic protective mechanism. The victims will thus be able to look to the international system for remedies. This is particularly relevant for the southern African region, which lacks a functional human rights tribunal (Fritz, 2015).

Common BRICS position?

South Africa seems uncertain about the stance of the other BRICS countries. Russia's and China's position on this issue is unclear, particularly given their ambitions as up-and-coming superpowers. The matter is further complicated by the fact that both China and Russia are host countries of TNCs as well as state-owned enterprises (SOEs).

At the time of the adoption of the HRC resolution, many countries that were later convinced to come on board did so upon the insertion of a footnote within the resolution, which made a distinction between domestic companies and TNCs and OBEs (other business enterprises). Russia and China were under immense pressure to support the resolution to avoid being seen in a negative light. It is unclear, as far as South Africa is concerned, how they will position themselves when negotiations commence, but South Africa plans on engaging them during bilateral discussions.

Domestic initiatives

South Africa has enacted new legislation which endeavours to balance the public interest and the promotion and protection of human rights, on the one hand, and the interests of investors who want to profit from their operations within the country, on the other. The purpose of the Promotion and Protection of Investment Act of 2015 is to ensure ethical conduct and respect for human rights. Countries such as Switzerland, Norway and Denmark have not welcomed this initiative and have used bilateral forums to voice their displeasure (Joubert, 2017).

DIRCO has taken the discussion of the treaty to other government departments, engaging with the Department of Labour, the Department of Mineral Resources, the Department of Water and Sanitation and the Department of Trade and Industry, to name a few. It has also approached the Social Protection, Community and Human Development cluster of ministries and the Anti-Poverty cluster to speak about this initiative. In addition, it has raised the matter with relevant Chapter 9 institutions,[7] notably the South Africa Human Rights Commission. DIRCO has also been in contact with research institutions, universities and human rights centres, such as the Centre for Human Rights at the University of Pretoria, the Dullah Omar Institute at the University of the Western Cape and the Centre for Applied Legal Studies (CALS) at Witwatersrand University; and civil society organisations such as the Legal Resources Centre (LRC) and the Foundation for Human Rights (FHR).

As some of the concerns raised have involved labour issues, DIRCO has also spoken to labour unions such as the Congress of South African Trade Unions, a federation of organised labour movements which has a key interest in the matter. DIRCO views this as essential for the working group session in October 2017 as it would be imperative for it to go to Geneva to represent the interests of the labour movement and present its crucial perspectives.

Considering that at the heart of the South African state's initiative there should be a commitment to ensuring that communities are protected from TNCs, it is vital that DIRCO engages with them.[8]

Collaboration with civil society

Despite opposition from the EU and the United States, which at some point asserted they would not participate, the Treaty Alliance, a coalition of NGOs from across the globe, seems determined to establish a treaty which can protect victims of corporate abuse and rein in corporate power (Treaty Alliance, 2016). One cannot imagine the treaty process having come this far without the invaluable support the alliance has provided to the treaty-initiating states. The energetic role played by civil society, particularly in raising awareness within governments, significantly propelled and bolstered the initiative. Most crucial and indispensable has been their central role in drawing attention to the need to protect vulnerable groups, such as women and girls, children, people with disabilities and indigenous peoples, who are usually the most affected by abuses by business enterprises. Indeed, many NGOs have provided substantial contributions to the debate, presenting rigorous legal and theoretical proposals during the working group sessions (OHCHR, 2017a, 2017b).

Another important role played by civil society has been in providing expertise and helping develop the content and scope of the draft treaty. This is an essential task for South Africa and Ecuador, which seek to have a draft convention ready for consideration and negotiation by the third session of the working group. This, South Africa believes, is crucial in countering opponents of the convention who propose a blank canvas and that everyone participate in writing the instrument together, paragraph by paragraph, thereby ensuring that the drafting process is drawn out indefinitely. The South African delegation is of the opinion that this is not necessary in view of the plethora of NGOs and institutions at the chairperson's disposal. Furthermore, given that stakeholders have already worked out the structure, nature and scope of the draft, South Africa proposes that members of civil society join as consultative experts in the development of a base document for negotiations.

Submissions regarding the content of the treaty

While South Africa is yet to release its own version of a model law, this section lays out the broad strokes of its position, which reflects similar positions held by various

South African NGOs and institutions such as the Legal Resources Centre, the Centre for Applied Studies and the South African Institute for Advanced Constitutional, Public, Human Rights and International Law, which made submissions to the working group in support of a binding treaty instrument.

The most contentious aspect of the treaty is its scope of application. South Africa agrees that domestic companies should be held accountable for human rights violations but disagrees with grouping them together with TNCs. It proposed that in the instrument there should be a chapter on state complicity in human rights violations, which can in turn address state-owned enterprises. As far as the government is concerned, there should be corporate accountability in respect of all human rights and not just gross human rights violations.

South Africa regards a TNC as a corporation that is registered in one country but has operations in other jurisdictions. Such an entity should have an obligation to uphold human rights wherever it operates and apply the same standards worldwide. It is untenable for TNCs to uphold the highest standards in the global North and substandard ones elsewhere. With regard to OBEs, they stand firmly behind the definition in the footnote of the resolution, which provides that OBEs in the context of the envisaged instrument include those that operate in other jurisdictions as well.

While this may be quite ambitious, South Africa would welcome discussion on the definition of globalisation and its impact, particularly considering TNCs are drivers of globalisation and owners of global wealth, which imposes a cost on everyone, with few reaping its benefits.

Submissions by the Legal Resources Centre

In essence, the Legal Resources Centre's proposals for the treaty were:
- that the right to development, as contained in the African Charter on Human and Peoples' Rights and as given content by the United Nations and the African Commission on Human and Peoples' Rights, be included as a founding principle and right in the treaty;
- that, as a means to recognise the disproportionate impact of the current resource wave on the rural communities of global South countries and to ensure the feasibility of implementing the right to development, community or people's' rights be recognised alongside individual rights (as per the African Charter); and
- that, as a baseline principle in ensuring the realisation of both the substantive and procedural aspects of the right to development, the free, prior and informed consent of affected communities be required as a condition for development projects. Only if a community has the option of saying no could it have any real bargaining power in its engagements with TNCs and states. That is the basis of the right to development.

Submissions by the Centre for Applied Legal Studies

The submissions by CALS proposed that a gendered lens and poverty be added to both the process for the development of the binding instrument and the content of the binding instrument. They further called for poverty to be considered by the working group in both the process and the content of the binding instrument. In summary, the CALS submissions called on the working group to use the treaty process as an opportunity to address the multifaceted and intersectional human rights impacts of corporate activities (CALS, 2015).

Submissions by the South African Institute for Advanced Constitutional Public, Human Rights and International Law

The submissions of the director of SAFAIC, David Bilchitz, focused on possible approaches that a treaty on business and human rights could adopt in apportioning obligations to promote or protect individuals against the violation of their rights by third parties such as corporations. Bilchitz considered both the direct and indirect model approach to be adopted for purposes of such a treaty. The indirect model, which focuses on the obligation of the state to protect individuals against the violation of their rights by third parties, would place an international legal obligation on the state to ensure that corporations do not violate the human rights of individuals. Corporations would, however, have no direct obligations flowing from international human rights law. The direct model, in contrast, imposes direct obligations on corporations by international human rights law or provides for their creation by states (SAFAIC, 2015).

Bilchitz advocates a direct approach. This would start with a beneficiary- or victim-orientated evaluation of whether particular actions or omissions of corporations have an effect on the interests protected by fundamental rights. This would then be followed by a consideration of reasons to limit the obligations of corporations in such circumstances, either for reasons relating to their nature or for reasons relating to the nature of the normative considerations underlying any potential limitation.

Conclusion

In the current circumstances, South Africa and Ecuador face a mammoth task. Both countries will have to find more efficient methods of advocacy and lobbying to nurture and capitalise on the support of the powerful countries which sponsored the resolution. It is crucial to ensure that African states, whose people are among the most severely affected by TNCs, stand firmly behind the initiative.

While the UN Guiding Principles are deficient, their proponents are well resourced and have made advances in terms of popularisation and public awareness. South Africa must proceed with caution given that this process could drag on indefinitely, proceeding along a well-trodden path from which past sojourners have returned empty-handed. DIRCO's concern with globalisation and divestment and its lack of contact with communities on the ground might do more to undermine the South African initiative than the UN Guiding Principles. Having come so far and expended a lot of energy and limited resources, it would be regrettable if, as Professor Ruggie cautioned, a successful treaty ended up as a largely symbolic gesture, of little practical use to affected communities on the ground.

Notes

1. John G. Ruggie is the Berthold Beitz Professor in Human Rights and International Affairs at the Harvard Kennedy School, Affiliated Professor in International Legal Studies at Harvard Law School, and Faculty Chair of the Corporate Responsibility Initiative.
2. The UN Guiding Principles on Business and Human Rights are a set of guidelines for states and companies to prevent, address and remedy human rights abuses committed in business operations. See www.business-humanrights.org/en/un-guiding-principles and www.un.org/press/en/2005/sga934.doc.htm.
3. Vienna Convention on the Law of Treaties (23 May 1969) 1155 UNTS 331, enacted on 27 January 1980.
4. Established in terms of UN Doc. A/HRC/RES/17/4 of 16 June 2011, para. 12 in order to accompany the Guiding Principles and promote dialogue and cooperation on issues linked to business and human rights, including challenges faced in particular sectors, operational environments or in relation to specific rights or groups, as well as identifying good practices. See also www.ohchr.org/EN/Issues/Business/Forum/Pages/ForumonBusinessandHumanRights.aspx, accessed 20 July 2017
5. General comment no. 24 (2017) on state obligations under the International Covenant on Economic, Social and Cultural Rights in the context of business activities has since been adopted; see E/C.12/GC/24, www.ohchr.org/EN/HRBodies/CESCR/Pages/CESCRIndex.aspx, accessed 13 September 2017.
6. At the regional level, a new Protocol on Amendments to the Protocol on the Statute of the African Court of Justice and Human Rights (article 46C) expands the jurisdiction of the court to try a number of crimes when committed by corporations.
7. Chapter 9 Institutions, named after their place in the Constitution, are 'State Institutions Supporting Constitutional Democracy', consisting of the Public Protector (PP), the Auditor-General (AG), the Independent Electoral Commission (IEC), the South African Human Rights Commission (SAHRC), the Commission for Gender Equality (CGE) and, lastly, the Commission for the Protection of the Rights of Cultural, Religious and Linguistic Communities. They are independent of government, subject only to the Constitution and the law, and report annually to Parliament.
8. Owing to the lack of interaction with communities, LRC tried to convene a roundtable in collaboration with DIRCO and other NGOs. This was in the hope that affected communities would be able to engage government and representatives from the mining sector on harmful practices by corporations and discuss how a binding treaty would assist in protecting them. This, however, did not materialise.

References

CALS (2015) *Submission by the Centre for Applied Legal Studies to the Intergovernmental Working Group on the Elaboration of a Binding Instrument on Business and Human Rights regarding the Content of the Binding Instrument* (June), www.wits.ac.za/media/wits-university/faculties-and-schools/commerce-law-and-management/research-entities/cals/documents/programmes/bhr/resources/CALS%20Submission%20on%20Binding%20Instrument%20on%20Business%20and%20Human%20Rights%20June%202015.pdf, accessed 20 July 2017

CESCR (2017) Committee on Economic, Social and Cultural Rights holds general discussion on state obligations in the context of business activities (21 February), *OHCHR*, www.ohchr.org/EN/NewsEvents/Pages/DisplayNews.aspx?NewsID=21210&LangID=E, accessed 20 July 2017

CETIM (2015) TNCs and human rights: Success of the first meeting of the United Nations working group, 19 September 2015, www.cetim.ch/tncs-and-human-rights-succes-of-the-first-meeting-of-the-united-nations-working-group/, accessed 18 March 2017

ECCJ (2016a) UN Treaty talks day 1: The EU is in the room, but is that enough? (25 October), www.corporatejustice.org/news/321-un-treaty-talks-day-1-the-eu-is-in-the-room-but-is-that-enough, accessed 17 July 2017

ECCJ (2016b) UN Treaty talks day 5: Morality cannot be legislated, but behaviour can be regulated (2 November) <www.corporatejustice.org/news/329-un-treaty-talks-day-5-morality-cannot-be-legislated-but-behaviour-can-be-regulated, accessed 17 July 2017

Feeney, P. (2013) NGOs should expose the limitations of pragmatism, *Conectas Human Rights*, 12 February, www.conectas.org/en/actions/business-and-human-rights/news/8495-ngos-should-expose-the-limitations-of-pragmatism, accessed 20 July 2017

Fritz, N. (2015) In smoke: The SADC Tribunal and rule of law in the region, *SAFPI Policy Brief* 11, www.osf.org.za/wp-content/uploads/2015/08/Up-in-smoke-The-SADC-Tribunal-and-Rule-of-Law-in-the-region.pdf, accessed 17 July 2017

ICJ (2016) *Proposals for Elements of a Legally Binding Instrument on Transnational Corporations and Other Business Enterprises* (October), www.icj.org/wp-content/uploads/2016/10/Universal-OEWG-session-2-ICJ-submission-Advocacy-Analysis-brief-2016-ENG.pdf, accessed 20 April 2017

Joubert, N. (2017) New Protection of Investment Act: The implications for foreign investors, www.caveatlegal.com/new-protection-of-investment-act-the-implications-for-foreign-investors, accessed 30 July 2017

OHCHR (2017a) www.ohchr.org/EN/HRBodies/HRC/WGTransCorp/Session1/Pages/Session1.aspx, accessed 24 April 2017

OHCHR (2017b) www.ohchr.org/EN/HRBodies/HRC/WGTransCorp/Session2/Pages/Session2.aspx; accessed 24 April 2017

Ortiz, L. (2017) UN treaty on transnational corporations and human rights progressing, *Friends of the Earth International*, 13 March, www.foei.org/news/un-treaty-transnational-corporations-human-rights-progressing, accessed 17 July 2017

Ruggie, J.G. (2014) A UN business and human rights treaty? An issues brief (28 January 2014), www.hks.harvard.edu/m-rcbg/CSRI/UNBusinessandHumanRightsTreaty.pdf, accessed 20 March 2017

SAFAIC (2015) What provisions should a treaty on business and human rights contain governing corporate obligations?, *OHCHR*, www.ohchr.org/Documents/HRBodies/HRCouncil/WGTransCorp/Session2/DavidBilchitz_Determining_Nature_Extent_Corporate_Obligations.docx, accessed 20 July 2017

Treaty Alliance (2016) Discussions on scope of the treaty on day four of the intergovernmental working group session in Geneva (28 October 2016), www.treatymovement.com/news/4ec8df00-6690-4dc2-8178-aca3be143e31, accessed 20 July 2017

UNGA (2014) Res. 26/9, Elaboration of an international legally binding instrument on transnational corporations and other business enterprises with respect to human rights (14 July), A/HRC/RES/26/9, *IHRB*, www.ihrb.org/pdf/G1408252.pdf

UN (Subcommission on the Promotion and Protection of Human Rights) (2003) Res. 2003/16, Norms on the Responsibilities of Transnational Corporations and Other Business Enterprises with Regard to Human Rights (13 August), UN Doc. E/CN.4/Sub.2/2003/L.1 1

Van Huijstee, M. (2012) Statement on the quality of the UN annual forum on business and human rights (10 December 2012), *OHCHR*, www.ohchr.org/Documents/Issues/Business/ForumSession1/SubmissionsStatements/MarietteVanHuijsteeSomo.pdf, accessed 20 April 2017

Weissbrodt, D. and M. Kruger (2003) Norms on the responsibilities of transnational corporations and other business enterprises with regard to human rights, *American Journal of International Law* 97

▶ **pp. 236/237** *Our values: Transparency*. Lonmin image campaign in Marikana and surroundings, recorded in Marikana West, 2015.

▶ **pp. 238/239** Air shaft close to Marikana. More than one third of all miners die of lung diseases caused by the toxic particles underground and attributed to insufficient ventilation.

13. RATHER PART OF THE PROBLEM THAN THE SOLUTION: ON THE FUNCTIONS AND EFFECTS OF SOCIAL AUDITS

Carolijn Terwindt

On 11 September 2012, in a fire at the Ali Enterprises factory in Karachi, Pakistan, 260 workers died and more than 30 were injured.[1]

Only three weeks earlier, on 21 August, the Italian company RINA S.p.A. provided the factory with an SA8000 certification, designed to indicate good working conditions.

The privatisation of governance in supply chains

The SA8000 certificate was awarded after a social audit conducted by a RINA subcontractor in Karachi. Moreover, the German retailer KiK commissioned three social audits between 2007 and 2011 to justify its purchases from the Pakistani factory. Despite the multiple audits and the SA8000 certificate, on the day of the fire the factory had an (illegal) wooden mezzanine, lacked a functioning fire alarm and did not have sufficient emergency exits. None of the factory audits identified these flaws. The incident thus tragically revealed the inadequacy of the current practice of private certification: independent and diligent audits seem rare and require, at best, a sort of 'checklist compliance'.

Social audits have become ubiquitous as a tool to diagnose adherence to social and environmental standards in supply chains. They were popularised during the 1990s in the textile industry, which during the past decades outsourced some, if not all, of their garment and textile production to profit from lower wages elsewhere. Under pressure from consumer campaigns, retailers developed codes of conduct in terms of which they voluntarily committed themselves to certain minimum standards throughout their supply chains (van Tulder et al., 2009). Such efforts in the textile industry are premised on the assumption that in buyer-driven value chains, the retailing brands have considerable control over manufacturers (Gereffi and Memedovic, 2003:4). Retailers drafted codes of conduct to set standards for suppliers on child labour, forced labour, working hours and health and safety. Social audits emerged as a means to demonstrate conformity to the social standards adopted (Clean Clothes Campaign, 2005:12).

Already in 2005, the Clean Clothes Campaign published a book titled *Looking for a Quick Fix: How Weak Social Auditing Is Keeping Workers in Sweatshops*, in which many problems with social audits were identified, such as their superficial nature and the likelihood of deception. Academic research since then has similarly documented that, as a stand-alone measure not integrated in management structures and without a bona fide trade union, codes of conduct and audits are not likely to lead to significant improvements in working conditions (Locke et al., 2013; Locke et al., 2007; Anner, 2011).

The problems with audits have not only been recognised in the textile industry. Early 2017, the Sustainable Agriculture Network decided to dispense with certification in agriculture. They concluded that certification audits are mostly done as a 'policing exercise', thus failing to actually improve the situation at the level of the producer. They further warn that certificates may end up 'misstating the actual reality on the ground' due to an auditor's lack of expertise or time: 'after working with this tool for over 20 years, we could look back and conclude that certification was not the best approach to improve the sustainability of most farmers in the world' (Freitas, 2017). Even the Association of Professional Social Compliance Auditors (APSCA) acknowledges that 'currently, you could ask anyone to conduct a social audit and there is nothing stopping them, and no way to verify their qualifications' (interview with executive director Rona Starr in Verisk Maplecroft, 2017:7).[2]

Despite these criticisms of social audits in the textile industry and elsewhere, this tool continues to be adopted by other industries. While consumer pressure was the driving force in the textile industry, the London Bullion Market Association (LBMA) developed the Responsible Gold Guidance, which they claim has ensured that 'all 71 gold refiners have completed their independent third party audit with no instances of zero-tolerance non-compliance' (LBMA, 2017). In 2011 the chemical companies BASF, Bayer, Evonik Industries, Henkel, Lanxess and Solvay founded the Together for Sustainability (TfS) initiative. Since then, a number of other companies have joined the initiative, including AkzoNobel, DSM, DuPont, Merck, Syngenta and Wacker (BASF, 2017a). The proclaimed goal of TfS is the global standardisation of supplier evaluations and auditing.

Just like retailers in the textile industry, the chemical company BASF has a Supplier Code of Conduct. If suppliers fail to fulfil these standards, BASF can terminate the business relationship, which it did with four suppliers in 2015 (BASF, 2017a). Audits thus play a role in the sourcing decisions of BASF and can also serve to justify continued sourcing. For example, in November 2015, BASF commissioned a third-party audit at its supplier mining company Lonmin in South Africa. On the basis of the audit report on Lonmin, BASF concluded: 'While the audit noted room for improvement, primarily in the areas of environment and safety, there were no critical findings of Lonmin's governance, human rights or labour practices nor any performance violations that prevented BASF's continuation of its relationship with Lonmin' (BASF, 2017b).

While the Lonmin audit thus reports 'no critical findings', for miners South Africa is still one of the most dangerous places in the world. In 2016 alone, 27 workers died in the platinum mines (Bergermann et al., 2017). This raises the question whether social auditing and certification schemes can frustrate more fundamental solutions addressing working conditions by giving the impression that something is being done. Some argue that audit schemes can be improved to accommodate criticism. For example, after the first audit at Lonmin, in 2017 a follow-up audit included 90 mining-specific questions which were not asked in the first audit. Still, in personal conversations with the author, labour organisers in the garment industry in Bangladesh and Pakistan voiced the opinion that private audits have inherent limits and that it is probably better if they were not conducted at all. As the deaths at the Ali Enterprises factory have shown, unduly flattering audit reports are a real concern. If a social audit report fails to signal instances of non-compliance with social and safety standards, lead firms may continue to source from suppliers, without implementing measures urgently needed to protect workers.

Based on the author's experiences, this chapter looks primarily at the problems with social audits in the textile industry and assumes that key structural issues like conflicts of interest are likely to characterise social audits in other industries, such as the mining sector. It then proposes that as long as social audits continue to exist – whether in the textile industry or elsewhere – in order to avoid the risk of unduly flattering auditing reports, audits should always be accompanied by accountability and liability mechanisms.

The problem with social audits

A social audit of a garment factory is a workplace assessment conducted over just a few days by one auditor or an auditing team. During this process, the auditors should review documentation supplied by management to check whether, for example, wages and hours are in line with the applicable labour standards; physically inspect the factory floor to ensure the presence of requisite health and safety measures like functioning emergency exits, ventilation, cleanliness and safety equipment; and conduct interviews with management and some workers to discover whether payslips and so on are accurate in practice and whether, for example, union activity is suppressed (Clean Clothes Campaign, 2005:23). Diagnostic social audits are generally followed by corrective action plans, the implementation of which should also be inspected by social auditors in follow-up visits.

Taking stock, the results of 25 years of corporate social responsibility in the textile industry are not encouraging. The widespread practice of private audits reduces the pressure on producing country governments to establish a functioning system for labour inspections. Academic research has documented that as transnational corporations have become entrusted with governing themselves and reporting on their efforts to government and the public, there has been a persistent decline in the state-based monitoring of production processes in many countries (LeBaron and Lister, 2015). In addition, most audits fail to substantially involve workers in assessment and subsequent improvement efforts.

A major problem with the privatisation of inspection lies in the negative incentive structure for auditors, which can lead to flawed if not faked audit results. Conflicts of interest are inevitable as commercial auditing companies are interested in keeping their clients operating in an increasingly competitive market (Jahn et al., 2003:9). Contrary to most current models of social auditing, an independent auditor should not be paid either by the buyer or the supplier. The competitive auditing market creates incentives to hold down auditing standards, costs, and efforts. When suppliers wish to receive a quality certificate without undertaking the relevant investment, there is an economic incentive to seek out lenient auditors (Jahn et al., 2003:11). Announced visits pose the additional problem that factory owners can manipulate the appearance of working conditions. Unfortunately, fake documentation is not an exception either.

There is another cause for manipulated or poorly conducted audit reports: while international textile brands and retailers require their suppliers to obtain certification, they also exert price and time pressure on them, thereby pushing them to engage in practices leading to poor working conditions. Even if audits identify gaps in adherence to certain standards, they do not help in finding ways of implementing corrective action plans. The race to the bottom for the cheapest prices should thus be replaced by responsible purchasing policies, i.e. longer delivery deadlines and fair prices.[3] Also, the costs of compliance with codes of conduct should not be exclusively externalised from lead firms to their suppliers. Audits should therefore not narrowly focus on the conditions in a given supplier, but include in their scope the purchasing practices of buyers that create the incentives for such conditions. Corrective action plans should include recommendations for the lead firms on how they can adapt their sourcing demands to enable the supplier to meet social and environmental standards.

Apart from deliberate falsifications, social audits frequently have methodological shortcomings that make it difficult for auditors to identify abusive conditions. Audits tend to be snapshot observations. Also, not all relevant aspects of working conditions are easy to measure, such as discrimination or freedom of association. Already in 2006, an industry representative was reported to have said that 'what is easy to measure is being measured, but what's hard to measure isn't' (Casey, 2006:3). Further, information on sexual harassment is frequently shared only after a long period of confidence-building, making it highly unlikely that auditors will reveal such problems, even if they are common.[4]

As a more fundamental critique of social audits, sociologists LeBaron and Lister argue that auditing produces standardised metrics, measurements and rankings, which create the appearance of independent supply chain monitoring; but the information produced through and derived from audits is partial, highly political and fundamentally shaped by the retail audit client. Public and governmental trust in the metrics generated by audits ends up concealing real problems in global supply chains. Furthermore, the choices made regarding the scope and design of audits tend to omit the portions of supply chains (beyond the first tier) where labour abuse is most likely to take place (LeBaron and Lister, 2015).[5] In particular, this issue of the scope of the audit was raised by critics of the 2015 BASF-commissioned audit at Lonmin, who asked why it only focused on the situation at the mine, while publicly available NGO reports had highlighted the precarious living conditions around the mine (Bahadur et al., 2017:34).[6]

Accountability and liability: How to control the controllers

As long as audits are carried out, the question is how to effectively control their quality. In order to implement effective quality control and ensure accountability, firstly, the likelihood of detecting deficient audits has to be increased. Further, auditing companies must face penalties if they deliver a deficient audit. Changing the incentives for the audit industry could be simply and effectively achieved by increasing the chances of liability. Currently, auditing companies are generally not held accountable on the basis of their reports, neither by textile brands or factory owners, nor by workers, who supposedly benefit from auditing.

One barrier to effective oversight is that audit reports are not made public. Contrary to claims of 'transparency', audit reports are regarded as confidential and the property of the auditor's client and therefore generally not made public. Therefore, workers or unions have no means of verifying the veracity of such reports. Audit transparency should go beyond publishing lists of suppliers, which has recently become more common. Access to audit reports is, however, a precondition for the identification of unduly flattering audit reports, oversight of audit quality, and accountability. Pleas for transparency are often countered with claims of a relationship of trust between supplier and buyer or because of trade secrets. At the same time, the publication of audit reports of garment factories by the Bangladesh Accord shows that it is possible to overcome these concerns.[7] Presumably, such transparency is possible in other industries as well. Vattenfall, for example, in addition to publishing a list of its coal suppliers, made public a human rights risk assessment of its coal supply chain in Colombia (2017).

It is generally accepted that social audits are only snapshot observations and that real and continued monitoring can best be done by the workers on the shop floor themselves. A problem with workers' involvement in social audits is that they are frequently threatened with dismissal, as well as the risk of losing orders for the factory as the result of lay-offs if they report abusive working conditions. This tends to influence worker interviews. A solution could be to implement special protections against such dismissals. A clause to that effect could be a standard part of the code of conduct, global framework agreements or multi-stakeholder initiatives. As workers may not be able to demand enforcement of such protection clauses, this can only have effect in combination with the other factors mentioned here. The involvement of trade unions is often made difficult by several practical issues, such as the absence of trade unions in garment factories and the severe repression faced by many unionists. This is particularly so in the textile industry in Bangladesh (Human Rights Watch, 2016). In other sectors, unions may be able to play a stronger role. At the same time, though, workers across industries prefer to keep their jobs and are all too easily put under pressure by the threat of a lead firm to terminate the business relationship. Just as in the textile industry, workers in other sectors have reported feeling inhibited from speaking freely with social auditors.

Grievance mechanisms in factories can play a role in revealing abusive working conditions and thus exert quality control over social audits. Discrepancies between unduly flattering audit reports and complaints filed through local grievance mechanisms can serve to reveal substandard audits. Grievance mechanisms are, however, not always used or even known to workers. What is more important, and often politically underestimated, is that the accompanying reduction of workers and trade unions to the status of mere 'witnesses' of working conditions undermines their role as a necessary party in collective bargaining.

So far, the mechanisms described to create accountability do not have any legal implications but are based on the voluntary commitment of lead firms, auditors and social compliance initiatives to create accountability. While these efforts may all be necessary, the question remains how to hold auditors to account if their negligent audits have severe consequences for the lives of workers. Here, legal liability comes into play. When lead firms request audits, they are – in their role as the client of auditing firms and suppliers – in a position to set the standards for quality audits. On the basis of the audit contract, the commissioning party is able to take steps against sloppy auditors.

Lead firms generally do not have an incentive to hold their auditors liable. This might change if and when they face legal claims for injuries due to abusive working conditions in their supply chain. A remarkable example here is the recent move by retailer KiK to hold auditing companies legally liable for findings in their report. A KiK spokesperson commented that 'KiK is the first company in Germany and possibly in Europe with a contract in place with its auditing firms, which makes them legally liable for their findings on the ground for a period of three months following the audits. […] For example, if an auditing company visits a factory and fails to spot the fire extinguisher has expired, and this is then discovered during a physical check in the factory, we can go back to the auditing firm and ask them to pay a penalty' (Barrie, 2017). Referring to their own risk of liability, KiK representatives indicated that they 'need to have a picture of the factory that properly reflects what we find there, because we are the ones facing the risk later on' and thus want auditors to 'make their job 150% accurate' (Barrie, 2017).

In addition to the contract parties holding auditing companies accountable for poor reports, there is a role for governmental justice systems. If workers are exposed to life-threatening working conditions (such as the absence of adequate fire-safety measures), the granting of a CSR certificate to such a workplace might impede necessary improvements. If workers are subsequently injured, prosecutors should investigate whether a negligent audit report led to the certification of an unsafe factory.

Thus far, workers have very few possibilities to hold auditors to account for their reports. As workers are not parties to the auditing contract, they cannot file claims for not fulfilling the contract service adequately. A simple and direct legal remedy should be in place for workers, whom social audits are intended to benefit. This can easily be done, for example, in the contracts entered into by auditing companies with the client. Such contracts could contain a clause explicitly conferring third-party beneficiary rights on those workers whom the auditing cycle is intended to benefit. Non-performance or a deficient audit would constitute a breach of the obligations of the auditing company under such a contract. A reversal of the burden of proof should facilitate such claims. If auditors fail to identify major non-compliances, negligence should be assumed unless they can prove that relevant professional standards were adhered to. It should be noted, though, that such a claim depends on workers filing cases. When workers do not even dare to speak up on smaller things, it is unrealistic to expect them to file such claims.

Outlook

Despite the critique of audits, human rights due diligence and disclosure laws are actually increasing the demand for social auditing (Verisk Maplecroft, 2017:7). The meagre or even counterproductive results of social audits in the textile industry should, however, be taken seriously in other sectors. Ultimately, certificates generate a high level of trust while incurring almost no legal risk. Despite notorious shortcomings, the continuing practice of social audits is too often understood as a means to monitor working conditions effectively. Buyers and suppliers in a supply chain can then claim to have met their corporate social responsibility by relying on audit reports. No incentives are given to undertake effective measures such as structural changes in purchasing practices. By declaring they are conducting audits and supervising corrective action plans, lead firms display their commitment, while at the same time avoiding any real change in their business model. On the contrary, companies often successfully portray their own actions as responsible, while identifying the supplier as the only problem. Lead firms frequently claim that there is not much that they can do and all too easily hide behind the argument that terminating a business relationship would not be responsible to the workers either. While true, this argument conceals many other aspects where lead firms have an influence on production practices, such as price, delivery deadlines and contributions to necessary investments.

Social audits are thus part of the problem rather than a solution, providing minor remedies while upholding a neoliberal framework and legitimising endemic features of global supply chains. It is a real problem that codes of conduct and the accompanying audits are extra-contractual tools, whereas agreements on price, volume, delivery date and product quality are contractually enforced. LeBaron, Lister and Dauvergne quote one of their interviewees: 'There is no greater power than a purchase order. The power relation begins and ends with the buyer's signature. All the rest that floats around it is talk. [...] Until your buyer says you care [about the environment and workers] in the purchase order, you don't care' (2017:108).

This concern was reflected in the criticism of the BASF-commissioned audits at Lonmin. The South African non-profit organisation Bench Marks Foundation and the German organisation Bread for the World took issue with BASF for not exerting contractual leverage over Lonmin. In its mining labour plan of 2006, Lonmin committed itself to building 5,500 houses. But in 2014, only three houses had been built (Rajak, 2016:943). The NGOs argued that despite this failure to comply with the required target, 'long term contracts between BASF and Lonmin have recently been renewed' and, according to these NGOs, 'do not include any enforceable clauses on Lonmin's SLP [social and labour plans] obligations' (Bahadur et al., 2017:6). Such apparent lack of enforcement fits with the conclusion of the economist Forslund, who after analysis of Lonmin's sustainability reports noted that as long as Lonmin keeps 'display[ing] public awareness of its failures' and 'promises to correct failures in the coming years', it can continue its mining operations. 'No sanctions of any kind have ever been meted out against Lonmin' (Forslund, 2013).

LeBaron, Lister and Dauvergne point out that attention to private audits is all too often focused on improving 'operational quality', while the social and environmental outcomes remain the same (2017:111). They conclude that the audit regime benefits corporations while 'failing workers and the planet'. In her analysis of the South African mining industry, Rajak similarly realised that the real question is not 'how CSR has helped workers, but how it has helped corporations to confront specific challenges' (2016:930). She observed that the logic of corporate social responsibility enabled South African mining companies to portray workers' health and housing as externalities instead of 'core operational costs' (2016:933). These scholars argue that audits make it all too easy for governments to ignore calls for stricter regulations and proper investments in adequate state inspections.

Despite the criticisms, for the moment social audits seem to be here to stay. As audits are increasingly adopted by companies to fulfil their human rights due diligence obligations, transparency and liability should be minimum conditions. Essential to any system that claims to ensure quality audits is a mechanism ensuring deficient audits are identified and penalised. This should involve independent workers' organisations and workers. On this point, the Bench Marks Foundation and Bread for the World criticised BASF as 'the audits commissioned in 2015 and 2016 are not public, methodology and results have not been communicated or consulted with NGOs, unions and communities' (Bahadur et al., 2017:6). Without access to audit reports, trade unions, workers and communities cannot independently verify whether the auditors were able to observe all instances of non-compliance with the relevant standard.

Auditor liability can contribute to necessary changes in the power relationship between lead firms, suppliers, workers, trade unions, communities and auditors. However, this will only happen if auditor liability is not only a theoretical possibility on paper but is also demanded in practice. This demand should come from lead firms, governments, compliance initiatives and workers. Efforts towards enforcing accountability should raise questions about the misleading scope of audits, draw attention to unduly flattering audit reports and criticise the lack of implementation of audit recommendations – thus revealing the mechanisms that currently perpetuate the status quo in which audits are carried out but social and environmental outcomes fail to improve. A firm like BASF can lead the way on this path towards accountability by including a clause for third-party beneficiary rights in its next auditing contract.

Notes

1 Significant parts of this chapter were previously published as C. Terwindt and M. Saage-Maaß, 'Liability of social auditors in the textile industry', ECCHR and FES Policy Paper, December 2016.
2 The Association of Professional Social Compliance Auditors now plans to create a certification programme for auditors.
3 Depending on the number of buyers and suppliers as well as the price mechanism in a particular value chain, the room for manoeuvre of lead firms may vary. While retailers are free to determine the price of fashionable clothing, the price of commodities like coffee and platinum is decided on the world market. Further, garment factories are not bound to specific places, allowing clothing companies to threaten going elsewhere, while mining companies are less likely to change their location. Owing to the specialised uses of platinum, the number of buyers is actually fairly small, just like the number of suppliers, thus creating a power dynamic unlike many others (see the interview with Gavin Capps).
4 An audit at Lonmin actually *did* note this particular problem, as it observed that sexual harassment of female employees at the company's facilities, near Rustenburg in the North West province, was 'common and pervasive' (McKay, 2017).
5 The challenges with subcontracting are relevant beyond the textile industry. For example, Rajak observed that subcontracted mining workers in South Africa do not have the same (social) rights as other employees (2016:940).
6 The 2017 audit at Lonmin actually led to the recommendation that 'Lonmin should take steps to better understand how the mining operation affects local communities and which measures can be derived from this' (BASF 2017b).
7 The Accord on Fire and Building Safety in Bangladesh is a legally binding agreement between global brands and trade unions and mandates factory inspections by building engineers. The reports are published on the Accord website (Accord, 2017).

References

Accord on Fire and Building Safety in Bangladesh (2017) Inspections, www.bangladeshaccord.org/inspections/, accessed 28 September 2017

Anner, M. (2011) Corporate social responsibility and international labor rights: The quest for legitimacy and control, Paper presented at the MIT Institute for Work and Employment Research Seminar Cambridge, MA, 1 November 2011

Bahadur, A., L. Kadel and S. Lincoln (2017) *Platinum for the World Market, Iron Shacks for the Workers: Living and Working Conditions in Marikana Five Years after the Massacre*, Bench Marks Foundation, Johannesburg, and Bread for the World, Berlin

Barrie, L. (2017) How KiK is raising the bar on working conditions: Interview, 11 April 2017, www.just-style.com/interview/how-kik-is-raising-the-bar-on-working-conditions-interview_id130409.aspx

BASF (2017a) Chemical initiative 'Together for Sustainability' (TfS), www.basf.com/en/company/about-us/suppliers-and-partners/sustainability-in-procurement/together-for-sustainability.html, accessed 7 November 2017

BASF (2017b) *Controlling Standards: Evaluation and Audit of Lonmin*, www.basf.com/en/company/about-us/suppliers-and-partners/sustainability-in-procurement/ensuring-sustainability-in-the-supply-chain.html, accessed 7 November 2017

Bergermann, M., S. Book, A. Busch, L. Deuber and M. Seiwert (2017) Das dunkle Geheimnis der Autoindustrie, *WirtschaftsWoche* 45

Casey, R. (2006) Meaningful change: Raising the bar in supply chain workplace standards, Working Paper No. 29, prepared for John Ruggie, Special Representative of the Secretary General for the Consultation on Business and Human Rights, November 2006

Clean Clothes Campaign (2005) *Looking for a Quick Fix: How Weak Social Auditing Is Keeping Workers in Sweatshops*, Clean Clothes Campaign, Amsterdam

Clean Clothes Campaign (2016) Input paper for Asian Living Wage Conference in Pakistan, May 2016

Forslund, D. (2013) Coping with unsustainability, Bench Marks Policy Gap 7 (Lonmin), Bench Marks Foundation, www.bench-marks.org.za

Freitas, A.d. (2017) It is time to recognize the limits of certification in agriculture (commentary), 16 November 2017, news.mongabay.com/2017/11/it-is-time-to-recognize-the-limits-of-certification-in-agriculture-commentary/

Gereffi, G. and O. Memedovic (2003) *The Global Apparel Value Chain: What Prospects for Upgrading by Developing Countries*, United Nations Industrial Development Organization

Human Rights Watch (2016) *Whoever Raises Their Head Suffers the Most: Workers' Rights in Bangladesh's Garment Factories*, www.hrw.org/report/2015/04/22/whoever-raises-their-head-suffers-most/workers-rights-bangladeshs-garment, accessed 1 March 2016

Jahn, G., M. Schramm and A. Spiller (2003) Zur Glaubwürdigkeit von Zertifizierungssystemen: Eine ökonomische Analyse der Kontrollvalidität, Paper presented at Institut für Agrarökonomie, Georg-August Universität Göttingen, Diskussionsbeitrag 0304

LBMA (2017) *A Guide to the London Bullion Market Association*, www.lbma.org.uk/assets/downloads/presspack/LBMA_Overview_Brochure.pdf, accessed 15 November 2017

LeBaron, G. and J. Lister (2015) Benchmarking global supply chains: The power of the 'ethical audit' regime, *Review of International Studies* 41, pp. 905–924

LeBaron, G., J. Lister and P. Dauvergne (2017) The new gatekeeper: Ethical audits as a mechanism of global value chain governance, in A. Claire Cutler and Thomas Dietz (eds.), *The Politics of Private Transnational Governance by Contract*, Routledge, London

Locke, R., B A. Rissing and T. Pal (2013) Complements or substitutes? Private codes, state regulation and the enforcement of labour standards in global supply chains, *British Journal of Industrial Relations* 51, pp. 519–552

Locke, R., T. Kochan, M. Romis and F. Qin (2007) Beyond corporate codes of conduct: Work organization and labour standards at Nike's suppliers, *International Labour Review* 146, 1–2, pp. 21–40

McKay, D. (2017) Lonmin says sexual harassment of women 'common and pervasive', *Miningmx*, www.miningmx.com/news/platinum/30861-lonmin-reports-sexual-harassment-women-common-pervasive/, accessed 17 November 2017

Rajak, D. (2016) Hope and betrayal on the Platinum Belt: Responsibility, violence and corporate power in South Africa, *Journal of Southern African Studies* 42, 5, pp. 929–946

Tulder, R. van, J. van Wijk and A. Kolk (2009) From chain liability to chain responsibility, *Journal of Business Ethics* 85

Vattenfall (2017) *A Human Rights Risk Assessment in Colombia*, www.news.vattenfall.com/en/article/new-report-human-rights-risks-colombia, accessed 17 November 2017

Verisk Maplecroft (2017) *Human Rights Outlook 2017*

▶ *Our values: High Performance, Respect for Each Other, Integrity, Honesty & Trust.* Lonmin image campaign in Marikana and surroundings, recorded in Wonderkop, 2015.

▶ **pp. 254/255** BASF conducted a first audit at Lonmin at the end of 2015, and a key result was the commitment to support the expansion of the Lonmin plant fire department. This fire station building in Marikana West is probably connected to it. It was built in 2016 and has not been used since then.

▶ *We dig to build this company*: Promotion booth of Lonmin on the occasion of the commemoration of the fourth anniversary of the massacre on 16 August 2016.

▶ In connection with the panel discussion, 'Supply chain responsibility: From airy voluntariness to binding rules' in Berlin on 21 April 2016. Thorsten Pinkepank, head of BASF's CSR department, once again defends the voluntary nature of supply chain responsibility in an interview with Stefan Buchen for the show *ARD-Panorama*. The manager for social responsibility refers to the chemical company's magnanimous efforts. *Translation: Our consequence of this is that we want to continue working to improve the living conditions of the workers.*

▶ Lonmin website's homepage, accessed a few months prior to the massacre.

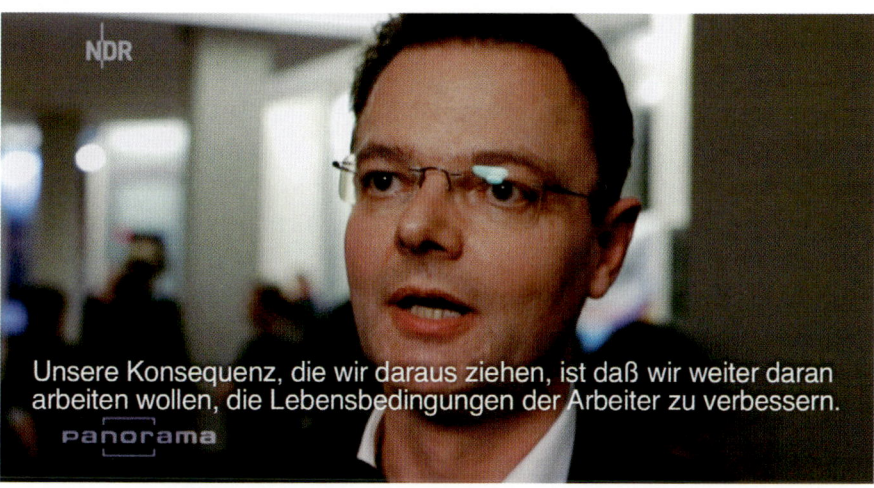

Unsere Konsequenz, die wir daraus ziehen, ist daß wir weiter daran arbeiten wollen, die Lebensbedingungen der Arbeiter zu verbessern.

14. POWER AND THE POLITICS OF CORPORATE RESPONSIBILITY ON THE PLATINUM BELT

A conversation with Dinah Rajak

Maren Grimm In 2016 you published a study with the title 'Hope and betrayal on the Platinum Belt: Responsibility, violence and corporate power in South Africa'. Investigating Lonmin, you argue that the rise of corporate social responsibility (CSR) strategies had actually enabled mining companies to externalise and dispense with their social obligations rather than fulfilling them.

It has enabled companies to accrue moral authority while displacing claims of entitlement and their attendant costs. And that Marikana actually highlights this paradox in the workings of CSR.

But to begin with: corporate social responsibility. Do you know when the term was first used and how the concept emerged?

Dinah Rajak You certainly have people using terms like CSR back in the 1950s. But it was not a concept in the way that it is now. If you talk to somebody in a business school, they would probably track it back to management scholar Carroll's pyramid of responsibility (1991), which presented CSR as a pyramid of corporate responsibilities of descending importance, or, let's say, priority, as the pyramid ascends. At the bottom (the primary responsibility of a company, according to Carroll) is the economic responsibility to shareholders; then comes the responsibility or the duty to obey the law; on top of legal responsibility sits ethical responsibility (i.e. professional ethics, or ethical employment practices that go beyond those that are legally regulated); and finally, on the very top, what Carroll terms 'philanthropic responsibilities', often framed as the rather nebulous idea of good corporate citizenship, that a corporation should 'give something back', though to whom or what is not specified. Of course, Milton Friedman used the language of responsibility already in 1970 in his much-quoted statement beloved of free marketeers, 'the only responsibility of business is to do business',[1] which suggests that increasingly corporations were confronting societal expectations that went beyond economics and beyond just complying with the law.

Those would be key points in the conventional history of CSR, but if I was to chart the history of CSR I would say that initially it evolved in response to activists campaigning against corporate *ir*responsibility. Corporations then reappropriated the discourse of critics (as they have shown themselves very adept at doing) and claimed the terrain of corporate responsibility as a mode of self-governance along the lines of 'there's no need to discipline our power or regulate our behaviour because we will discipline ourselves'. So you have a seamless shift, from campaigners saying, 'Stop doing harm!' to corporations responding, 'We are the solution, not the cause, of social or environmental damage', and projecting themselves as champions of sustainable development and architects of social responsibility. This is one of the reasons I find responsibility such a problematic notion. It has derailed and continues to derail demands for accountability from below by asserting responsibility from above. Responsibility is a fundamentally paternalistic relation as it is in the control of those claiming a position of responsibility and so in effect can undermine people's capacity to make claims of entitlements and rights. In other words, CSR has, time and again, shown itself to empower corporations rather than the supposed targets or beneficiaries of corporate-sponsored efforts at empowerment.

MG When did you start researching CSR? Was the South African mining industry in the focus from the beginning or why did you decide to look specifically at South Africa?

DR I started in 2003. CSR had been on the rise since the launch of the Global Compact at Davos in 1999 and the World Summit on Sustainable Development in

Johannesburg in 2002 when the UN announced Type II partnerships,[2] i.e. international development partnerships with multinational corporations. At the World Summit, multinational corporations took centre stage not only as partners in development (whether partners of governments, IFIs, NGOs or bilateral donors) but as architects of development policy. Particularly interesting was that companies in sectors often dubbed the 'harm industry', e.g. extractives, petrochemicals and so on, emerged as the vanguard of this movement. Those companies that had just the previous decade been at the forefront of media attention for misuse and abuse of people and the planet – Shell in the Niger Delta, BP in Colombia, Rio Tinto in Papa New Guinea, and so on – emerged at the forefront of the CSR movement as standard-bearers of ethical capitalism and champions of sustainable development. And it's not just specific companies – the global oil and mining companies – that feature prominently in this new global development agenda but specific figures. Which is why I think it's important to bring actors back into the analysis to identify and understand the power of elite agency *within* structures of corporate capitalism that drive, shape and sustain social and political change of this order. In the case of CSR, one can trace a cadre of top executives, CEOs and chairpersons of global companies – the captains of global industry of our age of late capitalism who emerge as individual visionaries or warriors of the CSR movement, almost like successors of Victorian industrialists who established a new order of industrial philanthropy for their age, such as Cadbury and Lever Brothers. You can identify a roster of key people who emerge as figureheads of the various compacts, conventions, norms or initiatives that constitute the amorphous global architecture of CSR. Meanwhile, the companies they head routinely top the indices of responsible investment and scoop up the awards at the annual cycle of CSR prize-giving events.

With mining companies, their social, political and environmental footprint is so immense that they have for hundreds of years been in the business of administering some form of social control around their operations. This is why they are necessarily at the forefront of questions around development, though that is quite distinct from being heralded and elevated as guardians and architects of human well-being, social upliftment, human rights and development more generally.

And what led me to South Africa? Well, in 2003 when I started researching CSR I was intrigued by how, on the one hand, it had garnered both such strong support from the arenas of international development as a supposed panacea for poverty and how, on the other hand, the academic response had been preoccupied with the normative question 'Is it a good or a bad thing?' Yet there was very little empirical research investigating the effects and outcomes of CSR in practice. So I set out to track it and see what it actually *does*. What does it enable? And for which actors? Who does it empower? And who does it disempower? What are the outcomes of CSR, expected and unexpected, intended and unintended, both in the so-called global arenas of international development and on the ground? The obvious companies to look at were those leading the CSR charge: the extractives. And South Africa became an obvious choice for me for various reasons. I had spent a lot of time in South Africa and one thing that always fascinated me was how deeply embedded mining is in the social and historical imagination, how everyone seemed to have one degree of separation from mining, and, in fact, one degree of separation from Anglo American (the most powerful mining company operating in South Africa), the company my book focused on, which had by the dying days of apartheid controlled around 52 per cent of private industry in the country (Rajak, 2011a). It was a company, not unlike BASF in many ways, that was omnipresent. It had this sense of immense political and social power that both authenticated and bolstered its economic might. I wanted to look at a country in which extractive industries played a central role in the political economy, so South Africa was the obvious choice.

MG In the 1990s, we have a changing political landscape, notorious 'harm industries' emerge as philanthropists and are even taking a leadership role in the discourse. Is this a specific historical situation for CSR concepts to enter the scene?

DR Too often when people try to understand what CSR is doing, they do it in an ahistorical way. What I find very interesting is that CSR is always responsive to particular challenges (whether social, political or economic) that companies are facing at a particular historical moment. Its power as a resource for companies lies precisely in its capacity as a malleable discourse that can be reshaped and deployed to meet and head off those specific, historically contingent challenges or critiques. In studying CSR empirically, from global headquarters to local implementation, boardroom to coalface as it were, it became clear that while CSR does something for companies at the global level, its power rests on its capacity to absorb and reappropriate particular local challenges. For South African mining companies, at the point when I started analysing CSR in the early 2000s, a key dimension of the 'local' challenge they faced was achieving some kind of post-apartheid (ethical) rehabilitation. This was, I would argue, one of the chief areas of social, political and moral 'work' that CSR was required to perform for extractive companies in the decade or so post-1994 when the terms (and spoils) of the new mineral economy were, in theory, up for grabs. And so a key focal point for the CSR agendas of mining companies eager to maintain their economic and political foothold in South Africa was reappropriating (and reorienting) the register of Black Economic Empowerment (BEE) under the banner of patriotic capitalism so that it became a corporate resource rather than a framework of redistributive justice or empowerment from below. From 1994 on there were two critical concerns for mining companies. On the one hand, they were nervous about, if not the threat of nationalisation, the imperative to democratise the industry and to be seen to share more widely the fruits of the profits of what soon emerged as an unprecedented commodity boom; and to show how these were being reinvested as part of the national patrimony in the development of the country as a whole. On the other was their desire to diversify their portfolio globally and release a good part of their asset base and capital that for so long had been tied up in South Africa, to quell investor anxiety about what they saw to be the 'political risk' of overexposure to the democratically elected post-apartheid government. So as you can imagine, this posed quite a dilemma for mining companies: how to show that they were fully committed to and invested in the new South Africa, to emerge as self-proclaimed engineers of economic emancipation (in an industry that had co-authored the blueprint for the exploitation and oppression of black workers under apartheid) while at the same time to facilitate divestment of capital *away* from South Africa, establishing new headquarters close to the capital markets in the United States or Europe and relocating their primary listing to the FTSE[3] or New York Stock Exchange. Anglo American was the first mining company to do this, but the others soon followed suit. After decades of internal and external constraints – economic sanctions on investing abroad and apartheid government regulations to prevent capital flight – South African mining companies saw in democratic South Africa both an opportunity to diversify globally and a new threat of 'political risk', much to the understandable fury and frustration of the new democratic government headed by Thabo Mbeki, who at the time publicly denounced the CEO of Anglo American for profiting from apartheid for 50 years and then turning round and crying 'political risk', implying a state of political instability and uncertainty the moment a democratic South Africa was released from the shackles of apartheid. And this, I would argue, is precisely where CSR comes into play as a set of discursive tools, strategies and practices that provides exactly that kind of moral valorisation and political legitimacy. In short, it enabled mining companies to kind of reinvent themselves and say, 'We are patriotic capitalists, we are collaborators in building the new South Africa, we are midwives of a new economic democracy in which all citizens are free' (and freedom becomes synonymous with a free market). At the same time, the very fact that companies are so vociferously embracing this role as good corporate citizens, as purveyors of corporate social responsibility, affords the government a moral authentication for embracing hyper-neoliberal economic reforms which enable companies to expatriate huge amounts of their capital out of South Africa. So the logic of CSR – which rests on companies claiming a duty to care for workers, communities, stakeholders, human rights, national development or the environment – enables corporations to turn instruments that could and should have been used to discipline them into instruments to serve their interests.

    MG In 2015, we invited Bishop Seoka to Germany to address management and shareholders at BASF's annual general meeting. It was the first time that a representative from the beginning of the platinum supply chain informed BASF shareholders about their connection to Marikana. Since then, we established the campaign Plough Back the Fruits and have been at BASF's AGM every year. We address them not only as long-term business partners of Lonmin but also as a company that claims to be a world leader in 'supply chain responsibility'. Until now we have heard a lot of lip service being paid. The answers we keep on hearing from BASF mainly revolve around the statement that they are concerned about the tragic events but generally they regard Marikana as a problem that has to be solved first in South Africa. In other words, they see it as a domestic problem. On one occasion Kurt Bock, the CEO of BASF, said, 'I am not sure whether we can give advice to solve those things, those labour struggles in a more civilised and peaceable manner that could have avoided these regrettable human losses.'[4] So rather than blaming their partner Lonmin, BASF points to the political sphere in South Africa. I think this is symptomatic of the strategic performance of transnational companies in addressing all the stakeholders in these processes differently and as it fits them best for the particular situation. And it also shows the capacity of CSR to shift responsibility to the political sphere.

DR In my experience of attending AGMs, this seems to me a common corporate strategy deployed by managers during the public performance of the AGM: a ritual of the AGM theatre almost. Representatives of affected communities bring acts of corporate irresponsibility to the attention of shareholders (forcible relocations or other human rights violations, environmental destruction or the dispossession of land and livelihoods). Corporate executives express genuine dismay combined with gratitude for the work of representatives in championing the needs of the company's 'stakeholders'. But ultimately, responsibility for these violations is deflected back onto local or national government (who may either have a large stake in the venture through a parastatal company with which the corporation has partnered or may merely have signed the licence and thereby sanctioned the corporation's activities). It's a very effective technique of displacing responsibility. But still, the AGM is a public performance. And it doesn't mean that as a focus, a site of campaigning, shareholder meetings are not one of the most effective, because actually what happens afterwards behind the scenes is more important. It's more important that BASF, however it responds to you within the public forum of the AGM where of course it has to put on a face for shareholders, the public and so on, gets on the phone to Lonmin, for example, and says, 'Look, guys, this is looking pretty bad for us, so you need to sort it out. However you do it, as compensation or something else, this is coming back on us now politically.' In a way then, as a point of pressure, it's incredibly important, even though I have been discouraged by how easy it seems for companies to deflect calls for accountability.

While this kind of activism has long existed, what is particularly innovative about the Plough Back the Fruits campaign is that you are taking it to a new point in the global supply chain, to the *buyer* so as to exert pressure on the minerals and metals *suppliers* in relation to their labour practices. This has, of course, been done with the retail sector where activists look to end-consumers to exert pressure down the supply chain. It is not new, of course, to use the supply chain as a point of leverage for the garment industry, for example. It's not new even for, say, diamonds (in relation to conflict diamonds and the Kimberley Process) if we are looking at extractive industries, where you have clear consumers at the other end. And more recently, a very, very small niche market for ethical gold has attempted to replicate this in the gold industry. But in metals, and especially in platinum group metals used predominantly for industrial applications, the supply chain has always posed a big challenge for campaigners. Consumers rarely know or think about the microscopic amounts of industrial minerals and metals they consume in their phones or catalytic converters in their cars. Meanwhile, the buyers – petrochemical giants such as BASF – seem more impenetrable than the extractive companies themselves. This is the first time that I've heard of a campaign that says, 'Let's track platinum and let's see where it goes and look to the next points in the chain, the companies buying the platinum, as another point of vulnerability, of pressure that can be put on the mining companies in relation to their treatment of workers, communities, environments and so on.' Ultimately this may well have consequences that will ripple out. That's a very important new front that you've opened up.

MG BASF has incorporated sustainability and ethical guidelines into their corporate identity. So that's how we addressed them: that it is in their interest to invest in the improvement of the mineworkers' situation and the situation of the mining communities. We never demanded disinvestment from Lonmin. On the contrary, we encouraged them to comply with their own narrative.

DR Disinvestment (whether it is disinvestment from a pension fund or disinvestment in terms of 'we'll find other suppliers of platinum') is very problematic. The leverage lies in the threat of divestment rather than its fulfilment. Once you divest, you lose your leverage and corporate managers have no more reason to stop whatever it was they were doing (violating workers' rights, polluting environments and so on). While managers may claim that the power of shareholders is inviolable and an impediment to their own ethical visions of sustainability, shareholder rebellions have not proved particularly powerful tools for holding corporations to account for social, environmental or political infractions (Gillan and Starks, 2007). (It's possible this is starting to change with the success of action by institutional investors in 2017 demanding much greater levels of climate change accounting at Exxon.) I agree with you, it is a very problematic line to pursue, especially given the fact that mining companies, particularly platinum mining companies in South Africa, have this constant rejoinder that they introduce, which is, 'If you protest like this, if you do anything that threatens the bottom line (i.e. the production and price of platinum), we will have to close shafts.' And ultimately that means another 1,000, 2,000, 5,000 workers retrenched. They always have that trump card in their back pocket, which they play. And since 2008, and the mass job losses in the mining industry that came in the wake of the commodity slump following the global economic downturn, mining companies have not held back from playing that card. In South Africa in the context of mass joblessness, 'those with jobs', as William Gumede (2012) puts it, 'cling on to them, for fear they may never get one again'. Yet they are all the more vulnerable to the dictates of a volatile global market and the shibboleth of shareholder value invoked by corporate management as a rejoinder to their struggle for better conditions and a fairer wage. This highlights the precariousness that has come to define having a job as well as joblessness (Barchiesi, 2011). As many people, such as Gumede, have pointed out, this profound and chronic level of insecurity, though much longer in the making, was further entrenched in the wake of the global financial crisis. However, the direct correlation between crisis and wage worker precarity in fact replicates the very discourse of mining companies themselves. The turn from boom to bust, from soaring profits to cutting costs, points to something further, beyond the vulnerability of the labour force to the ineluctable fluctuations of the global market. It speaks to the power of corporations to instrumentalise narratives of financial hardship and crisis to justify cuts of any order and constrain worker agency. In this vein, the South African business commentator Sipho Ngcobo (2012) rebukes Marikana's striking rock drillers for their unrealistic expectations: 'This is not 1999, 2002, 2006 and 2008 when platinum was the most profitable business in the world,' he writes; 'the good times are gone [...] The fact of the matter is platinum mines are not providing sufficient returns to satisfy shareholders, let alone double salaries overnight [...]. The workers and the trade unions (those who still have unions) would be well advised to hold on to their jobs'. Ngcobo neglects to mention that worker wages actually fell in real terms during the platinum boom of the early 2000s.

During the commodity super-cycle companies were posting record profits (back in 2005), and the *Financial Times* was reporting that mining companies were 'making so much money they didn't know how to spend it!'. Since the slump in metals and mineral prices that followed, at every industry event I have attended, executives have been racking their brains and looking terribly pained at corporate austerity and belt-tightening due to plummeting prices. But ultimately, it has provided them with this incredible weapon against any kind of struggle for better pay, better conditions: anything can be taken as a threat to a precarious bottom line in these apparently hard times. While workers did not share in the rewards of the boom years, they are expected to bear the sacrifice of the lean years.

MG So how would you assess the use and the effectiveness of dialogue between companies and activists?

DR One of the great claims of CSR is that it has brought formerly disparate parties with divergent interests, like NGOs and multinationals, and former combatants – corporations and campaigners – together as collaborators in a mutual project of sustainable development. And I think we have a deep-seated tendency to assume that the shift from combat to collaboration is always progress, that the evolution from, for example, the Publish What You Pay campaign to the Extractive Industry Transparency Initiative, championed by leading global extractives, is evidence of success (Rajak, 2011b; see also the chapter by Michael Reckordt). But I think one thing that the rise of CSR has shown us is that the quest for collaboration, for consensus between parties with divergent worldviews and indeed interests, can be quite dangerous. In fact, ongoing and constant struggle, or at least maintaining that oppositional position, can provide better protection and better checks, greater accountability, than partnership. For partnership all too easily enables the terrain, the agenda, to be controlled and, dare I say it, colonised by the interests and ideologies of the most powerful actor. The pursuit of consensus inevitably demands a lowest-common-denominator calculation of the points that can be agreed on and therefore a sidelining of those critical deal-breakers that can't be agreed on and threaten to unsettle the partnership. This not only neutralises the points of pressure but it can serve to co-opt those actors who effectively become advocates for corporate interests rather than the interests of those weaker affected groups whom they are supposed to represent. After all, whoever pays the piper calls the tune (Stirrat and Henkel, 1997). For workers, a consensual relationship between their union and management can well become a vehicle for corporate co-option, leaving them more exposed and less protected.

MG As you said, BASF is one of the leading German enterprises and they have been a world-leading chemical company for quite a while. In late 2014 there was a complaint filed with a New York court for illegal platinum price-fixing on the London stock exchange against HSBC, Goldman Sachs, Standard Bank and BASF. The complaint was lodged by a Florida-based jewellery business, Modern Settings, that produces and imports jewellery and police and army badges. When we first confronted BASF at their AGM, they answered: 'Well, we are astonished, our lawyers are checking this and we are collaborating, but we don't see that this complaint has any substance.' I would argue that the complaint itself reflects the power BASF must actually have on the PGM market (Rajak, 2016; Brot für die Welt, 2017:33).

DR The fact that the jewellery industry collectively brought that complaint is an intriguing discovery – it does seem to suggest that other actors perceive the company as exerting a cartel-like influence over the supply chain. And so it would certainly be a potentially fertile avenue to pursue in order to see how that influence could be used for other, more socially focused ends.

MG One is reminded of the so-called vitamin cartel in 2001, when BASF was compelled to paying almost 300 million euro compensation to the European Union.

In 2016, we had a picket in Zug in Switzerland at the offices of BASF Metals GmbH. Zug is the tax haven of Switzerland, and the Green Party in Zug lodged a parliamentary inquiry into the value of the platinum trade through this Swiss letterbox company. BASF Metals was closed a few months later and the business was moved to London. But the figures we have about the business volume of this subsidiary company do not match the figures we have about the trade volume with Lonmin.

What is significant for chemical companies is that as a normal consumer, you don't find yourself in a supermarket and ask yourself, 'Should I choose this item by BASF or should I choose another brand?' You normally don't see products with the BASF label. They are selling components for a wide range of things, also things you are surrounded by in everyday life: sneaker soles, vitamins, synthetic materials or catalytic converters for cars. And, of course, insecticides. But they are not known for particular products. And as a chemical company, this is probably what they prefer. But, on the other hand, BASF is very prominent in German business news and the performance of BASF shares is an important indicator for the German financial index.

DR I think the pre-eminence of companies like BASF, so deeply embedded in the national economy and national consciousness, exerting such wide-reaching influence globally, presents both a challenge and an interesting opportunity. In some ways their octopus-like omnipresence, with tentacles reaching into every domain of the economy, makes them very hard to track and hold to account. On the other hand, it also means they offer a critical juncture and potential pressure point for activists looking to influence or transform a range of different industries and effect change right down complex supply chains.

MG If you look at the city of Ludwigshafen, where their principal offices have been for 150 years and where BASF maintains the world's largest connected chemical unit, you will not find an action committee monitoring the company; in fact, quite the opposite. In 2015 we had difficulties finding a cinema that would screen *Miners Shot Down* because the owners would rather not be recognised as hosts of a screening or a talk that criticised BASF. BASF and their CSR department invest a lot in cultural activities and other visible and recognised programmes. Interestingly, Ludwigshafen is constantly to be found among the poorest municipalities in Germany, but as the largest employer in the region, BASF is generally very well regarded and has very strong roots in the region. The AGMs are attended by 5 to 7,000 shareholders, mostly workers and retired workers.

DR Workers as well – that's interesting!

MG Yes, a lot of BASF employees are also shareholders. In the 1950s, BASF started a participation model that allowed all employees to invest parts of their regular pay into shares. And that's a difference with England: generally at AGMs in Germany you have quite a large audience you can address. As shareholder, you have the right to speak and to ask questions and the board is required to answer. Thus the AGMs are quite a valuable source of information, about BASFs business dealings with Lonmin, for example.

DR One thing I just wanted to ask you about BASF: am I right in thinking that they are essentially a kind of fifth-generation successor of IG Farben?

MG Yes, exactly. In short: the cartelisation of the German chemical industry started at the beginning of the 20th century. In 1925 IG Farben was founded and in 1952 the cartel was broken up again, and BASF, Bayer, Hoechst and some other smaller units became independent again. But the final winding-up only happened in 2013, when IG Farben was deleted from the trade register. This is a broad field of inquiry in itself, but of course you could also draw a connection between IG Farben's continued existence alongside its successors for such a long time and the externalisation of war compensation claims. I think the decartelisation of IG Farben also involved a lot of other aspects that need to be considered, like the restructuring of the West German economy in a pre-Cold War constellation, for instance. But also the transformation process BASF undertook in the 1990s should be seen in relation to changes in the broader political landscape after German reunification and the collapse of the Eastern Block (see the chapter by Maren Grimm and Jakob Krameritsch). It is another example of early CSR strategies and the instrumentalisation of political transformation processes.

DR Again, going back to what we were saying earlier about the power of CSR to reinvent a company in the public imagination, this seems particularly relevant in relation to BASF, which has managed to rehabilitate its history and itself to the extent that they almost occupy a kind of higher ethical ground, which is amazing given that there were ongoing lawsuits against them for profiting from forced labour in Nazi concentration camps until relatively recently. That really speaks to the power of corporate public relations and CSR as a political technique that is crucial to the reinvention (from some of the darkest corporate histories), survival and reproduction of corporate power. And not just rehabilitate but reinvent themselves as a kind of ethical paragon. I think the tools, the devices, the resources that corporations use in order to reinvent themselves, to gain moral and political currency and capital, are much more global in that sense.

MG In your article you mention a blind spot or a repeated mistake of critics in regarding the phenomenon of CSR and its performative capacity to turn things around as an inherently logical process of the neoliberal system itself. Could you explain this?

DR With critical scholars and activists concerned with resistance to dispossession and exploitation, the tendency has been to reveal the hidden intricacies of subaltern agencies while reifying corporate power as systemic, monolithic and omnipresent. In focusing on the weapons of the weak, we overlook the weapons of the powerful and specifically the weapons, resources and techniques that corporations draw on to deal with or forestall the challenges they face, whether by incorporation or by deflection. The unfortunate side effect has been to 'conjure what we critique' (Mitchell, 2002), to reinforce the perception of corporate omnipotence, which is essential to sustaining market value and enabling managers to pursue their goals. Yet extractive corporations confront constant challenges, never more so than over the past five years with the convergence of a triple-bottomed crisis of plummeting commodity prices, unruly shareholders and intensified social and ecological pressures (particularly around climate change). And, as the challenges and the critique evolve, so too have the narrative techniques and tools of spin that corporations employ to deal with them – becoming more sophisticated, adding new discursive weapons to their armoury, as the old ones become depleted.

Let us take extractive industries and climate change as an example. In a world where the Paris Agreement represents a lowest common denominator consensus on climate ('a broad tent', as sustainability managers and consultants often call it), and to degrees the conservative (if unlikely) collective goal to which most oil transnationals have signed up, denial of the facts of climate science is no longer an option for extractive corporations attempting to manage critics, as it once was. In fact, the more oil and gas companies have engaged with (and ostensibly embraced) global climate governance, the greater their power to shape the terms of the debate and designate certain concerns as no-go areas. The evolving power of CSR has always relied on appropriating the language of critics, accruing moral authority, embracing the cause in a bid to keep control of the terrain and win a seat at the table where attempts are made to govern their actions. Meanwhile, the lines between what is *on* the table in debates over climate change mitigation and between what is not, as Michael Blowfield (2005) puts it, the negotiables and the 'non-negotiables' are fiercely guarded. Energy economists and climate analysts frequently refer to these as 'blind spots' hampering meaningful progress on decarbonisation. It quickly becomes clear that these 'blind spots' – chief among which is the incompatibility of sustainability with continued growth – are taboo subjects.

MG How was it possible for Lonmin to not meet their social obligations to such a degree, even after the massacre, when the company was in the spotlight? And could you examine it at the actual practical level of applied CSR techniques of control?

DR This is the key question. It alerts us to the need to consider the specific resources and techniques corporations deploy in order to head off challenges and avoid regulation through the logic of self-governance and the deeply problematic yet apparently persuasive claim that regulation only breeds compliance whereas self-discipline leads to creative solutions. There's been a lot of really powerful analysis of Marikana that has shown convincingly the convergence of NUM, state and corporate action against the striking rock-drillers (cf. Alexander, 2013; Chinguno, 2013; Sinwell and Mbatha, 2016). But how this state-union-corporate synergy, which ultimately served to safeguard corporate interests as opposed to basic worker rights and welfare, was achieved and validated remains something of an open question. Such a collaboration cannot be explained (or sustained) simply by elite pacting to divide and defend the spoils of the mineral economy at the violent expense of workers, as it often is. Rather, all such acts of violence to suppress dissent that impedes the workings of extractive capitalism require the ideological work of legitimation. The new authority of mining corporations rehabilitated and replenished in the post-apartheid political economy required just such a set of new discursive and ideological tools – in step with the orthodoxies of the post-revolutionary South Africa – in order to garner political support and moral validation. For this, I would argue, CSR – as a benevolent tyranny or tyrannical benevolence – has proved indispensable, first in reshaping the terms of worker welfare and social responsibility to make them amenable to corporate interests, and, second, in making possible (and politically correct) new alliances between civil society, labour unions and the government on which they depend. Responsibility is, after all, always a relation of power.

MG After the massacre a lot of evidence of failed social and labour plans (SLPs) and embezzled International Financial Corporation money turned up and a lot of research, survey and published work has been done to draw attention to working and living conditions around the mines. And, of course, to the vast ignorance about Lonmin and the government against the families of the killed, the injured and the arrested strikers; that no compensation has been paid and no judicial investigation into the police operation has taken place despite pertinent questions about the decisions that led to the massacre. Even before Marikana but definitely after the massacre, Lonmin has been probably one of the best monitored mining companies, even on a global level.

DR I think Marikana was so shocking because it was reminiscent of the Sharpeville Massacre (1960) over half a century ago as the embodiment of the brutal repression of the apartheid state. And so, half a century later, as Marikana became the symbol of a resurgence of state-backed violence against poor, disenfranchised South Africans, people asked: how could this happen in democratic South Africa, almost 20 years after the end of apartheid? It resonated very strongly, very painfully, locally, but it also gained a great deal of attention globally as a symbol of the vulnerability, the precarity and exploitation of workers at the bottom of global supply chains. In that sense it acted like a flashpoint, or wake-up call, much like the Rana Plaza building collapse in Bangladesh, when the quotidian structural violence experienced by industrial workers in the global South turns into overt physical violence, unsettling the wilful blindness of the public whether in the United Kingdom or South Africa or Germany. But after the initial shock and horror, we all too quickly move on, and it's important that four, five, six years on, we maintain the momentum and retain that symbolic significance as a focus of the struggles of workers for decent work and dignity under millennial corporate capitalism. That is why your project is so important; why the indefatigable work of activists and advocates such as Jim Nichol[5] is crucial not just for the local outcomes of Marikana and the commission of inquiry for those directly affected, but for its global significance and how it resonates with struggles faced by workers in other industries and other countries around the world. This requires fighting on both an ideological and very pragmatic level. I learnt a lot, for example, speaking to Jim Nichol, who was on the front line and took a much more pragmatic approach to CSR as a possible point of leverage in a battle where the victims of Marikana (the injured, the widows of those killed and their dependants) had so few resources at their disposal. When trying to understand what CSR *does* and for whom, my argument has been that CSR empowers companies rather than workers, or those it claims to empower. And while I think that is still very much the case, and it makes me very circumspect about corporate claims to CSR, it is also possible to think pragmatically and creatively about how the discourse of CSR could be reappropriated by workers, communities, activists, to hold companies to those very claims, just as companies themselves reappropriated the register of sustainable development from those looking to hold them to account in the first place. How might it be used as a pressure point? How might CSR be claimed back, as it were, as a point of bargaining to extract compensation or other concessions in negotiations between workers and corporate management? And that was a lesson to me. After all, if corporations such as Lonmin, Anglo and BASF are to be taken seriously in their declarations of corporate social responsibility, it stands to reason that workers (as well as all those affected in one way or another by their activities) must try to compel companies to make good on their promise, by whatever means they can.

Notes

1. 'There is one and only one social responsibility of business – to use its resources and engage in activities designed to increase its profits so long as it stays within the rules of the game, which is to say, engages in open and free competition without deception or fraud.'
2. For a short explanation of Type II partnerships, see www.en.wikipedia.org/wiki/Type_II_Partnerships.
3. Financial Times Stock Exchange, the major British stock index.
4. At the annual presentation of BASF's financial statements, 24 February 2016.
5. James Nichol, British activist and lawyer.

References

Alexander, P. (2013) Marikana, turning point in South African history, *Review of African Political Economy* 40, 138, pp. 605-619

Barchiesi, F. (2011) *Precarious Liberation: Workers, the State and Contested Social Citizenship in Postapartheid South Africa*, SUNY Press, Albany, NY

Blowfield, M. (2005) Corporate social responsibility: Reinventing the meaning of development, *International Affairs* 81, 3, pp. 515-524

Brot für die Welt (2017) Platinum for the world, iron shacks for the workers, 2017, www.brot-fuer-die-welt.de/fileadmin/mediapool/2_Downloads/Fachinformationen/Analyse/Analyse75-Nd1-en-v01-Web.pdf

Carroll, A.B. (1991) The pyramid of corporate social responsibility: Toward the moral management of organizational stakeholders, *Business Horizons* 34, 4, pp. 39–48

Chinguno, C. (2013) Marikana: Fragmentation, precariousness, strike violence and solidarity, *Review of African Political Economy* 40,138, pp. 639–646

Friedman, M. (1970) The social responsibility of business is to increase its profits, *New York Times Magazine*, 13 September.

Gillan, S. and L. Starks (2007) The evolution of shareholder activism in the United States, *Journal of Applied Corporate Finance* 19, 1, pp. 55–73

Gumede, W. (2012) Marikana is South Africa's turning point, *Gulf News*, 1 September, www.gulfnews.com/opinions/columnists/marikana-is-south-africa-s-turning-point-1.1

Mitchell, T. (2002) *Rule of Experts*, University of California Press, Berkeley

Ngcobo, S. (2012) The economic tragedy of Marikana, *Moneyweb*, 17 September, www.moneyweb.co.za

Rajak, D. (2011a) *In Good Company: An Anatomy of Corporate Social Responsibility*, Stanford University Press, Stanford

Rajak, D. (2011b) Theatres of virtue: Collaboration, consensus and the social life of corporate social responsibility, *Focaal: Journal of Global and Historical Anthropology* 60, pp. 9–20

Rajak, D. (2016) Hope and betrayal on the platinum belt: Responsibility, violence and corporate power in South Africa, *Journal of Southern Africa Studies* 42, 206, pp. 929-946

Sinwell, L. and S. Mbatha (2016) *The Spirit of Marikana: The Rise of Insurgent Trade Unionism in South Africa*, Wits University Press, Johannesburg

Stirrat, R.L. and H. Henkel (1997) The development gift: The problem of reciprocity in the NGO world, *Annals of the American Academy of Political and Social Science* 554, pp. 66–80

▶ **pp. 274/275** Two flyers of the network for gene ethics (Gen-ethisches Netzwerk), an NGO that monitors developments in bioengineering, genetic engineering and reproduction technologies, and critically reviews them for the public, such as on the occasion of BASF's 150th anniversary.
Translation:
After 150 years of BASF there are many reasons to congratulate and be thankful.
CONGRATULATIONS
Congratulations – you've made the (German) Federal Government squander State Development Assistance funds to open new markets for you and other agribusiness companies in developing countries. So instead of these funds assisting people in poor countries, they've ended up in the coffers of corporations.
We congratulate BASF for the success of its genetically modified potatoes in the EU. Nobody wanted them to begin with. Also, they're banned in Europe now. The rest of the world was also less than enthusiastic about them.
Congratulations on exemplifying the polar opposite of honesty and transparency! In the US, BASF opposes the labelling of genetically modified foods and generally identifies the genetic modifications when released in the USA as confidential trade secrets.
Congratulations on more and more patents on life itself. With an unshakeable refreshing mind, you seek attributes and genes developed by Nature in order to privatise them.

Congratulations on your idea of the innovation principle, which you and partner companies use to supplant any notion of precaution that a rational human would take.
BUSINESS GOALS
Keyword: 'effective climate protection'. In 2008, the former CEO announced that 'a warm winter is not yet a disaster for the climate'.
Keyword: 'trustful cooperation with worker committees'
Thank you for the reduction of 350 jobs in the Basel region after the CIBA takeover.
Keyword: 'responsibility along the value chain'
A strike at Lonmin's Marikana mine in South Africa, which supplies BASF, sees 34 miners shot dead by police.
THANK YOU
Thank you for a shareholders' meeting, which is a mix of show, power management, ritualised processes, spectacle and catering for the shareholders.
Thanks for your sincere consideration of the public. 'It hardly smells in Ludwigshafen anymore, although smell is the hardest to control in chemistry', notes Bock.

Biotechnologische
Agrar
Science
Fiction

BASF
Der Gentechnik-Gigant

Nach 150 Jahren BASF gibt es viele Gründe zu *gratulieren* und sich zu *bedanken*.

GLÜCKWÜNSCHE

Herzlichen Glückwunsch, Sie haben die Bundesregierung dazu gebracht, staatliche Entwicklungshilfe zu verwenden, um Ihnen anderen Agrarkonzernen neue Märkte in Entwicklungsländern zu eröffnen.
Statt Menschen in armen Ländern zu helfen füllt der Staat die Kassen der Konzerne.

Wir beglückwünschen die BASF zu dem nachhaltigen Erfolg ihrer gentechnisch veränderten Kartoffeln in der EU.
Erst wollte sie niemand, mittlerweile sind sie Europa verboten. Im Rest der Welt waren sie nie ein Thema.

Herzlichen Glückwunsch zu Ihrer vorbildlichen Offenheit und Transparenz!
In den USA setzt sich die BASF gegen die Kennzeichnung von gentechnisch veränderten Lebensmitteln ein und kennzeichnet die gentechnischen Veränderungen bei Freisetzungen in den USA im Regelfall als geheime Geschäftsinformationen.

rzlichen Glückwunsch zu immer mehr
enten auf Leben.
unerschütterlich erfinderischem Geist
hen Sie Eigenschaften und Gene in der
ur, um sie zu privatisieren.

rzlichen Glückwunsch zu Ihrer Idee des
ovationsprinzips.
Partnerunternehmen haben Sie so endlich
en adäquaten Begriff gefunden, um dem
igen Vorsorgeprinzip zu begegnen.

TERNEHMENSZIELE

chwort „effektiver globalen Klimaschutz"
8 verkündete der damalige Vorstands-
sitzende „ein warmer Winter ist noch keine
makatastrophe"

chwort „vertrauensvolle Zusammenarbeit
den Arbeitnehmervertretungen"
nke für den Abbau von 350 Arbeitsplätzen in
Region Basel nach der CIBA-Übernahme.

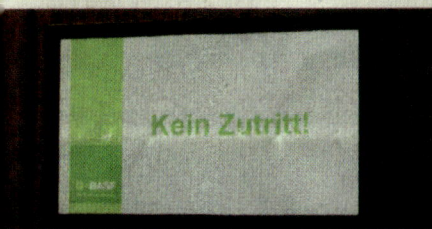

Stichwort „Verantwortung entlang der Wertschöpfungskette"
Nach Streik beim BASF Zulieferer Lonmin in Südafrika werden 34 Minenarbeiter von der Polizei erschossen

DANKE

Danke für eine Aktionärsversammlung, die eine Mischung aus Show, Machtverwaltung, ritualisierten Abläufen, Spektakel und Verpflegung für die AktionärInnen ist.

Danke, dass Sie die Öffentlichkeit für dumm verkaufen: „Es riecht praktisch nicht mehr in Ludwigshafen, obwohl Geruch das am schwierigsten zu kontrollierende ist in der Chemie', weiß Bock."

15. THE CHEMISTRY IS RIGHT: THE CORPORATION AND POLITICS

Jan Pehrke
Translated by Simon Phillips

Since its founding in 1865, the chemical corporation BASF has been ready to wield its economic power in order to ensure that its interests are effectively represented in the political arena. Even during its decision about where to locate its headquarters, BASF was able to skilfully play off the cities of Mannheim and Ludwigshafen against each other and ensure that the corporation could secure a location that met all of its needs. From this point on, BASF continued to deploy its expertise with considerable success, irrespective of which form of government it was dealing with at the time. Whether during the German Empire, the Weimar Republic, the Third Reich or the Federal Republic, BASF has always found the ways and means with which to exert its influence and to secure its profits. This, of course, has required political flexibility, but it has meant that BASF has always made a profit. The corporation's flexibility is also clear from its readiness to participate in the preparations for war that were conducted during the German Empire – doing so promised BASF attractive returns on its investments.

Planned influence

After 1918 and the end of the German Empire, BASF and other companies quickly came to terms with the new rulers and immediately regained their access to power. This enabled them to win a 10-year tax waiver. In 1925, corporations including Bayer, BASF and Hoechst merged to form the conglomerate IG Farben. IG Farben was the world's largest chemical company at the time, and the merger considerably strengthened the corporations' political clout. IG Farben made lavish donations to the bourgeois parties, but it also had emissaries within them who met regularly as part of a working group attached to the conglomerate's supervisory board. This illustrious circle was known as the Kalle Circle, and it was named after Wilhelm Ferdinand Kalle, a member of IG Farben's administrative board. Kalle was also a representative of the German People's Party. However, the managers of these corporations were not content with merely joining political parties; they also adopted important offices within the governments of the Weimar Republic. Thus, between November 1929 and June 1930, Paul Moldenhauer, a member of IG Farben's supervisory board, became minister of economic affairs under Chancellor Hermann Müller and then minister of finance under Chancellor Heinrich Brüning. Moldenhauer's colleague Hermann Warmbold, a long-time member of BASF's executive board, served as minister of economic affairs between October 1931 and January 1933 under chancellors Brüning, Franz von Papen and Kurt von Schleicher. This approach to politics is also clear from a statement made by Carl Duisberg, the chair of IG Farben's supervisory board, who explained, 'I've given up trying to influence the parties using reason! All difficulties can be overcome through planned influence' (Schneckenburger, 1988:46).

When the NSDAP (Nazi Party) rose to power, however, IG Farben maintained its distance from the party for a long time. This only changed once the conglomerate had realised that the Nazis could help it out of a tricky economic situation. IG Farben was incurring losses in Germany owing to its attempts to extract petrol from coal. In the early 1930s oil prices began to fall, and IG Farben's venture proved to have been an enormous error of judgement. In June 1932, however, the conglomerate plucked up its courage to arrange a meeting with the NSDAP. Heinrich Bütefisch, head of the BASF plant in Leuna, and Heinrich Gattineau, who was responsible for trade policy at IG Farben, visited the party leader – Adolf Hitler – who signalled his support. During the Nuremberg trials, Bütefisch was to state for the record that 'Hitler promised to provide our petrol production with the necessary protection' (Gattineau, 1947:231).

Following the meeting with Hitler, IG Farben's board of directors immediately decided to proceed with coal hydrogenation rather than write off losses of 300 million Reichsmarks. This decision paid off when Hitler kept his word. In December 1933, Hitler sealed the Petroleum Agreement with representatives of the conglomerate; it granted IG Farben a guaranteed price, a return of 5 per cent and write-off options. Bütefisch later expressed how happy he was with this decision: in 1941, he wrote, 'Now we know that our haste was necessary [...] The reassuring certainty provided by ensuring that the Luftwaffe's and the other significant sections of the Wehrmacht's supply of fuel in Germany were free of foreign influence would have been at risk if we had acted more hesitantly' (Köhler, 2017).

As had been the case during the First World War (the 'Saltpetre Promise'),[1] the chemical industry proved indispensable to the warlords. In fact, IG Farben even took care of planning the minute details. Carl Krauch, who was a member of the conglomerate's board and had managed BASF's Merseburg ammonia plant since 1912, prepared a memorandum entitled *Zur Vorbereitung der Industrie auf den Krieg* (Preparing industry for war) for the Ministry of War. Moreover, in his role as *Wehrwirtschaftsführer* (head of a company that was essential for the war effort), Krauch decisively shaped the 'four-year plan' that was intended to make industry ready for war. This placed IG Farben in a position where it could make rich pickings from the plundering undertaken by the Nazis. Only a few days after the Anschluss of Austria, Krauch and colleagues drew up a memorandum aimed at restructuring Austria's chemical industry, and this pattern was to be repeated throughout the Second World War. Joseph Borkin went on to describe IG Farben's actions in the following terms: 'IG Farben followed the Wehrmacht into the countries it was overrunning like a jackal following a lion' (Borkin, 1979:91).

IG Farben also played a decisive role in other crimes committed during the Nazi regime. The conglomerate's subsidiary Degesch supplied Zyklon B for the gas chambers, and IG Farben not only operated a plant close to Auschwitz but also had its own concentration camp to guarantee its facility with a supply of forced labourers.

After 1945

After the demise of the Third Reich, the directors of IG Farben sensed that problems might be looming: Georg von Schnitzler, a member of its executive board, pointed out that 'should financial claims be made, the material that would be relevant to these cases would rob our defence lawyers of their sleep' (Greiner, 1995:219). Initially, things did not seem to be going particularly well for the conglomerate. A team under US Treasury Secretary Henry Morgenthau collected evidence against IG Farben and concluded that 'if Allied policy aims to ensure that "Germany will never again be able to threaten its neighbours or the peace of the world", then IG Farben must be destroyed, together with its factories that are vital for war' (Greiner, 1995:243). However, things were to turn out differently. Morgenthau's hard line was forced into the political defensive in the United States. US industry, which had extensive business relations with German corporations, played a significant role in this U-turn, as it demanded that the US government secure their markets instead of implementing a 'tabula rasa strategy' in Germany. Furthermore, the anti-Hitler coalition had split, and this led the Allies to change their priorities. The Cold War also meant that a strong Germany was needed to act as a 'frontline state'. As a result, the Americans, British and French distanced themselves from the destruction of IG Farben and, instead, a break-up of the conglomerate was now on the agenda. However, the Allies still shied away from completely untying the areas in which the conglomerate was most strongly intertwined. Although the original plan had been to divide IG Farben into 50 'independent units', this was reduced to 12; ultimately, however, IG Farben was split into just four successor corporations: BASF, Bayer, Hoechst and Casella.

There was no *Stunde Null* (zero hour) for IG Farben's staff either. The new corporations continued to rely on their 'well-deserved' IG Farben personnel. In 1952, Dr Carl Wurster, a former *Wehrwirtschaftsführer* (rank of an NSPAP party member officer who was responsible for economic relations) who had been in charge of the inorganic chemistry laboratory and pilot plants at BASF in Ludwigshafen, returned to his previous employer to chair its executive board. It was not long before the corporations regained their old strength: just 20 years after their 'restart', BASF, Bayer and Hoechst were already as big as IG Farben had been during its heyday.

'Action Kohl'

The 'planned influence' exerted over the political parties, as described by IG Farben's director-general, Carl Duisberg, in the 1920s, was to reach an interim peak around 50 years later as part of 'Action Kohl'.

BASF developed a particularly intimate relationship with politics during the Kohl era. Helmut Kohl had worked at BASF during his studies and had remained true to the chemical industry, returning after a short intermezzo at an iron foundry. Between 1959 and 1969, Kohl was an adviser to the Rhineland-Palatinate section of the German Chemical Industry Association (VCI), which is located in Ludwigshafen, alongside the headquarters of the association's largest member, BASF. In 1959, Kohl was elected to the state parliament in Frankfurt as its youngest member. It was no coincidence that Kohl's political career had begun to pick up speed at this time. The publicist Werner Rügemer emphasises, 'Kohl's employer not only paid Kohl for his advisory role, but also promoted the politician's simultaneous and costly rise within the Christian Democratic Union at the national level' (Rügemer, 2017). Kohl's rise within the party reached its climax when he became minister president in 1969.

From 1973 onwards, Helmut Kohl's advance through the ranks of the CDU at the national level was mainly supported by the corporations Flick and Henkel – represented by Eberhard von Brauchitsch and Kurt Biedenkopf. They were 'committed to Action Kohl' because they did not trust the CDU leader Rainer Barzel politically and believed that he had very little chance of winning an election. As such, they intended to ensure that 'Dr Kohl takes over the party chairmanship and the task of renewing the party at the organisational level and its manifesto' (*Neues Deutschland*, 26 August 1995). This plan was drafted by Kurt Biedenkopf, the CEO of the Henkel corporation in May 1973. Chemistry was in Biedenkopf's blood: his father had been a director of IG Farben and a *Wehrwirtschaftsführer*. In May 1973, the first '100,000 Deutschmarks due to Kohl' (*Neues Deutschland*, 26 August 1995) were provided to manage the political landscape – the corporations soon reaped the benefits of their plan, as Kohl was made party chair. However, neither Brauchitsch nor Biedenkopf wanted to permit Kohl to go it alone, and Biedenkopf therefore decided to join him as CDU general secretary.

During Biedenkopf's time in the CDU, he was able to 'top up' his pay to ensure that he did not incur any loss of salary: Biedenkopf received payments via the CDU's slush fund – which Flick[2] and colleagues had largely financed via the Staatsbürgerliche Vereinigung (Civic Association). The Civic Association, which was founded in 1954, had plenty of money – between 1969 and 1980 it received about 100 million euro. Unsurprisingly, BASF was also one of its donors. In fact, this situation even resulted in BASF's former CEO Matthias Seefelder having to answer to the courts after he was investigated by the Bonn public prosecutor's office in 1985 for tax evasion.

Kohl's intimate relationship with BASF is also illustrated by an object that he always carried with him: a BASF diary. When Kohl died, the corporation expressed a commensurate level of sympathy: BASF director Kurt Bock stated, 'Helmut Kohl had a lot to do with BASF: he visited us as a member of parliament, as minister president of Rhineland-Palatinate and as federal chancellor of Germany. In 2015, nothing could stop Helmut Kohl from celebrating our 150th anniversary with us and showing his commitment to the company – in fact, this was one of his last personal appearances' (*Handelsblatt*, 18 July 2017).

Securing access to raw materials

Today, BASF is still heavily involved in political 'landscape management', especially when it comes to securing access to raw materials. The three-way catalytic convertors that BASF produces are a good example. These products provide around 10 per cent of the corporation's sales, but catalyst production requires huge amounts of platinum. BASF acquires platinum worth around 2 million euro every day from a single South

African mining operator, Lonmin. The corporation also requires a significant amount of cobalt, nickel, rhodium and rare earths. Moreover, it even produces and sells crude oil and natural gas through its Wintershall subsidiary. BASF also trades in platinum and palladium and holds a 6 per cent stake in Deutsche Rohstoff AG, which has access to minerals such as tin, rare earths, tungsten, molybdenum, gold and silver.

At the same time, BASF acts as a service provider to the mining sector. The solutions provided by the South African branch of BASF's Global Mining Solutions in Johannesburg, for example, include processes to separate ores from rock, reagents for further processing, as well as technologies for water recovery and solvent extraction.

However, it is hard to speak of any form of 'business as usual' within the commodities sector, as the industry faces numerous uncertainties. In many places, low mineral deposits are compounded by rising demand now that China has entered the market, and modern developments such as electric motors are leading to a run on many of these resources. In addition, minerals hold tremendous political power. In cases where they are not directly causing civil wars, they are often being used to finance them, as was the case with the Congo. Moreover, if peace has been established in a resource-rich country, it is often because a deadly calm is being enforced by an authoritarian regime. Finally, the latest BASF annual report (2017) points to a further risk: 'We expect many commodity suppliers to expand their value chains.' In this context, South Africa is planning on preventing large corporations from receiving the lion's share of the revenues they gain from selling minerals.

These are the reasons why corporations seek assistance from politics. Above all, businesses are particularly concerned with securing access to resources. In 2005, the Federation of German Industries (BDI) sounded the alarm and organised its first Raw Materials Congress, stating, 'Raw materials that are essential to industry are becoming increasingly scarce, because of increasing demand from China, other emerging economies, and the growing global economy.'[3] The lobbyists at the BDI were even able to summon up a prominent guest to attend their event – the incumbent German federal chancellor, Gerhard Schröder, who would have certainly understood the pertinence of the question 'What must politics in Germany and Europe do to secure the supply of raw materials and energy in the future?'[4] The BDI already had the answer: it called on the German government to develop a 'raw materials strategy'.

Importantly, the Raw Materials Congress was not only dedicated to the 'need' for a raw materials strategy. It also covered issues such as 'resource availability and geostrategic risks', 'future developments in the commodity markets' and 'commodity problems in the value chain'. The BASF manager Gabriel Tanbourgi took to the podium to speak about the last of these issues.

The BDI argues that the German government should treat the issue of securing access to resources as a cross-departmental task and not merely focus on its economic aspects. The association maintains that German foreign policy in general and development policy in particular should also play an important role in securing corporate access to raw materials. In 2007, at the panel discussion 'Raw Material Security: A Challenge for Development Policy', which was organised by the Konrad Adenauer Foundation, a BDI representative contended that 'development policy can contribute to our raw material security when it promotes the stability of these countries, ensures that mining concessions are awarded transparently, and enables raw materials to be transported faster and more easily'.[5]

The Commodity Alliance, which was co-founded by BASF and has recently been reintegrated into the BDI, even wanted to involve security policy; if necessary, access to their coveted treasures was to be secured by force. This led *Handelsblatt* to summarise an interview it conducted with Dierk Paskert in the following manner: 'Businesses are worried about free access to oil, gas and minerals. The head of the Commodity Alliance [...] demands support from the German government – and, if necessary, the help of the military' (*Handelsblatt*, 18 February 2013).

Paskert's comments caused quite a stir, and the Commodity Alliance was forced to issue a denial: 'Military conflict is not a suitable means of sustainably securing the supply of raw materials.' Although Paskert did not directly call for the implementation of a gunboat policy to maintain 'resource security', certain statements clearly point in this direction: 'We need a strategic foreign trade and security policy [...] Therefore, together with our partners in the EU and in NATO, we will have to take on even more responsibility in foreign trade and security issues to achieve this goal' (*Handelsblatt*, 18 February 2013).

A similar approach has long been part of Germany's official military doctrine. The 1992 Defence Policy Guidelines, which set out the tasks of the Bundeswehr, include 'preserving free world trade and securing unrestricted access to markets and raw materials throughout the world'.[6] In addition, a recent White Paper lists 'a secure supply of raw materials and energy' as one of Germany's strategic priorities (Bundesministerium der Verteidigung, 2016:47).

The German government takes action

The German government listened to the signals that these companies were sending out and acted on them. In October 2010, Rainer Brüderle (FDP), then minister for economic affairs, announced that 'Since early summer, the Federal Ministry of Economic Affairs and Technology has been involved in extensive discussions as part of several working groups that include representatives of the BDI, the raw materials processing industry, the recycling industry and trade unions. The working groups' findings have been included as part of this raw materials strategy.' Brüderle also emphasised that the government's package set out 'the further path towards a sustainable supply of raw materials in Germany'.[7] He was convinced that the strategy would provide industry with the protection it was demanding. Moreover, Brüderle claimed that the strategy meant that 'we are facing up to new global challenges, in particular the growing international competition for important industrial raw materials'.[8] He announced investment guarantees, the inclusion of commodity projects during the promotion of foreign trade, the creation of a raw materials agency and raw material partnerships with resource-rich countries. Importantly, these partnerships shape the 'economic and political framework'[9] that provides the foundation access to platinum and other minerals. In addition, Brüderle argued that they provide 'important support to German industry's capacity to access a secure supply of raw materials'.[10]

Germany is not particularly selective when it comes to finding partners for cooperation – and this is particularly the case whenever Berlin heeds the 'call of gold'. In 2013, Günter Nooke, Chancellor Angela Merkel's personal Africa representative, stated: 'The demand for responsible, non-corrupt governments remains central to all forms of development and any meaningful use of a country's resources. However, it would be naïve to demand that raw materials should not be extracted if certain political, legal and administrative conditions are not met. That is not the way that the world works, especially not in Africa.' Nooke was speaking at an event jointly organised by the Konrad Adenauer Foundation and the Sub-Saharan Africa Initiative of German Business (SAFRI) (Wahlers, 2013:11). He concluded by stating, 'Political experience demonstrates that, in the end, it is not WTO rules that govern the game, but power interests' (Wahlers, 2013:11–10).

The German Mineral Resources Agency (DERA) plays a key role in Germany's raw materials strategy. DERA describes itself as 'the economic competence centre for raw materials and the central information and advisory platform for mineral and energy resources for German businesses'.[11] DERA, which is attached to the Federal Institute for Geosciences and Natural Resources (BGR), tracks international commodity markets, carries out risk analyses and conducts research into the potentials of raw materials. The agency prides itself on having a 'sound regional knowledge of raw materials and economics', and in particular good relations with developing countries. It works with countries such as Mongolia, Kazakhstan, Chile, Peru and South Africa and implements projects to explore and extract raw materials in these countries. It also prepares studies, such as *Sicherung der Rohstoffversorgung bei der BASF im Allgemeinen und im Falle der seltenen Erden* (On the possibilities of engagement of German companies in the South African raw materials sector),[12] that provide the basis for new raw materials partnerships. DERA also holds events that provide information about the industry. The trade seminar 'Energy and raw materials for tomorrow: Securing raw materials for the German economy', which was organised in 2012 together with the German Chambers of Industry and Commerce, was also attended by Gunther-Alexander Kellermann, a representative of BASF. Kellermann gave a speech about 'Securing the supply of raw materials at BASF in general and particularly in the case of rare earths'.[13]

For some time, the German Chambers of Commerce Abroad has operated 'competence centres on mining and raw materials' in countries that are rich in minerals, and German embassies are also active in these areas. The German Chamber of Commerce in Peru has launched a coalition of German companies that includes BASF, VW and Canasta Tecnológica Alemana, and it organises trips to the mines.

Development policy is also expected to play its part. In 2010, the Federal Ministry for Economic Cooperation and Development (BMZ) published the *Entwicklungspolitische Strategiepapier Extraktive Rohstoffe* (Development Policy Strategy Paper Extractive Raw Materials) and pointed out that action needed to be taken on cobalt, platinum, and tantalum in terms of 'advice and competence development for modern, efficient and environmentally friendly mining and production methods' (BMZ, 2010).

Conflicts over conflict minerals

Corporations such as BASF do not merely undertake political activities in order to secure access to raw materials; they also focus their political intervention on what are known as 'conflict minerals'. Conflict minerals are raw materials that trigger, fuel or at least finance war-like conflicts, and, therefore, come to the attention of supranational organisations and governments. The brisk business that is currently being conducted in conflict minerals has led the United Nations to adopt guiding principles on business and human rights, and the OECD has also issued policies urging companies to exercise a special duty of care in their supply chains. The German government responded with its National Action Plan on Business and Human Rights. In this context, a hearing took place on 1 October 2015 at the Federal Ministry for Economic Cooperation and Development, and representatives of BASF also attended. During the hearing, BASF's Thorsten Pinkepank pointedly rejected placing excessively high demands on the industry. The minutes of the meeting record him as stating, 'Businesses cannot be expected to take on the statutory role of protecting human rights. If they do have to adopt this role, they can only be expected to do so to a very limited extent.'[14] Pinkepank also argued that transparency was not an end in itself and stressed the importance of 'maintaining proportionality at all times between the efforts involved, the information gained, and privacy and business secrets'. Furthermore, he was even unhappy about the term 'human rights'. Pinkepank argued, 'It is important to remember that whenever the issue of human rights is raised, companies feel like they are under accusation; as such, the term does not have positive connotations.'[15] He continued by arguing that the National Action Plan should focus on providing support to corporations and helping them, for example, by providing information and country-specific risk databases. Pinkepank made these comments despite the fact that the corporations are fully aware about what is going on in certain resource-rich countries.

When the governing coalition took Pinkepank's concerns to heart as part of its December 2016 National Plan, Bread for the World, Amnesty International and other organisations reacted with disappointment. 'All of them "should" implement human rights diligence processes to prevent human rights violations in their supply chains. This will be "verified" on a random basis. If companies ignore these requirements, however, they will not face any consequences' (see the chapter by Sarah Lincoln) (VENRO et al., 2017:3).

Despite the fact that the situation had looked quite hopeful for them at first, the corporations were less fortunate at the EU level. The BDI initially praised the plan that Brussels had drawn up to deal with conflict minerals, calling it a 'balanced proposal'. This should come as no surprise, since the EU had intended to encourage companies to voluntarily comply with the plan and left it up to businesses to certify their own supply chains. However, this was before the European Parliament got involved. The parliament not only improved the Bill, but also put in place rules governing the disclosure of procurement practices. Nevertheless, national authorities were left to assess whether the provisions were being properly implemented.

BASF also uses industry-specific organisations such as the International Platinum Group Metals Association (IPA) to exert further pressure. The IPA quite openly describes itself as an 'early warning system for the PGM industry that monitors legislative projects (emissions control, REACH,[16] recycling, etc.) and industry-related topics such as trade, health and safety, and sustainable development'.[17] The last time that IPA president Steve Phiri, head of the South African platinum mining company Royal Bafokeng Platinum, rang the alarm bells was in June 2017. At that time, the South African government had adopted the Mining Charter III as a means of strengthening the position of black people in the extractive industries. Previously, at least 26 per cent of a mining corporation had to be owned by black shareholders; Mining Charter III increased this percentage to at least 30 per cent. In addition, it forces companies to use at least 1 per cent of their turnover to finance black empowerment. This situation led Phiri to label the charter as 'the last nail in the coffin' of the mining industry (Vanek, 2017). Moreover, he immediately announced a law suit in his capacity as vice-president of the Chamber of Mines, which includes industry giants such as Glencore and Lonmin. However, it may no longer be necessary for the Chamber of Mines to pursue the case because, when President Jacob Zuma resigned, Mining Minister Mosebenzi Zwane also lost his position – and the mining charter played a considerable role in his replacement.

REACH out, BASF is there

The IPA considers that part of its work should involve lobbying against REACH – the European regulation that regulates chemicals. It believes that REACH poses a threat to the mining industry, and for good reason: Brussels requires assessments to be undertaken of the health risks associated with the processing of certain substances, including platinum. Although platinum is not linked to any direct health risks, its salts can cause cancer, damage organs, cause genetic mutations and increase the toxicity of other substances.

BASF has not only used IPA lobbying to ensure that the REACH requirements are set as low as possible; it also lobbies to hinder their implementation. This has been achieved at the European level through the merger of the European Chemical Industry Council (CEFIC) and Business Europe, and at the German federal level through the Chemical Industry Association. However, BASF also took up the initiative itself and sent a member of staff to the EU working group that drew up the REACH directive. Later, this person continued to work with REACH as an 'external employee' of the Federal Ministry of Economic Affairs and Technology. Moreover, despite the fact that he was still employed by BASF, he claimed to be representing the Ministry of Economic Affairs during a presentation he gave for MEPs, so as to provide his agenda with the appearance of an official remit.

BASF's representative in Berlin was soon in a position to report back to Ludwigshafen. The representative's lobbying led the Ministry of Economic Affairs to water down plans that had been drawn up by the Federal Ministry for the Environment, Nature Conservation and Nuclear Safety to use REACH to implement far-reaching precautionary measures to protect people's health. The former secretary of state for the environment, Rainer Baak, was angered when he learned of the details. Speaking on the ARD programme *Monitor* (3 April 2008), Baak stated, 'If it is true that a salaried BASF employee was involved in drawing up European legislation with the Ministry of Economic Affairs on chemicals law, it is scandalous. This would mean that some people in the Ministry of Economic Affairs do not understand that they are committed to neutrality and that they are not there to represent the interests of individual companies in Germany.'

It is unlikely that BASF, which has also installed its emissaries in the German government's press service, the Ministry of Finance and the Ministry of the Environment, believes that it has crossed a red line. On its website, the company argues, 'BASF supports personnel transfers and temporary personnel exchanges between BASF and political organisations and institutions or the public administration. The aim is to gain knowledge and experience from different working environments and thus an improved understanding of the specific political and business contexts, structures and processes involved.'[18]

Extreme corporate lobbying such as this has succeeded in drastically reducing the number of substances that have to be assessed as part of the REACH directive. Moreover, these companies now only have to submit detailed data sets on substances with an annual level of production that exceeds ten tonnes. And they have plenty of time to do so – even though it was adopted 12 years ago, the REACH directive has yet to be fully implemented. The transitional period for full registration for substances with an output of between one and a hundred tonnes per annum, however, expires in June 2018.

As a major emitter of climate-damaging carbon dioxide – BASF produced around 22 million tonnes in 2016 – the corporation has successfully lobbied the German government to ensure that its emissions do not get the corporation into trouble. Moreover, in cooperation with other multinationals and associations such as CropLife, the European Roundtable of Industrialists, Business Europe and CEFIC, BASF succeeded in making the EU emissions trading system largely ineffective. The programme was launched in 2006, but has never achieved its goal of ensuring that economics has a positive impact on the environment. The concept of charging companies for every tonne of greenhouse gas that they emit above the limit has so far failed to influence their actions. This is because industry persuaded Brussels to set the emissions limits too generously. In addition, companies were granted numerous licences to emit CO2 free of charge and did not even have to register all of their plants with the EU Emissions Trading System (ETS).

This has resulted in regular attempts by the EU to reform emissions trading; however, as global players immediately intervene whenever they do so, the reforms have only ever resulted in minor fixes. In 2014, BASF and 13 other companies even approached the European Commission president, José Manuel Barroso, about this issue. Bock and colleagues argued that 'the ETS should continue without changes until 2020'.[19] The company directors even threatened to relocate their production facilities if changes were made. Moreover, Bock also rejected the EU's target of reducing carbon dioxide emissions by 40 per cent by 2030, compared with 1990 levels. In 2014, Bock warned that 'if we take the 2030 climate targets seriously, European industry – and chemistry – will have to shrink'.[20] Moreover, BASF has also provided generous campaign donations to Republican climate change deniers in the United States. In fact, the corporation's 'commitment' to these issues earned BASF the dubious title of being one of the most effective lobbyists when it comes to preventing climate change policies: BASF was ranked sixth in this context by InfluenceMap (*taz*, 12 September 2017).

BASF also extensively uses its channels of influence in the field of genetic engineering. For example, the corporation wrote a letter to DEFRA, the United Kingdom's environment ministry, to argue that new techniques such as oligonucleotide-directed mutagenesis (OgM) should not be treated as genetic engineering. BASF was trying to ensure that OgM – a procedure for changing the genetic material in plants by activating the repair mechanism within their cells – would not have to undergo a lengthy approval procedure. In general, BASF is committed to simplifying the approval of genetically modified (GM) crops through EuropaBio and other organisations. Even in the case of laboratory-grown crops that enter EU soil illegally and that may infiltrate the DNA of conventionally bred species, the corporations urged Brussels not to fall back into its 'fortress Europe' mode and instead called on them to welcome them to Europe.

BASF was particularly persistent in its lobbying when attempting to pave the way for the introduction of Amflora – its GM potato. The company wrote nine letters to the European Commission president, José Manuel Barroso, and the environment commissioner, Stavros Dimas. Moreover, because BASF was unhappy with the speed of the process, the corporation even sued the European Commission for inaction. It also threatened Berlin and Brussels by promising to shift its research activities to more 'innovation friendly' countries if the potato – with its artificially high starch content – were not to receive approval.

BASF not only influences European Union policies from the outside; it is also well connected within the EU's political structures. For example, the Advisory Forum of the European Food Safety Authority (EFSA), which conducted the scientific assessment of Amflora, included many faces that were familiar to BASF.[21] Joe Perry, for example, had a long history of working for a company that received research contracts from the corporation. In addition, Howard Davies was employed by the Scottish Crop Research Institute, which also received orders from BASF. Moreover, BASF even directly contracted Jeremy Sweet to produce a study for the company. Finally, Detlef Bartsch wrote an article for the journal *Nature Biotechnology* together with colleagues from the corporation; Bartsch also belongs to the Society for Plant Breeding, which was co-founded by BASF.

Unsurprisingly, in 2009, the EFSA approved Amflora. The panel argued that resistance to the antibiotics neomycin and kanamycin, which BASF researchers had incorporated as markers into the potato to control successful gene transfer, posed no risk to health. At the same time, the EFSA did not seem to be worried about the fact that these genes could spread into the environment and promote the development of pathogens that are immune to neomycin and kanamycin because, it claimed, these two substances have 'little or no therapeutic relevance'. The World Health Organization sees this very differently and classifies neomycin and kanamycin as 'critically important antibacterial agents for human medicine'.[22]

This situation led a number of EU member states to take court action against the approval of Amflora – and they won the case. In December 2013, the European Court of Justice revoked Amflora's approval, citing errors in the approval procedure.

As if that were not enough, BASF also lobbies Brussels to ensure that the EU does not impose stricter controls on pesticides and hormonally active substances. The corporation also focuses on the EU's research, chemicals, health and trade policies (such as TTIP) and pulls the strings from its office for 'EU–Government Relations' in rue Marie de Bourgogne in Brussels. However, although its lobbying headquarters has just 19 employees, it swallows up 3.2 million euro a year. Ten members of staff have access to the European Parliament and some even sit on EU working groups, such as on occupational safety. Furthermore, BASF sends out its own invitations to events such as parliamentary evenings, dinners and dialogue events in the Belgian capital and the corporation also maintains further 'liaison offices' in Berlin, Washington, New Delhi and Beijing.

A review of corporate lobbying

BASF does not sit on its laurels; it assesses the influence it has and uses every trick in the book to ensure that its interests are represented. In the course of setting up its office in Berlin, BASF commissioned a 'government relations study' to find out how its lobbying policy could be made as successful as possible in the German capital. In 2000, as part of the study, the corporation interviewed over 200 members of the German parliament, around 100 members of parliamentary staff, 50 representatives of the press and about 1,000 people from Berlin. The corporation was interested not only in the general level of acceptance of lobbying, but also in identifying the acceptance of lobbying in specific situations, such as during legislative processes. The corporation sought to understand politicians' preferred manner of dealing with corporations by asking for information about the importance that the politicians placed on contacts with board members, experts from specialist departments and liaison officers. In addition, BASF also enquired as to whether the politicians would like to visit production sites or needed further information about the corporation.

BASF is very open about the results of its study. The former chair of 'Young Union' (Leif and Speth, 2003:98–114), Klaus Escher, who led the liaison office from 2000 to 2002, presents the findings in his contribution to *Die stille Macht. Lobbyismus in Deutschland* (The Silent Power: Lobbyism in Germany).[23] Escher is happy to state, 'The overwhelming majority of respondents from politics and the media view corporate participation in political debates as desirable or essential.' In contrast, although the general population accepts lobbying or the 'participation of companies in political debates', it is 'much more sceptical about it than the political or media elite' (Leif and Speth, 2003:102–104). The latter take a more positive view of lobbying by BASF and others, with 71 per cent attesting to a strong or very strong corporate influence on politics and 89 per cent considering this to be the case with industry associations.

Escher draws a number of conclusions from the study: a company's political office should not simply be involved in public relations; rather, it should ensure that corporate strategies 'are translated into economic policy interests' (Leif and Speth, 2003:112). Clearly, this is best done within familiar circles that do not leak information to the outside world – groups such as the Tuesday Circle. This group, which now operates under the name Collegium, includes representatives of large national and international corporations. They regularly invite high-ranking politicians and officials to their meetings, who clearly make for an attentive audience. A former TUI lobbyist described the exclusive club in the following terms: 'The Collegium is a form of focused lobbying power that no minister or secretary of state can ignore.'[24] In 2012, the Collegium was chaired by the head of BASF's liaison office in Berlin.

Escher also recommends deploying the extra weight provided by terms such as 'investment' and 'innovation' in meetings with members of parliament. However, he maintains that points can also be scored with other topics that are 'derived from internal fields of competence' such as the world economy or taxes. Escher, speaking from his own experience, points out, 'This is what happens when BASF's tax experts meet with important financial politicians' (Leif and Speth, 2003:113) He also speaks with pride about the visit to BASF that was conducted by the Bundestag's inquiry into the effects of globalisation. Once again, he sees no reason for modesty and shamelessly reveals how the company moulds the political landscape.

The work that BASF undertakes to ensure that it wields influence at the political level displays a remarkable level of continuity across time and political systems. The corporation has always sought the proximity of the powerful – whoever they have been – in order to enforce its economic agenda. It is certainly not worried about mixing with the powerful and is as at home with dictators as democrats. It seems that BASF has something to offer every taste. It was even ready to supply the products needed when past rulers lusted after war.

The corporation does not even shy away from directly entering into politics. It greatly helped pave Helmut Kohl's road to power. At the same time, if necessary, BASF's employees change sides and adopt important political positions: on the corporate march through the political institutions, BASF's emissaries have taken up posts within ministries and governments. Clearly, the state's constitutional foundation does not provide for the power of industrial players, and industry has no political mandate. Therefore, corporations use informal channels that deal with public affairs within networks that lack any form of transparency. However, it is for good reason that the lobbyists do not attempt to gain a political mandate. It would be difficult for them to do so because they represent highly particular interests. Furthermore, in the case of BASF, these interests are often explicitly directed against the common good, such as whenever the corporation demands fewer climate protection measures, less regulation of hazardous substances or the unhesitant deployment of risky technologies. As Günter Grass once said, it is practices such as political landscape management that lead 'democratically elected parliaments to degenerate into the playgrounds of economic interests' (*Neue Westfälische*, 14 April 2015). Lobbyism clearly represents something of a blind spot in terms of parliamentary democracy.

Notes

1. Saltpetre is indispensable for explosives production. When the British naval blockade prevented Germany from importing saltpetre from Chile, German industry jumped at the chance to fill the gap: BASF boss Carl Bosch and his Bayer counterpart Carl Duisberg gave the Supreme Command the 'Saltpetre Promise'. In return for the commitment to further develop the Haber-Bosch Process, which offered an alternative method of large-scale nitric acid production, BASF received generous subsidies, purchase guarantees and interest-free loans.
2. The Flick party sponsoring affair was one of the largest corruption scandals of post-World War II Germany.
3. See https://www.presseportal.de/pm/6570/654117
4. See www.german-foreign-policy.com/news/detail/1219/.
5. See Rohstoffsicherheit. Herausforderung für die Entwicklungspolitik, www.kas.de/wf/de/33.12174/.
6. See *Deutschlands Beteiligung am weltweiten Krieg um Ressourcen*, 16 January 2007, www.ippnw.de/frieden/energie-krieg-frieden/artikel/de/deutschlands-beteiligung-am-weltweit.html.
7. *Bundesregierung bringt neue Rohstoffstrategie auf den Weg*, 20 October 2010, https://www.pressebox.de/pressemitteilung/bundesministerium-fuer-wirtschaft-und-technologie-bmwi/Bundesregierung-bringt-neue-Rohstoffstrategie-auf-den-Weg/boxid/382841
8. Ibid.
9. BMWi, *Rohstoffpolitik*, www.bmwi.de/Redaktion/DE/Artikel/Industrie/rohstoffpolitik.html.
10. Ibid.
11. *Rohstoffe Subsahara*, p 6, https://www.bgr.bund.de/DERA/DE/Downloads/rohstoffstudie-subsahara.pdf
12. Answer by the Federal Government to a minor inquiry posed by Bündnis 90/Die Grünen, Drucksache 17/13434, 10 May 2013, p. 5, http://dip21.bundestag.de/dip21/btd/17/134/1713434.pdf
13. See www.bit.ly/2CkZK5L.
14. See *Dokumentation Nationaler Aktionsplan Wirtschaft und Menschenrechte*, 3 November 2015, www.auswaertiges-amt.de/blob/273846/65c4e91657273906cba5c7b6348e6d6f/expertenanhoerung8-data.pdf.
15. Ibid.
16. The European Chemicals Regulation REACH is a directive that governs the assessment of health hazards linked to chemicals.
17. See ipa-news.com.
18. *BASF: Regeln für die politische Interessenvertretung*, www.on.basf.com/2CntoYj.
19. InfluenceMap, *Corporate Carbon Policy Footprint*, www.influencemap.org/score/BASF-Q11-D6.
20. Ibid.
21. Approving the GM potato: Conflicts of interest, flawed science and fierce lobbying, 7 November 2011, www.bit.ly/2EzFi7d.
22. Commission Decision of 2 March 2010 authorising the placing on the market of feed produced from the genetically modified potato, document 32010D0136.
23. Joint youth organisation of CDU and CSU, two German political parties.
24. See www.lobbypedia.de/wiki/Das_Collegium.

References

BASF (2017) Annual Report, www.basf.com/documents/corp/en/about-us/publications/reports/2017/BASF_Report_2016.pdf

BMZ (2010) *Entwicklungspolitisches Strategiepapier Extraktive Rohstoffe*, Berlin www.bmz.de/de/mediathek/publikationen/archiv/reihen/strategiepapiere/Strategiepapier299_04_2010.pdf

Borkin, J. (1979) *Die unheilige Allianz der IG Farben. Eine Interessengemeinschaft im Dritten Reich*, Campus, Frankfurt am Main

Bundesministerium der Verteidigung (2016) *Weißbuch 2016. Zur Sicherheitspolitik und zur Zukunft der Bundeswehr*, Berlin

Gattineau, H., Eidesstattliche Erklärung, 13 March 1947, NI-4833, Archive of the Fritz Bauer Institute, Nuremberg follow-up case, Case VI, Prosecution Exhibits, reel 016, pp. 227–232

Greiner, B. (1995) *Die Morgenthau-Legende. Zur Geschichte eines umstrittenen Plans*, Hamburg.

Handelsblatt, 18 February 2013, Expedition ins Erdreich: Deutschlands neuer Kurs

Handelsblatt, 18 July 2017, Wirtschaftslenker würdigen Helmut Kohl

Junge Welt, 26 June 2017, Otto Köhler: Gestatten Sie, dass ich stehen bleibe

Leif, T. and R. Speth (eds.) (2003) *Klaus Escher: Die Stille Macht. Lobbyismus in Deutschland*, Wiesbaden

Monitor, 3 April 2008, Heimliche Interessensvertreter: Lobbyisten in Bundesministerien. www.meinepolitik.de/wdrmonit.pdf

Neues Deutschland, 26 August 1995, Die Biedenkopf-Flick-Aktion

Rügemer, W. (2017) Nichts zu danken: Helmut Kohl war nicht nur zufällig korrupt, 18 June, www.arbeitsunrecht.de/nichts-zu-danken-helmut-kohl-war-nicht-nur-zufaellig-korrupt

Schneckenburger, A. (1988) Die Geschichte des IG-Farben-Konzerns. Bedeutung und Rolle eines Großunternehmens, cited in Coordination gegen BAYER-Gefahren et al. (eds.) (2015) *IG Farben. Von Anilin bis Zwangsarbeit. Zur Geschichte von BASF, Bayer, Hoechst und anderen deutschen Chemiekonzernen*, Stuttgart

taz, 12 September 2017, Apple gegen ExxonMobil, www.taz.de/!5443530/

Vanek, M. (2017) *SA's revised Mining Charter is 'the last nail in the coffin'*, Chamber of Mines, 15 June, www.cnbcafrica.com/news/southern-africa/2017/06/15/chamber-mines-seek-legal-opinion-mining-charter/

VENRO et al. (2017) *Kein Mut zu mehr Verbindlichkeit. Kommentar deutscher Nichtregierungsorganisationen zum Nationalen Aktionsplan Wirtschaft und Menschenrechte der Bundesregierung*, updated edition, 6 February,germanwatch.org/de/download/17288.pdf

Wahlers, G. (ed.) (2013) *Deutsche Wirtschaftsinteressen und afrikanische Rohstoffe. Nachhaltigkeit und Transparenz in der globalisierten Welt*, Konrad-Adenauer-Stiftung, Berlin

▲ View from the headquarters of Rosa Luxemburg Stiftung looking onto one of BASF's Berlin offices. In the background, the building of the insurer Allianz, which is also one of the companies on the DAX 30 Index. In the foreground Berghain, one of the most famous techno clubs in the world.

16. CORPORATE STRUCTURES AND TAX AVOIDANCE BY BASF:
THE PLATINUM PERSPECTIVE

Christoph Trautvetter
Translated by Simon Phillips

Multinational corporations can use different forms of internal transfer pricing […] to make adjustments […] to their subsidiaries' stated earnings […]. Their principal motive is to hide information about where profits are being made and to balance out their losses – largely in order to pay less tax.
– Ernst Piehl[1]

BASF is one of the largest chemical companies in the world and has annual revenues of 60 billion euro. The corporation makes just under 5.3 billion euro in profit and pays out approximately 1.1 billion euro in taxes[2] and 2.6 billion euro in dividends.[3] This makes BASF one of Germany's and the world's largest taxpayers and most profitable companies. A share price increase of 7,000 euro, plus dividends worth 2,500 euro, means that anyone who bought 100 shares from BASF 10 years ago (when they were valued at around 2,000 euro) would now make a profit of 9,500 euro.[4] In contrast, subcontracted miners in South Africa earned a daily wage of between 13 and 14 euro[5] – they would have to work for almost three years (nearly 700 days) to earn 9,500 euro. A study commissioned by the Greens–European Free Alliance in the European Parliament shows that BASF used tax loopholes to save approximately 923 million euro during the five-year period between 2010 and 2014; this amounts to just under 200 million euro in taxes every year. The loopholes the corporation employs are clear from its publicly available financial statements.

BASF has 359 production sites in over 80 countries and 114,000 employees. Its publicly listed parent company, BASF SE, with its headquarters in Ludwigshafen in Germany, owns just under 600 companies throughout the world. South Africa is both a production site and a major source of the platinum used in the catalysts the corporation produces. BASF has nine subsidiaries and associates in South Africa, four of which are listed in its consolidated financial statements. Catalyst production is part of the company's largest business segment ('functional materials and solutions', amounting to 33 per cent) and accounts for approximately one-tenth of the corporation's annual revenues (6 billion euro). The company buys platinum valued at about one-tenth of this price (600 million euro). BASF's UK subsidiary, BASF Metals Limited, which manages BASF's platinum trading, is one of the largest platinum traders on the London Metal Exchange.

BASF's tax and corporate structure: What we know, what we think, and what we can only guess

Every year, BASF publishes countless reports describing its economic situation; some are aimed at investors, others are provided to the tax authorities. The most important report for investors is the Financial Statements and Management Report published by the corporation's parent company, BASF SE. This report sets out the corporation's consolidated financial statement and its profits, which also determine the dividends that are paid out to shareholders, and, once BASF has offset internal transactions with its subsidiaries, the corporation's tax liability. The consolidated financial statement also lists BASF's 294 major subsidiaries and associates. In addition to its annual report, BASF prepares reports for its individual subsidiaries, some of which are publicly available (for example, those published in the Netherlands, Belgium, the UK and Germany) whereas others (such as those from South Africa and Switzerland) are not. Sometimes, these reports enable conclusions to be drawn about the business relations that BASF has with its individual subsidiaries. However, even if the corporation were to publish all of these reports, the figures they provide would not be directly comparable with those set out in the financial statements as various adjustments are made for consolidation. BASF files separate tax returns for its subsidiaries in each of the countries in which they operate. The regulations that apply in each case, such as when profits have to be posted, the expenses that are deductible and the way in which investments are valued, differ from country to country and thus also from the regulations that apply to the BASF's consolidated financial statement. Combined with the fact that tax disputes may take many years to resolve and because tax returns may face future legal challenges, these issues mean that the figures provided by BASF in its publicly available financial statements are of limited value. Importantly, tax returns almost always remain confidential.

Where BASF earns its money

According to BASF's 2016 annual report, almost 50 per cent of its 114,000 members of staff are employed in Germany. Despite this, the companies that BASF has registered in Germany generated a 'mere' 30 per cent of its sales and 25 per cent of its operating profits; sales to German customers constituted 'just' 13 per cent of total sales. At first glance, this probably means that German employees, in particular the 35,000 employees at its corporate headquarters, take on tasks such as administration or research for subsidiaries located in other countries and that German subsidiaries export their products abroad. The regulations on segment reporting mean that – apart from the details that it provides in its annual report – BASF does not have to publish any further information about its staff, the breakdown of its revenues or the profits it makes throughout the world.

If the figures that BASF posts on sales are compared with the profits it reports from the various regions in which it operates, the rest of Europe appears to be highly profitable, particularly when compared with Germany and North America. In fact, the figures seem to suggest that although BASF only generated 17 per cent of its revenues in the rest of Europe, these locations were responsible for 33 per cent of its operating profits. Moreover, as only 15 per cent of BASF's employees work in the rest of Europe, these figures imply that the company's staff there are far more productive than those in Germany and North America. However, this situation could also be due to various operational differences – for example, if the oil and gas business were to be stronger in some regions than in others (80 per cent of the company's revenue in this sector is generated in Europe) or if it employs a different relation between revenue and profit than its other fields of business. However, it could also be caused by profit shifting.

Figure 1: Revenue and profits by region (BASF Report, 2016: 91)

BASF can use internal transactions and the transfer prices it sets to shift both its revenue and the profits it makes from one country to another – preferably, of course, to a country where it is taxed as low as possible. When a BASF subsidiary in the Netherlands, for example, provides a credit to a subsidiary in the US, it can charge interest on the loan. This interest is then deducted from any profit made by the US subsidiary and added to that made by the Dutch subsidiary. (Figure 4 provides further examples of how such internal transactions work.)[6]

Although the table does not provide any separate data for BASF's South African subsidiaries, these are probably not particularly significant. Unlike Germany, the South American, African and Middle Eastern regions generate more revenue from local customers than can be accounted for by BASF's subsidiaries in these regions. On the one hand, this could just mean that they import more than they export. However, it could also mean that BASF is transferring goods between its subsidiaries or internally charging them for services, trademarks and other intangible assets.

Regions (million euro)

	Sales by location of company			Sales by location of customer			Income from operations by location of company		
	2016	2015	Change in %	2016	2015	Change in %	2016	2015	Change in %
Europe (excl. Germany)	27.221	38.675	(30)	26.039	36.897	(29)	3.632	4.174	(13)
Germany	17.540	28.229	(38)	7.412	13.483	(45)	1.582	2.303	(31)
North America	14.682	15.665	(6)	14.042	15.390	(9)	1.113	1.295	(14)
Asia Pacific	11.512	11.712	(2)	12.165	12.334	(1)	1.098	445	(147)
South America, Africa, Middle East	4.135	4.397	(6)	5.304	5.828	(9)	438	334	(29)
	57.550	70.449	(18)	57.550	70.449	(18)	6.275	6.248	0

Figure 2: Profits and revenue according to the subsidiary's or customer's location (BASF Report, 2016: 90)

Where BASF pays its taxes

Like all companies, BASF has to pay taxes in the country in which its economic activities take place. Therefore, it has to pay property taxes where it owns factories, payroll taxes where it employs people and sales taxes either in the country in which it sells a product or where its consumers are located. Importantly, the corporation only partially discloses information about these taxes in its annual report.[7] Instead, the report – as well as the international debate on profit shifting – focuses on income tax; in Germany this applies to business and corporation tax. According to BASF's 2016 report, the corporation's tax bill amounted to 1.654 billion euro. After deducting deferred taxes and taxes due at a future date (mainly due to pension provisions), in 2016 BASF was required to pay 1.140 billion euro in taxes (21.1 per cent of its profits). About one-third of its tax liability was payable to Germany (589 million euro) with two-thirds going to other countries (1.184 billion euro).

As the corporation does not provide a more detailed breakdown of its tax liability, the details of the way in which its taxes are distributed between Germany and other countries are of limited significance. However, if its extraordinary expenditure (deductions, interest) is distributed evenly across the regions, the company paid a tax rate of 29.8 per cent in Germany and 20.2 per cent in the other countries in which it operates.

Million Euro	2016	2015
Current tax expense	1.654	1.610
Corporate income tax, solidarity surcharge and trade taxes (Germany)	598	514
Foreign income tax	1.184	1.231
Taxes for prior years	(119)	(135)
Deferred tax expense (+) / income (-)	(514)	(363)
From changes in temporary differences	(473)	(314)
From changes in tax loss carryforwards / unused tax credits	(43)	(59)
From changes in the tax rate	(6)	7
From valuation allowances on deferred tax assets	8	3
Income taxes	1.140	1.247
Other taxes as well as sales and consumption taxes	272	302
Tax expense	1.412	1.549

Figure 3: Tax expenditure (BASF Report, 2016, Appendix, n.11)

How BASF reduces its tax liability

'BASF attaches great importance to strict compliance with tax laws throughout the world [...]. Taxes are a cost factor and have an impact on business decisions. In the interests of its shareholders, BASF seeks to reduce this cost within the framework offered by current tax legislation.'[8]

According to *Toxic Tax Deals*, a report drawn up by the Greens–European Free Alliance in the European Parliament, BASF managed to save at least 923 million euro in taxes between 2010 and 2014. This amounts to 10 per cent of the corporation's total tax liability during this period. The report demonstrates that BASF used a variety of mechanisms and country-specific tax laws to reduce the tax it was required to pay, and that these schemes generally involve profits being shifted from high-tax countries (such as France and the US) to low-tax countries or those with special rules for foreign profits (such as Switzerland and Puerto Rico). This is often done by charging subsidiaries in low-tax intermediates (the Netherlands, Belgium or Malta) for services, such as loans, the use of patents or trademark rights and administrative services. The taxes that this enables BASF to avoid can then either be reinvested or paid out as dividends.

Path of transaction	Type of transaction	Savings (in million euro)[9]
from France	A subsidiary producing in France makes very little profit (0.41% of its revenues).	37.7
to Puerto Rico	Thanks to various exemptions, BASF effectively pays just 2.4% tax on profits in Puerto Rico.	163.3
to Switzerland	Profits in the Zurich office of BASF Agro BV (the Netherlands) and other subsidiaries in Zug (Switzerland) benefit from lower foreign tax rates (of between 5% and 8%).	255.2
via the Netherlands	BASF's Dutch holding company receives almost 6 billion euro in tax-free dividends from its foreign subsidiaries. If this money had been transferred to Germany, it would have faced a minimum 5% tax rate.	73.3
	A Belgian subsidiary provides a loan to a subsidiary in the US. In the US, interest payments for 'hybrid loans' are tax-deductible; they are then converted into tax-free dividends in the Netherlands.	177.9
	The tax rate on research expenditure and patents is only 5% instead of the usual 25%.	72.1
	Profit reduction due to write-down on investments in subsidiaries of 288.5 million euro.	
via Belgium	Income of 618 million euro in corporate loans of 15.39 billion euro is almost tax-free in Belgium thanks to a special rule.	202
	An agreement existed with the Belgian tax authorities on surplus profits. The European Commission has since deemed this agreement to be illegal state aid.	46
via Malta	A tax rebate is provided to a Malta-based German company for income as interest.	?
Total		923 million euro

Figure 4: An overview of the tax loopholes used by BASF and documented by *Toxic Tax Deals*

In most cases, the tax savings listed in the report are based on a comparison of the average BASF tax rate paid in the years concerned (26.5 %) and are therefore only approximate.

Toxic Tax Deals uses publicly available data from trade balances (notably from BASF's Dutch subsidiaries) to illustrate a whole range of ways in which BASF could be shifting its profits. These are summarised in Figure 4. The report explains the advantages of using a Dutch holding company by demonstrating how BASF Nederland BV can shift profits around the world. Profit shifting ensures that profits are subject only to marginal levels of taxation, and, if a company's income has been taxed elsewhere, it can be transferred back to the EU almost tax-free. BASF Nederland B.V. has at least 56 direct and indirect subsidiaries in 13 countries around the world, including South Africa and BASF Metals GmbH in Switzerland.

During the five-year period covered by the report, these companies transferred almost 6 billion euro in dividends to the Netherlands. As these dividends – in theory at least – should have been taxed in the country from which they were transferred, they are tax-exempt in the Netherlands. In practice, however, these funds would have either been taxed at a very low tax rate or not at all. If they had been transferred to Germany, a flat-rate tax would have been imposed on at least 5 per cent of the dividends. This clearly demonstrates that BASF can save taxes by transferring its profits to its Dutch subsidiary. Importantly, the company's 2016 consolidated financial statement reports that its subsidiaries made retained profits of just under 9 billion euro – BASF either paid no tax on these profits or will simply reinvest them for an unspecified period. Be this as it may, the lack of data means that it is impossible to determine whether, and the extent to which, this situation came about through profit shifting.

In another example, the report compares the profit margins of three interconnected agrochemical corporations: a subsidiary with three factories in France; a branch of a Dutch subsidiary with a factory in Puerto Rico; and a Dutch management company with 39 employees and its headquarters in Switzerland. Whereas the French subsidiary made a profit of just 0.41 per cent and therefore paid very little tax, BASF's subsidiary in Puerto Rico – a country in which BASF enjoys generous tax exemptions – made 39.9 per cent profit. Furthermore, BASF's subsidiary in Switzerland, which mainly trades with other subsidiaries (including the French subsidiary), still recorded 14.2 per cent profit. It is highly doubtful that these differences are due to Swiss diligence or the country's inspiring alpine panorama, or even the better climate in Puerto Rico. Instead, it is far more likely that these discrepancies are due to internal profit shifting. Until 2017, BASF Metals GmbH, which handles the corporation's platinum trading, was also based in Switzerland, and the corporation's annual report states that it made 25 million euro in profits between 2010 and 2013.[10]

All of the examples and figures presented above are based on publicly available trade balances (and particularly those provided by BASF's Dutch subsidiaries). Unfortunately, this means that they are only rough estimates and based on speculation.

In response to *Toxic Tax Deals*, BASF stated: 'The report appears to be very detailed regarding the alleged structures, but it is not always accurate.' Moreover, BASF stressed 'the sovereignty of individual countries to encourage investment through tax incentives'. Although the company's documented approach uses existing laws and loopholes and interprets them in a specific manner, this need not necessarily imply that BASF's conduct is illegal. The very nature of tax loopholes means that they are neither legal nor illegal until they have been contested by a tax authority and a court has issued a binding judgment about them. Nevertheless, this has already occurred in one of the cases documented by the report: a Belgian law of 2004 that permitted companies to transfer 'excess profits' from foreign companies to Belgium was declared illegal by the European Commission in 2016. However, the European Court of Justice has been dealing with this case since the beginning of 2017 and has yet to make a final judgment.[11] Nevertheless, once it does, BASF's argument that everything is 'completely legal' may be on shaky ground.

Figure 5: The corporate structure of BASF Nederland BV
(Auerbach, *Toxic Tax Deals*:11)

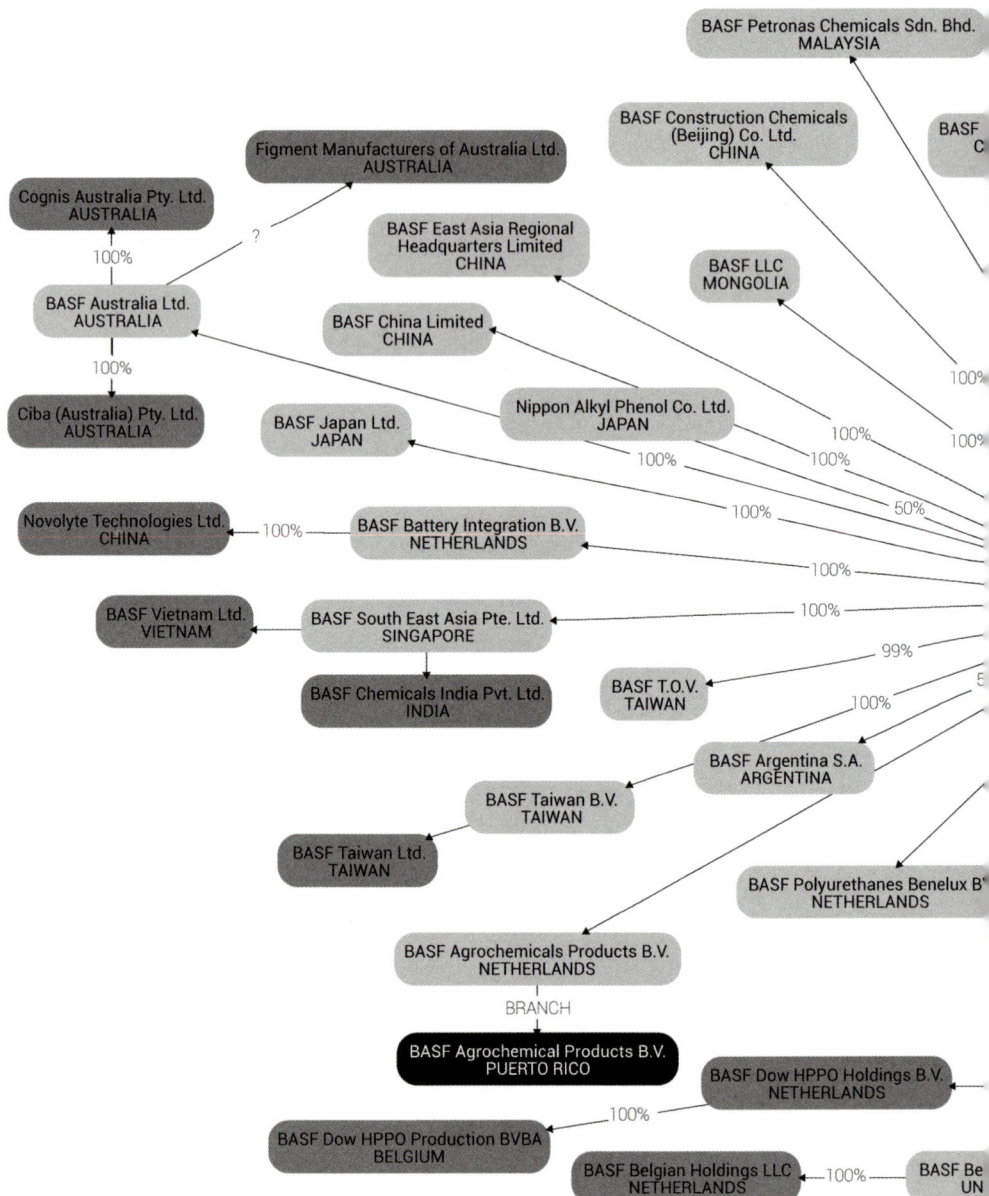

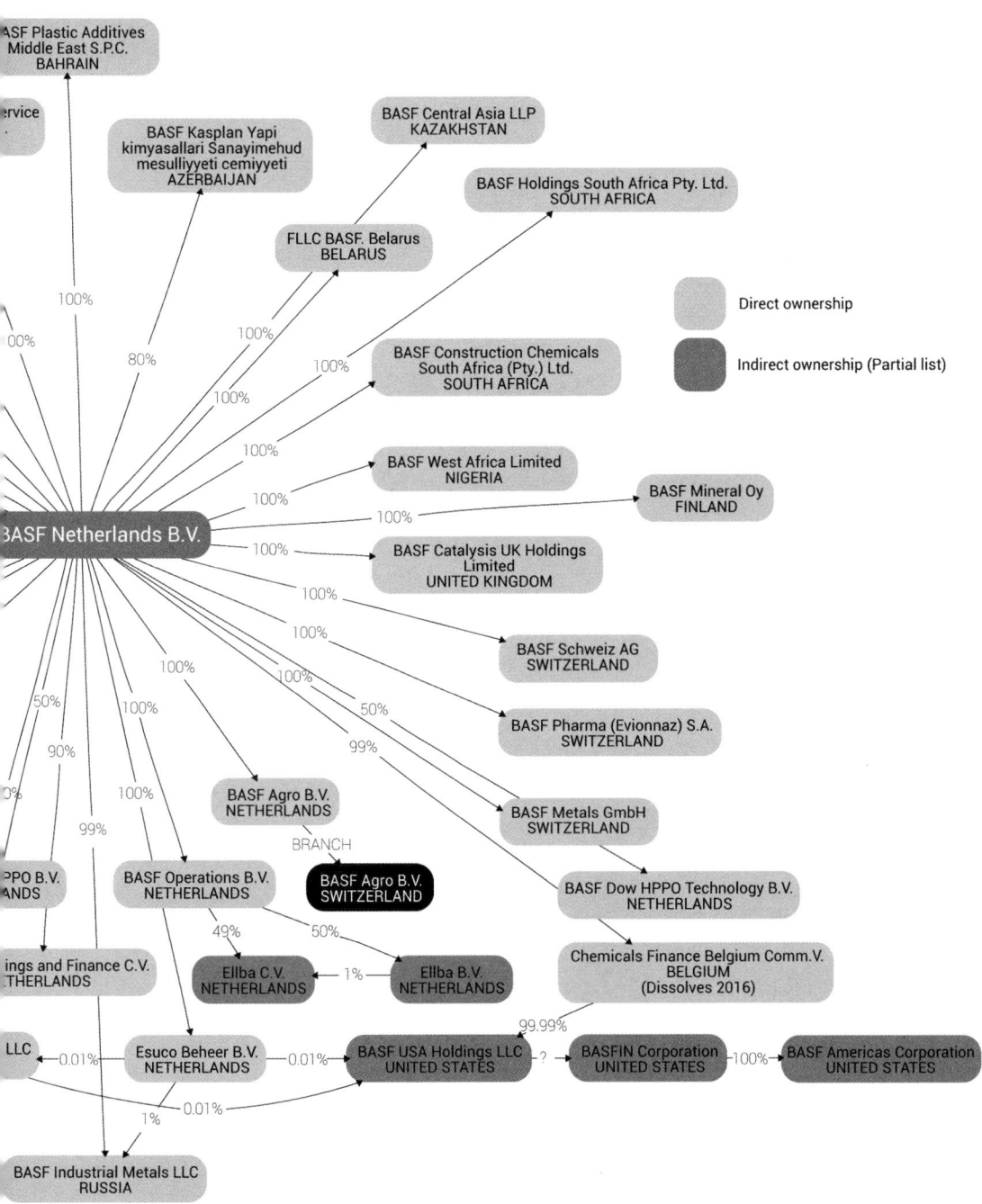

How platinum is exported from South Africa throughout the world

South Africa is the world's largest producer of platinum, the majority of which is used to produce catalysts. In 2016, almost 280 tonnes of platinum were produced worldwide, including 66 tonnes from recycling and 213 tonnes from mining (the majority of which – 70 per cent or 150 tonnes – is mined in South Africa). Nearly half of South Africa's total production (42 per cent or 116 tonnes) was used to produce catalysts with the rest mainly required for jewellery (33 per cent) and other industrial products (24 per cent).[12] The chain between miners in South Africa and car buyers in Germany involves a whole series of actors and mechanisms that ensure that profits are more likely to remain in Germany than South Africa. According to BASF, most of the platinum used for catalysts ends up in Europe.

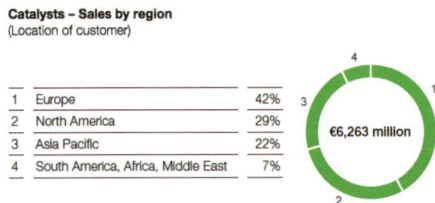

Figure 6: **Revenue from catalysts by region (BASF Report, 2016: 78)**

Most of the platinum in South Africa is mined by a small number of large companies. Lonmin, the owner of the mine in Marikana, owns the third-largest platinum reserves after Amplats and Implats.[13] However, much of its reserves are located in the traditional mining zones close to Rustenburg, where the mines are older, deeper, more labour-intensive and, therefore, more expensive. After several years of very high profits, Lonmin began making losses in 2010 due to the sharp fall in world market prices and the rising costs of wages, security and development. Whereas back in the boom year of 2002, Lonmin's annual report stated that 12 per cent of the company's income was spent on wages, 17 per cent on taxes and 56 per cent went to shareholders. In 2015 80 per cent was spent on wages, 0.3 per cent on taxes while shareholders received no dividends at all.[14] The sharp drop in prices was probably caused by oversupply due to a lack of coordination between producers and the increasing availability of recycled platinum. Recycling chains and dealers also have an impact on price.

Organisations such as Global Financial Integrity (GFI) continue to stress that capital is being illegally shifted from poorer producer countries to richer countries with large international capital markets. GFI argues that companies are declaring the wrong quantities and prices at customs and estimate that this applies to between 4 per cent and 11 per cent of global trade volume;[15] this results in annual losses of up to 20 billion euro. GFI's estimate is based on discrepancies in trade data – in other words, between the levels of exports reported by South Africa and the levels of South African imports declared by the country's trading partners. Moreover, a comparison of data from the UN Comtrade database[16] on platinum demonstrates that both the volume of platinum that is recorded as having been exported and its value are far below the actual volume and the price of what is being imported. The data from Switzerland and Britain are particularly worth emphasising as these countries report that they receive far fewer imports than South Africa states that it exports to them.

	Exports from South Africa (reported by South Africa)		Imports from South Africa (reported by South Africa's trading partners)	
	kg	US$	kg	US$
All	143.229	4.223.830.580,00	197.252	6.203.694.682,00
Switzerland	8.611	265.246.779,00	3.587	114.816.740,00
UK	39.289	1.136.173.743,00	34.685	1.042.879.734,00
Germany	18.655	551.366.123,00	20.777	653.518.556,00
China	5.609	171.325.913,00	44.546	1.449.968.554,00

Figure 7: **Platinum exports from South Africa (data from UN Comtrade)**

Owing to numerous problems with this data,[17] a detailed interpretation is beyond the scope of this chapter.

What role does BASF Metals play?

Although BASF obtains some of its platinum from Lonmin, it provides no information about the exact extent of the companies' business relations. Until 1 September 2017, BASF's platinum trade was conducted by BASF Metals GmbH in Switzerland; it is now the responsibility of BASF Metals Limited in London,[18] a subsidiary of BASF Catalysts UK Holding Limited, which, in turn, is a subsidiary of BASF Nederland BV.

In 2016, BASF Metals Limited had a total of 27 employees trading in precious metals (including platinum) yet made a profit of 24 million euro and paid 4.8 million euro in taxes. BASF Metals Limited is one of the largest platinum traders on the London Metal Exchange (LME) and, together with the three banks Goldman Sachs, HSBC and Standard Bank and, more recently, Johnson Matthey (a further catalyst manufacturer), fixes the price for the physical trading of platinum twice a day.[19] In a 2014 indictment, BASF, among other companies, was accused of price manipulation by a jewellery producer.[20]

Conclusion

A range of additional data would be needed before a conclusion could be made about how BASF distributes its profits from the platinum trade and its subsequent catalyst production throughout the world. The same applies to the distribution of BASF's social insurance contributions in the form of taxes on the huge profits it makes. However, the available data certainly indicate that the corporation's profits from the platinum trade and its taxes are being unfairly distributed.

A number of small changes could be made to improve this situation. The European Union could oblige BASF to disclose the revenues and profits the corporation makes and the taxes it pays in the countries in which it operates. This would make it easier for the public and for tax authorities to assess whether BASF really is involved in profit shifting. Thanks to the OECD 2015 initiative on profit shifting (BEPS) and its implementation via the EU anti-tax avoidance directive,[21] most of the world's major corporations have had to share this data with certain tax authorities since 2016 – this also applies to South Africa. However, this data is still inaccessible to most other tax authorities in Africa and developing countries. This issue could be resolved by publishing country-by-country reports, and this would also increase the pressure on tax authorities to take action. Some companies – including EU banks and mining companies – already have to publish their reports, and a directive adopted by the European Parliament in 2017 aims to extend this obligation to all companies with revenues of more than 750 million euro.[22]

South Africa could ensure that companies operating in its territory publish their accounts in the country, and could also strengthen tax and customs controls while continuing to work for a full-fledged UN committee on taxation.[23] Furthermore, South Africa has yet to join the global Extractive Industries Transparency Initiative (EITI) (see the chapter by Michael Reckordt) doing so would provide more transparency in the mining sector.

Finally, BASF could end the lobbying it undertakes against existing tax legislation and, instead, call for improvements to be made to corporate taxation, such as by supporting the EU's proposed common consolidated corporate tax base. Finally, there are no legal frameworks that prevent BASF from providing increased transparency in its annual reports and opting for a more serious level of corporate responsibility. This also applies to its supply chain, its many public statements and the measures it already implements.

Notes and references

1. Piel, E. (1974) *Multinationale Konzerne und internationale Gewerkschaftsbewegung*, Schriftenreihe der Otto-Brenner-Stiftung, vol. 2, Frankfurt/Main p. 48.
2. Taxes payable in 2016, excluding deferred taxes (100 million euro) and deferred tax income (514 million euro).
3. BASF's shares are mainly owned by German private investors (29%) and German institutional investors such as banks and funds (11%) as well as institutional investors from the US (18%), Britain and Ireland (11%) and the rest of Europe (17%).
4. www.finanzen.net/dividende/BASF
5. According to Lonmin's 2016 annual report, permanent underground workers earn between 20 and 22 euro whereas subcontractors (and their number is increasing) earn between 13 and 14 euro. See p. 312 (for payslips from a temporary worker at Lonmin from February 2016).
6. International regulations do not specifically stipulate how revenues and profits should be delineated. BASF initially used operating profit excluding special items until its second quarter and has since switched to earnings after special items (but before taxes and interest). However, this does not constitute a particularly large overall change. Figure 1 is also available as an Excel table from www.bericht.basf.com/2016/de/konzernlagebericht/regionenbericht.html.
7. 109 million euro for property taxes and 163 million euro for sales, consumption and other taxes.
8. BASF's response to Marc Auerbach, *Toxic Tax Deals: When BASF's Tax Structure Is More about Style than Substance* (The Greens–EFA Group, 2016), www.greens-efa.eu/legacy/fileadmin/dam/Documents/Studies/Taxation/ToxicTaxDealsVF2.pdf
9. In most cases, the tax savings listed in the report are based on a comparison of the average BASF tax rate paid in the years concerned (26.5%) and are therefore only approximate.
10. Since 2014, BASF no longer publishes the profits made by its individual subsidiaries as part of its consolidated financial statement.
11. See http://curia.europa.eu/juris/ case Celio International v Commission can be found by searching for case number T-832/16
12. See www.platinuminvestment.com/supply-and-demand/platinum-quarterly/.
13. See www.fes-southafrica.org/fileadmin/user_upload/documents/SWOP_BREAKFAST_PAPERS_2.pdf, p.10.
14. BASF Report 2016, p. 35.
15. See, for example, www.gfintegrity.org/report/illicit-financial-flows-to-and-from-developing-countries-2005-2014/.
16. See www.comtrade.un.org/data. Data refer to product codes 711011 (platinum, unwrought or in powder form) and 711019 (platinum, semi-manufactured).
17. For an overview, see www.cgdev.org/sites/default/files/trade-misinvoicing-developing-countries.pdf/.
18. BASF Media Release, 19 October 2016, www.basf.com/documents/ch/20161019-BASFMetals-PI-DE-final.pdf
19. www.lme.com/metals/precious-metals/platinum/.
20. Case reference: 1:14-cv-09391-GHW, www.law360.com/cases/547e094848511a63b6000003
21. Directive 2016/1164 of 12 July 2016, www.eur-lex.europa.eu/legal-content/EN/TXT/PDF/?uri=CELEX:32016L1164&from=EN.
22. Co-decision procedure COD 2016/0107: https://eur-lex.europa.eu/legal-content/EN/TXT/PDF/?uri=CELEX:52016PC0198&from=EN
23. See www.un.org/esa/ffd/wp-content/uploads/2017/04/ICTM2017_Presentation_SouthAfrica.pdf.

▶ Pay slip of a worker from October 2016 who is employed indirectly by Lonmin via a temporary employment agency. The wage amounts to the equivalent of approx. 220 euro; health and pension insurance as well as social benefits are not included. For a long time, workers, trade unions, scientists and activists have argued that temporary workers do the same work as Lonmin employees but receive less than half of the regular wage.

▶ **pp. 310/311** Some members of the German activist-artist collective Schwabinggrad Ballett at the Solidarity Without Borders demonstration against the G20 Summit in Hamburg on 8 July 2017.

COMPANY NAME		PERIOD	DATE
PHAKWE MINING SERVICES (PTY) LTD		8	31/10/2016
EMPLOYEE CODE	EMPLOYEE NAME		COST CENTRE
	M B W SITHOLE		NEWMAN SHAFT

EMPLOYEE CODE		EMPLOYEE NAME	M B W SITHOLE	COST CENTRE	NEWMAN SHAFT	
DESIGNATION		MINER ASSISTANT			PERIOD	8
COMPANY NAME		PHAKWE MINING SERVICES (PTY) LTD			DATE	31/10/2016
POSTNET SUITE 383						
PRIVATE BAG X82245				0300	RATE	24.92
RUSTENBURG						

INCOME

DESCRIPTION	QUANTITY	RATE	AMOUNT
Hourly Wage	192.00	24.92	4,784.64
Bonus			354.78
Living Out Allowance			950.40

GROSS EARNINGS   6,089.82

BENEFITS   **COMPANY CONTRIBUTIONS**

DEDUCTIONS

DESCRIPTION	BALANCE	AMOUNT
Query Already Paid	0.00	354.78
AMCU	0.00	47.85
UIF Contribution	0.00	51.39

TOTAL DEDUCTIONS   454.02

LEAVE DAYS DUE	3.50	NETT PAY	5,635.80
3699 Gross Remuneration	4103 Total Employee's Tax	4005 Medical Aid Contributions	4001 Pension Fund - Current
31,147.42	0.00	0.00	0.00

17. FROM BASF TO VOLKSWAGEN AND THE WORLD BANK: GERMAN FINGERPRINTS AT THE SCENE OF LONMIN'S MARIKANA MASSACRE

Patrick Bond

In December 2017, London and Johannesburg investors witnessed what seems to be the death of Lonmin, a firm born as the London and Rhodesian Mining and Land Company Limited in 1909 (Bond, 2017). One reason for the company's death was the backlash against the Marikana massacre. Lonmin's 16 August 2012 massacre of 34 workers and a variety of other crimes it has committed against communities, workers and the environment should be seen within the context and logic of world capitalism, especially where linkages to firms like BASF, and subsequently to Volkswagen and other automobile manufacturers,[1] and to the World Bank, implicate Germany.

If the bigger picture is considered, this will not be merely a case study of inadequate corporate social responsibility – a black sheep in the otherwise supposedly exemplary mining industry – but an incident that unveils many relationships that would otherwise be pushed into the background. Without addressing the larger connections between Lonmin and the metabolism of profit, leading to two major German firms – BASF and Volkswagen – and at least one agency of international neoliberal power, the World Bank, even a partial fix for the problems at Marikana is unlikely, as unfortunately has been proven to be the case.

It is tempting to begin with the highest-profile individual – Cyril Ramaphosa – who still receives blame for the massacre. Incriminating email evidence shows that the day before, as the main local owner of Lonmin, Ramaphosa repeatedly insisted that the police move in for 'concomitant action' against 'dastardly criminals' who were engaged in a wildcat strike. Only around five years later did Ramaphosa apologise for the choice of words in his email. He certainly would not have wanted a massacre, as subsequently unfolded a day later. Yet testimony by police underlings to the Farlam Commission indicates in no uncertain terms that as they surrounded the mineworkers in Marikana gathering on the hill the day after Ramaphosa's emails, they interpreted their duty as, suddenly, lethal.

In his book *How Europe Underdeveloped Africa*, Walter Rodney (1973) used a British multinational corporation (Unilever) to draw the links between North and South. As Rodney explained:

> The question as to who and what is responsible for African underdevelopment can be answered at two levels. Firstly, the answer is that the operation of the imperialist system bears major responsibility for African economic retardation by draining African wealth and by making it impossible to develop more rapidly the resources of the continent. Secondly, one has to deal with those who manipulate the system and those who are either agents or unwitting accomplices of the said system.

But in the subsequent five years, as Ramaphosa rose to the presidency of South Africa in February 2018, a useful myth circulated. Among others (e.g. Everatt, 2018), *New York Times* journalist Norimitsu Onishi (2018) claimed, 'Ramaphosa was accused of using his political influence to press for a police crackdown, though an official inquiry into the massacre eventually absolved him of guilt.' And to be sure, Justice Farlam and his commission (2015:438) indeed concluded, 'There is no basis for the Commission to find even on a *prima facie* basis that Mr Ramaphosa is guilty of the crimes he is alleged to have committed.'

The inability to consider structural processes and corporate privileges – including those 'critical to the operation of the imperialist system', as Rodney put it – behind the Marikana massacre led to some important silences in the Farlam Commission.

Thus, on the one hand, the Farlam Commission could not avoid consideration of the obvious misery that characterised Marikana mineworkers' daily lives. Lonmin 'created an environment which was conducive to the creation of tension, labour unrest, disunity among its employees' (Farlam, 2015:522). It repeated this finding twice more, stressing how Lonmin 'created an environment conducive to the creation of tension and labour unrest by failing to comply with the housing obligations' it was legally committed to within the firm's social and labour plans (SLPs), which were required by the state for it to gain mining rights to South Africa's platinum (Farlam, 2015:557). Lonmin's SLP commitment called for 5,500 houses to be built between 2007 and 2011, at a cost of R665 million (US$106 million at peak rand value in mid-2011, but far less when the rand declined, e.g. to the value of just $37 million at the very lowest point in early 2016). But by the time of the Marikana massacre, Lonmin had only built three show houses and even they were uninhabitable. Lonmin repeatedly violated its SLP even though it openly acknowledged in risk assessments that one result of not building houses could be 'withdrawal of our Mining Licences resulting from failure to deliver commitments made' (Farlam Commission, 2015:534). Drawing out the irresponsibility of Lonmin was one of the merits of the Farlam Commission.

On the other hand, the commission report had telling silences, for it did not even mention the Lonmin board's Transformation Committee, which was responsible for labour and social conditions, including housing. It did not mention that Ramaphosa chaired that committee starting in November 2010, when he could have directed an emergency housing construction programme to make up for lost time. Lonmin's refusal to build the houses was due to a variety of shifting excuses (Amnesty International, 2016). But the firm's most important excuse was also Ramaphosa's own when testifying to the Farlam Commission: a lack of funding within the firm, due to the 2008 world financial meltdown which temporarily reduced demand for platinum. As a 2009 Lonmin report claimed, 'The financial situation of the company impacted by the global economy on the price of platinum resulted in a review of the housing and hostel upgrade programme' (Farlam Commission, 2015:534). The rebuttals are simple:

- First, the construction should have begun in earnest in 2007–8, when the first 2,000 houses were to be built (hence even the Farlam Commission termed this excuse 'irrelevant').
- Second, $148 million in revenues were removed from South Africa to the tax haven of Bermuda in the same period, ostensibly for the purpose of paying a major marketing wing of the firm. In reality there was no such marketing operation, and the Bermuda office had just two employees. Ramaphosa was directly implicated in

the tax-avoidance scandal via his Shanduka firm's control of the Black Empowerment partner Incwala Resources, and according to Lonmin's lawyer, 'Incwala for very many years refused to agree to the new structure' to halt the outflow.[2]
- Third, there were from 2007–11 more than $600 million in profits and dividends repatriated to shareholders of Lonmin and Incwala, so merely redirecting around 15 per cent of that surplus would have provided the housing stock.[3]
- Fourth, Ramaphosa's committee had access to a $100 million World Bank loan that had been pre-authorised well before the meltdown and that stood available for housing construction had Ramaphosa and his Lonmin colleagues so desired.

In testifying to Farlam, Ramaphosa did not mention the role of the World Bank, even though it considered its Marikana community development a success story. Hence when it comes to financing, the links from the police massacre of wildcat striking platinum workers up to the highest levels of global capitalism – especially the tax havens and multilateral lenders which transnational corporations regularly access – were specifically obscured by the Farlam Commission. Likewise, as for the consumption of Lonmin's output, the commission failed to consider a series of upstream purchases of platinum that also deserved consideration. For example, the most important links are to the German firm BASF, which purchased and processed platinum for use by Volkswagen in its diesel engines. Those engines became the source of intense controversy given the firm's subsequent corporate malfeasance in respect of emission controls.

Before we consider solidarity campaigning, the two cases of linkages from Germany to the Marikana massacre deserve more attention: BASF and, concomitantly, Volkswagen buying Lonmin platinum, and Germany's role in the World Bank, which committed serious crimes while earning a share of Lonmin's illegitimate profits. The Bank's prolific contribution to the super-exploitation of Africa deserves comment in this instance, for even the Bank's own researchers acknowledge how much the looting of Africa's minerals by multinational corporations causes its underdevelopment: at least $100 billion annually in natural capital depletion uncompensated by corporate reinvestment (Lange et al., 2018; Bond, 2018). As for Walter Rodney, the story of how 'Europe underdeveloped Africa' can be updated because Lonmin (Britain), BASF and Volkswagen are obviously the core firms involved in this case. To be sure, the story of African underdevelopment has subsequently expanded to include firms not only from the North but more recently also from the Brazil-Russia-India-China-South Africa BRICS bloc (Bond and Garcia, 2015). They may well follow in the footsteps of the once-lucrative – now financially and morally bankrupt – German–British arrangements with Lonmin.

Volkswagen's platinum-demand distortion and Lonmin's demise

The world capitalist system's extraordinary capacity to generate crises helps explain the rise and fall of commodity prices, as witnessed in the 2002–11 'super-cycle' rise in the platinum price from $500/ounce to $2,270/ounce in 2007. But after the crash, the price settled at below $1,000 after 2016. The impact of not only the price crashes but Lonmin's mismanagement was profound, driving the firm's share value from $28.6 billion in 2007 to $383 million when it was purchased by Sibanye-Stillwater in late 2017.

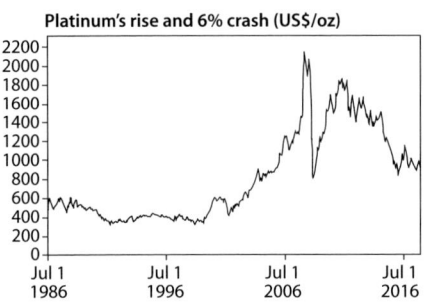
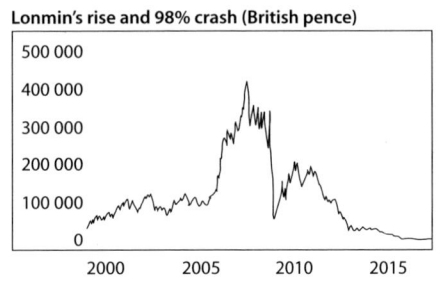

The price declined during 2015 from $1,500 to $900 and subsequently it remained at the latter low level, at which nearly half of South Africa's mines were unprofitable. One reason is that Volkswagen was exposed for its abuse of platinum in diesel engines, which were falsely marketed as having lower emissions than they had in reality. The world's largest car manufacturer was prosecuted and paid more than $15 billion in fines for installing 'defeat device' software in diesel-powered vehicles. The scam allowed 40 times the legal limit of nitrogen oxide emissions, a chemical not only dangerous when generating smog (and asthma) but also as a greenhouse gas, 300 times more damaging than carbon dioxide.

One of the world's leading platinum marketers, Huw Daniel, told *Mining Weekly* in 2017 that one reason vast oversupply of platinum persisted was that 'demand took a knock following vehicle manufacturer Volkswagen's emissions scandal and extensive anti-diesel sentiment, losing market share to palladium'. Of 8.5 million tonnes of demand for platinum in 2016, Daniel noted that 40 per cent was generated in the automotive sector (Solomons, 2017). As the scandal broke, reporter Jo Confino (2015) complained about VW's broader damage 'to the corporate sustainability movement'.

> Volkswagen's actions will fuel the cynics who believe businesses are just paying lip service when it comes to issues like climate change and resource scarcity. [...] What the Volkswagen scandal illustrates is that profit maximisation is so deeply

embedded in corporate culture that when push comes to shove, the vast majority of companies will put the bottom line above any moral case for change and sometimes even cheat to keep the short-term profits coming in (Confino, 2015).

The bottom line for Lonmin should have included longer-term support for emissions cuts, including platinum fuel cells in new automobiles, buses and other vehicles. As one of the competing mining leaders, Royal Bafokeng Platinum CEO Steve Phiri, put it in late 2017, 'Our message to particularly the regulators and government is that you cannot produce 80 per cent of the world's platinum group metals and still be on emission standard euro 2' (Creamer, 2017). He was referring to the terribly low anti-pollution standards that the rest of the minerals-energy complex had compelled the state to adopt over the years.

The crash of Lonmin is terribly important because at the time of writing in early 2018, the platinum market remains glutted. The new owner – the Johannesburg firm Sibanye-Stillwater, led by a corporate manager notorious for squeezing margins to improve profits, Neil Froneman – announced when buying Lonmin in December 2017 that it had one overarching objective in acquiring the firm: its relatively cheaper smelting overcapacity for use by other firms. Closure of Lonmin mine shafts will accelerate so as to save more than $100 million annually by 2020. As a result, 38 per cent of Lonmin's 33,000 employees are due to be retrenched within the next three years, according to Froneman. He also immediately warned critics to cease attacking Lonmin for repeated, ongoing SLP violations: 'Communities that are unhappy, the Department of Mineral Resources that is unhappy – need to stop and allow us to complete this so that in the longer term we can do more.'

This proved an unconvincing plea, judging by the response of the main trade union leader representing Lonmin workers, Joseph Mathunjwa of the Association of Mineworkers and Construction Union (AMCU): 'We are prepared to join forces with communities around Lonmin to ensure that the interests of mineworkers' mine-affected communities are defended. We want to warn the new owners and current shareholders that we will fight and not sit quietly as our members' future is destroyed.'

Banking on Marikana misery

Berlin's influence at the World Bank is considerable, for as one of five top Bank officials, its 'Executive Director represents Germany in meetings at the World Bank and engages in direct consultations and negotiations with other Executive Officers in efforts to gain support for the World Bank's efforts in reducing poverty', according to the Bank (2017) website. Thanks to its citizens' generosity since it joined the Bank in

1952, Germany now holds a 4.31 per cent share ownership, ranking it fourth behind the United States (17.17 per cent), Japan (7.39 per cent) and China (4.76 per cent).[4] German financing of the Bank, though impossible to calculate, is also lucrative to its numerous bondholders. More importantly, as the strongest European Union economy, Germany has oversized influence in the Bank, with Berlin co-serving with Beijing as global neoliberalism's most important capital city, now overtaking Trump-ruled Washington DC and Brexit-sabotaged London. Indeed, the power of Germany over the World Bank was revealed when in late 2016, Berlin's federal development minister Gerd Müller told Bank president Jim Yong Kim to halt any further financing of fossil fuel projects, and within six months Kim then publicly announced this as Bank policy.[5]

Recent Bank directors have included Ursula Müller (2014–17) and, currently, Claus-Michael Happe and Jürgen Zattler. Even though controversies have been raging for several years about Bank profiteering by Lonmin, none of the German directors has made any recorded statement on the scandal. On rare occasions, the German representative to the Bank takes critical stances against projects, e.g. against Newmont Mining in 2006 following lobbying by Bread for the World (Brot für die Welt).

In 2015, the Farlam Commission's failure to fully connect the dots was reflected in how explicitly its leaders and researchers ignored the glaring role of the World Bank. At the same time that Lonmin workers were meant to live in housing that was not even of 19th-century quality, the firm was removing R1.3 billion ($148 million) to Bermuda from 2007 to 2011, ostensibly for marketing expenses (Forslund, 2015). In addition, from 2007–11 Lonmin paid dividends of more than $600 million while ignoring 'its much lesser R655 million legally binding commitments to build social housing for its workers' (Higginbottom, 2017:17). One beneficiary of these profit and dividend outflows was the Bank's private-sector investment arm, the International Finance Corporation (IFC).

From 2007, the IFC had invested $15 million in an equity position in Lonmin, via the Johannesburg Stock Exchange, to support 'the development of a comprehensive, large-scale community and local economic development program'.[6] This stake, along with another $35 million share purchased subsequently, brought with it the IFC's Investment and Advisory (I&A) services, which was meant to support Lonmin's community development strategies. In addition to the $50 million equity investment, World Bank president Robert Zoellick authorised a further loan facility of $100 million, although Lonmin never drew this down. As the well-read business journalist Rob Rose (2007) reported at the time in one of the country's main newspapers:

Lonmin CEO Brad Mills said the plan was to use the [$100 million] cash to create 'thriving communities' around Lonmin's projects so that when the platinum was depleted and the miners left, the communities would be 'comfortably middle-class' and able to support themselves. 'We intend to use 100 per cent of this facility to facilitate partners in our business,' Mills said. Lonmin would use part of the cash to build 5,000 houses in the next five years for community members, with 600 scheduled to be built this year.[7]

From Washington, meanwhile, the IFC regularly bragged about Lonmin's 'developmental success' thanks to the introduction of IFC 'best case' practices, ranging from economic development to racially progressive procurement and community involvement to gender work relations (IFC, 2006, 2010).[8]

Feminist activist Samantha Hargreaves (2013) highlights the general imbalance of power between women and men and reaches back into the migrant labour system itself: 'The Marikana story is about much more than a strike for higher wages, it is also a story about a crisis in social reproduction. State neglect and corporate greed have fomented household crises stretching from the mines back to the sources of migrant labour in far-flung regions and neighbours'.

The Bank was especially delighted with Lonmin's 'gender equity' work (Burger and Sepora, 2009). Moreover, according to its own 2012 *Sustainable Development Report*, Lonmin has established community resettlement policies which comply with the World Bank Operation Directives on Resettlement of Indigenous Peoples and Cultural Property. There were no resettlements of communities and no grievances lodged relating to resettlements. In terms of the Restitution of Land Rights Act 22 of 1994, the company is in the process of addressing several land claims lodged against it before 2011. The resolution of these claims is being managed within the legislative framework of the regional Land Claims Commission and Land Claims Court (Lonmin, 2012).

Mismanagement at Lonmin's Marikana operation was endemic, in spite of IFC marketing propaganda. The church-founded Bench Marks Foundation reported in 2007 (just as the IFC was getting involved) and 2012 (after the main IFC work had been completed) about the ways Lonmin had demonstrably failed in the main areas of corporate social responsibility: job creation and subcontracting (including labour broking); migrant labour, living conditions and the living-out allowance; ineffectual community social investments and lack of meaningful community engagement and participation; and environmental discharges and irresponsible water use, especially in relation to local farming (Bench Marks Foundation, 2007).

The Center for International Environmental Law (CIEL) (2012) argued that the World Bank had ignored critical information before making its Lonmin investments:

Despite attesting to a close working relationship with the South African police force on matters of security, a statement made yesterday [16 August 2012] by

Lonmin chairman Roger Phillimore characterised the violence as 'clearly a public order rather than a labour relations associated matter'. [...] In addition to seeking a full investigation into the violence and what led to it, CIEL has called on World Bank President, Jim Yong Kim, to revisit the Bank's investment in this project in light of recent events, specifically, and its approach to lending in the extractive industries more generally.

Exactly two weeks after the massacre, Kim went to nearby Pretoria and Johannesburg for a visit. Tellingly, he neglected to check on his Lonmin investment in Marikana and instead gave a high-profile endorsement to an IFC deal with a small junk-mail firm (Mailtronic Direct Marketing) that was prospering from state tenders. The other systems of accountability within the Bank were also deficient, as women residents of Marikana would later find. From 2012 to 2013, an investigation by the IFC's independent Compliance Advisor Ombudsman (CAO) took place, in which the CAO (2013) objected to the IFC's evaluation of 'industrial relations and worker security' problems that were apparent over at least 18 months before the August killings. The CAO found the IFC had inadequate monitoring systems at several crucial points:

- the IFC's response to Lonmin's dismissal of 9,000 employees in 2011;
- the limited discussion between the IFC and Lonmin over worker-management relationships;
- the IFC's response to the death of one employee and the assault of five others on their way to work in April 2012; and
- the adequacy of IFC reports after visits to Lonmin, especially since sections of some of the reports seemed to have been copied from previous years (Dasnois, 2014).

However, in the absence of a formal complaint from workers, the CAO dubiously argued that no link could be established between these concerns and the deaths at Marikana, and closed the case in 2014. As Alide Dasnois (2014) remarked:

> Neither the IFC evaluation teams nor the World Bank's own evaluation team, which reported in June 2012, had much to say about employment issues at Lonmin in the run-up to the events in August. After the killings, the IFC team 'noted violence at Lonmin occurring in the context of increasing tensions between rival unions in the mining sector in South Africa, mines being shut down, worker lay-offs and declining workers' bonuses'.

'Stakeholders' emerge from the shacks to attack the Bank

As a result, furious women residents of the Nkaneng shack settlement formed a group, Sikhala Sonke ('We cry together', later the subject of a major film, *Strike a Rock*), aided by leading Johannesburg-based public interest lawyers at the Wits University Centre for Applied Legal Studies (CALS) (Marinovich, 2015). In 2015, they placed a complaint against the IFC with the CAO (CALS, 2017:1), citing:

> [...] an absence of roads, sanitation and proper housing, as well as accessible, potable, and reliable sources of water. Further, the Complainants allege that to the extent the mine offers benefits in the form of employment, less than 8 per cent of employees currently are women. The complainants also allege environmental pollution, specifically relating to air and water. They further allege failure by Lonmin to provide the Nkaneng community with adequate health and educational facilities which were promised at the inception of the project.

Indeed, there were persistent problems with men forcing women mineworkers into unwanted underground sexual relations, and Lonmin was no better than other mining houses in spite of the IFC intervention, according to research by Asanda Benya (2009, 2015). Instead of monitoring community development and gender equity directly, 'the IFC has played the role of an "absentee landlord", relying on the annual reports of the company. The IFC should have been more vigilant around their investment, but at least they have a mechanism to receive complaints,' according to CALS director Bonita Meyerfield (Davis, 2015). The Sikhala Sonke complaint (CALS, 2015: 17) pointed out that even a year before it invested in Lonmin, the IFC itself held a high-minded, self-congratulatory stance on development finance 'performance standards'. IFC statements about gender equity at Marikana have focused upon the rising (albeit still small) share of women in the workplace. IFC mining principal investment officer Robin Weisman claimed Lonmin as a success story in 2017, simply ignoring local women's critiques.

Lonmin's 2008 Sustainability Report noted a substantial decrease in community support. The 2009 and 2010 Sustainability Reports contained no data on community support, likely because it was in free fall. Then in Lonmin's 2011 report, received by the IFC, a 'principal risk' identified within Lonmin's staff and community stakeholder engagement was that 'poor community and employee relations' could result in 'strike action and civil unrest'. In the light of all this information, the IFC ought to have been aware of the significant deterioration of mine-community relations. The IFC ought to have been aware that Lonmin was failing to provide adequate housing, water and sanitation to the local communities and ought to have known that Lonmin was failing to reach its targets for gender mainstreaming in the mine. Even the most basic review would have identified the very serious, detrimental impact of the mine on the local community and the failure of the I&A Project to deliver the benefits it promised.

As for Sikhala Sonke's demands, they were posed in reasonable terms, within the confines of what an international investor in Lonmin should be expected to do, bounded by the constraints of CSR: 'Consequently they urge the CAO to conduct a Compliance Investigation irrespective of the outcome of any Dispute Resolution process' (CALS, 2015:25). That process was adopted with strong endorsement from the CAO, but during 2016 – after three meetings – it broke down:

> In March 2017 the Complainants informed CAO that they were withdrawing from the dialogue process, citing, from their perspective, the lack of progress and failed implementation of undertakings given by Lonmin as part of the dialogue. The Complainants are of the view that none of their grievances have been resolved. Accordingly, the complaint will be transferred to CAO Compliance (CAO, 2017:2).

In all of this oversight, perhaps most important was what did not appear on the agenda: the broader nature of the World Bank's role in financing the underdevelopment of Marikana. Such an agenda would bear in mind the Bank's prolific support for apartheid, its role in introducing and cementing neoliberalism in public policy between 1990 and 1996, its other dubious IFC investments in the post-apartheid economy (including the highly profitable Net1 CPS extraction of funds from the poorest social grant recipients), its largest-ever loan ($3.75 billion) given for the corruption-riddled Medupi power plant, its bizarre research on inequality and various other features of Bank advocacy and investment (Bond, 2014).

Campaigning for justice at Marikana

The struggles for fair wages by AMCU workers and decent living conditions by Sikhala Sonke women activists have been joined by solidarity campaigns, of which the Plough Back the Fruits campaign is exemplary. The Plough Back the Fruits movement consists of the German branches of the Association of Ethical Shareholders, Bread for the World, the Rosa Luxemburg Foundation, KASA (Ecumenical Services on Southern Africa), the Swiss-based KEESA (Swiss Apartheid Debt and Reparations Campaign) and SOLIFONDS. From South Africa, the participants are Bench Marks Foundation, Khulumani Support Group and Widows of Marikana.

BASF resists acknowledging this secondary pressure but in 2017 was finally compelled to admit, 'We note that the development of living conditions for Lonmin workers is not progressing as quickly as one would expect or hope. This is due to the fact that the situation in South Africa is extremely multi-faced and cannot be solved in the short term by one institution alone' (Faku, 2017). Indeed, it must be observed that solutions to these problems have not been found in disparate civil society strategies that followed the Marikana massacre. One strategy was the demand for higher wages, which the workers are gradually winning, though the R12 500/month (in 2017 just $925/month) requested will only be achieved in 2019 when inflation will have eroded that sum by more than a third. Another strategy was community development, advocated most strongly by Sikhala Sonke women who, in part, attacked the World Bank for its failures, followed by further Bapo community grievances.

In future months and years, can these forces – women, mineworkers, the Bapo people, environmentalists – find common cause? As Hargreaves (2013) insists, 'Narrow male-dominated trade union and worker interests mean that hope for a radical resolution lies in the struggles of women in places like Wonderkop. The challenge is linking these with (mainly male) worker struggles and environmentalist solidarity to challenge the extractivist model of development, the social, economic and environmental costs of which are principally borne by working-class and peasant women.'

It may well be, in this context, that both shop-floor and grassroots forces require assistance from institutions with larger agendas, including those challenging the broader economic agenda of transnational corporations. For example, in mid-2015 Lonmin's tax avoidance was raised by AIDC director Brian Ashley (a leading AMCU adviser): 'As the AIDC, we will pursue a campaign for the company's licence to be revoked and for the state owned mining company to take over the company. [...] We need to hold these huge corporations to account. You cannot have a company in a country that needs to be rebuilt sucking the resources dry' (Faku, 2015b).

At the same time, the leftist Economic Freedom Fighters (EFF) party also demanded mine nationalisation and, in the case of the massacre, punishment, including both jail for Lonmin leaders and compensation: 'The EFF will institute a process of reparations against Lonmin to demand reparations and payments of all the families of deceased mineworkers of R10 million ($1.1 million) per family and R5 million ($0.55 million) per injured worker' (Faku, 2015a, 2015b). Even the centre-right Democratic Alliance announced that it also supported forcing Lonmin to compensate massacre victims' families. These are the sorts of demands that should be put to Sibanye-Stillwater.

With Lonmin unable to continue as a growing concern, much bigger questions about political strategy can be raised. To think creatively about the options for Lonmin (via Sibanye-Stillwater) not only requires a revived debate about whether or not to take away the firm's mining licence (as AIDC advocates and as was threatened by the South African government in late 2016) or to nationalise it with – or preferably without (given such immense liabilities) – compensation to traditional overseas owners (as the EFF argues).

If we put aside the particular problems at Marikana, the disastrous recent period of mining capital's over-accumulation and ruinous competition also compels much wider considerations of the need for new priorities that would radically change the corporate financing parameters now in place. These might include:

- developing a world platinum cartel centred in South Africa;
- establishing a genuinely green economic strategy to move the minerals-energy complex away from its traditional roots in coal, iron ore, manganese, gold and diamonds (and not simply to hydrogen fuel cells for individualised electric vehicle production);
- incorporating natural capital accounting into state (and corporate) decision-making so that the true costs and benefits of mining can finally be understood in full cost-accounting terms; and ultimately,
- ensuring a 'just transition' to low-carbon, post-extractivist economic activities that are especially friendly to women's needs, within not just the sphere of production but also the reproduction of society, as the AIDC Million Climate Jobs campaign advocates.[9]

These are the kinds of big-picture strategic questions that can be raised as a result of the injustices that continue at Marikana. For there, we find not the power but also the overlapping, interlocking vulnerabilities associated with Lonmin's historical abuse of people and the planet (and Sibanye's likely amplification of these). The vulnerabilities that even huge mining corporations face have so far generated fragmented campaigns for reform. As the limits of reformist strategies are reached in each of these, it is still possible for much greater unity to be established between disparate groups of mining capital's victims. If these victims soon include investors representing South Africa's large civil service as well as financiers, it will be up to the grassroots, shop-floor and environmental activists to ensure that an even more exploitative regime of extraction in the platinum belt does not emerge in coming years.

Given the German establishment's role along the value chain – from supporting the IFC's private-sector investment regime (no matter how wicked, as in the Lonmin case) to BASF's and Volkswagen's roles in the ups and downs of platinum and their failure to conduct minimal oversight – there may be a vital factor that can shift the balance of forces: international solidarity. For just as Germans came to the anti-apartheid movement to heed the call of Tambo, Mandela and the liberation movements, it will not be long before the contradictions in Marikana again demand a unifying support base. Plough Back the Fruits is one model, and it may be that, once made aware of the crimes to which German financing and shareholding are contributing, there will be new opportunities for even more extensive solidarity. For what is being revealed at Marikana about the way platinum is financed, mined, purchased and remoulded within a system of increasingly brutal, ecologically destructive international capitalism should compel Germans of goodwill to examine the full extent of their own responsibilities – as well as their liberatory potential.

Notes

1. BASF is the world's largest supplier to the automotive industry.
2. This was the third such public incident involving Ramaphosa's dubious international financial relations, for as the Paradise Papers revealed in late 2017, Ramaphosa's firm also retained Mauritius accounts for nefarious purposes. Furthermore, as chair of Africa's largest cellphone operator, MTN, he suffered continent-wide criticism for illicit capital flight.
3. One standard approach would have been to rent the houses for a nominal maintenance fee, thereby ending Lonmin's 'living out allowance', which in turn could even have allowed the housing to remain a company asset. Thus decent housing for workers would have been supplied, even – as Lonmin complained – if the workers lacked sufficient financial capacity of their own, or if they desired the retention of their rural housing as their main priority because they viewed their Marikana migrant labour commute as temporary and thus not meriting a major residential investment in a desolate site whose lifespan was limited in any case by the wasting platinum asset.
4. Similar voting arrangements prevail at the Bank's sister institution, the International Monetary Fund, which was led by Horst Köhler from 2000 until he resigned to take up the German presidency in 2004.
5. The Bank's $3.75 billion loan to Eskom, to finance construction of the fourth-largest coal-fired power plant in the world, remained a source of ongoing embarrassment, even leading to a controversy in early 2018 over Eskom's inability to repay the Bank. That loan, originally made by the widely discredited Bank president Robert Zoellick in 2010, should be considered odious debt and repudiated by a non-corrupted South African government, once one is finally elected (Bond, 2012).
6. It should be pointed out that in making hard-currency (US dollar) investments in Lonmin during the height of the commodity super-cycle (when at peak in 2011, the South African rand was valued at R6.3 to the US dollar), the World Bank perpetuated its dubious record of compelling repayments in hard currency even though soft currencies like the rand devalued radically after the commodity super-cycle ended in 2011, in the South African rand's case to as low as R17.9/$ by early 2016, before stabilising in the R12–R14/$ range in subsequent years.
7. The actual numbers should have been 5,500 and 700 if the SLP had been followed to the letter.
8. The IFC was not the only agency to laud Lonmin's Marikana management. In 2008, the South African commercial bank most actively green-washing its record of minerals and coal investment, Nedbank, awarded Lonmin and the World Bank its top prize in the socio-economic category of the Green Mining Awards (*Daily Business News*, 2008). By 2010, Lonmin's *Sustainable Development Report* was ranked 'excellent' by Ernst and Young.
9. See www.aidc.org.za/programmes/million-climate-jobs-campaign/about/.

References

Amnesty International (2016) *Smoke and Mirrors: Lonmin's Failure to Address Housing Conditions at Marikana*, Johannesburg, www.amnesty.org/en/documents/afr53/4552/2016/en/

Bench Marks Foundation (2007) *The Policy Gap: A Review of the Corporate Social Responsibility Programmes of the Platinum Industry in the North West Province*, Johannesburg

Bond, P. (2012) *Politics of Climate Justice*, University of KwaZulu-Natal Press, Pietermaritzburg

Bond, P. (2014) *Elite Transition*, Pluto Press, London

Bond, P. (2017) In South Africa, Ramaphosa rises as Lonmin expires, *Pambazuka*, 20 December, www.pambazuka.org/democracy-governance/south-africa-ramaphosa-rises-lonmin-expires

Bond, P. (2018) Economic narratives for resisting extractive industries in Africa, forthcoming in *Review of Political Economy*

Bond, P. and A. Garcia (eds.) (2015) *BRICS: An Anti-Capitalist Critique*, Jacana Media, Johannesburg

Burger, A., and B. Sepora (2009) A mine of their own: The women of Lonmin, *World Bank*, http://siteresources.worldbank.org/INTGENDER/Resources/NewsletterPage6.pdf?cid=PREM_GAPNewsEN_A_E

CALS (Centre for Applied Legal Studies) (2015), Complaint by affected community members in relation to the social and environmental impacts of Lonmin PLC's operation in Marikana, Complaint to the International Finance Corporation Compliance Advisor Ombudsman, Washington DC, 15 June, www.caoombudsman.org/cases/document-links/documents/ComplaintbyAffectedCommun-itMembersin

RelationtoSocialandEnvironmentalImpactsofLonmin20150615.pdf
CALS (Centre for Applied Legal Studies) (2017) Social and labour plans, University of the Witwatersrand, Johannesburg, www.wits.ac.za/cals/our-programmes/environmental-justice/social-and-labour-plans/
CIEL (Center for International Environmental Law) (2012) CIEL calls on World Bank to revisit investment in Lonmin, Washington DC, 17 August, https://www.ciel.org/news/ciel-calls-on-world-bank-to-revisit-investment-in-lonmin-operator-of-violence-plagued-south-african-mine/
Confino, J. (2015) After the Volkswagen emissions scandal, why should we trust companies to protect the environment?, *Huffington Post*, 21 September
Creamer, M. (2017) Introduce stringent anti-emission laws – Royal Bafokeng Platinum, *Mining Weekly*, 2 August, http://www.miningweekly.com/article/introduce-stringent-anti-emission-laws-royal-bafokeng-platinum-2017-08-02/rep_id:3650
Dasnois, A. (2014) Lonmin investor rapped over the knuckles, *GroundUp*, 3 December, www.groundup.org.za/article/lonmin-investor-rapped-over-knuckles_2499
Davis, R. (2015) Women of Marikana lodge World Bank complaint against Lonmin, *Daily Maverick*, 30 June
Everatt, D. (2018) South Africans are trying to decode Ramaphosa (and getting it wrong), *The Conversation*, 10 January, https://theconversation.com/south-africans-are-trying-to-decode-ramaphosa-and-getting-it-wrong-89886
Faku, D. (2015a) Lonmin repatriated R400m annually, says AIDC report, *The Mercury*, 3 June
Faku, D. (2015b) Lonmin's licence is under attack: Share slid 13 percent after report, *The Mercury*, 6 July
Faku, D. (2017) BASF in 'threat to walk away from Lonmin', *The Mercury*, 3 November, https://www.iol.co.za/business-report/companies/basf-in-threat-to-walk-away-from-lonmin-11832486
Farlam Commission (2015) *Marikana Commission of Inquiry: Report on Matters of Public, National and International Concern Arising out of the Tragic Incidents at the Lonmin Mine in Marikana, in the North West Province*, Pretoria
Forslund, D. (2015) Briefing on the report 'Profit shifting, inequality and unaffordability at Lonmin 1999–2012', *Review of African Political Economy* 42, 146, pp. 657–665, https://www.tandfonline.com/doi/pdf/10.1080/03056244.2015.1085217
Hargreaves, S. (2013) More misery in Marikana, *Third World Resurgence*, https://www.twn.my/title2/resurgence/2013/271-272/cover08.htm
Higginbottom, A. (2017) The Marikana massacre in South Africa, Unpublished paper, London, Kingston University
IFC (International Finance Corporation) (2006) *Lonmin: Summary of Proposed Investment*, Washington DC, World Bank Group
IFC (International Finance Corporation) (2010) *Strategic Community Investment*, Washington DC, www.scribd.com/document/96448930/IFC-Handbook-Sustainable-Investments-to-Emerging-Market
International Finance Corporation Compliance Advisor Ombudsman (2013) *IFC Investment in Lonmin Platinum Group Metals Project, South Africa*, Washington DC, www.cao-ombudsman.org/cases/document-links/documents/CAO_Appraisal_LONMIN_C-I-R4-Y12-F171.pdf
International Finance Corporation Compliance Advisor Ombudsman (2017) *Dispute Resolution Conclusion Report – Lonmin-02/Marikana*, Washington DC, http://www.cao-ombudsman.org/cases/document-links/documents/Lonmin02DRConclusionReport_May252017.pdf
Lange, G., Q. Wodon and K. Carey (eds.) (2018) *The Changing Wealth of Nations 2018*, Washington DC, World Bank, doi:10.1596/978-1-4648-1046-6
Lonmin (2012) *Sustainable Development Report*, London
Marinovich, G. (2015) How the women of Marikana are taking on the World Bank, *Daily Maverick*, 4 July
Onishi, N. (2018) Meet Cyril Ramaphosa, South Africa's new president and a Mandela favorite, *New York Times*, 15 February, www.nytimes.com/2018/02/15/world/africa/south-africa-cyril-ramaphosa.html
Rodney, W. (1973) *How Europe Underdeveloped Africa*, Bogle-L'Ouverture Publications, Llondon
Rose, R. (2007) World Bank body to put $150M into Lonmin,' *Resource Investor*, 13 March, www.resourceinvestor.com/2007/03/13/world-bank-body-put-150m-lonmin
Solomons, I. (2017) Platinum industry redoubling marketing efforts in the midst of oversupply, *Mining Weekly*, 28 July,http://www.miningweekly.com/print-version/platinum-industry-redoubling-efforts-to-promote-the-metals-uses-2017-07-28
World Bank (2017) *Voting Powers*, www.worldbank.org/en/about/leadership/votingpowers

▶ Proposal for a Transnational Development Plan. Projection onto a company sign of Lonmin in Marikana, 2016.
▶ **pp. 330/331** Marikana cash & carry. Discount store in Marikana, 2013.
▶ **pp. 332/333** Police photo in Germany. Millerntorplatz on 7 July 2017 during a blockade against the G20 summit in Hamburg. Several thousand people tried to hinder the arrival of the heads of state and government and their delegations with blockades all over the city.

TRANSNATIONAL DEVELOPMENT PLAN

LONMIN

We declare our responsibility for the Marikana Massacre and for our active participation in all sorts of other exploitative shit. We apologize! Lonmin's money belongs to all who laboured in the mines. The Bermuda bank accounts will be transferred to the families and friends of the killed mineworkers. Security and police forces will from now on serve as guards in the subterranean "Museum of Capitalist Horror as a Result of the Imperial Colonial Regime" that will be installed in the mine shafts. Instead of wasting our energy

18. IMPERIALIST RAW MATERIALS STRATEGIES IN EU POLITICS

Boniface Mabanza
Translated by Sally McPhail

2017 was declared 'Africa year' in Germany. As part of its G20 presidency, the federal government provided a focus with high media impact and in so doing responded to the challenges which have arisen from the new migration movements. More specifically, three federal ministries worked out different concepts which are in competition with each other.

They bore distinct names: Compact with Africa (Federal Ministry of Finance), Marshall Plan with Africa (Federal Ministry of Economic Cooperation and Development) and Pro! Africa (Federal Ministry of Economics and Technology). In all the diversity of their nuances, each of these three concepts 'discovered' Africa – as did their European counterpart, the Foreign Investment Plan – as a 'continent of the future', a 'continent of opportunities' which called for the mobilisation of private investment.

Old power – new game

As one of the continents with the least amount of raw materials in the world, Europe boasts a high level of raw material consumption (EEAS Strategic Planning, 2003).[1] About three times as many resources are consumed per capita in the countries of the European Union as in Asia and four times as much as in Africa. Most of all, European industry is reliant on raw materials – and on secure and controlled access to them. During the colonial era, direct access was guaranteed, even if the colonial powers were sometimes in competition with each other. The Berlin Conference of 1884–1885 managed these conflicts and legitimised the exploitation of the territories that were reduced to colonies (Buch, 2011:114). 'Colonisation', as the state secretary of the German Reich's Imperial Colonial Office defined it in 1907, 'means the cultivation of the earth, its treasures, the flora, the fauna and above all the people to the benefit of the economy of the colonising nation, and the latter is in exchange obliged to bestow in return its higher culture, its moral concepts, its better methods' (cited in Melber, 1992:91). With the end of colonisation and the formal independence of African states, it became necessary for the industrialised nations to develop mechanisms which, after the loss of direct control of the political sphere, could guarantee continued access to the resources required.

This chapter analyses the continuities of the imperial access to resources and demonstrates that the new battles for access to raw materials reproduce previous colonial patterns. The construction of the 'other' continues till today: as an uncivilised subject reduced to its labour in the colonial era, as an inexperienced and malleable political subject on the way to supposed independence, as a dependent recipient of development aid and as a seemingly equal negotiating partner in international bodies. The narratives are changeable – but the power relationships, political structures and the economic dominance resulting from them have remained shockingly stable. Jointly articulated criticism by African states is slow to take shape. At the 11th Ministerial Conference of the World Trade Organization (WTO) in Buenos Aires in December 2017, the Africa Group acted as one in order to evade the divide-and-rule strategy of the imperial powers. Although the group managed cohesively to formulate their criticism of the architecture of trade, which favours the global North at the expense of the global South, the overcoming of the centuries-old power imbalance nonetheless seems a long way off.

World Bank and IMF Structural Adjustment Programmes

A whole host of African countries strove for economic reforms after gaining political independence; however, their efforts did not go far enough. This was to a certain extent due to the fact that the newly emerging states were not actually released into independence. The mines and plantations formerly owned by the colonial powers were often simply transferred over to private sector actors from the former colonisers. They in turn could not allow the collapse of the existing privileged relationships, because the colonial division of labour had ensured that the manufacturing industries for raw materials came into existence in Europe while the materials themselves could only be found in the colonies.

At the end of the 1970s, Structural Adjustment Programmes (SAPs) were developed by the World Bank and the IMF. They were introduced as 'debt relief programmes' for the countries targeted. In order to be able to receive loans from the World Bank, individually tailored programmes to combat poverty and for economic growth were imposed on these countries, entailing significant interventions in the national budgets and further restrictions on their sovereign rights. In addition to a reduction in subsidies and budgetary discipline, this also included restrictions on foreign currency transactions and the privatisation of public sector companies. Representatives of the World Bank and IMF involved themselves directly in the budgetary reforms related to the SAPs and, through them, regulated not only industry and the financial sector, but also agriculture, health and education. These fiscal and economic political measures, which were effectively forced through by the IMF and World Bank,[2] led to even greater controls over countries than were already exerted through the legacies of the colonial era. This all happened in the spirit of neoliberalism, according to which the creative strength of the market was to be freed from the clutches of state regulation and bureaucratisation. Transnational corporations now found themselves dealing with countries weakened in this way. As part of an unprecedented wave of privatisation in the 1990s, the TNCs were able to secure the most valuable concessions of the resource-rich African countries at absurdly low prices.

The triumphal procession of the neoliberal spirit continued during the first stage of South Africa's political transformation after apartheid was formally overcome. The country considered itself to be under dual pressure: on the one hand, in order to end political apartheid without risking the privileges of the white minority, a compromise had to be negotiated with the National Party regime involving the participation of the most important Western countries. On the other hand, the international financial institutions exerted pressure for liberalisation, in order to once again strengthen their grasp on the South African economy, which had ground to a halt in the last decade of the apartheid regime's self-isolation, and extend their hold from South Africa across the entire continent.

When the 'raw materials boom' started at the turn of the millennium (Rowden, 2016), most African governments were not able to profit all that much, especially as they were forced to compete with one another. The terms which most

African governments had conceded to the transnational corporations were often so exceptionally generous that their own share of the profit was very small. Jörg Goldberg summed up their plight in 2007: 'The African governments [were] shortly before the start of the raw materials boom at the turn of the century in an especially unfavourable negotiating position [...]. The privatisation requirements of the SAPs had brought about the dissipation of state ownership; favourable investment conditions, generous tax regulations and cheap concessions were supposed to attract foreign capital. Foreign investors were frequently conceded long-term tax holidays' (Goldberg, 2007). Many countries accepted the diktat of the international financial institutions, as they expected economic growth and therefore a positive impact on the local employment market and the consolidation of government funding.

However, it became clear that the economic benefit of the structural adjustment programmes in most countries remained modest, while the social situation stagnated at best and the ecological impact was often abysmal. In addition to this, governments were bound to a long list of projects, known to be 'white elephants', in terms of development policy. This included prestigious major projects such as the Inga dam in Congo, which cost a great deal of money and consequently paved the way for worsening debt. The Inga dam was built in west Congo in order to supply the mining region in the south–west with electricity. This required the construction of a high-voltage power line of over 2,000 kilometres, which pushed the costs up even further. Today, Congolese people see the power lines running above their heads, but they themselves have no electricity. Cheaper decentralised solutions using small hydroelectric power plants, which would have been feasible in many places due to the Congo's rich water landscape, were out of the question for the World Bank. The Inga project was a bad investment, at least for the local population. The company which was responsible for the construction of the plant, however, made hefty profits, as did the operating company. This is a recognisable outcome of the funding model of the World Bank and the IMF: the enrichment of private companies and industrialised nations at the expense of the countries in which prestige objects are built. Such dynamics can also be observed in the case of Lonmin in South Africa. Financial cooperation between Lonmin and the International Finance Corporation of the World Bank group[3] was supposed to contribute to improving the living conditions of the Marikana community. To date, there is no visible evidence of this (see the chapter by Patrick Bond).

The rules of the World Trade Organization

From the turn of the millennium, the rapid rise of China and other emerging countries and their increasing demands for agricultural, energy and mineral raw materials increased competition with Western industrialised nations. From the mid-2000s, China not only introduced export restrictions on its own rare earth metals, but secured its own access to other strategically important raw materials, particularly in Africa, in an increasingly proactive way. 'Western powers have for centuries viewed developing countries as suppliers of cheap raw materials. The new factor is, however, the emergence of competitors. During the past decade China, India and other emerging economies have entered traditional European and US preserves and are vying for control over these resources' (Curtis, 2009). In so doing, China employed methods which had to date not been used by the Europeans, such as the exchange of raw materials for infrastructure. On the one hand, this guarantees a return to the raw materials-producing country, while, on the other, this infrastructure (roads, ports and supply of energy) facilitates the extraction and transportation of the raw materials. But the EU regarded these measures as a distortion of competition and as an encroachment on their economic interests. In reaction, the EU Commission developed – at least within the framework of bilateral agreements with individual developing countries – measures such as the Raw Materials Initiative and other tools, which are described below.

First, we should however take a look at the activities of the World Trade Organization, whose multilateral policies are interpreted by the EU in its own favour. Given the increasing scope of influence of 'emerging countries', the industrialised nations are themselves being confronted with growing resistance at WTO level. Consequently, the Doha Round, which began in 2001 in the capital of Qatar and which was due to be completed in 2005, ground to a halt because the industrial nations were not prepared to abolish protectionism and competition-distorting subsidies, in order to protect their own agricultural industries (Tangemann, 2006). At the same time, they demanded from emerging and developing countries the liberalisation of their industries and new trade sectors such as services, public procurement, regulation of investments, trading of data and protection of intellectual property. In the end, negotiations at the 11th Ministerial Conference in Buenos Aires also failed: while the developing countries demanded a conclusion to the Doha Round, the industrialised nations insisted instead upon focusing on new issues such as e-commerce. In terms of protectionism, double standards are clearly applied: if Europe and the US protect the interests of their farmers, the WTO rules are not questioned; however, as soon as China took up similar trade and industrial policy measures after 2008 to promote its industrialisation and to participate in the global value chains, adverse reactions came from Europe and the US, which referred to precisely the same WTO rules which they constantly breach themselves to protect their own farmers.

The World Trade Organization's awareness of the conflicts surrounding these different interpretations is reflected in the 2010 *World Trade Report*. The report deals with the raw materials trade and highlights the different mechanisms of the raw materials markets. The WTO's general secretary at the time, Pascal Lamy, a long-standing advocate of neoliberalism, who wrote the preface, questioned the pure doctrine of international trade theory, according to which free trade always leads to the best result for all countries involved. In order to prevent overexploitation, he called for the strengthening of independent management of raw materials by the developing countries. To this end, according to Lamy, it would be necessary to amend and clarify the WTO's rules for the trade in raw materials. He maintained that conflicts between producer and consumer countries are pre-programmed and, in order to defuse them, more precise rules are required. Lamy argued for a rapid conclusion of the Doha Round so that new challenges and trade conflicts could finally be dealt with under the umbrella of the WTO. But the disagreements within the Doha Round prevented a rapid conclusion – it was only declared a failure in 2016. It was primarily the leading industrialised nations who profited from this by using the existing imbalance of power relations to their advantage. For many of the emerging countries, most of the developing countries and in particular the African states, this meant that they were forced increasingly by the EU into bilateral agreements. Two instruments are particularly worth mentioning here: the EU's Raw Materials Initiative and the Economic Partnership Agreements (EPAs).

The EU's Raw Materials Initiative

The EU's Raw Materials Initiative came into existence at the urging of European corporations and their lobby associations, among them the Federation of German Industries (BDI), which in view of the intensifying competition from emerging countries claimed that the governments of EU member states were not doing enough to secure the supply of raw materials for their own industries. They referred to the need to close this gap with the same commitment as the governments showed in creating outlet markets for European manufactured goods. As Dieter Ameling, president of the German Steel Federation, stated at the Federation of German Industries' first raw materials congress in March 2005: 'In the past, politics did not take sufficient account of the key significance of the supply of raw materials. [...] We in Germany can only remain export world champions if the companies receive free and fair access to the international raw materials markets' (Ameling, 2005).

Whatever Ameling might have understood by 'fair access', it is a fact that the German federal government's raw materials strategy, which was developed in 2010 under the overall control of the Federal Ministry of Economic Cooperation and Development, stresses that 'development aid' also plays a vital role in Germany's raw materials supply: 'Development policy measures by the Federal Government can help to create the policy framework for a pro-investment climate in the partner countries via the establishment of a stable and efficient raw materials sector and competent state players, and German commerce can also benefit from this' (BMWi, 2010:23).

Based on this raw materials strategy of the German government, consultations were held between several EU governments as well as with industrial and lobby associations which resulted in the idea of an EU-wide Raw Materials Initiative. This was introduced by the EU Commission in 2008. It essentially rests on three pillars: the procurement of raw materials from European sources, reducing European consumption of primary raw materials and, above all, securing access to raw materials on the global markets. The last pillar has gained significance because the EU Commission was or became increasingly convinced that neither the mining of raw materials from the limited European sources nor recourse to substitute raw materials nor recycling could guarantee the competitiveness of the EU's industries. In view of the EU's dependence on imports of strategically important raw materials such as the high-tech metals cobalt, platinum and titanium as well as other resources such as wood, chemicals, furs and skins, the focus on the two other thematic pillars of this initiative was somewhat of a red herring.

The EU Commission pointed out 'that the extent of the EU's import dependency on minerals lies between 48 per cent for copper ore, 64 per cent for bauxite and 100 per cent for metals such as cobalt, platinum, titanium and vanadium' (cited in Curtis, 2009:9). The fact that access to strategic raw materials abroad is the core interest of the EU's raw materials policy was once again confirmed in November 2013 by an ad hoc working group (EC, 2013:6). The working group identified 41 minerals and metals which are important to the EU, of which 14 were categorised as critical 'since a high share of world production comes from a small number of countries, mainly China, Russia, the Democratic Republic of Congo (DRC) and Brazil' (cited in Curtis, 2009:9). In view of this, the European Council explicitly called on the Commission and member states to use their aid programmes to secure access to raw materials. The May 2009 Council meeting, for example, concluded that, to promote the 'raw materials diplomacy', the EU should not only raise the issue in all appropriate fora but also 'give adequate consideration to the opportunities provided by projects undertaken in the context of development cooperation', adding that 'the specific situation of poor developing countries has to be taken into consideration' (cited in Curtis, 2009:9).

In addition to the influence exerted through development cooperation, bilateral trade agreements offer the EU the opportunity to nullify two additional significant trade policy instruments of the raw material-producing countries: export taxes and restrictive investment rules. In the view of the EU, the latter distort the international trade in raw materials and consequently are included in a regulated way in the economic partnership agreements (EPAs). The investment rules, like the regulation of competition, services, public sector procurement and protection from intellectual property, form part of the 'rendezvous clause' with individual countries, which lists topics whose negotiation had to be deferred because of the resistance from African countries. Export taxes are already part of the trade agreements which were negotiated as part of the EPAs with different African regions. The following section deals with the problems surrounding export taxes and their inclusion in the EPAs, with a particular focus on the agreement with the SADC region,[4] which provisionally came into effect in October 2016.

Economic Partnership Agreements and export taxes

Even if its humanitarian rhetoric suggests something else, the EU proactively pursues an interest-based policy with the EPAs, which have been under negotiation since 2002. This is articulated in the document 'Global Europe: Competing in the World' (October 2006) by the trade commissioner, Peter Mandelson:

> our prosperity is directly linked to the openness of the markets we try to sell to. [...] Alongside our commitment to the WTO we have, through bilateral negotiations, sought to remove trade barriers behind borders – barriers beyond the reach of WTO rules [...] Building on the WTO, our aim will be to go beyond what can be achieved at the global level by seeking deeper reductions in tariffs; by tackling non-tariff barriers to trade; and by covering issues which are not yet ready for multilateral discussion, such as rules for competition or investment (EC, 2006).

A document of 2015 entitled 'Trade for All' adds:

> In view of the EU's dependence on imported resources, access to energy and raw materials is critical for the EU's competitiveness. Trade agreements can improve access by setting rules on non-discrimination and transit: by tackling local content requirements; by encouraging energy efficiency and trade in renewables; and by ensuring state owned enterprises compete with other companies on a level playing field according to market principles (EC, 2015).

According to Mandelson, the aim of the EU's trade policy was therefore 'an open global market completely free of all distortions on trade in energy and raw materials' (cited in Curtis, 2009:21). In order to emphasise the interdependency between the multilateral (WTO) and bilateral levels (for instance, between the EU and the ACP countries – the African, Caribbean and Pacific group of states) intended by the EU as part of the EPAs, it should be noted that the existing WTO agreements in no way forbid export taxes for raw materials-producing countries:

> Measures which control or limit the export of goods are effectively not at all regulated in the WTO and consequently are not part of the rules for regional trade agreements. Attempts by the EU and other industrialised countries to introduce this aspect into current WTO negotiations have been largely unsuccessful. However, it [the EU] is attempting this via other channels, for example, it made the limitation of export taxes a condition for the Ukraine's entry into the WTO (Reichert et al., 2009).

On the contrary, export duties as instruments of economic policy have proved to be effective incentives for the further processing of raw materials at local level by contributing to the increase in export earnings and adding value through diversification of exports. In this way, the vulnerability of national economies could be reduced (KASA, 2014). Furthermore, export taxes generate government revenue, which can be used for investments in health and education.

At the start of the EPA negotiations, the EU made a radical demand: the ban on all export duties and restrictions immediately following the EPAs enforcement: 'The basic EU position is that export restrictions and taxes must be eliminated. The Commission states that "our aims are generally to secure non-discriminatory access to key inputs for the EU economy" and that "one particular problem" is export duties. It argues that export taxes are counter-productive' (DG Trade Priorities, cited in Curtis, 2009:21).

The EU was able to achieve its original aim of having export duties completely abolished in some cases only. Most agreements have been allowed to maintain existing export duties and the introduction of new ones is subject to conditions. For instance, export taxes are contained in the South African Development Community's EPA agreement, with exceptions that limit their effectiveness to a large degree: they can only be introduced for a maximum of 12 years, are only valid for a maximum of eight products per SADC country and cannot exceed 10 per cent of the value of the raw materials. Furthermore, the SADC countries must exempt exports into the EU from export tax for the first six years; only after the seventh year may export taxes be levied on 50 per cent of the products exported to EU countries. In addition to this, the countries intending to raise export taxes still have to substantiate their effectiveness in increasing government revenues, the protection of new industries or the environment. For this reason, the implementation of even these limited export taxes felt like a victory for many governments of the SADC region, as it was the very export tax conditions negotiated by them that, among other things, served to justify the final signing of the EPAs (ICTSD, 2014).

Beyond pure material interests: Dialectics of the colonised mind

As far as Africa is concerned, an analysis of all EPAs demonstrates that the regions of the continent have to reckon with other negative effects in addition to the subversion of export taxes. These include the threat to spheres of political action, de-industrialisation, loss of government revenue through tariff dismantling, and in a few cases even the threat to food security. The question is why African 'elites' sign such Economic Partnership Agreements at all.

There are several reasons why a number of African governments have signed these agreements after many years of tough negotiations, despite all the disadvantages. One of them has to do with the EU's 'divide-and-rule' negotiating strategy, which is expressed in its market access reforms. Discussed by the EU Commission for the first time in 2011, the Market Access Regulation (MAR) was meant to reform the pre-existing regulation MAR 1528/2007. In this sense, a total of 18 ACP countries would lose their preferential access to the EU market on 1 October 2014, in the event that they had not initiated any steps towards ratification of an interim agreement. This deadline as part of the MAR reform was unilaterally decided by the EU without prior consultation with the African 'negotiating partners' and significantly increased the pressure on the countries concerned. These included the Ivory Coast, Ghana and Cameroon, as well as Botswana and Namibia from the Southern African Development Community (SADC). In particular, the governments of the latter two countries have experienced increasing pressure from certain economic sectors, particularly those involved in export, to sign the agreement. The interests of the export-oriented economic sectors are sharply opposed to those of the domestically oriented small producers. This is a new dynamic which the EU knew how to make skilful use of in the negotiations. In addition, the threat of export-oriented sectors had a direct effect on the self-interest of some African elites. Although European companies dominate the trade in and export of bananas, coffee, tea, cocoa, cut flowers, beans, beef and fish to Europe, African elites have stakes in a number of these companies. The decision to sign the agreements was therefore often made for personal material advantages and at the expense of the long-term interests of their countries.

A good example for this is Black Economic Empowerment (BEE) in South Africa. What has been praised as an instrument for the greater participation of the black majority in the economy, from which black people were excluded during the colonial era, has emerged as an instrument for the co-opting of black elites. From the moment when elites begin to enjoy the privileges of participating in an 'imperial mode of living', they forget their agenda of transformation, with which they formerly mobilised the masses as part of the freedom movement.

A second factor which has impacted on the EPA negotiations is the political change taking place in West Africa. The change of government in the Ivory Coast and Senegal had a direct influence on the negotiations: with Alassane Ouattara, the Ivory Coast gained a head of state who had a long career at the International Monetary Fund (1968–1990) and in his former role as prime minister of the Ivory Coast (1990–1993) expressed his allegiance to neoliberal ideology in a remarkable way. What is even more serious is that he owes his renewed accession to power to a controversial French military intervention in his country. Together with his Senegalese counterpart Macky Sall, whose personal commercial ambitions and activities were as renowned as they were notorious, Ouattara campaigned for the EPAs. In Ghana, too, the approach to the EPAs changed after the sudden death of the President John Atta Mills in July 2012.

Both the MAR reforms and the changes in government in West Africa may also be viewed from a postcolonial perspective. Indeed, it cannot be otherwise explained why the black elites signed agreements such as the EPAs, despite the fact that studies (Kramml et al., 2017) clearly show that their countries have more to lose in the long term than they can gain through trade with the EU, including the trade-related development policies accompanying the EPAs: these measures have assumed the role of the very 'colonial plunder machine' which they aimed to replace after achieving their hard-fought political independence.

Nobel Prize laureate Amartya Sen describes this phenomenon as part of the 'dialectics of the colonised mind', which finds expression in a kind of 'obsession with the West'. He says that this obsession can cover a wide spectrum: from 'slavish imitation through to categorical enmity' (Sen, 2007:100–112). Sen discusses the issue of the lasting effectiveness of former colonial patterns: these are not only revealed in the continuing dominance and paternalism of the former colonial powers. Rather, according to Sen, the experience of humiliation and its enforced feeling of inferiority have also imprinted themselves on the colonised populations with lasting effect. This is certainly one explanation for the corruptibility of the African elites.

The perception of corruption is, however, often selective. The corruption scandals which shook South Africa in 2017 involving global companies like McKinsey, KPMG and Bell Pottinger are often discussed in a different way from the corruption scandals surrounding Jacob Zuma. While it was generally insinuated that Zuma's case had to do with a trait characteristic of all black people, the scandal-ridden companies and their managers were portrayed as exceptions who only acted as they did because of the (black) context. Sisonke Msimang was right when she stated: 'Exposing corruption

[...] will only yield results when the crimes of white South Africans and global corporations are as thoroughly investigated and debated by whites as those of their black compatriots' (Msimang, 2017). This applies not only to South Africa but also in a global context. In Germany, one often meets people at public events who have not seen the documentary about the 'Paradise Papers' on TV and who get enraged about corrupt elites in Africa, without mentioning a single word about the role of the mainly white protagonists in the Paradise Papers scandal. Corruption is only used in connection with 'others' and not with 'civilised Europe'.

Raw materials policy as a security policy

What would actually happen if African states were to develop resistance to trade agreements to such an extent that Europe's supply would actually be at risk? In the EU and in the US, in the last 15 years the concept of security has been redefined in such a way that it is actually no longer about defending oneself against dangers from within and outside but rather about asserting and securing economic interests by military means wherever necessary, in particular when it comes to access to raw materials and energy. From this perspective, a raw materials policy forms part of the security policy, as the Bundeswehr's 2006 White Paper reveals: 'Like many other nations [Germany] is highly dependent on a secure supply of raw materials and safe transportation routes around the world. [...] A secure, sustained and competitive supply of energy is of strategic importance for the future of Germany and Europe. [...] Energy issues will play an ever more important role for global security in future' (BMVg, 2006).

Many elites in the global South are aware of the risks of resistance to the interests of the Western industrialised nations, exercising anticipatory obedience and ingratiating themselves practically voluntarily. Ultimately, they know the fate of those who attempted to do things differently in the past, like Thomas Sankara and Patrice Lumumba. Speaking about her home country, Nadine Rosa-Rosso illustrates how France, known as the country of the Enlightenment, does not hesitate 'to decree wars, torture and political murder if it has to do with defending her colonial empire and the interests of her multinational corporations such as Elf, Total, Areva, Bolloré, Eramet, Technip, Bouygues, Orange, Geocoton, Rougier, etc. And this is not about ancient history but about everyday life for millions of Africans' (Rosa-Rosso, 2016).

In his day, Robert Cooper, chief civil servant of the European Union, openly declared that the EU did not fight shy of using any means in order to pursue its interests:

Postmodern imperialism takes two forms. First there is the voluntary imperialism of the global economy. This is usually operated by an international consortium through International Financial Institutions [...] The challenge to the postmodern world is to get used to the idea of double standards. Among ourselves, we operate on the basis of laws and open cooperative security. But when dealing with more old-fashioned kinds of states outside the postmodern continent of Europe, we need to revert to the rougher methods of an earlier era – force, pre-emptive attack, deception [...] Among ourselves, we keep the law but when we are operating in the jungle, we must also use the laws of the jungle' (Cooper, 2002).

In Germany, the federal president, Horst Köhler, resigned in May 2010 because his statement that the Bundeswehr could be used to protect access to raw materials provoked major criticism. Although there has since been no incident of such use,[5] the discussion remains in the political arena. Defence experts increasingly stress the need to structure the training of soldiers in such a way that they can be deployed anywhere in the world. In view of the fact that European industry is dependent on mineral and energy resources which are not available in Europe or cannot be extracted due to the high environmental standards or lower economic profitability, the following question presents itself: what would happen if a country such as the Democratic Republic of Congo, which delivers 60 per cent of the EU's required cobalt supply, were to put a stop to these deliveries for some reason or other? And if South Africa did the same with platinum and other countries followed suit? I suspect that what Robert Cooper calls 'force, pre-emptive attack, deception' would reach a new dimension. At this point it is perhaps helpful to remind ourselves of the fact that the Second Congo War, which began in August 1998, began because the government under Kabila had, from the perspective of Western countries, introduced a 'false' raw materials policy. In the interim, more than six million people have died as a result of this war and millions live as internally displaced persons or refugees in neighbouring countries, but the raw materials of the Congo continue to supply the global markets.

Closing remarks

In 1999 Ignacio Ramonet, director of *Le Monde diplomatique,* wrote, 'the world's real masters are no longer the politicians who hold the formal reins of power'. Based on the history of Africa, the following can be said with certainty: African countries never really became independent, as the rationale behind the organisation of national economies to cater to the advantage of foreign beneficiaries has remained intact. The actual holders of power are those who determine the rules. African elites have stakes in this power but often operate under conditions which they themselves do not determine.

From the independence of African countries to the most recent bilateral free trade agreements via the structural adjustment programmes of the international financial institutions and the terms of the World Trade Organization, Europe (along with other industrialised nations) has displayed great ingenuity in safeguarding its continued privileged access to the resources of Africa and other developing countries, which existed during the colonial occupation, and survives even after formal legal independence. Here, control of the global market prices remains a constant factor: because the countries that are rich in raw materials, particularly in Africa, control neither their resources nor the markets on which they are traded, they never receive a fair price for their contribution to the global economy. The 'invisible hand', which determines the fluctuations in price, is active when it comes to getting the resource-rich countries to mitigate the 'burden' of companies for each price drop in such a way that they can 'survive', i.e. remain profitable. If prices shoot up and corporations bring in large profits, the invisible hand remains inactive. The South African journalist Khadija Sharife accordingly appealed to African governments: 'Where countries hold the monopoly on finite resources and pricing is opaque, governments in Africa must revisit the role in price setting in the global economy, both for resources and labour' (Sharife, 2016).

In addition to the control of prices for imported raw materials, Western countries also have an additional tool which is at least as powerful: they claim for themselves the power of defining how the raw materials markets are organised and the instruments of its regulation. In a 2017 interview with the German magazine *taz.FUTURZWEI*, the film and theatre director Milo Rau explained how this definition of power works, using the example of the law on conflict minerals:

> Let's take the coltan or gold extracted in Congo. The EU Parliament passes a law which says: We don't want any conflict minerals, we want clean production conditions. This sounds great at first but then you ask the EU raw materials experts the question: What does 'conflict mineral' actually mean? And they answer in quite a relaxed manner: this is a mineral which we don't have but which we need in Europe. Therefore, we need this law on regulation in order to criminalise the Congolese producers and get the raw materials to Europe at the cheapest possible prices (Rau, 2017).

In response to the question of whether the law should police the link between conflicts, human rights violations and our consumption of everyday items, Rau (2017) replied:

This is precisely the moral demand. However, in truth this is an imperial monopoly law: that's because only the European multinationals get the label 'clean'. The Congolese small producers have no lobby in the EU parliament. It's as if the central committee of the Chinese Communist Party were to adopt ethical laws for the German automotive industry, close down Volkswagen (VW) and then import Chinese cars. This sounds completely absurd; for the Congolese people and large parts of the world, however, this is an everyday thing.

Notes

1. In its strategic concepts, the EU follows the US both in its claim to intervene globally and 'preventively', and in its emphasis on the question of energy. 'Energy dependence is a special concern for Europe. Europe is the world's largest importer of oil and gas. Imports account for about 50% of energy consumption today. This will rise to 70% in 2030.'
2. The measures implemented as part of the structural adjustment policy included the lowering of government spending and rates of tax, the creation of incentives to attract foreign investment, the liberalisation of trade by reducing customs duties and abolishing import restrictions, the privatisation of public sector companies and bodies and the strengthening of rights to property.
3. See IFC and World Bank Group, *Lonmin plc, South Africa: Investing in Success and Sustainable Development*, www.ifc.org/wps/wcm/connect/industry_ext_content/ifc_external_corporate_site/ogm+home/priorities/mining/mining_case_studies_lonmin_plc.
4. The SADC, which was founded in 1992, emerged from the SADCC or South African Development Coordination Conference, which was the amalgamation of the front-line countries of Angola, Zambia, Zimbabwe, Tanzania, Mozambique, Botswana, Lesotho, Malawi, Swaziland and Namibia. After overcoming political apartheid, South Africa, Mauritius, the Seychelles and the Democratic Republic of Congo joined. The SADC is a heterogeneous group, whose membership criteria combine geographical, historical, ideological as well as economic motives. This heterogeneity is reflected in the implementation of the group's joint projects. The defined economic aims, such as the creation of a joint economic area, a customs union and a common currency, are behind schedule. In particular, the political aims, which were to find expression in the consolidation of democracy, have suffered major setbacks in the last few years.
5. Even if the deployment of the French army in Mali is itself seen by many African civil society forces as a mission to defend the raw materials supply in relation to uranium in the neighbouring country and the development of new raw materials sources in Mali, the Bundeswehr is only in Mali to 'relieve' France, according to the words of the German defence minister Ursula von der Leyen.

References

Ameling, D. (2005) Speech held at the first Raw Materials Conference of the Federation of German Industries, cited in Entwicklungsforum Bangladesh e.V. (2013) *Wie viele Menschen trägt die Erde? Im Fokus: Bangladesch*, www.bit.ly/2tJsDJR

BMWi (Federal Ministry of Economics and Technology) (2010) *The German Government's Raw Materials Srategy. Safeguarding a sustainable supply of non-energy mineral resources for Germany*, Berlin, www.ec.europa.eu/growth/tools-databases/eip-raw-materials/en/system/files/ged/43%20raw-materials-strategy.pdf

BMVg (Federal Ministry of Defence) (2006) *White Paper 2006 on German Security Policy and the Future of the Bundeswehr (Weißbuch 2006 zur Sicherheitspolitik Deutschlands und zur Zukunft der Bundeswehr)*, www.responsibilitytoprotect.org/Germany_White_Paper_2006.pdf

Buch, H.G. (2011) *Apokalypse Africa oder Schiffbruch mit Zuschauern*, Frankfurt

Cooper, R. (2002) The new liberal imperialism, *The Guardian*, 7 April, www.theguardian.com/world/2002/apr/07/1

Curtis, M. (2009) *The New Resource Grab: How EU Trade Policy on Raw Materials Is Undermining Development*, www.curtisresearch.org/wp-content/uploads/Raw-materials-report.pdf

EEAS Strategic Planning (2003) *European Security Strategy: A Secure Europe in a Better World*, www.europa.eu/globalstrategy/en/european-security-strategy-secure-europe-better-world

EC (European Commission) (2006) *Global Europe: Competing in the World. A Contribution to the EU's Growth and Jobs Strategy*, www.trade.ec.europa.eu/doclib/docs/2006/october/tradoc_130376.pdf

EC (2008) *The Raw Materials Initiative: Meeting Our Critical Needs for Growth and Jobs in Europe*, COM 699, Brussels

EC (2013) *Critical Raw Materials for the EU: Report of the Ad-hoc Working Group on Defining Critical Raw Materials*, www.ec.europa.eu/growth/tools-databases/eip-raw-materials/en/system/files/ged/79%20report-b_en.pdf

EC (2015) *Trade for All: Towards a More Responsible Trade and Investment Policy*, www.trade.ec.europa.eu/doclib/docs/2015/october/tradoc_153846.pdf

Goldberg, J. (2007) *Afrika im Weltkapitalismus. Überleben im Goldland*, ISW-Report 72

ICTSD (International Centre for Trade and Sustainable Development) (2014) *Why Should the SADC EPA Allow Export Taxes?*, www.ictsd.org/bridges-news/bridges-africa/news/why-should-the-sadc-epa-allow-export-taxes

KASA (Kirchliche Arbeitsstelle Südliches Afrika) (ed.) (2014) *Zeit zum Umdenken: Rohstoffe im Südlichen Afrika. Der natürliche Reichtum der Region muss endlich der Bevölkerung zugutekommen*, Heidelberg

Kramml, J., M. Kaufmann, K. Küblböck and J. Planitzer (2017) *Mehr Menschenrechte in Rohstoff-Lieferketten. Sorgfaltspflichten – Handelspolitik – öffentliche Beschaffung*, Vienna

Melber, H. (1992) *Der Weißheit letzter Schluss. Rassismus und kolonialer Blick*, Frankfurt

Msimang, S. (2017) Are South Africa's anti-corruption crusaders racist?, *Mail&Guardian*, www.mg.co.za/article/2017-11-14-are-south-africas-anti-corruption-crusaders-racist

Ramonet, I. (1999) The year 2000 (L'an 2000), *Le Monde diplomatique*, www.mondediplo.com/1999/12/01leader

Rau, M. (2017) Wir sind Arschlöcher durch Geburt, *taz.FUTURZWEI-Interview*, October

Reichert, T., Silke Spielmans, Carolin Mengel, Michael Frein and Kerstin Lanje (eds.) (2009) *Entwicklung oder Marktöffnung? Kritische Aspekte in den Wirtschaftspartnerschaftsabkommen zwischen der EU und afrikanischen Ländern*, n.p.

Rosa-Rosso, N. (2016) *Le mythe de l'Europe en paix depuis 1945: l'exemple français*, www.legrandsoir.info/le-mythe-de-l-europe-en-paix-depuis-1945-l-exemple-francais.html

Rowden, R. (2016) Das Ende des Mythos. Afrika hat sich nie wirklich entwickelt, *Internationale Politik und Gesellschaft*, www.ipg-journal.de/kommentar/artikel/das-ende-des-mythos-1254/

Sharife, K. (2016) The London fix: Price-making in capitalism, *Review of African Political Economy*, 25 February, www.roape.net/2016/02/25/the-london-fix-price-making-in-capitalism/

Sen, A. (2007) *Die Identitätsfalle. Warum es keinen Krieg der Kulturen gibt*, Bonn

Tangemann, S. (2006): Das Scheitern der Doha-Runde. Wie groß ist der Schaden?, *ifo Schnelldienst 17*

WTO (2010) *World Trade Report 2010*, www.cesifo-group.de/DocDL/ifosd_2006_17_1.pdf

▶ Announcement of the performance of DJ Mlungu (isiXhosa: *white person*) at Makwase Palace in Marikana. DJ Mlungu is a white South African, he speaks about half of South Africa's 11 national languages and is a respected house music DJ and music producer in the black community.

19. DISCOURSE (AS) OPPOSED TO THE FACTS: GERMANY'S LINKS TO THE MARIKANA MASSACRE HAVE LONG GONE UNNOTICED

Stefan Buchen
Translated by Simon Phillips

It is almost a truism to note that Africa does not make it into the German news very often. However, 16 August 2012 and the days that followed were quite different because 34 striking workers were shot dead by the police at a South African mine. *Tagesschau* viewed the events as newsworthy enough to justify a short film, and the following day the presenter on ARD's late night news programme described the shootings as 'reminiscent of the worst of the South African apartheid regime'.

And finally, *Tagesthemen* introduced a news report from the site in Marikana – a settlement in the Platinum Belt north-west of Johannesburg where precious metal mines are located – with the headline 'Police shoot mineworkers'.[1]

The initial dismay at the violence was soon followed by cautious attempts to establish the event's background: on 23 August 2012, the *Süddeutsche Zeitung* wrote that 'A whole nation is distraught because it cannot grasp what has happened here on the hill in Marikana'. It continued by arguing that 'The young democracy in South Africa has been cut to the core'. The reporters evidently viewed these events as extremely important: Marikana, they stressed, was set to become a 'symbol' of the violence occurring in post-apartheid South Africa. For both German and international news outlets, the massacre marked a 'turning point' in South African history.

Reports from Marikana described the grief and anger expressed by the workers and their families after the massacre. They also addressed the poor and unhealthy living conditions that people are exposed to in the slums, and the lack of running water and electricity, just as much as the low wages the workers receive of around 400 euro monthly, which, of course, were the reasons why the workers had gone on strike in the first place.

Analyses of the events focused on two aspects. In the first place, reporters attempted to determine who had been responsible for the escalation of violence: were the security forces or the workers mainly at fault? Whereas *Der Spiegel* (27 August 2012) accused the police of having 'lost their nerve' and of 'firing automatic weapons into the crowd', *Die Zeit* expressed understanding for the action that the police had taken. The newspaper quoted security expert Johan Burger from the Institute for Security Studies in Cape Town as saying, 'In that situation, I also would have given the order to open fire.' Similarly, *Welt am Sonntag* (19 August 2012) and *Tagesspiegel* (3 September 2012) stressed that it was the strikers' aggressiveness and readiness to use violence that provoked the security forces' sharp response.

Secondly, the reports emphasised that the violence pointed towards the existence of a deep domestic political crisis. 'Marikana', it was argued, was a symptom of the failure of the governing party – the African National Congress (ANC) – to create better living conditions for all South Africans since the 1994 victory over apartheid. At the same time, the reports linked people's rise through the ranks of the ANC to promises of personal wealth and implied that this had been the driving force behind the political commitment of people involved in the party. On 24 August 2012, the *Süddeutsche Zeitung* proposed that 'There is no one on the horizon to replace Mandela'.

All of these reports published by German correspondents share a common perspective: they treat the massacre in Marikana as a domestic political issue. Despite giving individual explanations for the massacre – a corrupt government, poorly trained police, violent workers or poor working conditions – the reports all depict it as an event whose causes and context were specifically South African.

This chapter does not question these claims. In fact, our research demonstrates that there are good reasons why the journalists came to these conclusions. However, in the days that followed the massacre, no one had as much time or opportunity to cover the events as meticulously as Greg Marinovich, the South African investigative journalist, whose recently published book, *Murder at Small Koppie: The Real Story of the Marikana Massacre* (2016), lays out the tragedy's background in detail. Marinovich had discovered internal police documents proving that senior officials in the security forces had planned early on to end the protests violently rather than to deal with the workers' demands for increased wages and improved living conditions – and that they had done so with the support of influential politicians such as Cyril Ramaphosa, a former trade unionist and colleague of Nelson Mandela. Marinovich's research culminated in the discovery that the police had murdered at least 34 miners in cold blood: some of the strikers had been shot in the back of the head after they had withdrawn from the main site of the protests to another area (Small Koppie) a few hundred metres away.

Instead, this chapter seeks to demonstrate that the reports published by German correspondents in August 2012 had something essential in common: they all blanked out the question of what the massacre had to do 'with Germany'. None of the reporters attempted to highlight possible links between Marikana and Germany. As such, news readers and viewers would have assumed that no such link existed. From the German point of view, therefore, the massacre was purely a foreign policy issue.

All of the television and most of the newspaper reports portrayed Lonmin – the company which was mining platinum in Marikana, and which was at the centre of the workers' protests against low wages – as a South African venture. This, of course, was not wrong, but a number of correspondents were more precise, referring to Lonmin as a 'South African-British company with its headquarters in London'. Even Greg Marinovich, whose book was published four years after the events, fails to provide further details.

Only a few of the German newspaper articles published in August 2012 vaguely indicate that South Africa's platinum mines are indeed embedded in the global economy. Bartholomäus Grill, a correspondent for the weekly newspaper *Die Zeit* at the time, stated on 23 August:

> There is a brutal labour struggle raging in Marikana, and it is a reflection of global conflicts. On the one side, we have a multinational corporation attempting to extract raw materials from the mine as profitably as possible; on the other, an army of wage slaves who feel exploited – and in between, irresponsible managers, power-hungry trade union bosses and state bodies that are failing miserably.

The *Süddeutsche Zeitung* (23 August) explained to its readers that Lonmin was finding it difficult to accept the workers' demands for higher wages because world market prices for platinum had crashed owing to the 'weak European car industry'.

None of the journalists, however, mentioned that BASF, a major German corporation with its headquarters in Ludwigshafen am Rhein, was Lonmin's most important customer – a detail they could have picked up from Lonmin's publicly available annual reports. In fact, the company's reports clearly state that no one else buys as much platinum from Lonmin as BASF and Mitsubishi (Japan). They also point out that the company would face serious economic difficulties if it were to lose either of its two major customers. It is therefore interesting to note that the connection between Lonmin and these companies was first highlighted not by a media outlet, but by the historian Jakob Krameritsch, editor of the collected volume *Das Massaker von Marikana. Widerstand und Unterdrückung von Arbeiter_innen in Südafrika* (2013).

BASF is a chemical company that requires large quantities of platinum to build catalytic converters for cars and diesel-powered cars in particular. Platinum is a precious metal with catalytic properties: it converts the nitrogen oxides produced during fuel combustion into less harmful carbon dioxides – at least in theory. It is clear that catalytic converters are not keeping the air clean, at least not to the extent to which industry wanted everyone to believe they would, and this is particularly the case with diesel engines. However, this point is mentioned here only to emphasise the irony of the irony. What matters is that BASF, like Bosch, the automotive supplier, was a member of the German automotive industry's 'diesel cartel' from the outset, a cartel that attracted extensive media scrutiny during the summer of 2017. In acquiring the American catalyst manufacturer Engelhard in 2006, BASF's executive board had taken the strategic decision to become the industry's global market leader. In Port Elizabeth, some distance away from the source of the platinum – which is indispensable to BASF – the company claims to have 'built a world-class factory' for the production of vehicle catalysts. The catalyst sector now accounts for about 10 per cent of BASF's total sales of around 70 billion euro.

Lonmin continued to speak openly about its excellent business relations with BASF right up until the publication of its 2012 annual report. The 2012 report was published in 2013 – close to the time when the massacre took place; and in the years that followed, BASF discreetly disappeared from Lonmin's reports. Yet this has not at all affected the companies' close business relations: during a press briefing on BASF's annual results held in February 2016 in Ludwigshafen, Kurt Bock, chair of BASF's board of executive directors, confirmed that 'We are a very, very large customer of that company [Lonmin]'.

BASF annually buys platinum worth 500 million euro from Lonmin – platinum that miners have hauled up to the surface from 1,200 metres below the veld. Without its

German customer, Lonmin's business model would collapse. Are these just abstract financial details, interesting only to economic experts? Is it not in the public interest in Germany or Europe as a whole to publish this information? Or are these actually important, relevant facts that help complete the media's coverage of an event like the bloodbath that took place in the Platinum Belt?

This chapter should be understood as arguing in favour of the wider importance and broader relevance of these seemingly marginal details; not mentioning the links between BASF and Lonmin constitutes a failure on the part of the media. In what follows the chapter therefore considers the reasons why this failure occurred, and the conclusions that can be drawn from them.

Describing the events that occurred in Marikana and her reaction as she watched them unfold on television from Johannesburg, Martina Schwikowski, a correspondent for the newspaper *taz*, recalled: 'It was a shocking experience; with the bullets raining down, the focus on the people dying in front of the camera. I jumped up as if I had been electrified. It was a traumatic experience' (*ZAPP*, 27 April 2016). Her reports for *taz* reflected that experience and then analysed the domestic political situation. This horror, amplified by the TV images, may well have been the initial reason why the massacre gained international media attention.

But 'unnatural deaths' in the numbers that occurred in Marikana happen every day somewhere in Africa, whether it is violent clashes in eastern Congo, famine in Somalia or a combination of both in South Sudan (to mention just a few recent examples). The world's press, however, rarely takes notice of these catastrophes, which are scarcely less terrible than those that occurred in South Africa. There must therefore be other reasons that triggered those relatively detailed reports from Marikana. On the one hand, many international Africa correspondents are stationed in Johannesburg or in Cape Town, making South Africa the second-largest reporter hub after Nairobi in Kenya. Even in today's era of social media, citizen journalism and other recent forms of news distribution, the physical presence of professional foreign correspondents certainly helps to ensure that information coming from 'their' countries is disseminated across the world.

What is more, South Africa continues to occupy a special role in Europe's cultural imagination, even after the collapse of the apartheid regime. The country's 'peaceful' transition to democracy and equality that occurred under the guiding hands of Nelson Mandela, and the Truth Commission, which addressed the wrongdoings of the past and planted reconciliation in the hearts of the people, have inspired an idealised image of hope that is essentially romantic. The extent to which the post-1994 media enthusiasm could be viewed as providing a form of recompense for the fact that European countries and companies – including BASF – benefited greatly from their cooperation with the apartheid regime is a subject that will have to be left to the psychologists. Daimler's promotional film *Labour of Love* (1994) could be interpreted as another possible example of such an act of recompense. The film, set to stirring music, depicts workers of all colours and creeds voluntarily renouncing part of their wages to build a red 500 SEL in the Mercedes factory in East London for President Nelson Mandela. Daimler's message was obvious: like South Africa, the car was composed of many different colourful parts that ultimately fit together to form a harmonious whole. Yet in the decades before then, Daimler had built Unimog armoured vehicles for the apartheid regime, which were then used to violently suppress the black population's struggle for equality. But why have hard feelings? South Africa was now the 'rainbow nation'.

Against this background, the massacre in Marikana undoubtedly fulfilled the criterion of journalistic relevancy (it was both an unexpected and an extraordinary event); therefore, it was clearly a 'man bites dog' story that stood outside the manner in which the 'new' South Africa is usually framed.

This meant that the reporters had to quickly find a new way of framing the events. As stated above, they turned to the narrative of 'domestic political failure' and perceived 'endemic levels of corruption' among the ANC government formed by Mandela's successors. The *Tagesspiegel*'s correspondent described the miners' strike on 3 September as 'completely out of control'. Marauding hordes were said to have 'laid entire inner cities lame', 'blocked motorways' and 'set fire to schools'. The newspaper even went as far as to claim that 'half of the black population is currently worse off than it had been during apartheid'. The message was clear: perhaps the black population would have been better off had apartheid never been abolished.

This tendency among European journalists to claim that Africa cannot be left to the Africans, at least not without it 'going to the dogs', was noted by the anti-colonialist Frantz Fanon in *The Wretched of the Earth* (1961): 'The report intends to verify the evidence: everything's going badly out there since we left.' Before the rise of communication studies and its specialised branches, and long before Edward Said's critical analyses of imperialism, Fanon, a psychiatrist, had already fully understood hegemonic Eurocentric discourse.

The intention here is not to accuse German correspondents of intentionally concealing the links between BASF and the massacre that took place in Marikana: that would be tantamount to a naive conspiracy theory. However, it does seem reasonable to suspect that, during the crisis, the reporters shied away from depicting the bigger picture. In this case, the bigger picture involves the relations of dependency and exploitation established over centuries by European conquerors and colonialists. It would probably be too much to ask of European journalists that they remember Fanon's point that 'Europe is literally the creation of the Third World'. Fanon was arguing that Europe had only been able to become as rich as it is by raiding various colonial territories with the aim of enslaving the people who lived there and stealing raw materials. However, it would certainly help if reporters were to read Fanon's views about the conditions under which decolonisation takes place. Fanon's arguments in *The Wretched of the Earth*, which were based on his own experiences in North and West Africa, have proved to be prophetic in relation to post-apartheid South Africa. Fanon pointed out that after a colony gains political independence, a small local bourgeoisie culturally aligned with the former colonisers takes over political leadership. It secures the economic interests of the former colonial powers despite independence, while the majority of the population continue to live in squalor – a situation that plays into the hands of the multinationals, as they can continue to tap into a reservoir of workers that will never run dry.

In post-apartheid South Africa, the rise of the local bourgeoisie has its own term: Black Economic Empowerment (BEE). For many years, the poor regions of the Eastern Cape and the failed neighbouring state of Zimbabwe have been acting as the Platinum Belt's bottomless reservoir of workers. BASF and Marikana is just one (extreme) example of how far German and European companies are willing to go in the pursuit of their interests in Africa. It is certainly worth taking a closer look: dam builder Lahmeyer, Siemens, Strabag and other stakeholders from the coal industry are just a few companies that could be mentioned.

Finally, when we asked various South African correspondents why they had not traced the relationship between BASF and Marikana after the massacre at the platinum mine, almost none of them wanted to answer. Only Martina Schwikowski from *taz* was ready to address the question. In an interview with NDR's media magazine programme *ZAPP* (27 April 2016), she stated: 'It's a pity that we were more focused on the shocking experiences that were unfolding at the time instead of looking further to see whether there were any links to Germany. In the North, most people don't really understand what people's working and living conditions are actually like [in the South]. But we benefit from these conditions, and I think this means that we also have to make people in the North aware of this situation.'

Notes

1   See also the *Panorama* television report broadcast on ARD on 28 April 2016, and the *ZAPP* report on NDR on 27 April 2016, as well as the article 'Der Platin-Komplex' published in *Die Zeit* on 28 April 2016.

▶ **pp. 360/361** Selection of media coverage in the context of the Plough Back the Fruits campaign. The campaign focuses on BASF's connection to Lonmin and the Marikana massacre.
▶ **pp. 362/363** Collage: Reference texts. Selection of literature, sources and reference material for this volume.

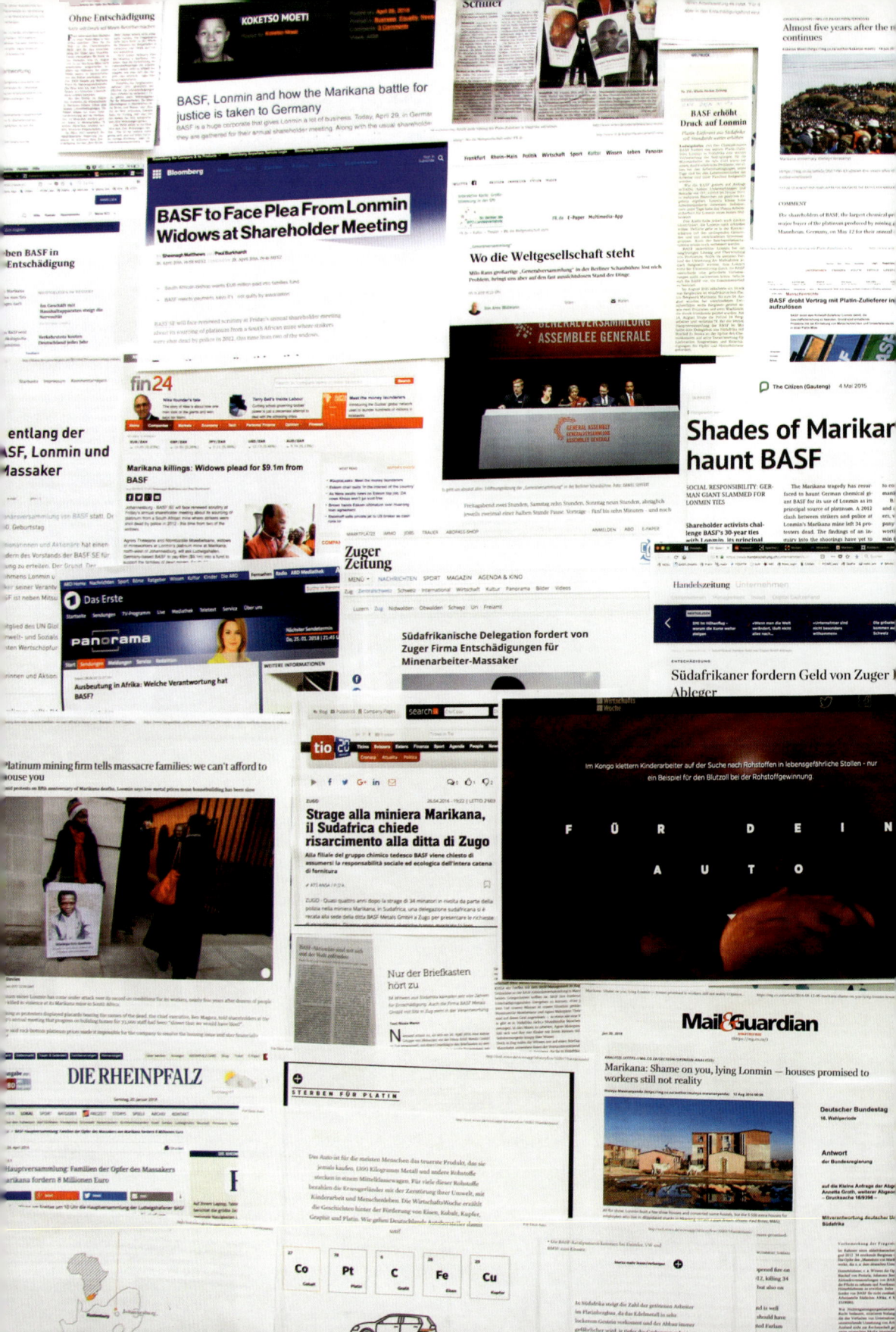

20. BARED LIFE: COLONIAL AND NEO-COLONIAL DEPICTIONS OF SOUTH AFRICAN MINERS IN THE PUBLIC IMAGINATION

Rosemary Lombard

The striking mineworkers at Marikana have become spectacularised. It is a stark reminder that the mine worker, a modern subject of capitalism, in these parts of the world is also the product of a colonial encounter.
– Suren Pillay (2014)

We need to understand how photography works within everyday life in advanced industrial societies: the problem is one of materialist cultural history rather than art history.
– Allan Sekula (2003)

I pick up the odd wood-and-metal contraption. This is a stereoscope, I am told. It feels old, in the sense that there is a certain worn patina about it and a non-utilitarian elegance to the turned wood and decoration, though not as if it were an expensive piece; just as if it came from an era when there was time for embellishment. It feels cheaply put together, mass-produced and flimsy as opposed to delicate, the engraving detail of the tinny sheet metal rather rough, the fit of the one piece as it glides through the other somewhat rickety in my hands.

I reach for the pile of faded stereographs, flipping through them slowly. There are 24, picked up in an antique shop in an arcade off Cape Town's Long Street together with the viewing device. A stereograph is composed of two photographs of the same subject taken from slightly different angles. When they are placed in the stereoscope's wire holder and viewed through the eyeholes, an illusion of perspective and depth is achieved as the two images appear to combine through a trick of parallax.

Susan Sontag remarks that 'photographs, which cannot themselves explain anything, are inexhaustible invitations to deduction, speculation, and fantasy' (1973:23). And Allan Sekula calls the photograph an 'incomplete utterance, a message that depends on some external matrix of conditions and presuppositions for its readability. That is, the meaning of any photographic message is necessarily context determined' (1982:4). In what follows, I will look more closely at two of these 24 pictures and, through a contextual discussion, begin to unpack a few aspects of the complex relationships of photography with its subjects and also with public circulation.

Each thick, oblong card with its rounded, scuffed edges discoloured by age has two seemingly identical images on it, side by side, and is embossed with what I guess must have been the photographer's or printing studio's name in gold down the margin: 'RAYMOND NEILSON, BOX 145, JOHANNESBURG'. The images depict miners underground. Some are very faded, to the extent that the figures in them appear featureless and ghostly. There is virtually no annotation on most of the photos. On just a few of them, spidery white handwriting on the photo itself, as if scratched into the negative before it was printed, announces the name of the machinery or activity in the picture and the name of the mine: 'Crown Mines'.

I pick up the first card, slot it into the stereoscope and peer through the device. On the left of the two images, the writing announces: 'Ingersoll hammer drill cutting box hole. C215. Crown Mines.'

I slide the holder backwards and forwards along the wooden shaft to focus. I'm seeing two images, nothing remarkable, until suddenly, at a precise point on the axis, the images coalesce into one which is three-dimensional. The experience is that of a *gestalt* shift, the optical illusion uncanny. I blink hard. It's still there. It feels magical, as if the figures in the photos are stepping right out of the card towards me. Their eyes stare into mine through over a century of time, gleaming white out of dirty, sweaty

▲ Stereographic image of miners in the Crown mines at the beginning of the 20th century

faces. Startlingly tangible, here stand two young white men in a mine shaft, scarcely out of their teens, leaning against rock, each with a hand on the hip and a jauntily cocked hat. They are very young ... yet very old too, I immediately think: definitely dead now and perhaps dead soon after the picture was taken, living at risk, killed in a rockfall or in the First World War. A pang of indefinable emotion hits me. I am amazed at how powerfully this image has flooded my imagination. Even with the difficult viewing process, the effect is astonishing.

I am reminded of Sontag's contention that all photographs are *memento mori*: 'To take a photograph is to participate in another person's (or thing's) mortality, vulnerability, mutability. Precisely by slicing out this moment and freezing it, all photographs testify to time's relentless melt' (1973:11; cf. Berger, 1972 and Barthes, 1981:14).

I also notice that the trick of parallax (and, concurrently, the evocativeness) works most pronouncedly on the figures in the foreground, probably due to the camera angle and vanishing points of the perspective. Behind the two white youngsters, almost fading into the darkness, is a black man, holding up a drill over their heads that seems to penetrate the tunnel of rock in which they are suspended. He appears to have moved during the shot as his face is blurred. This could also be due to the low light in the shaft. Though he is looking straight at me, I can't connect with him as I do with the figures in front. He is very much in the background, a presence without substance. The way the photo was set up and taken has placed him in that position, and this viewpoint is indelible no matter how hard I try to look past it.

I line up the next image. There is no writing on this one except for what seems to be a reference number: 'C269'. The figure in the foreground is a black man, miming work with a mallet and chisel against the rock face though clearly standing very still for the shot as he is perfectly in focus, his sceptical gaze directed at us, a sharp shadow thrown on the rock behind him. This is no ordinary lamp light: it seems clear that these pictures have been professionally illumined by the photographer, perhaps using magnesium flares, because the shots definitely predate flash photography.

To the left of the man with the chisel stands a white man, face dark with dirt. He is holding a lamp in one hand and his other grasps a support pile which bisects the shaft and also the photo. Tight-jawed, he stares beyond us, his eyes preoccupied, glazed over. Behind the two men in the foreground, there are more men: parts of two, perhaps three workers can be seen, one a black man crouched down at the rock face behind the man with the chisel.

What strikes me most about this picture – the *punctum*, after Barthes (1981:27) – is the man with the chisel's bare feet. He is at work in an extremely hazardous environment without shoes. If one looks at all the photographs, every white worker is wearing boots, but there are several pictures where it is clear that many of the black workers are barefoot. This is shocking visual evidence of an exploitative industry which does not take its workers' safety seriously, placing these men at incredible risk without the provision of adequate protective attire: none have hard protection for their heads, and the black workers are without shoes. Men not deemed worthy of protection are, by inference, expendable. From these photos, one surmises that black lives are more dispensable than white.

I am curious to find out more about these pictures. Perhaps the visual evidence here is echoed in literature. Or perhaps they can tell us things the literature does not. *Who were these people?* There is nothing on the back of the photos. No captions, no dates. *Who was the photographer? For what purpose were these pictures taken?* The lack of answers to these most mundane of questions lends the photos an uncanny, almost spectral quality. I have technical questions about how these pictures were taken, too, such as about the lighting and the camera used. Surely it was large and difficult to manoeuvre down into the mine, and probably an expensive exercise.

With virtually no background information, there is little direct means of understanding how or why these stereographs came into being. I assume that as a viewer now, my experience and interpretation of the images would be informed by a very different paradigm from that inhabited by viewers at the turn of the 20th century. Hence, I attempt to examine the broader historical and theoretical milieu. As John Tagg reminds us, 'The photograph is not a magical "emanation" but a material product of a material apparatus set to work in specific contexts' (1988:3).

From the information I have at my disposal, I cannot tell for what exact purpose these photographs were intended. I cannot imagine an overtly business-related use for them, as the annotation is too intermittent: if there were a commercial value to

▲ Stereographic image of miners from Johannesburg at the beginning of the 20th century

naming the machinery in some of the shots, it would most likely have been named more consistently. If they were to be used for advertising or documentary purposes, this would be of a 'cabinet of curiosities' type, in which the spectacle of seeing something usually invisible to the audience would be the main attraction. Perhaps the photos could have had an educational function, although the documentation is too imprecise to serve any real use as an inventory record.

I google 'Raymond Neilson', trying various permutations and keywords in conjunction with the name, with no luck. I google 'old South African mining photographs'. I find only one promising reference, in a forum post from 30 April 2013 on heritageportal. co.za, a 'discussion, education and marketing platform serving the South African Heritage Sector'. The post describes a cache of 46 stereographs found with a stereoscope in a cellar in North Yorkshire, England. The writer's description is strikingly similar to the images I have in hand, right down to her observation of the black workers' bare feet. Her images, too, are undated and unannotated, except for the names of the mines on Johannesburg's gold reef where they were taken, and the printer's name and address: 'G.B. Neilson, 15 Victoria Street, Georgetown'. The writer of the post indicates that Museum Africa has agreed to add these stereographs to their collections.

I follow up with Diana Wall, collections manager at Museum Africa in Newtown, Johannesburg, and former curator of the Bensusan Museum of Photography, who chats to me at some length about the historical context of these photographs. Diana is not familiar with the name 'Raymond Neilson' and says that dating the images precisely is impossible, but they were most likely made around the turn of the 20th century. The stereoscope, she tells me, is typical of those used in Victorian homes for education and amusement; looking at stereographs was a widespread form of entertainment until around 1920 (Wall, pers. comm., 26 May 2014).

Victorian voyeurs

The stereoscope's heyday followed the popularisation of the device at the Great Exhibition in Hyde Park, London, in 1851, where Queen Victoria herself ordered one (Strasser, 1942:117). Popular in Victorian parlours for over half a century, mass-produced stereographs provided entertainment and vicarious travel opportunities for the emerging middle class. In this sense, they were predecessors of later forms of media that occupy a similar niche: cinema, television and the Internet (Spiro, n.d.:3).

Aimed at the sector of society whose consumption fuelled the industrial economy, stereographs reinforced and extended claims supporting and justifying industrial capitalism. Shelley Staples (2002) discusses how turn-of-the-century stereograph depictions of industrial life in America emphasised machinery and products over labourers in industries as varied as textile, lumber, meatpacking and mining. She argues that these images offered 'standardised views (both aesthetically and ideologically) of labour and industry', a focus which reflected the rise of technocratic ideas about workers being 'nothing more than parts of the machinery they work' (Schlereth, 1991:56). This is certainly the case in the pictures I am looking at: while the miners are in the frame, they remain anonymous, while the machinery is labelled. It therefore seems likely that the stereographs may have been intended as this type of voyeuristic 'edutainment'.

The act of photography functions as a control mechanism exerted upon the world, upon our experience of it and upon others' perception of our experience, argues Sontag (1973:2): 'To photograph is to appropriate the thing photographed. It means putting oneself into a certain relation to the world that feels like knowledge — and, therefore, like power.'

As Elizabeth Edwards (1992:6), among others, has discussed, the collection of photographic evidence has also been a tool of colonial knowledge production in both the strict sense of, for instance, anthropometric photography and the more 'leisurely' sense of the photographic postcards that circulated in Victorian society, creating audiences (Krautwurst, 2009).

Epistemic violence

The will to knowledge as power and dominion: this is the quintessential colonising mindset (cf. Foucault, 1976). These stereographs allowed their audience, from the safety and comfort of their drawing rooms, to see underground into the hot, filthy, dark, dangerous bowels of the earth, to survey and thus to 'own' the workings of the very source of the wealth driving the expansion of the South African economy. I imagine that a strange mixture of romance and detachment accompanied this Victorian parlour experience, a voyeuristic frisson and perhaps an element of disavowal, too (Staples, 2002; Lehmann, 2009:100). That the men in the pictures are all unnamed reduces them to mere exemplars of hive workers, stereotypes void of individual identity and thus as interchangeable as ants or moles in burrows, existing in a liminal, abject state, almost already buried alive, even as they engage us with their eyes in the moment of being 'shot'.

Shot. The thought immediately brings to my mind images of South Africa's Marikana massacre. On the five-year anniversary of this event, I watched an interview with Joseph Mathunjwa (2017), the Association of Mineworkers and Construction Union (AMCU) leader who was present during the Marikana strike negotiations. If colonial photography stripped miners of their individual identities, rendering them nameless cogs in the machinery of the capitalist economy, it is striking that Mathunjwa speaks of the workers in the very same terms: 'Tomorrow we'll be gathering at the same koppie [...] commemorating the lives of the comrades who told Capital that "Enough is enough". We are human beings, we are not just pieces of equipment that [are] thrown underground [to] get the wealth without benefiting from it.'

Photography played a central role in what unfolded at Marikana, too: not only did it shape interpretations and understandings of the massacre after it happened but the presence of cameras in fact changed the course of subsequent events themselves.

In the first weeks after the massacre, what appeared in the press was coloured by partial coverage of the shootings. Owing to restricted access from behind police cordons, photojournalists could only cover what was later understood as 'Scene One' of two where shootings occurred that day (Duncan, 2012; Fogel, 2012). From where they stood, journalists saw what appeared to be the armed miners running at police and police opening fire to defend themselves. Later research and aerial footage would show that the miners were in fact herded chaotically in that direction by razor wire cordons, tear gas and rubber bullets as they tried to leave the koppie where they had been congregated in compliance with police orders (see, for example, Rehad Desai's 2014 documentary film, *Miners Shot Down*). According to forensic evidence gathered, 'Scene Two', out of sight of journalists, was where 17 of the killings took place at close range (Tolsi and Botes, 2015). This was not covered by media until a pivotal investigative piece by Greg Marinovich (2012) appeared in the *Daily Maverick*, three weeks after the shootings (Alexander et al., 2012; Moodie, 2012).

In this way, a lopsided picture of events appeared in the press, the narrative shaped by Lonmin representatives, police and government, who spun the available footage to their advantage, exonerating themselves from culpability. Jane Duncan has shown that, in coverage of the week before and after the Marikana massacre, the miners themselves were almost absent as news sources. When they were represented, she argues, 'they had little agency in shaping the coverage and defining its overall direction'. As a result, the story that the viewers of initial news reports were told was that the massacre was, at worst, 'an example of police panic at the workers' growing and increasingly violent militancy' (Duncan, 2013; Rodny-Gumede, 2015). This dominant narrative had already coalesced when more complex perspectives emerged in which surviving miners were directly consulted, such as that of Marinovich and of the book *Marikana: A View from the Mountain and a Case to Answer*, which was published in December 2012. Duncan, following George Gerbner, calls this silencing of the miners 'symbolic annihilation'.

Of docile bodies

In thinking about Marikana, I recall my conversation with Museum Africa's Diana Wall about conditions in the mines for black workers at the turn of the 20th century.

The Victorian stereographs were taken less than 20 years from the day in 1886 when gold was discovered on the Rand. Johannesburg mushroomed out of the veld with the rise of the gold mining industry. People flocked to the cities in search of economic prosperity. To facilitate the extraction of the seams of precious metal from the earth, an enormous reservoir of labour was required that had until then not existed (First, 1961). Government in concert with mine owners set up an ingenious system of laws and controls which coerced workers who had previously lived as subsistence farmers into joining the capitalist machine. Deprived of access to land and subject to taxation, people were forced to enter the wage economy to survive. Many migrated to the mines in search of employment, becoming tied into perpetual servitude by impossibly low wages and the enervating bureaucracy set up to regulate their coming and going.

Through the systematic exploitation of the workers on its lower rungs, South Africa's burgeoning mining industry enriched society's privileged upper echelons, sowing the seeds for the vast socio-economic inequalities and abuses that persist to the present day (Legassick, 1975; Callinicos, 1981).

Photographs sometimes allow us to access information about material conditions that may be otherwise obscured. Diana Wall tells me that men had to pay for their own protective clothing from the meagre wages they earned. This would explain why those workers who probably earned the lowest wages, the black workers, do not wear shoes in the stereographs: they were probably unable to afford them.

Bare life. The stereographic images give a literal sense of South African mineworkers living in a paradoxical state of exception akin to Agamben's *Homo Sacer*, outside the protection of basic human rights yet simultaneously under total control of the juridical system: constructed as docile black bodies (Foucault, 1976; Agamben, 1995). Each mineworker occupies a role that is utterly essential to the entire economy, yet he remains unindividuated, underground, absent from view as long as no violence erupts. The extreme force and lack of accountability which characterised Lonmin's and the South African government's actions to quash the 2012 Marikana miners' strike reveal that this status of exception continues to the present (cf. Pillay, 2014).

In looking again at the stereographs in relation to coverage of Marikana, it has become clear to me that the precedent for treating mineworkers and, indeed, industrial labourers in general as less than human, as depersonalised inputs, stretches right back to the beginnings of capitalist industrialisation in South Africa. In fact, exploitation in the Marxist sense, which involves the relative devaluation and dehumanisation of the worker, is necessary for profitable business. Corporations have always treated workers as less than fully human, in the sense that their material well-being has always come second to their utility as inputs for production: this instrumentality is a form of objectification. It is thus no surprise that media embedded in an industrial society would reflect this objectifying viewpoint.

Concluding remarks

> The life of a person who is working in the mines is cheaper than even chewing gum.
> – Andile Yawa, a relative of one of the victims of Marikana (in Nicolson, 2014)

Historically, the growth of South Africa's mining industry has tended to be recounted, especially within the industry itself, as a 'story of "progress" – of modernization, technological achievements, an expanding economy' (Callinicos, 1981:iv). This is the story told by the stereographs, which named the machines in the pictures yet not the workers. It is a tale of the technical conquest of corporations, which obscures the fact that none of this triumph would have been possible without the backbreaking labour of countless workers who hewed the riches from the ground, bodily.

This is still the story being told. Although the workers now feature in that narrative, they are acknowledged only in lip service paid by mine owners and the South African government to the neoliberal concepts of corporate social responsibility and basic human rights discourse. On the ground, their lives continue to be devalued, and the precarity the stereographs reveal persists. This is borne out by the statistics of broken promises by Lonmin to its workers, which stoked tensions in the build-up to the massacre. For example, of a promised 70 hostel block upgrades and 3,200 new houses by 2009, only 29 upgrades and three houses were delivered by that year (Lewis, 2017).

What I take from this example is that the mineworkers' human needs – for shelter and decent housing, for security and warmth, for fair remuneration – have been neglected. As long as they have showed up for work, as long as they have continued to extract the precious minerals from the ground, mine owners have been content to let these needs go unaddressed and to leave their own promises unfulfilled (Frankel, 2012; Lewis, 2017). The Marikana survivor Mzoxolo Magidiwana's speech, given in May 2017 at the annual general meeting of BASF (reproduced in this book), underlines how mineworkers continue to be regarded as inputs rather than as human beings deserving of the dignity and care accorded to other people in society. Viewed from this angle, the Marikana massacre itself was just an extreme example in a long history of treating the lives of workers as expendable.

Yet, despite this abjection, in how they live their lives and in representing themselves, workers have insisted on their humanity being recognised. This, too, has always been the case. The choreographed stereographic tableaux in which miners were posed as dutiful units of labour power belie the rich ways in which workers on the Witwatersrand *did* find means for self-representation, exercising sophisticated, creative agency despite the conditions they endured (Abrahams, 1946; Tracey, 1952; First, 1961; Callinicos, 1981; Coplan, 1994; Van Onselen, 2001; Allen, 2005). Their stories and songs have rarely reached audiences beyond their own communities.

While the oppression of the capitalist system endures, compounded by the legacy of apartheid and racism, there *have* been paradigmatic shifts in critical social perspective between the moment of the stereographs' origin and the present. As one example, there is now a greater space for narratives that speak of the agency of labourers, even as mainstream media representations still tend to elide their perspectives (Nicolson, 2014; Tolsi and Botes, 2015).

The iconic photographic image by *City Press* journalist Leon Sadiki of rock drill operator and strike leader Mgcineni Noki (also known as 'Mambush' and the 'Man in the Green Blanket') testifies to this. This image of Mambush raising his fist and his voice, bright green blanket pinned around his shoulders as he addressed striking Lonmin workers just hours before he and 33 others died in a hail of police bullets, has broken loose from its immediate context and come to stand for resistance to corporate and government oppression in general. Now it is used in other struggles: a stylised stencil of the figure, created by the Tokolos collective (www.tokolosstencils.tumblr.com/), makes a regular appearance in South African urban space, usually accompanied by the words 'REMEMBER MARIKANA' or 'WE ARE ALL MARIKANA'.

This image is being mobilised in a wider public domain, drawing mainstream attention to the plight of working-class people in South Africa, despite continued efforts by neoliberal corporations and government to maintain the status quo that would hold mineworkers and other labourers in silent servitude.

References

Abrahams, P. (1946) *Mine Boy*, Dorothy Crisp & Co., London
Agamben, G. (1995) *Homo Sacer: Sovereign Power and Bare Life*, Stanford University Press, Stanford
Alexander, P. et al. (2012) *Marikana: A View from the Mountain and a Case to Answer*, Jacana, Johannesburg
Allen, V. (2005) *The History of Black Mineworkers in South Africa*, 3 vols.), The Moor Press, Keighley and Merlin, London
Barthes, R. (1981) *Camera Lucida: Reflections on Photography*, Hill and Wang, New York
Berger, J. (1972) *Selected Essays and Articles: The Look of Things*, Penguin, London
Callinicos, L. (1981) *A People's History of South Africa, Volume One: Gold and Workers 1886–1924*, Ravan Press, Johannesburg
Coplan, D. (1994) *In the Time of Cannibals: The Word Music of South Africa's Basotho Migrants*, University of Chicago Press, Chicago
Desai, R. (2014) *Miners Shot Down*, documentary film, RSA, 90 mins, Uhuru Productions, Johannesburg
Duncan, J. (2012) Marikana and the problem of pack journalism, *SABC News.com*, www.sabc.co.za/news/a/00f7e0804cfe58899b00bf76c8dbd3db/Marikana-and-the-problem-of-pack-journalism-20121007, accessed 15 November 2014
Duncan, J. (2013) South African journalism and the Marikana massacre: A case study of an editorial failure, *The Political Economy of Communication* 1, 2, polecom.org/index.php/polecom/article/view/22/198, accessed 5 October 2017
Edwards, E. (1992) Introduction, in *Anthropology and Photography 1860–1920*, Yale University Press, New Haven, in association with the Royal Anthropological Institute, London
First, R. (1961) 'The gold of migrant labour', in D. Pinnock, *Voices of Liberation*, HSRC Press, Cape Town, 2012, pp. 118–140

Fogel, B. (2012) The selling of a massacre: Media complicity in Marikana repression, *Ceasefire*, Monday, 5 November, ceasefiremagazine.co.uk/south-africa-marikana/, accessed 9 October 2017

Frankel, P. (2012) Marikana: 20 years in the making, *IOL Business Report – Opinion*, 21 October, www.iol.co.za/business-report/opinion/marikana-20-years-in-the-making-1407448, accessed 19 October 2017

Foucault, M. (1976) *Discipline and Punish: The Birth of the Prison*, Pantheon, New York

Krautwurst, U. (2009) The joy of looking: Early German anthropology, photography and audience formation, in A. Hoffmann (ed.), *What We See: Reconsidering an Anthropometrical Collection from Southern Africa: Images, Voices, and Versioning*, Basler Afrika Bibliographien, Basel

Legassick, M. (1975) South Africa: Forced labour, industrialisation and racial differentiation, in R. Harris (ed.), *The Political Economy of Africa*, John Wiley, New York

Lehmann, A. (2009) *Exposures: Visual Culture, Discourse and Performance in Nineteenth-Century America*, Stauffenburg, Tübingen

Lewis, P. (2017) Marikana: Lonmin's dodgy housing record, *GroundUp*, 4 September, www.groundup.org.za/article/marikana-lonmins-dodgy-housing-record/, accessed 10 October 2017

Marinovich, G. (2012) The murder fields of Marikana: The cold murder fields of Marikana, *Daily Maverick*, 8 September, www.dailymaverick.co.za/article/2012-08-30-the-murder-fields-of-marikana-the-cold-murder-fields-of-marikana, accessed 19 October 2017

Mathunjwa, J. (2017) WATCH: AMCU boss speaks about Marikana 5 years after the massacre, *ENCA.com*, video interview with Joseph Mathunjwa, published 16 August, www.enca.com/south-africa/watch-amcu-boss-speaks-about-marikana-5-years-on-since-the-massacre, accessed 19 October 2017

Moodie, G. (2012) Where were the miners' voices at Marikana?, *Journalism.co.za*, 15 October, www.journalism.co.za/index.php/news-and-insight/insight/170-backstory/5097-where-were-the-miners-voices-at-marikana.html, accessed 20 August 2017

Nicolson, G. (2014) Marikana Commission: Families speak, *Daily Maverick*, 14 August, www.dailymaverick.co.za/article/2014-08-14-marikana-commission-families-speak, accessed 5 October 2017

Pillay, S. (2014) Marikana: The politics of law and order in post-apartheid South Africa, *Al Jazeera*, 21 March, www.aljazeera.com/indepth/opinion/2012/09/2012916121852144587.html, accessed 15 November 2014

Rodny-Gumede, Y. (2015) Coverage of Marikana: War and conflict and the case for peace journalism, *Social Dynamics*, 41, 2, pp. 359-374

Schlereth, T. (1991) *Victorian America: Transformations in Everyday Life, 1876–1915* (The Everyday Life in America Series, vol. 4), Harper Collins, New York

Sekula, A. (1982) On the invention of photographic meaning, in V. Burgin (ed.), *Thinking Photography*, Macmillan, London

Sekula, A. (2003) Reading an archive: Photography between labour and capital, in L. Wells (ed.), *The Photography Reader*, Routledge, London and New York

Sontag, S. (1973) In Plato's cave, in *On Photography*, first electronic edition (2005), RosettaBooks, New York

Sontag, S. (1977) Photography unlimited, *New York Review of Books*, 24, 11, 23 June, www.nybooks.com/articles/1977/06/23/photography-unlimited/, accessed 5 October 2017

Spiro, L. (n.d.) A brief history of stereographs and stereoscopes, Part 1 of a 4-part course, *History through the Stereoscope*, cnx.org/contents/s3OUU76y@5/A-Brief-History-of-Stereograph, 5 October 2017

Staples, S. (2002) The machine in the parlor: Naturalizing and standardizing labor and industry through the stereoscope, American Studies Program, Fall 2002, University of Virginia, www.xroads.virginia.edu/~ma03/staples/stereo/home.html, accessed 5 October 2017

Strasser, A. (1942) *Victorian Photography*, Focal Press, London and New York

Tagg, J. (1988) *The Burden of Representation: Essays on Photographies and Histories*, Macmillan, London

Tolsi, N. and P. Botes (2015) Marikana: The blame game – A special report, laura-7.atavist.com/mgmarikanablamegame, accessed 20 August 2017

Tracey, H. (1952) *African Dances of the Witwatersrand Gold Mines*, African Music Society, Johannesburg

Van Onselen, C. (2001) *New Babylon, New Nineveh: Everyday Life on the Witwatersrand 1886–1914*, Jonathan Ball, Johannesburg

REMEMBER MARIKANA

▲ Remember Marikana. Download the stencil at: tokolosstencils.tumblr.com.

21. POSTCOLONIAL INTERNATIONALISM: THOUGHTS ON REDEFINING GLOBAL NORTH–SOUTH SOLIDARITY IN THE 21ST CENTURY

Alexander Behr and Trevor Ngwane

Beginning with the Algerian war in the late 1950s, solidarity with anti-colonial liberation movements in African countries has played an important role in the Western European internationalist movement for at least 30 years. Internationalist activities also came from the Soviet Union and China, including from post-colonial anti-capitalist states such as Cuba. Most broadly established were the diverse (boycott) campaigns against the South African apartheid regime in the 1980s. International awareness of apartheid atrocities rose considerably when police shot and killed 69 anti-pass demonstrators in Sharpeville in 1960.

This massacre provoked a global outcry which, sadly, was absent when, on 16 August 2012 – long after the end of apartheid – South African police shot dead 34 striking miners in Marikana. On this day Mandela's famous refrain and promise – 'Never again!' – was muffled by the loud noise of automatic gunfire. The ensuing silence of the world underlines the horrifying extent to which transnational solidarity with the working class and Africa's poor has declined, especially since 1989. Even the anti-globalisation movements appear to have succumbed to the dominant view of Africa as a continent of catastrophes rather than supporting its social struggles – solidarity was largely turned into charity. However, it is gratifying to note that there is a slow turnaround. Over the past few years, numerous contacts have been established between grassroots initiatives in Africa and Europe.

Analysing the virtual collapse of internationalist practice after 1989 and arguing from a perspective that examines specific campaigns, this chapter deals with the question of what shape the tentative efforts of the Left – one that is interested in tangible transnational cooperation and campaigns – might take in this era of climate change, European border regimes, a unipolar world order and the seemingly untrammelled power of transnational corporations. It focuses on advancing 'international solidarity in support of freedom, justice and development' (Katjavivi, 1999:1). Aware that all three terms remain highly contentious, we approach this question from two vantage points, namely, that of the global North and of the global South, and attempt to bridge the chasm between these historical and geographical political entities. In this process, it is crucial to also examine the debate surrounding migration, which has – at least for some time – displayed a void that makes clear the ignorance shown by the Left in the global North.

The history of internationalist practice

It is important to note that the internationalist movement of recent decades has never been a homogeneous entity. There have always been different, diverse and overlapping groupings – anti-imperialists of various backgrounds, Moscow-loyal traditional communists, the churches and autonomous and social revolutionary groupings. Many changes in strategy made in the new internationalism have come about from the revolt of the Zapatistas in Mexico in 1994, in particular because of their refusal to regard the acquisition of state power as an emancipatory goal.

Unfortunately, it has to be noted that there have been monstrous mal-developments in different countries in which the internationalist movements had high hopes. In Vietnam, Cambodia, Mozambique and Ethiopia, it became clear what seemingly progressive liberation movements are capable of – often this became apparent during the liberation struggle and certainly once state power had been obtained.

Frantz Fanon, a man renowned not least as a theoretician of the Algerian revolution, appears to have anticipated this in his writings, which are scathing in their critique of the post-colonial nationalist elite. Kwame Nkrumah, first president of the liberated Ghana, warned repeatedly of the dangers of neocolonialism from a Marxist perspective. In South Africa, the Marikana massacre shockingly underlines how one of the greatest international solidarity movements in history, the Anti-Apartheid Movement, unwittingly helped put a regime into power that turned its guns on its own supporters: the black working class. According to Anthony O'Brien, the outcome of the bitter national liberation struggle in South Africa has ultimately cemented 'a de facto racist status quo' and 'black stewardship of racial capitalism'. The reason for this failure lies in the inability to wrest substantive control and ownership of the country's wealth from the '*white* South African system and international corporate hands' (O'Brien, 2001:4).

But for all the trials and tribulations, there can be no doubt that the collapse of internationalist practice was a serious political disaster – and for at least three reasons. Firstly, because of the increasing failure to analyse power and violence in a global context. Particularly problematic was the loss of an empirically proven understanding of the interplay between successful capital accumulation in the centres and the aggressive peripheralisation of whole regions of the world, i.e. the processes of externalisation. Also, concrete issues that are directly linked were gradually marginalised or tacitly delegated to NGOs – whether it was hunger, indebtedness or lack of health care. Secondly, knowledge of the diversity and strength of social movements in the global South has largely disappeared from the Northern mental map, in terms of political alliances as well. Many of the collaborations between Southern and Northern grassroots initiatives that emerged in the 1970s and 1980s have also declined (one exception was the PGA – the People's Global Action – which was relatively strong in the 1990s). Thirdly, the often apocalyptic conditions of existence in the periphery were scarcely regarded as a scandal, let alone a call for action, either intellectually or emotionally. As a bitter consequence, a question that has been debated so extensively over the last decade has become increasingly marginalised, namely, the extent to which it is, for reasons of social and ecological justice, imperative to lower the material standard of living in the global North and, conversely, fundamentally redefine what is understood as 'a good life' and thus as social development (Bernau, 2010).

Social movements and state power

The consequence of all this is that the relevant points of reference are now less left-wing governments but rather state-independent social movements. All around the world people are fighting for political, civil and social rights, and they are organised in a variety of ways, whether they are fighting for free access to land, water, health care, political participation, or against union repression, privatisation, free trade agreements, approval of genetically manipulated seed and structural adjustment programmes. Here it is important to stress that it is not just politically articulated battles that deserve attention; we must also note and take seriously individual strategies of appropriation as they emerge, for example, in the struggles of migration. This is due to the simple but significant reason that a shift of the overall social power relations is only possible if the different fields of force interact on a large scale. In the old internationalist movement, this view did not gain acceptance for a long time as the focus tended to be exclusively on the achievement of state power, and often all forces concentrated on activities related to this goal.

In many cases, the focus on taking state power certainly stood to reason: it arose from the observation that it was the most effective weapon used by imperialism to control the state and its institutions and ultimately enforce its will upon people in its colonies. However, this assessment, correct in and of itself, was undermined and distorted when the liberation movements relinquished the idea of tearing down the colonial state and replacing it with something completely new. Instead, the goal became taking over the state with its existing structures left intact. Subsequently, more often than not, this resulted in what was nothing more than a de facto leadership change. The need to tear down the bourgeois state and replace it with a participatory workers' state had been the conclusion drawn by Marx from his analysis of the Paris Commune. The fact that most liberation movements have simply aspired to take over the state institutions as they already existed was often a major detraction from the internationalist nature of the movement. As a consequence, one strand in the movement gained the upper hand as it was more or less based on nationalist perspectives and strategies focused on winning state power in individual countries; i.e. the notion of building 'socialism in one country'. This approach was always problematic; today, however, it is completely obsolete, especially – in a world where nations are inextricably linked – when discussing effective solidarity in struggles for justice.

Another crucial question is how global solidarity might look beyond paternalistic intercession or only presenting the interests of others. How can specific political struggles, which result from different social conditions, fight together without individual movements being subsumed or coopted? Communication across 'established borders and boundaries' would appear to be crucial as we otherwise run the risk of 'imposing our own views, needs, and conceptions of the good life on other people', and thereby overlook the fact that solidarity has to be conceived as a dialogic process (see the chapter by Franziska Dübgen). An important requirement is to deal openly with differences and to reduce organisational pressures and tempo in the common processes and to respect the realities of the opposite ('reflexive solidarity' in Dübgen's words).

'We are here because you destroy our countries'

Internationalist solidarity efforts cannot ignore the issue of migration. But it is apparent that even in anti-racist contexts the focus has, for a long time, been on the situation of migrants in the so-called 'receiving countries', with the result that the structural causes of migration are overlooked. There have been few exceptions to this narrow perspective. However, in recent years there has been a turnaround in policy on migration between Europe and Africa. A new line of discourse was initiated with the slogan 'We are here because you destroy our countries'. The truth is, whether it is large-scale 'land-grabbing' in the Congo, overfishing of the coastal waters off Senegal by European fleets, the devastation of vast swathes of land by the extraction industry, the tax-avoidance and profit-shifting practices of transnational corporations, the structural adjustment programmes imposed by the IMF, cheap imports of food from the EU or the effects of climate change on small-scale farming in many African countries, anti-racist struggles in Europe, as well as in campaigns for the right to stay or for the legalisation of people, must take into account the circumstances that force people to leave their countries. Such a transnational perspective is important because it opens the door to establishing North–South solidarity with social movements in migrants' so-called countries of origin.

With this in mind, struggles of migration can be seen as struggles that challenge the exploitative economic relations between the North and the South. If local struggles that take place in the global South, such as those for access to water, land, seeds or education, are understood in this context, then paternalistic concepts used by traditional Western NGOs are no longer necessary. This has been impressively demonstrated in the last two decades by the international peasant and landless organisation Via Campesina. A string of progressive NGOs have also distanced themselves from paternalistic or charitable approaches. In terms of examples from the German-speaking world, one NGO that is certainly worth mentioning is Medico International, which has proclaimed that it is 'beyond aid': 'The problem in the world is not too little aid, but rather the conditions that make more and more aid necessary. [...] We operate on the maxim "Defend, criticise and overcome aid".'[1]

Solidarity along the value chain

Like Candeias (2011), we argue that real linkages between labour struggles can be created along the value chain when solidarity and protest are no longer merely moral, but a product of well-intentioned self-interest – if they become 'subjectively functional'. In this sense, a major challenge of international or transnational solidarity is to ensure that an articulation of common interests can take place between wage-dependent persons along the value chain, not forgetting the crucial unpaid labour performed in domestic households, mostly by women, such as taking care of children and the elderly. The fact that this labour is performed without remuneration clearly amounts to a subsidy for the capitalist class and their system (see the chapter by Asanda Benya and Judy Seidman).

The solidarity of actors who are not directly involved in the value chain can be crucial for a particular campaign. As Olaf Bernau (2009) emphasises: 'Not only politically, but also materially and strategically the success of social struggles is decisively dependent on the extent to which external support can be mobilised.' An important function of campaigning is always to disseminate media reports about the current social situation on the ground. This allows a greater number of activists and interested people to be involved in the debate concerning the next possible steps in a campaign.

In the age of neoliberalism, monopoly capitalism is characterised by huge transnational companies whose wealth easily dwarfs that of many nation states. Often their production and distribution processes traverse the entire globe and many aspects of the value chain, including forward and backward linkages. This gives them tremendous power to manipulate prices, including those of production inputs. They are also able to structure their production processes so that various aspects and stages are located in different countries. This spatial fragmentation of the production process is always arranged so that it benefits the company rather than humanity or those countries in which production takes place. Here the role of the nation state is often restricted to playing handmaiden to the companies' profit-mongering schemes (see the chapter by Britta Becker and Boris Kanzleiter). The need for more up-to-date forms of international solidarity must therefore be understood against this grim backdrop of the almost untrammelled power of these economic monsters and the 'imperial mode of living' that sustains them.

The imperial mode of living, critique of consumerism and the role of unions

The term 'imperial mode of living' describes the material and cultural integration of the global middle classes into the international division of labour (Brand et al.,

2007:67). The relative stability of capitalist relations can only be explained by the inclusion of further sections of the subaltern classes in the global North, or the middle classes in the so-called emerging countries, in certain patterns of consumption that occur at the expense of subaltern classes in countries of the global South. These patterns are deeply anchored, highly routinised and unintended. Combined with the individualising logic of neoliberalism, they present a major obstacle to building transnational solidarity.

Such solidarity cannot therefore be achieved through moral appeals or the individualisation of consumer choices. Rather, common interests between different groups of socially disadvantaged people must be found. Consumption boycotts are only capable of developing a wider political effect if they are coordinated with those who are struggling to end misery in the places of production and distribution (e.g. wage earners in the mines and the factories or workers in transport and logistics). Through the organised, collective pressure of consumers – ideally, combined with protests or strikes on site – there is a chance that court proceedings will be conducted properly, wages increased, working conditions improved, *sans papiers* legalised and works councils set up. Ultimately, processes of solidarity along the value chain require stable and credible trade unions, which are able to represent the interests of the wage earners at the various places of production or marketing.

However, we live in a world where labour movement support for proactive campaigning as part of an international solidarity effort can no longer be taken for granted, either in South Africa or Europe. In South Africa this stance has led to much more severe consequences than in Europe: the events that culminated in the Marikana massacre included the National Union of Mineworkers of South Africa (NUM) refusing to take up the wage grievances of its own members, leading the Marikana workers to call a wildcat strike. Workers criticised the NUM for being 'a pocket union', meaning its officials stood to benefit personally from the policy of appeasement with Lonmin management (Sinwell and Mbatha, 2016). Indeed, independent research after the massacre concluded that the bosses of leading South African mining companies have found ways to systematically contain autonomous worker actions by incorporating union leaders into their power structures and granting them special privileges (Bezuidenhout and Buhlungu, 2008).

In other words, transnational corporations in the mining sector such as Lonmin have successfully devised strategies of coopting working-class leaders so that they sit at the bosses' table at the expense of ordinary workers. Critics of post-apartheid South Africa have repeatedly argued that political and economic leaders of the new state have gone the same way (McKinley, 2017). In fact, it was the 'toxic collusion between state and capital', a phrase coined by Dali Mpofu, legal representative of the slain and injured Marikana miners at the state-appointed Farlam Commission into the massacre, that, together with the connivance of the NUM (then the biggest union in the mining sector), led to the massacre. Buhlungu (2016:140) notes that 'Although the strike at Marikana was triggered by a wage dispute involving rock-drill operators, the heavy-handed action of the union, management and the police had everything to do with the fact that Lonmin and other platinum workers in the region had dared to challenge a trade union monopoly underwritten by management, the ruling tripartite alliance and the state'.

All the members of the tripartite alliance, the ANC, the Communist Party and the Congress of South African Trade Unions (COSATU) had condemned the workers' strike. Buhlungu (2016:145) points out that the striking workers were disowned not only by the alliance, but also by the NUM, the government and management. Hence the massacre of workers did not elicit a whimper of protest from COSATU or the NUM; instead, they blamed it on the workers themselves, as did the Farlam Commission, which suggested that 'overall responsibility for triggering the violence should be attributed to the conduct of the strikers' (Forrest, 2015:29). Organising local and international solidarity with the workers in the aftermath of the massacre had to contend with this hostile political reality. Attempts by the Marikana Solidarity Campaign, a civil society initiative, to form an alternative 'people's tribunal' to investigate the massacre came to naught owing to funding and legal problems. Such a tribunal would have challenged the narrative of the state-sponsored Farlam Commission, whose overall findings raise the question whether its investigation led to 'unearthing the truth or burying it' (Forrest, 2015).

Marikana is a prime example of how semi-peripheral economies such as the BRICS (Brazil, Russia, India, China and South Africa) often play the role of 'sub-imperialist' states in that they facilitate the continued exploitation of other countries and subaltern classes by advanced capitalist societies (Bond and Garcia, 2015). They frequently position themselves as challengers of imperialism but, in reality, they legitimise and connive with its logic to the detriment of less economically strong former colonies. Cyril Ramaphosa, whose political intervention indirectly led to the Marikana massacre, became president of South Africa on 15 February 2018 following the resignation of Jacob Zuma.

The survivors of the Marikana massacre decided to exchange the 'union of the mountain' (where they had camped throughout their strike and where they were shot at by the police) for the 'union of the office' (withdrawing en masse from the NUM and joining a small union called the Association of Mineworkers and Construction Union – AMCU). In all of the three major platinum mining companies, Amplats, Lonmin and Impala Platinum, the workers had gone on strike separately in the same year (2012) and each time the strike was led by a workers' strike committee. The decision to join AMCU derived from the need to have a 'proper' union that would actually represent the interests of workers. It was also part of a plan to call a 'protected' (legal) nationwide strike across the entire sector, which indeed took place in 2014. Recent developments in the South African Platinum Belt suggest that independent workers' committees have a crucial role to play, in stopping the unions from becoming 'pocket unions' and in holding the union leadership accountable to the membership. The 'union of the mountain' should be kept alive inside the 'union of the office'.

Reform and revolution: Forms of organisation

Although the prospect of a world without domination should be the aim of any emancipatory approach, concrete commitment cannot solely be based on a distant goal. On the way there, changes, within a realistic framework, must be won, for through successful battles, the social distribution of power and the social and economic contexts of the conflicts can be changed. Fighting for reforms (e.g. certifications and social standards, compliance with collective agreements, reduced working hours, legalisation of *sans papiers* and defence of peasant agriculture against land-grabbing) should always be linked to the struggle for a fundamentally different society – which is why it is problematic to play so-called 'reformist' and 'revolutionary' strategies off against each other. After the failed revolutionary voluntarism of the 1960s and 1970s, perceptions on how capitalism could be overcome changed, and it became more and more thought of as a transformation – as a longer historical process. The struggle for hegemony, the carving out of positions and open spaces against the powerful and their order, led to molecular processes of change becoming the focus. However, as seen in the revolts and revolutions in the Arab world during 2010 and 2011, moments of rupture can be of decisive importance in emancipatory processes. These do not, however, fall from the sky, but are the expression of prolonged processes in which experience has been collected from social struggles, and disappointment and anger accumulate.

Revolutionary ruptures constantly raise the question of the relationship of spontaneity and conscious planning, a classic conundrum of the Left. While the Egyptian uprising successfully removed the dictator Mubarak, the counter-revolution subsequently emerged triumphant. While the Egyptian revolution is far from over, its course of development suggests the need for better preparation, programmatic intervention and tactical leadership by future revolutionary forces. It became amply clear that there was not enough unity, coherence or direction at decisive moments of the revolution, which allowed the ruling class and the army generals to confuse and put down the people's movements and organisations. The centralised army structure cut through resistance like a hot knife through butter because there was no symmetrical centralised force on the people's side to frustrate its intervention.

Broad fronts put together for the purpose of action require political platforms, as well as collective strategies and goals that bind the various strands together, i.e. a programme. It is the programme which, if taken seriously, helps to provide coherence and binds the movement together. However, a programme is pointless if it is adopted today and ignored by half the organisations of the alliance tomorrow. This is neither democratic nor does it show integrity; it is also a sure-fire recipe for failure. An action alliance will work if its various components consist of reasonably developed organisations – those that have spent some time developing their own politics and positions at least in relation to the alliance and have a leadership that is able to marshal and keep intact its organisational forces. This will be crucial as the enemy does not sit waiting to be hit; it actively seeks to weaken, divide and undermine any organised attempt to challenge its hegemony. Ultimately, it is up to strong political organisations or movements to prove whether they are capable and efficient enough to provide clear leadership and direction from the centre of the action alliance while not being fooled into using undemocratic or sectarian methods. This is the only way to ensure the success of broad fronts.

Movements of solidarity remain trustworthy if the original direction of their policy remains recognisable, and when their effort increases the possibilities to act for social struggles from below. That is why there is a need for coherent organisation. The alternative is failure due to the individualistic tendencies of individual groups. This approach may momentarily impress with short-lived revolutionary effervescence, which undoubtedly makes a political statement but nothing more, except lessons of how struggles for reforms should not be conducted if they are to be effective and sustained.

The organisation of counter-hegemony in the global North is undeniably a long-term task. Olaf Bernau mentions the conditions and preconditions for counter-hegemonic strategies:

> Protest and offensive resistance do not run by themselves; they cannot be derived from objective macro data such as massive closures or the drop of real wages. Those who argue like this project their own conception of justice onto society, with the consequence that it becomes inexplicable as to why conflicts, even militant ones, are interrupted by defensive, often long-lasting phases in which social struggles are noticeably diminishing and their character changes, possibly continuing to bubble under the surface – usually as individual survival strategies (Bernau, 2009).

The subjective factor of embedding experience plays a key role in the development of social struggles: 'The pressure might be big but resistance and protest are only there when the experiences are interpreted as unjust. But this is by no means a given since the social actors – regardless of their willingness for rebellion – are currently more or less bound to the prevailing conditions in a habitual sense, i.e. cognitively, normatively and affectively. Therefore, it is reasonable that left theorists have always dealt with this simple and fundamental issue – important concepts are, for example, "ideology as necessarily false consciousness" (Marx and Engels), "objectified consciousness" (Lukácz), "authoritarian character" (Adorno), "spontaneous consensus, everyday understanding and cultural hegemony" (Gramsci), "sense of one's own place" (Bourdieu), etc.' (Bernau, 2009).

The linkage and the mutual promotion of transnational labour struggles and solidarity therefore do not appear automatically. While economic tensions and crises of capitalism have the potential to promote emancipatory movements, they can also increase racism, patriarchal gender relations and a further intensification of the uneven distribution of the world's resources. Crisis impacts are often externalised from the centre to the peripheries. In some places, social cohesion rapidly disintegrates; in other areas, hegemony is more or less precariously sustained by concessions to the subaltern. What is certain is that a new kind of impoverishment theory – that everything has to get worse and worse so that alternatives can prevail – is not useful and is ultimately cynical. The change in the prevailing conditions is rather the result of social struggles in episodes that involve processes of enlightenment and self-enlightenment (Bernau, 2009).

Central to the desire to bring about a socio-ecological shift is the creation of a crossover of movements and groups: the creation of bridges between the struggles of workers, critical shareholders, consumers, trade unions or environmental groups. One must always have the courage to embrace the 'troubles of the ground', or, in other words, the shift of social forces in the sense of a socio-ecological revolutionisation of society on a global scale. The duty of those who, because of their origin, their economic status or the specific identity assigned to them, are in a relatively privileged position within the global division of labour should be in solidarity with those who are denied these privileges. But if we wish to avoid recreating a paternalistic model, it is those who are deprived of these privileges who should be taking a central role in this fight. Ultimately, universal liberation is only conceivable through the abolition of any particular privileges and the full development of the collective productive forces of humankind for the benefit of all within the ecological limits of this planet.

Notes

1   See www.medico.de/en/about/medico-international/.

References

Bernau, O. (2009) Runter vom Beobachtungsturm, *AK: Zeitung für linke Debatte und Praxis* 541, 21 August 2009, www.akweb.de/ak_s/ak542/13.htm

Bernau, O. (2010) Internationalistische Praxis nach dem Internationalismus? Interviews mit Vertreter_innen von NoLager/transact!, Stop the Bomb und Fels, *Phase 2-37*, September 2010

Bezuidenhout, A. and S. Buhlungu (2008) Union solidarity under stress: The case of the National Union of Mineworkers in South Africa', *Labour Studies Journal* 33, 2, pp. 262–287

Bond, P. and A. Garcia (2015) *BRICS: An Anti-Capitalist Critique*, Jacana, Johannesburg

Brand, U., B. Lösch and S. Thimmel (2007) *ABC der Alternativen*, VSA-Verlag, Hamburg

Buhlungu, S. (2016) The paradox of trade union action in post-apartheid South Africa, in T. Kepe, M. Levin and B. von Lieres (eds.), *Domains of Freedom: Justice, Citizenship and Social Change in South Africa*, UCT Press, Cape Town

Candeias, M. (2011) Handlungsfähigkeit und Transformation, *Luxemburg* 2, pp. 6–13

Forrest, K. (2015) Marikana Commission: Unearthing the truth or burying it?, Working Paper No. 5, Sociology of Work, Society and Development (SWOP) Institute, University of the Witwatersrand, Johannesburg, https://www.swop.org.za/working-papers

Katjavivi, P. (1999) A tribute to international solidarity support for Southern Africa, Paper presented at the symposium 'The Anti-Apartheid Movement: A 40-year Perspective', South Africa House, London, 25–26 June

McKinley, D.T. (2017) *South Africa's Corporatised Liberation: A Critical Analysis of the ANC in Power*, Jacana, Johannesburg

O'Brien, A. (2001) *Against Normalisation: Writing Radical Democracy in South Africa*, Duke University Press, Durham and London

Sinwell, L. with S. Mbatha (2016) *The Spirit of Marikana: The Rise of Insurgent Trade Unionism in South Africa*, Wits University Press, Johannesburg

World Bank (2017) *The World Bank in South Africa: Country report*, www.worldbank.org/en/country/southafrica/overview, accessed 17 December 2017

▶ Bongani Sithole, contract worker at Lonmin, in conversation with Jakob Krameritsch in February 2017 at Makwase Palace, a popular club and grill house in the centre of Marikana.
▶ **pp. 392/393** Cleaning of the Freedom Charter Monument at Walter Sisulu Square in Kliptown, Soweto. Adopted by the Congress of the People in 1955, the Freedom Charter was a central document of the anti-apartheid movement and is still frequently referred to today.

03
THE
EOPLE
HALL
ARE IN
THE
UNTRY'S
ALTH!

02
ALL
NATION
GRO
SH
EQ

22. 'THE RIGHT TO HAVE RIGHTS': GLOBAL SOCIAL RIGHTS AS A TOOL AGAINST THE POWER OF TRANSNATIONAL CORPORATIONS AND CAPITALIST EXPLOITATION

Boris Kanzleiter and Britta Becker
Translated by Joanna Mitchell

On the eve of the First World War, socialist theorists were already concerned with the globalisation of capitalism and the emergence of large corporations.

The Austrian Marxist economist and Social Democratic politician Rudolf Hilferding was an important contributor, outlining the growing monopolisation of capital and assimilation of smaller businesses by new, large corporations in his 1910 magnum opus, *Finanzkapital*. He postulated the end of 'free competition', which was considered one of capitalism's essential traits in classical economic theory.

In the ascent of these large corporations and their close ties with finance capital, he foresaw the emergence of 'organised capitalism'. This in turn would lead to the growing fusion of economy and state, a form of 'state monopoly capitalism' characterised by the formation of cartels. In this system, the large corporations would dominate government activity: 'Economic power also means political power. Domination of the economy gives control of the instruments of state power. The greater the degree of concentration in the economic sphere, the more unbounded is the control of the state' (Hilferding, 1955).

Over a hundred years later, these observations are more relevant than ever. In early 21st-century global capitalism, large corporations have amassed a hitherto unprecedented degree of power. While Hilferding primarily describes corporations operating within national borders, we are today confronted with the phenomenon of transnational corporations (TNCs). TNCs operate on a global scale via subsidiaries, financial investments or other economic affiliations, and their economic power often surpasses entire national economies. For example, in 2016 the turnovers of BASF and Lonmin jointly amounted to approximately the gross domestic product (GDP) of Luxembourg and approximately one-fifth of South Africa's GDP (IMF, 2017; BASF, 2016; and Lonmin, 2016). In 2010, private companies made up almost half of the world's 100 largest economies. Therefore, it is not surprising that Royal Dutch Shell's turnover is higher than Austria's GDP and that British Petrol's turnover is approximately as high as that of Denmark (Attac, 2016).

The economic power concentrated by transnational corporations is accompanied by the polarisation of wealth and increasing social inequality. According to a recent study by the French economist Thomas Piketty, social inequality has increased globally since 1980. Increasing privatisation is seen as the major reason for this (Piketty, 2017). Furthermore, studies of annual global wealth distribution performed by the NGO Oxfam have documented the increasing concentration of wealth in the hands of few: 'In 2016, the eight richest billionaires – all men – own more wealth than the entire half of the poorer world population'. Further, the richest 1 per cent of the global population owns 50.8 per cent of the global wealth – more than the remaining 99 per cent combined. Oxfam provides important background: 'This is also connected to the power held by international corporations: they employ tax evasion techniques, transfer their profits to tax havens and drive countries into a ruinous race for low tax rates' (Oxfam, 2017).

The enforcement of TNCs' profit- and power-oriented interests has devastating global consequences for people's living conditions worldwide. These include the polarisation of wealth, exploitation of workers, ecological devastation in the wake of environmental degradation and the infringement and undermining of democratic rights. As exemplified by Volkswagen's 'Dieselgate' or Monsanto's glyphosate scandal, the power held by TNCs also poses a threat to democracy in Germany and the European Union. In both cases, strong ties exist between lobbyists and government within a system of influence and collusion. Imke Dierßen, political managing director of the non-profit organisation Lobbycontrol, draws a disillusioning conclusion: 'Our democracy is in a deep crisis. More and more people do not see themselves represented in politics, and right-wing populists are on the rise. One reason for this is an unbridled, non-transparent lobbyism with few rules, but nonetheless imbued with the belief that giving lobbyists free rein best serves the collective good. This is a dangerous misconception' (Dierßen, 2016).

Another criticism of the lack of transparency in government is voiced in the broad protest movement against the Transatlantic Trade and Investment Partnership (TTIP) and other free trade agreements. One of the main reasons for civil society's enormous support of these protests is the secrecy surrounding the contractual negotiations of these agreements.

In all of this, what becomes apparent is that the weaker that democratic controls are upheld by the public and the constitutional structures of a country, the more brutally the TNCs push forward with their purely profit-oriented agenda. The Marikana massacre serves as a sad example, taking its place in a long list of similar cases.

In order to create a more equitable world living in solidarity, one must therefore examine the question of how the power of TNCs can be broken down. One hundred years ago, Rudolf Hilferding assumed that, at the highest stage of monopolisation, corporations could be socialised by a revolution and thus brought under democratic control, thereby creating the basis for a socialist system of production.

From a current perspective, the issue at hand is far more complex. Beyond changing ownership conditions, breaking down existing power structures and democratising the production process, there are two important additional aspects that must be considered. Firstly, an ecological transformation of the mode of production must be achieved in order to sustain humanity's natural livelihood. Secondly, in the face of the rapidly advancing process of transnationalisation, the global interconnection of production processes and the increase in power held by TNCs, a global course of action must be adopted. An emancipatory and socio-ecological transformation can only be conceived as a global process.

Envisioning a global social rights policy

Rising up to meet these enormous challenges is a difficult endeavour. The discourse on global social rights (GSR) offers the opportunity to consider the multiple crises and problems from a global perspective, to identify the inner ties and contradictions of seemingly opposing interests and to formulate appropriate solutions (for an introduction to global social rights, see Oehrlein, 2009; and Fischer-Lescano and Möller, 2012). This places a political and anti-authoritarian parenthesis around the different ties between corporate power and human rights along the platinum supply chain examined in the individual chapters of this book. Global social rights connect social and political human rights and view these as indivisible from one another. This in turn gives rise to the vision of a global transformation which brings together the different dimensions of our global challenges as inseparable parts of a whole and develops holistic courses of action which, in contrast to nationally anchored or citizenship rights, are not tied to particular conditions.

The unconditional demand for universal social and democratic rights for all humans is central to the concept of global social rights. Every person has the 'right to have rights' (Arendt, 2001), irrespective of their place of residence or religious affiliation (Oehrlein, 2009). These social and democratic rights are based on the right to a dignified life as established by international treaties and documents, such as the International Covenant on Economic, Social and Cultural Rights (ICESCR) and the conventions of the International Labour Organization (ILO), but exceed these in scope. As such, global social rights must also be fought for outside and against institutions, as exemplified in the Treaty Alliance movement (see the chapter by Akhona Mehlo). Global social rights thus create the link between local and international struggles for the enforcement of social rights, which include the universal right to humane working conditions, health care, education and housing. Furthermore, the concept of global social rights helps unify struggles for democratic and political rights, such as the right to free movement and assembly, in order ultimately to achieve their legal enforceability, while also focusing on existing relations of power that hinder their implementation. Global social rights do not only criticise the violation of social or political human rights, but also strive to overcome current relationships of production and rule. Equally fundamental is the perspective of the ecological transformation of production and societal reproduction. The 'imperial mode of living' must be conquered by a 'solidary mode of living' (Brand and Wissen, 2017). It is here, in the confrontation with the TNCs' global reach of power that the potential of a policy of global social rights resides.

Breaking down the power of transnational corporations

As the exploitation of cheap labour by TNCs and reports of inhumane working conditions in the world-market factories of the global South are long-known facts among the critical public of the North, the German government is under pressure to act. In 2014, as a response to fatal accidents in textile factories in Bangladesh and Pakistan, the German federal minister for economic cooperation and development, Gerd Müller, initiated the Partnership for Sustainable Textiles, in which actors from politics, business and civil society are represented. The partnership strives to improve working conditions along the global textile production supply chain. In accordance with the partnership's requirements, its members, which include the companies C&A, Aldi and Adidas, set their own goals for social, ecological and economic improvements to the entire textile supply chain and deliver an annual progress report (Partnership for Sustainable Textiles, 2018). Following the Partnership's fundamental philosophy of 'individual responsibility', all members are committed to implementing the jointly agreed goals: 'Taken together, the individual measures implemented by each member gradually lead to improvements in the environmental and social conditions within the textile sector, especially in the producer countries' (GIZ, 2018).

The Partnership for Sustainable Textiles thus constitutes a benchmark example for corporate social responsibility (CSR), a catchword which, over the past 20 years, has attracted a discourse on corporate voluntary commitment to social and ecological standards (see also the interview conducted with Dinah Rajak in this book). TNCs have warmly – and with great PR effect – welcomed these initiatives, in particular as a means to secure their own power of action and influence within the emerging institutions. CRS Europe, for example, a network of business enterprises founded by the European Commission, is committed to mainstreaming corporate social responsibility and sustainability in European Union policies (CSR Europe, 2018). Founded in 1999 by the UN secretary general, Kofi Annan, the UN Global Compact initiative also follows the principle of entrepreneurial self-regulation and is run by TNCs (Karaaslan, 2017).[1] As one of the founding members, BASF remains a member of the UN Global Compact Board to date (BASF, 2015).

The UN Guiding Principles on Business and Human Rights and their implementation within the German National Action Plan on Business and Human Rights represent yet another failure to establish binding legal regulations on human rights responsibilities in business relations abroad (VENRO et al., 2016). Civil society organisations have criticised the Action Plan, which took effect in December 2016, as 'bearing the signature of the private sector' and as 'a textbook example of lobbyism' (Dierßen, 2016). From the global social rights perspective, these voluntary multi-stakeholder initiatives, rather than effectively safeguarding proper working conditions and compliance with ecological and human rights standards in the supply chain, are completely insufficient or even counterproductive (see also the chapter by Sarah Lincoln). With its focus on voluntary commitment, this type of corporate self-commitment actually leads to the obstruction of specific standards and legally enforceable rights. Simultaneously, the creation of institutions which actually enforce these rights and standards is undermined (see the chapter by Carolijn Terwindt).

Global social rights, on the other hand, focus on approaches which develop and expand such legally binding regulations on a global scale. An example of such a civil society approach is the Global Campaign to Reclaim Peoples Sovereignty, Dismantle Corporate Power and Stop Impunity, a network of over 200 social movements, organisations and affected communities combating land-grabbing, resource exploitation, inhumane wages and environmental destruction at the hands of TNCs in different regions of the world, with a focus on Africa, Asia and Latin America (www.stopcorporateimpunity.org). Founded in 2012 during the UN Conference on Sustainable Development (Rio+20), the campaign demands an International Peoples Treaty, which would serve as a grassroots framework for social movements to unite in the global struggle against the power of TNCs. Based on economic, social and cultural rights, as well as the universal rights that are already enshrined in key documents of the ILO, the OECD and the United Nations, such a Peoples Treaty would further develop mechanisms for implementation. Milestones include the extension of parent company's legal responsibility to affiliates, suppliers and subcontractors, as well as the development of mechanisms for defining and enabling personal criminal liability for management positions within TNCs. In addition, the treaty foresees the subordination of TNCs and their business practices to the control of host-state governments, as well as the creation of an international tribunal for the punishment of human rights violations committed by TNCs (Peoples Treaty Working Group, 2014).

In light of the transnationalisation of production and the growth of TNCs, a debate concerning international treaties on human rights violations and environmental destruction ensued within the UN as early as the 1970s; however, when blocked by industrialised countries of the global North, these approaches made no headway. Led by Ecuador and South Africa, a coalition of states from the global South are currently organising a renewed approach (see the chapter by Akhona Mehlo) (Martens and Seitz, 2016; CorA-Netzwerk für Unternehmensverantwortung, 2017).

In June 2014, the UN Human Rights Council voted for the establishment of an Intergovernmental Working Group for the development of binding regulations for TNCs. In the meantime, this working group has convened several times, and has successively grown from 60 member states during the first session in 2015, to 101 in 2017. Along with other industrialised nations, the EU member states initially blocked, later observed and finally participated in the process, but they continue to try to slow down or even hinder the drafting of an agreement (van Schaik, 2017). While this type of treaty would not help achieve Hilferding's goal of socialisation, it would at least create a framework for exerting steady pressure on TNCs. In the meantime, the chances of practically enforcing such a treaty depend on many factors, such as the stance of governments which support the process. Simultaneously, civil society and human rights organisations must develop international alliances and campaigns in order to increase public pressure on TNCs, and should call on governments to take a stand on legally binding human rights measures within the UN and other international institutions.

One of the problems is the unequal distribution of power at the UN level. In contrast to the Intergovernmental Working Group, which is predominantly sustained by countries of the global South and civil society initiatives, its competitor, the UN Forum of Business and Human Rights with its focus on voluntary commitment approaches, is backed by the global North and large-scale industry participation and thus is significantly better equipped both in terms of funding and political power.

Trade union organisation along production chains

The dedication with which progressive and left-wing governments, human rights organisations and further critical voices of civil society push for legally binding standards for humane working conditions and environmental requirements is of central importance. But what is necessary for the effective enforcement of social rights and human rights standards is the presence of trade unions along the production chain, through which affected parties can articulate and represent their own interests. This involves strategies for generating international solidarity among employees through self-organisation at the local level. After all, only the common representation of workers' interests along the production chains can limit the power of the TNCs to play employees off against each other (see the chapter by Alexander Behr and Trevor Ngwane).

It is here that three challenges become apparent. First of all, European trade unions often follow a Eurocentric perspective which prioritises the preservation of domestic jobs and can thus hardly achieve a cross-border solidarity. Secondly, trade unions themselves are often actors in political decision-making processes or are otherwise involved in political processes. In South Africa, for example, as a member of the Tripartite Alliance alongside the ANC and the Communist Party, the umbrella trade union body COSATU is brought into conflict with the direct representation of workers' interests. Thirdly, serious differences in costs of living hinder the development of a common vision: despite increasing pressure on working standards in the highly competitive global North, the standard of living nonetheless remains significantly higher than in the global South. 'According to the World Bank, in 2013 the 210,000 predominantly working class Bangladeshis living in the Great Britain sent approximately 4,000 US Dollars to relatives in Bangladesh. In the same year, the average annual workers' salary in Bangladesh was 1,380 US Dollars. This means that Bangladeshis working some of the lowest-paid jobs in a country with one of the highest costs of living worldwide were still able to save three times the amount of money that their relatives in Bangladesh even earn in the first place' (Kuhn, 2017). Against this background, what could trade union strategies for organisation along production chains look like?

An important starting point can be found in existing legal norms. In 1998 the ILO created a legally binding framework for all 187 of its member states in its Declaration on Fundamental Principles and Rights at Work (DGB Bundesvorstand, 2009). The document includes four fundamental principles which are integral to the development of a strong and effective trade union movement: a) freedom of association and the effective recognition of the right to collective bargaining; b) the elimination of all forms of forced or compulsory labour; c) the effective abolition of child labour; d) and the elimination of discrimination in respect of employment and occupation (ILO, 2010).

Further, the 1966 UN ICESCR, which in articles six and eight also guarantees fundamental individual and collective workers' rights, and the Treaty Alliance's demands for legally binding regulation and control of corporate activities, both include important steps towards the development of a global social rights policy towards TNCs. In working towards a legally binding guarantee of workers' social and trade union rights, existing rights must be defended in some countries and extended in others. What is also required is the stronger inclusion of such measures in international treaties and conventions and the development of effective instruments for their implementation. The concept of an international tribunal analogous to the UN War Crimes Tribunal in The Hague appears to be one possibility, but it depends on increased pressure on TNCs from all sides: progressive and left-wing governments, trade unions, farmers' associations, human rights organisations, the movement for global solidarity, critical media workers and academics must all increasingly develop common strategies and campaigns, some of which have already proved successful in individual cases.

Global social rights and socio-economic transformation

In the light of the multiple crises of modern-day globalised capitalism, one thing is clear: the strategy of unfettered profit maximisation practised by powerful TNCs does not only brutally exploit and threaten workers' social livelihoods and democratic rights, but also leads to the destruction of the ecosystems. Thus, it is not only a question of changing ownership structures, but also of how to achieve a social-ecological transformation of globalised production. Only by connecting the demand for a socio-ecological societal transformation with the concept of global social rights will the underlying mechanisms of domination and exploitation, which stand in the way of their realisation in capitalist society, be revealed. Global social rights thus constitute a part of the 'concrete utopia' (Bloch, 1985) which Raul Zelik and Aaron Tauss consider necessary for extending the debate on the dynamics of the current crisis to transformation strategies (Tauss, 2016).

Furthermore, 'Corporate power cannot be contained with a few minor changes in the law. As long as our economic system is based on the principles of profit orientation and competition, only limited changes can be made to these conditions. Breaking down the power of corporations means ultimately replacing the capitalist economy with another – one that focuses on human rights, democracy and a good life for all' (Attac, 2016).

In their 2010 declaration (Attac Österreich, 2010), the Attac Austria network outlined several necessary pathways for transformation, describing seven key areas in which fundamental changes must be made towards a post-capitalist society. These include changes that will help bring about a public welfare-oriented financial economy, localisation of the economy, food and energy sovereignty, the use of commons, the enforcement of the right to humane work and comprehensive democratisation.

The suggested measures for achieving these goals are manifold. However, specific struggles must be fought in order to develop the required practices and strategies. As Marx once stated, this is precisely 'the advantage of the new movement, for it means that we do not anticipate the world with our dogmas but instead attempt to discover the new world through the critique of the old' (Marx, 1981). Criticism of the status quo helps to exacerbate the existing cracks and tensions in the system, in order to create the basis for something new (Tauss and Ehs, 2016). Although the conquest of institutional power is necessary in order to change the prevailing conditions, it is also a matter of creating new institutions and redefining the relationship between government and civil society. Change within government can only take place through confrontation. New alliances between grassroots, trade union and municipal movements and parties that 'examine the question of power and implement societal reorganisation step by step through their actions' (Tauss and Ehs, 2016) are therefore integral to successful change.

Outlook

This is where the debate on global social rights, originating from the critical discussion forum Kritischer Bewegungsdiskurs, comes full circle. It constitutes a specific political horizon for criticism of the status quo, which is expressed almost everywhere in the world through struggles for rights and against very concrete grievances. This is particularly evident in the struggles fought against the power of TNCs along global supply chains.

The long-standing protests for better working and living conditions by South African mineworkers, as well as the international support and public awareness generated by the Plough Back the Fruits campaign, are exemplary for many other movements that deal with the application of global social rights at different levels. The crucial difference lies in the establishment of political, economic and legal interrelations. These become clear by addressing the consequences and demands to the TNCs responsible, BASF and Lonmin, by involving this process in European and international debates on raw material strategies, corporate responsibility and legal regulations at UN level and by clarifying the persistence of neo-colonial exploitation. What is problematic is that individual struggles, including their successes and defeats, mostly take place on a local or regional level. With an internationalised project for society as a whole currently still in its conception phase, the isolation of individual struggles must be overcome in favour of creating new connections and interrelationships. In this context, the category of 'class' – in the broad sense of a 'new class policy' which also includes the precariat – could also continue to prove relevant. As the growing phenomenon of precarisation highlights the expropriation of social rights as a general, social process which extends beyond national borders, the precariat also acquires a transformational potential (Candeias, 2008).

The challenge remains to continuously emphasise existing relationships and contradictions and connect individual struggles with one another. Currently an indispensable part of any political essay, the discourse on rights must be continuously reoccupied and reclaimed by the Left – not only in the struggle for its appropriation, but also as a political and societal ideal.

Notes

1 With over 13,000 participants from 170 countries, the UN Global Compact is the largest voluntary initiative for promoting sustainable management and responsible corporate governance. Members include 9,000 private companies and 4,000 organisations from civic society, government and the UN, associations, cities (Global Compact Cities Programme) and further actors from the public sector. The 340 participating German enterprises (including BASF, Daimler, Bosch, Deutsche Bahn) form the German Global Compact Network (DGCN) with about 70 participants from civil society, politics and research; see Karaaslan (2017).

References

Arendt, H. (2001) *Elemente und Ursprünge totaler Herrschaft. Antisemitismus, Imperialismus, Totalitarismus*, 8th edn, Piper, Munich
Attac (2016) *Konzernmacht brechen! Von der Herrschaft des Kapitals zum Guten Leben für Alle*, Kritik & Utopie, Vienna
Attac Österreich (2010) *Attac Deklaration 2010. Eine andere Welt gestalten! Ein gutes Leben für alle ermöglichen!*, Vienna, www.attac.at/engagieren/deklarieren/deklaration-2010.html
BASF (2015) Kurt Bock in United Nations Global Compact Board for another three years, www.basf.com/en/company/sustainability/whats-new/sustainability-news/2015/united-nations-global-compact-board.html, checked on 4/2/2018.
BASF (2016) *BASF Online Report 2016*, www.imf.org/external/pubs/ft/weo/2017/01/weodata/index.aspx
Bloch, E. (1985) *Werkausgabe*, 8th edn. Suhrkamp Taschenbuch Wissenschaft, Frankfurt am Main
Brand, U. and M. Wissen (2017) *Imperiale Lebensweise. Zur Ausbeutung von Mensch und Natur im globalen Kapitalismus*, Oekom Verlag, Munich
Candeias, M. (2008) Prekarisierung als Kampf um Globale Soziale Rechte und Perspektiven feministisch-sozialistischer Transformation, in R. Klautke and B. Oehrlein (eds.), *Globale soziale Rechte Zur emanzipatorischen Aneignung universaler Menschenrechte*, Munich, pp. 175–205
CorA-Netzwerk für Unternehmensverantwortung (2017) *Menschenrechte brauchen Verbindlichkeit! Der Prozess für ein UN-Abkommen über Wirtschaft und Menschenrechte*, www.cora-netz.de/cora/treaty/, accessed 4 February 2018
CSR Europe (2018) *Benefit from Our EU Expertise*, www.csreurope.org/benefit-our-eu-expertise, accessed 4 February 2018
DGB Bundesvorstand (2009) *Binding rules for one and all! 10-Point paper on CSR. Adopted by the German Confederation of Trade Unions (DGB) and its affiliates*. Available online at www.dgb.de/themen/++co++article-mediapool-d53cc7ab420124dd635aa3dc03429f87, checked on 4/2/2018.
Dierßen, I. (2016) *Nationaler Aktionsplan für Wirtschaft und Menschenrechte. Ein Lehrstück in Sachen Lobbyismus*, www.lobbycontrol.de/2016/12/nationaler-aktionsplan-fuer-wirtschaft-und-menschenrechte-ein-lehrstueck-in-sachen-lobbyismus/, accessed 4 February 2018
Fischer-Lescano, A. and K. Möller (2012) *Der Kampf um globale soziale Rechte. Zart wäre das Gröbste*, Verlag Klaus Wagenbach (Politik bei Wagenbach), Berlin
GIZ (2018) *Partnership for Sustainable Textiles: Annual Report 2016/2017*, Bonn
Hilferding, R. (1955) *Das Finanzkapital*, 2nd edn, Europ. Verlagsanst (Basis), Berlin
ILO (2010) ILO Declaration on Fundamental Principles and Rights at Work and Its Follow-up, 2nd edn, Geneva
IMF (2017) International Monetary Fund: World Economic Outlook Database, Update April 2017, www.imf.org/external/pubs/ft/weo/2017/01/weodata/index.aspx
Karaaslan, O. (2017) United Nations Global Compact: Global Impact?, www.wirtschaftsrecht-news.de/2017/02/united-nations-global-compact-global-impact/, accessed 10 December 2017
Kuhn, G. (2017) Der gemeinsame Kampf in einer geteilten Welt. Warum 'Neue Klassenpolitik' internationalistisch sein muss, *AK: Zeitung für linke Debatte und Praxis* 631
Lonmin (2016) Consolidated Income Statement 2016, www.imf.org/external/pubs/ft/weo/2017/01/weodata/index.aspx
Martens, J. and K. Seitz (2016) Auf dem Weg zu globalen Unternehmensregeln. Der 'Treaty-Prozess' bei den Vereinten Nationen über ein internationales Menschenrechtsabkommen zu Transnationalen Konzernen und anderen

Unternehmen, *Global Policy Forum / Rosa Luxemburg Stiftung*

Marx, K. (1981) *Briefe aus den Deutsch-Französischen Jahrbüchern* 1

Oehrlein, B. (2009) Perspektiven global oder das Recht, Rechte zu haben. Über das Konzept 'Globale Soziale Rechte (GSR)', *Standpunkte: Rosa-Luxemburg-Stiftung* 19, www.rosalux.de/publikation/id/905/perspektiven-global-oder-das-recht-rechte-zu-haben/, accessed 4 February 2018

Oxfam (2017) Just 8 men own same wealth as half the world, www.oxfam.org/en/pressroom/pressreleases/2017-01-16/just-8-men-own-same-wealth-half-world, accessed 4 February 2018

Partnership for Sustainable Textiles (2018) *Who We Are*, www.textilbuendnis.com/en/who-we-are/, accessed 4 February 2018

Piketty, T. (2017) *Soziale Ungleichheit weltweit gewachsen*, www.zeit.de/wirtschaft/2017-12/ungleichheit-privatisierung-thomas-piketty-studie, accessed 4 February 2018

Schaik, A. van (2017) UN Treaty negotiations: A chance for the EU to champion human rights, www.euractiv.com/section/economy-jobs/opinion/un-treaty-negotiations-a-chance-for-the-eu-to-champion-human-rights/, accessed 4 February 2018

Tauss, A. (2016) *Sozial-ökologische Transformationen. Das Ende des Kapitalismus denken*, Hamburg

Tauss, A. and T. Ehs (2016) *Das Ende des Kapitalismus denken? Fragmente für eine demokratisch-ökologische Linke im 21. Jahrhundert*, Hamburg

Peoples Treaty Working Group (2014) *Ideas and Proposals for Advancing Work on the International Peoples Treaty on the Control of Transnational Corporations: Base Document for Global Consultation*, www.stopcorporateimpunity.org/wp-content/uploads/2015/02/PeoplesTreaty-EN-dec2014.pdf, accessed 4 February 2018

VENRO, Forum Menschenrechte and Corporate Accountability (2016) *Kein Mut zu mehr Verbindlichkeit. Kein Mut zu mehr Verbindlichkeit*, www.venro.org/fileadmin/redaktion/dokumente/2016/NAP_Kommentar.pdf, accessed 4 February 2018

◀ **pp. 406/407** Sibonile Sobhopa, mine worker at Lonmin and survivor of the 2012 massacre, in Marikana in February 2016. He wears a T-shirt from the AMCU union, which went on strike at the Platinum Belt for six months achieving wage increases for Lonmin employees in 2014. However, the R12,500 the strikers demanded in 2012 has still not been achieved.

◀ **pp. 408/409** Taken the day before the massacre, this photo shows the meeting place of the striking workers. On the right in the background: the informal settlement Nkaneng.

◀ **pp. 410/411** 5 November 2017: Activists from the Ende Gelände campaign demonstrate in the German Hambach open-cast mine for abandoning fossil energy production and against the further destruction of the landscape by lignite mining.

◀ **pp. 412/413** London, 15 March 2018: Demonstration of London Mining Network, Decolonising Environmentalism and Plough Back the Fruits in front of the Lonmin shareholder meeting. The posters show the miners shot in the massacre.

▶ 'Women demand – We decide who represents and who governs us'. Adapted anti-apartheid silkscreen by Judy Seidman for the One in Nine campaign, Johannesburg 2017.

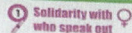

23. THE REAL ISSUES: POLITICS AGAINST 'NOT WANTING TO KNOW'

Stephan Lessenich
Translated by Simon Phillips

It doesn't take much to explain the real issues at hand. First, Marikana is everywhere; second, everyone knows that this is the case.

Marikana is everywhere...

Let's not deceive ourselves – an embarrassing secret lies behind the wealth amassed by 'highly developed' industrial capitalist societies: we didn't borrow our wealth, we took it forcibly, and we continue to withhold it from other people. Whether we are speaking about platinum mines in South Africa, textile factories in Southeast Asia or the plantation economy in Latin America, the situation is always the same: people have to die somewhere else so that we can live here as we have done since time immemorial.

The prosperous welfare-capitalist model of economic value creation and the – albeit limited and selective – social redistribution of revenues gained from growth largely rely on the unfettered exploitation of labour and the environment in other regions of the world – regions that also have to bear the ecological and social costs of local forms of production and consumption. The dominant living conditions in our part of the world have only become possible and can only be sustained because the majority of the population in the 'underdeveloped' societies within the global capitalist system work and live under conditions that we would consider completely unacceptable.

Clearly, wealth is also unevenly distributed here, and, recently, income inequalities and disparities in the distribution of wealth have even widened further. Nevertheless, these inequalities need to be understood as being embedded within the structure and dynamics of global inequalities. Globally, conditions that we view as socially acceptable, appropriate and bearable are made possible by societal conditions elsewhere that we would regard as absolutely unacceptable, inappropriate and unbearable – and rightly so, because this is precisely what they are. Compared to the rest of the world, consumption levels in our society – material and energy wise – are not only not 'sustainable' but should be regarded as downright absurd, if not insane. Moreover, we can only maintain this level of consumption because billions of people around the world consume far fewer natural resources than we do.

Let's face it: we live our lives at the expense of others.

... and everybody knows that this is the case.

But what do we do? We don't face up to it. We know what's going on, but we don't want to acknowledge it. What's more, there's no need for us to want to acknowledge it. Nobody forces us to be aware of what's going on, and we gladly accept every opportunity to remain ignorant.

To avoid any misunderstanding, this is not about blurring or ignoring individual responsibilities through appeals to generalised and vague notions of 'us'. After reading this book, there should be absolutely no doubt that it is the large multinational corporations and capital owners, with their economic power and political influence, that enable global business to exploit labour and the environment – and they are making an obscene profit from doing so. Therefore, it is right that these companies are the focus of criticism; and when it comes to naming names, it is also right that activists point to BASF.

Nevertheless, it is important to remember that BASF – and all of the others – operate on fertile ground. The games they play only work because so many people play along with them. I am not referring to the so-called 'power of consumers' here, but to people's depoliticisation.

Half a century of growth and a quarter-century of neoliberalism have left their mark on welfare capitalism's dominant subjectivity and in people's hearts and minds. Neither the desire for more, on the one hand, nor the concern for oneself, on the other, is the personal malignancy of individuals; they are not even anthropological constants in the sense of such infamous claims as 'that's just the way people are'. On the contrary, they are a result of the social conditioning that people have experienced in the rich societies of the West over a long historical period.

The desire for more is not just an individual self-indulgence or instinctive greed. Rather, it is the fundamental component of a form of social action that has made producing a 'surplus' (capitalist accumulation) an economic necessity and a social principle. In Western growth-based capitalism, everyone has to want more, irrespective of whether this is what they actually want. Capitalism, as the seminal sociologist Max Weber understood, produces the subjects it needs, and it needs growth subjectivity – the endless collective–individual desire for more.

A similar situation applies to the concern for oneself. It is not human beings per se but the neoliberal subject that is selfish, envious and competitive – or, at least, it should be. This position has been drummed into us time and again for decades by business institutes, economics professors, political leaders and the media: the individual comes before the collective, private before public, property rights before common goods and that which belongs to us over the things that belong to others. Although it would be better if this were not the case, the associated ideological indoctrination and politically institutionalised market pressures, have left their mark on us all.

This time I am indeed referring to the ominous, generalised, vague notion of 'us' as subjects of neoliberal growth (although without personally criticising or morally reprimanding anyone in particular) as well as our everyday actions that are imbued with the desire for more and a concern for ourselves. Being the neoliberal growth subjects that we are, or have become, we like to deceive ourselves. We like to believe that electricity simply comes from a socket in the wall or that e-mobility enables us to drive 'emission-free'. We are happy to hear that corporations are doing everything they can to improve supply-chain 'transparency'. And we gladly let ourselves be blinded by the social and sustainability awards that the nastiest exponents of transcontinental exploitation are pocketing and pinning to their lapels.

We want to believe in the good of global capitalism, in green lies and colourful glossy brochures. We don't want to know what hides beneath the facade – but it is not necessarily brilliant minds that are behind global capitalism, but broken bodies and souls, a devastated natural environment, and lives left in ruins.

What we need to do

If Marikana is everywhere and everyone knows that this is the case – but prefers not to acknowledge it – then there is a third element at stake here: ensuring that this becomes a political issue.

We need to use sound and appropriate arguments to courageously and deftly name those involved in this exploitation – BASF, for example. We also have to make the Potemkin facades that pervade the propaganda that surrounds us, and in which we also somehow participate, visible as such. We need to break through the tacit agreement that portrays these issues in a positive light, because we are also aware that we do not really want to know the truth. Finally, we need to expose the entire lie of growth and competition – a lie that we continue to live with; a staggering misnomer that we also let ourselves be controlled by.

This, of course, is easier said than done. Moreover, it is being stated from within the ruse itself – from a position that is not external to these relations, but caught – entangled – within them. To be sure, this does not make the right way of life wrong. On the contrary: in a way, it just makes the fight against the wrong way of life all the more self-evident, more evident to us.

What do we need to do? We need to look behind the facade, as this is the only way that we will be able to move forward.

▶ **pp. 420/421** Impression of the Solidarity Without Borders demonstration against the G20 summit in Hamburg on 8 July 2017 with over 75,000 participants.
▶ **pp. 422/423** Several generations of miners in February 2017 at Makwase Palace, a popular club and grill house in the centre of Marikana.
▶ **pp. 424/425** The women's organisation Sikhala Sonke at a demonstration in Marikana, 2012.
▶ **pp. 426/427** Group photo with some of the members of the General Assembly, Schaubühne Berlin, 5 November 2017.
▶ **pp. 428/429** 'An economy based on cheap labour is per se an economy of violence – all over the world,' says Oupa Lehulere, director of the Khanya College, who had the slogan 'We are all Marikana' painted on walls in various public spaces in Johannesburg and the surrounding area.

24. A BETTER LIFE FOR ALL?
SPEECH AT THE GENERAL ASSEMBLY BERLIN, 4 NOVEMBER 2017

Thumeka Magwangqana

To the president and all the delegates from all over the world, and the people in the audience, here in this room and also in other places – I greet you all. Thank you for letting me speak in this parliament.

My name is Thumeka Magwangqana, coming from Marikana, South Africa. Marikana is the place where police brutally killed 34 miners – our husbands and fellow brothers. I am here to represent the Sikhala Sonke Women's Organisation, which is based in Marikana, as their chairperson.

In 2012 our husbands went on strike, asking for an increase of their wages. They were sitting on the mountain in Wonderkop, waiting for their mine management to respond to their plea. But instead of them coming, the police came. We were amazed to see the police coming to our place in large numbers. And we heard that some of the government officials were interfering in this so that they can be killed. The police had the order to end the strike by any means. This means, they did it on purpose, it was already organized, that our fellow brothers should be killed. They were killed in a hail of bullets, as if they were criminals.

I did not know that asking for an increase is a crime.

Why is our black brothers' blood so cheap?

Our brothers' blood is cheaper than the money they were fighting for.

You can't replace the life of a person with money.

So now, after five years of the massacre, there is no one held accountable. No one has been compensated. No reparations were paid to the widows and to the injured mineworkers. The commission of inquiry was not appropriate. They did not even invite the perpetrators to the court. We never thought that under our black President there will be bloodshed. We never thought that after democracy there will be killings happening in South Africa. Still they want to remain in power, but they have blood on their hands.

There is no change in Marikana. Our government is sitting folding their arms as if nothing had happened. Our government has failed us. They have no remorse. They even don't care. The people are living in shacks, that are leaking, there is no sanitation, no running water, no electricity. And there are no roads.

Where is the better life for all?

All we have is violence, gender-based violence, domestic violence, rapes, the situation is very bad, also the poverty is driving these things to happen. The government should find ways to eliminate hunger.

The mine management – Lonmin – is also accountable for what has happened in Marikana. They did not protect the mineworkers. Instead they kept on saying they must go back to work. I am very disappointed in Lonmin, and the South African government. They are so cruel.

We were in the dispute resolution with Lonmin about the living conditions and the safety of the mineworkers. But that seems to be a waste of time, they did not come up with something, but only false promises.

I learned that BASF is the biggest customer of Lonmin's platinum. Buying platinum every day for a huge amount of money but ploughing nothing back to the communities to better the living conditions of their workers.

Where is the better life for all?

I think this democracy is for half, not for us all.

The whole South Africa is wounded about what has happened in Marikana.

We demand justice!

Amandla – awethu.

ABOUT THE AUTHORS

Britta Becker is a sociologist working as project manager in the Africa Department of the Rosa Luxemburg Foundation (RLS), with regional expertise on southern Africa.

Alexander Behr is a translator, journalist, and lecturer at the universities of Vienna and Klagenfurt. In addition to teaching at universities, schools, and trade unions, he is an activist in the network Afrique Europe Interact and the European Civic Forum.

Asanda Benya is a feminist activist and a lecturer in the Department of Sociology at the University of Cape Town, South Africa. Her research focuses on women in mining in Africa.

Patrick Bond is a distinguished professor in political economy at the University of the Witwatersrand School of Governance and an honorary professor at the University of KwaZulu-Natal School of Development Studies. He earned his doctorate in economic geography under the supervision of David Harvey at Johns Hopkins (1985–92). His recent books are *BRICS: An Anti-Capitalist Critique* (co-edited with Ana Garcia, 2015), *South Africa: The Present as History* (co-authored with John Saul, 2014), *Elite Transition: From Apartheid to Neoliberalism in South Africa* (2014, 3rd edition) and *Politics of Climate Justice: Paralysis Above, Movement Below* (2012).

Stefan Buchen works primarily as a TV journalist for the ARD politics magazine *Panorama*. For his investigative reports, he has been awarded several prizes, including the Leipzig Prize for the Freedom and Future of the Media. Additionally, he writes for national newspapers and the web portal www.qantara.de. In 2014, he published a book that deals critically with the prosecution of smugglers titled *The New Enemies of the State*. Stefan also studied Arabic language and literature at the universities of Mainz and Tel Aviv.

Gavin Capps is a senior researcher in the Society, Work and Politics Institute (SWOP) at the University of the Witwatersrand. He was awarded his PhD in development studies from the London School of Economics in 2010 and since 2013 has led the Mining and Rural Transformation in Southern Africa (MARTISA) Project at SWOP, which is funded by the Ford Foundation. Gavin has published a number of articles on the political economy of the platinum industry in post-apartheid South Africa and is currently writing a book on that subject with Andrew Bowman.

Franziska Dübgen holds a PhD in philosophy from the University of Frankfurt. She is currently researching theories of justice in the global South, African philosophy and the legal-philosophical critique of punishment and sentencing at the University of Koblenz-Landau.

María do Mar Castro Varela holds degrees in psychology and educational science and a PhD in political science. She is a professor of general pedagogy and social work with a focus on queer and gender issues at Alice Salomon Hochschule in Berlin. Her focus of work is postcolonial theory, critical migration research, critical educational science, queer studies, especially on questions of global justice. Her recent publications are *Postkoloniale Theorie. Eine kritische Einführung* (with Nikita Dhawan) and *Die Dämonisierung der Anderen. Rassismuskritik der Gegenwart* (edited with Paul Mecheril).

Maren Grimm is a filmmaker working for the Academy of Fine Arts in Vienna. She is the co-founder of the campaign Plough Back the Fruits (basflonmin.com).

Boris Kanzleiter has been the director of the Center for International Dialogue and Cooperation of the Rosa Luxemburg Foundation (RLS) since 2016. From 2009 to 2016 he headed the office of RLS for Southeast Europe in Belgrade. He holds a doctorate in history and journalism with a focus on Yugoslavia, Latin America, social movements, social human rights and left-wing actors. His studies and research projects are based in Berlin, Mexico City and Belgrade.

Simone Knapp studied ethnology, African studies and sociology in Mainz with a primary emphasis on African literature, human rights and southern African history. Since 2007 she has coordinated the Ecumenical Service on Southern Africa (KASA) in Heidelberg. KASA's work involves selected issues of social and economic justice, with a main focus on reparation, debt relief, trade, social security and land issues.

Jakob Krameritsch is an historian working for the Academy of Fine Arts in Vienna. He is the co-founder of the campaign Plough Back the Fruits (basflonmin.com) and co-editor of *Das Massaker von Marikana. Widerstand und Unterdrückung von Arbeiter_innen in Südafrika* (2013).

Stephan Lessenich is a sociologist at the Ludwig Maximilian University of Munich, chair of Social Development and Structures and special fellow of the DFG-Kollegforschergruppe Postwachstumsgesellschaften at the Friedrich Schiller University in Jena.

Sarah Lincoln is a lawyer and has been working for Brot für die Welt since 2012 as a consultant for economic, social and cultural human rights. In particular, she deals with the human rights implications of German and European companies, working closely with civil society organisations in the global South to document case studies and demand the accountability of German companies. Among other things, she has closely followed the German government's process of drafting a National Action Plan on Business and Human Rights and supports the United Nations treaty process for a binding agreement regulating transnational business.

Rosemary Lombard is currently completing a master's of philosophy in heritage and public culture at the University of Cape Town's Centre for African Studies. In collaboration with the Five Hundred Year Archive Project of the Archive and Public Culture Research Initiative at UCT, she examines processes of institutional knowledge production in relation to missionary colonial collections created at the beginning of the 20th century in KwaZulu-Natal, South Africa.

Mzoxolo Magidiwana is a retired mineworker. He started working for Lonmin in 2011 and participated in the strike for higher wages in 2012. He was hit by nine bullets from the police on 16 August 2012. Two bullets went directly through his body while seven bullets had to be removed in hospital. In Marikana he is known as 'the dead man walking', because it seems like a miracle that he survived the massacre.

Thumeka Magwangqana is a South African civil rights activist and the head of Sikhala Sonke (We Cry Together). This women's organisation was founded in Marikana on the day of the massacre. Since then, Sikhala Sonke has campaigned for better working and living conditions in the communities affected by mining. The film *Strike a Rock* (Aliki Saragas, RSA, 2017, 87 mins) portrays this struggle.

Boniface Mabanza Bambu was born in the Democratic Republic of the Congo under the military dictatorship of Mobutu. He studied philosophy, literature and theology in Kinshasa and holds a doctorate from the University of Münster. Since 2008 he has worked as coordinator of the Ecumenical Service on Southern Africa in Heidelberg. For years, he has been committed to a consistent change of perspective, especially in respect of the economic relations between African and European countries and the EU.

Akhona Mehlo is the business and human rights attorney at the Centre for Applied Legal Studies (CALS), based in Johannesburg. Previous to this, she worked at the Johannesburg office of the Legal Resources Centre (LRC) where her focus areas were gender, protests and policing, as well as openness and accountability of government and corporations. Before that she was a researcher in extractives, which is where her focus on holding transnational corporations accountable for human rights abuses began.

Barbara Müller coordinated the Swiss KEESA campaign for debt relief and reparation in southern Africa until December 2017. She is an ethnologist and her long-term work has focused on racism, decolonisation and international solidarity.

Trevor Ngwane is a post-doctoral research fellow at the Centre for Social Change, University of Johannesburg, and a member of the Marikana Support Campaign and the United Front of Johannesburg. He was a socialist-activist scholar in the anti-apartheid movement and is still active today.

Jan Pehrke is a member of the initiative Coalition against Bayer Dangers, which monitors the Bayer Group, and is responsible for the magazine *Stichwort Bayer*.

Dinah Rajak is senior lecturer in anthropology and international development at the University of Sussex. She is the author of *In Good Company: An Anatomy of Corporate Social Responsibility* (2011), co-editor of *The Anthropology of Corporate Social Responsibility* (2016) and co-founder of the Centre for New Economies of Development (http://www.responsiblebop.com).

Michael Reckordt is a graduate geographer and has been working at PowerShift since 2013 as the coordinator of AK Rohstoffe, a civil society network of environmental, human rights and development organisations that deals with German raw materials policy, human rights and ecological impacts of resource consumption.

Walter Sauer is a professor in the department of economic and social history of the University of Vienna, focusing on Austrian–African relations in history and the present. He is the chairperson of the Southern African Documentation and Cooperation Centre (www.sadocc.at), a successor organisation of the anti-apartheid movement.

Judy Seidman is a visual artist and activist based in Johannesburg. From the 1970s, she worked with South Africa's liberation movement, exploring ways to use the creative arts to give a voice to silenced and oppressed groups. Following this, in 2012 she facilitated art-making workshops with women from Marikana (with a South African feminist organisation, the One and Nine Campaign), then worked with Widows of the Marikana Massacre (through Khulumani Support Group), and worked on a research project about the impact of platinum mining on people in communities near the mines and in labour-sending areas. These in turn fed into the Plough Back the Fruits Campaign.

Jo Seoka is the former Anglican bishop of Pretoria and a political and social justice activist. His major ministry has been to the workers since his student days. He was the first church leader to visit the striking miners of Lonmin and has supported the Marikana strikers since the day of the massacre. It is said that he was the last person to speak with Mambushi Noki, 'the man in the green blanket', who asked, 'Bishop, where are you? They are shooting us!', before he was shot dead along with 33 other striking miners on 16 August 2012.

Carolijn Terwindt, graduate in law and anthropology from Utrecht University, joined the European Center for Constitutional and Human Rights in 2012, where she works closely with workers and their families in Pakistan and Bangladesh on cases of corporate liability in the textile industry. She has published on a wide range of topics, including supply chain liability, identity politics, anti-terrorism legislation, criminalisation of social protest, and the liability of pharmaceutical companies.

Christoph Trautvetter holds a master's in public policy from the Hertie School of Governance, Berlin and works with the Tax Justice Network on developing a fairer tax system in Germany and around the world.

INDEX

A
African Charter 231
African National Congress (ANC) 48, 92, 95, 118, 353, 357
  banning of 63
  member of Tripartite Alliance 400
  mineral and mining policies of 92, 94
Afrika Süd 131
Ahmed, S.
  On Being Included (2012) 174
AK Rohstoffe 184
AkzoNobel 242
Albers, Hans 137
Algeria
  War of Independence (1954–62) 378
Alliance Against Mining 185
Alternative Information and Development Centre (AIDC)
  Million Climate Jobs campaign 324
  personnel of 323
Amadiba Crisis Committee 184–5
Ameling, Dieter
  President of German Steel Federation 339
Amnesty International 285
Anglican Church 172
Anglo-Boer War (1899–1902) 85
Anglo Platinum (Amplats) 91–2, 107, 304
  Khomanani Mine 115
  Rustenburg Platinum Mines 87–9, 97
Apartheid Debt and Reparations Campaign (KEESA) 74
Areva 345
Argentina
  Buenos Aires 335, 338
ARMSCOR 68
Ashley, Brian 323
Association of Ethical Shareholders 322
Association of Mineworkers and Construction Union (AMCU) 48, 163, 216, 322–3, 370
  personnel of 317, 395–6
Association of Professional Social Compliance Auditors (APSCA) 242
Australia 135
Austria 33, 64, 75, 77, 79, 198
  Anschluss (1938) 278
  economy of 395
  Federal Chamber of Commerce 77
  government of 75
  Vienna 75, 144
Austrian anti-apartheid movement
  founding of (1976) 77–8

B
Bangladesh 242
  Rana Plaza Building Collapse 270, 398
  textile industry of 246
Bapo Ba Mogale 90, 96
Barroso, José Manuel
  European Commission President 288
Barzel, Rainer 280
BASF 23–4, 30–2, 37, 51, 64, 67, 88, 121, 131, 133–4, 138–42, 146, 169, 173, 175–6, 189, 217, 248, 264, 266–8, 279–81, 289, 291, 295, 304, 312–13, 355–7, 358, 403, 418, 432
  Amflora 288
  annual report of (2016) 296, 298
  ART 134
  BASF Metals Limited 295
  BASF Nederland B.V. 300
  BASF South Africa Ltd 135
  CHC Elastogran 134
  CSR efforts of 138, 140
  facilities of 278, 290
  founding of (1865) 276
  Global Mining Solutions 281
  personnel of 33–4, 131, 136–9, 164, 284
  shareholder meeting (2015) 130–1, 140, 173, 262
  shareholder meeting (2016) 120, 131, 146–7, 171
  shareholder meeting (2017) 33, 131
  subsidiaries of 295–8, 300
  Supplier Code of Conduct 242
  Sustainable Development Report 139
  tax evasion methods of 36, 295–300, 304–5
Bayer 134, 242, 268, 279
Belgium 296
  Antwerp 135
  Brussels 288–9
Bench Marks Foundation 23, 188, 322
Berlin Conference (1884–5) 335
von Bern, Erklärung 71
Bernau, Olaf 397
Bilateral Investment Treaties (BIT) 187
Bilchitz, David 232
Black Economic Empowerment (BEE) 94–5, 261, 315, 343–4, 358
Biedenkopf, Kurt 280
Blowfield, Michael 269
BMW 136, 284
Bock, Kurt 146, 149, 170, 172, 174, 287
  CEO of BASF 33, 131
Bolloré 345
Borkin, Joseph 278
Botswana 343
Bourdieu, Pierre 79
Bouygues 345
Bowman, Andrew 92
Brandt, Willy 67
Brazil 183, 227, 340
Bread for the World 188, 285, 322
Brüderle, Rainer 282–3
Brüning, Heinrich 277
Burger, Johan 353
Bushveld Complex 87
Business Europe 287
Bütefisch, Heinrich 277

C
Cambodia 379
Canada 135, 188
capitalism 32, 35, 312, 315, 369, 380
  corporate 261
  free market 35
  industrial 369, 418
  organised 395
Capps, Gavin 33
Center for International Environment Law (CIEL) 319–20
Chile 283
China, People's Republic of 92, 189, 227–9, 337–8, 340, 378
  Beijing 289, 318
Chinese Communist Party 348
Christian Democratic Union (CDU) 279
  members of 280
City Press 374
Civic Association
  founding of (1954) 280

437

Clean Clothes Campaign
  Looking for a Quick Fix: How Weak Social Auditing is Keeping Workers in Sweatshops (2005) 241
Cold War 63–4, 78, 279
  end of 138
Colombia 183–4, 245
  Cajamarca 186
  Ibagué 186
  Piedras 186
colonialism 78, 167
  postcolonialism 169, 206
Commerzbank 67
Committee on Economic, Social and Cultural Rights (CESCR) 225
Compact with Africa 36, 334
Confederation of German Employers' Associations (BDA) 215
Congress of South African Trade Unions (COSATU) 48, 385
  member of Tripartite Alliance 400
Cooper, Robert 345–6
corporate social responsibility (CSR) 38, 79, 138, 140, 207, 213, 216, 247, 258–60, 262, 266, 268, 270
  voluntary measures 215
Critchley, Simon
  Infinitely Demanding (2007) 169
Cronimet 187
CRS Europe 398
Cuba 378

D
Daily Maverick 371
Daimler 67
Daimler-Benz 136
Dasnois, Alide 320
Democratic Republic of the Congo (DRC) 183–4, 189, 337, 340, 382
Denmark 229
Der Spiegel 68, 137, 353
  editorial staff of 66–7
Desai, Rehad
  Miners Shot Down (2014) 371
Deutsche Bank 67
Die Zeit 353
Dierßen, Imke 396
Dimas, Stavros 288
Dresdner Bank 67

DSM 242
Düsseldorf Institute for Applied Marketing 137
DuPont 242
Duncan, Jane 371

E
Economic Freedom Fighters (EFF) 118, 323–4
Economic Partnership Agreements (EPAs) 339, 341–3
  negotiation of 342, 344
Ecosense 189
Ecuador 218, 227, 232
Ecumenical Services on Southern Africa (KASA) 322
Edwards, Elizabeth 370
El Salvador 186
  banning of metal mining in (2017) 185
ELG Haniel GmbH 187
Elf 345
Engelhard 134–5, 355
  acquired by BASF 139
Enlightenment 345
Eramet 345
Escher, Klaus 289
ESKOM 67
Ethical Globalization Initiative 224
Ethiopia
  Addis Ababa 135
EuropaBio 288
European Chemical Industry Council (CEFIC) 286–7
European Commission 189, 215, 288, 301, 340, 343, 398
  Market Access Regulation (MAR) 343–4
  personnel of 288
European Council 189, 340
European Court of Justice 288–9
European Parliament 189, 285, 299, 306
European Partnership Agreements 36
European Roundtable of Industrialists 287
European Union (EU) 36, 88, 184, 227, 285, 306, 318, 335, 338, 341, 343, 345, 398
  anti-tax directives of 304
  Emission Trading Systems (ETS) 287
  member states of 36–7, 288–9, 399
  personnel of 134, 345

Raw Materials Initiative 339
REACH 286–7
Evangelical Church in Germany 66
Evonik Industries 242
Extractive Industries Transparency Initiative (EITI) 186, 306
  founding of (2002) 186
  members of 187
  Standard 187

F
Fanon, Frantz
  Wretched of the Earth, The (1981) 177, 357–8
Farlam Commission 48, 51, 109, 314–15
  Report of 51
Federal Council of Switzerland 74
Federal Republic of Germany (West Germany) 64
Federation of German Industries (BDI) 189, 214, 281–2, 285, 339
  personnel of 282
  Raw Materials Congress 281
Financial Times 265
First World War (1914–18) 278, 394
Fleming, Ian 134
Flick 280
Ford Motor Company 67
Foundation for Human Rights (FHR) 229
fracking
  opposition to 186
France 64, 345
Freytag, Bernd 131
Friedman, Milton 259
Froneman, Neil 317

G
Gabriel Resources 188
Gattineau, Heinrich 277
Gencor 91–2
General Motors 67, 88
Genscher, Hans-Dietrich
  West German Foreign Minister 136
Geocoton 345
Gerbner, George 371
German Association of Chambers of Industry and Commerce (DIHK) 214
German Empire 276–7
  Imperial Colonial Office 335
German Mineral Resources

438

Agency (DERA) 50, 283–4
German Steel Federation
    personnel of 339
German Trade Union
    Confederation (DGB) 214
Germany 32–3, 37, 67–8, 79, 131–2, 134, 187–9, 191, 198, 276, 282–3, 286, 296, 304, 317, 334, 354
    Berlin 289–90
    Bonn 280
    Bundeswehr 280, 345–6
    Federal Institute for Geosciences and Natural Resources (BGR) 283
    Federal Ministry for the Environment, Nature Conservation and Nuclear Safety 286
    Federal Ministry of Economic Affairs 286
    Federal Ministry of Economic Cooperation and Development (BMZ) 36, 214, 217, 284, 334, 339–40
    Federal Ministry of Economics and Technology 36, 282
    Federal Ministry of Finance 36, 334
    Foreign Ministry 214
    Kiel 136
    Ludwigshafen 30, 37, 133, 138, 172, 267, 276, 286, 295
    Mannheim 121, 276
    Ministry of Finance (BMF) 214–15
    Ministry of War 278
    National Action Plan (NAP) 213–14, 284–5
    opposition to fracking in 186
    Reunification (1990) 268
    Rhineland 186
GFI Mining 97
Ghana 343–4
Glencore 285
Global Campaign to Reclaim Peoples Sovereignty, Dismantle Corporate Power and Stop Impunity 399
Global Financial Crisis (2007–9) 36, 96–7
Global Financial Integrity (GFI) 304–5
global social rights (GSR) 396–7, 399
Global Witness 183

globalisation 91, 290
    division of labour under 169
    legal 34
Gold Fields South Africa 97
Goldman Sachs 266
Gramsci, Antonio 203
Grass, Günter 291
Greece
    opposition to gold mining in 186
Green Party (Germany) 136
Green Party (Switzerland) 267
Greens-European Free Alliance 297–8
    Toxic Tax Deals 299–301
Group of Twenty (G20) 334
Gumede, William 265

H
Happe, Claus-Michael 318
Hargreaves, Samantha 319
Health and Safety Act 108
Heidelberg Institute for International Conflict Research 183
Henkel 242, 280
Hilferding, Rudolf 399–400
    Finanzkapital (1910) 394
Hitler, Adolf 277–8
Hoechst 268
HSBC 266
hydrogen fuel cell (HFCs) 98

I
IG Farben 65, 135, 268, 277
    founding of (1925) 268
    personnel of 277–80
Impala Platinum (Implats) 87–8, 108, 304
imperialism
    British 84
Incwala 95, 315
India 92, 183, 227, 338
    New Delhi 289
Indonesia
    Grasberg Mine 184
    West Papua 184
International Business Machine (IBM) Corporation 67, 136
International Council on Mining and Metals (ICMM) 190
International Covenant on Economic, Social and Cultural Rights (ICESCR) 225, 397, 401
International Finance Corporation (IFC) 318–22, 324

Compliance Advisor Ombudsman (CAO) 320, 322
Investment & Advisory (I&A) services 318, 322
International Labour Organization (ILO) 188, 226, 397, 399
    Convention Concerning Indigenous and Tribal Peoples in Independent Countries 188
    Declaration on Fundamental Principles and Rights at Work 401
    Safety and Health in Mines Convention 188
International Monetary Fund (IMF) 337, 344, 382
    Structural Adjustment Programmes (SAPs) 336
International Platinum Group Metals Association (IPA) 285–6
    personnel of 285
Investment Partnership Agreements 187
Ivory Coast 343–4

J
Japan 355
Jürgens, Udo 77

K
Kaleck, Wolfgang 207
Kalle, Wilhelm Ferdinand 277
Kalle Circle 277
Kampeter, Steffen
    CEO of BDA 215
Kant, Immanuel 170
Kazakhstan 283
Kellermann, Gunther-Alexander 284
Khulumani Support Group 67, 144, 322
Kim, Jim Yong 318–20
Kimberley Process 264
KiK 35
Kohl, Helmut 137, 279, 290
Köhler, Horst
    resignation of (2010) 346
Konrad Adenauer Foundation 283
Krameritsch, Jakob 131, 355
Krauch, Carl 278
Kritsichen AktionärInnen Deutschlands 147
Kritischer Bewegungsdiskurs 402–3

L

Labour Relations Act 108
labour sending areas (LSAs) 105–7, 111
   education of children in 120
   underdevelopment in 108
   women in 110–12, 114–15, 117–19
LafargeHolcim 70
Lahmeyer 358
Land Act (1913) 85–6
Land Act (1936) 85–6
Land Claims Commission 319
Land Claims Court 319
Länderbank AG 75
Lanxess 187, 242
Le Monde diplomatique 346
Legal Resources Centre 229, 231
Legal Rights and Natural Resources Center 185
Lessenich, Stephan
   concept of 'externalisation society' 37, 39
Lesotho 85
Lévinas, Emmanuel 201
Living Out Allowance (LOA) 93
London Bullion Market Association (LBMA)
   Responsible Gold Guidance 242
London Meeting Network 147
London Metal Exchange 295
Lonmin 23–4, 30, 32, 38, 46–50, 88, 90, 95–7, 107, 109, 119–20, 130–1, 142, 164, 169, 172, 176, 188, 191, 217, 242, 258, 270, 285, 313, 316–17, 319–21, 324, 337, 355–6, 373, 403, 432
   failure to implement SLPs 113, 248
   personnel of 147, 162, 322–3
   responses to Marikana Massacre 143–4
   Transformation Committee 314
Lonrho
   formerly London and Rhodesian Mining Company 87
   Western and Eastern Platinum mines 92
Lumumba, Patrice 345

M

Made in Germany 189
Madörin, Mascha 71
Magara, Ben
   CEO of Lonmin 147
Magidiwana, Mzoxolo 148, 373
   shooting of (2012) 33
Magwanqana, Thumeka 40, 430
Malindi, Stanley 90
Mandela, Nelson 25, 324, 354, 357
Marc Rich & Co AG 71, 74
Marikana Massacre (2012) 29–31, 33, 38, 40, 105, 107, 143, 147, 167–8, 182, 184, 312, 315, 364, 379
   media coverage of 38, 354, 357, 370
   political impact of 31, 51, 95, 118, 121, 140, 143–4, 176, 270, 323, 353–4, 380, 431
   weaponry used by police in 48–9
Marinovich, Greg 371
Murder at Small Koppie: The Real Story of the Marikana Massacre (2016) 354
Marshall Plan with Africa 36, 334
Mathunjwa, Joseph 163, 317, 370
Max Planck Foundation 183
Mbeki, Thabo 95, 262
Merck 242
Merkel, Angela 283
Mexico
   Zapatista Revolt (1994) 379
Mills, John Atta
   death of (2012) 344
Minerals Act (1991) 107
Minerals and Petroleum Resources Development Act (MPRDA)(2002) 95, 107
   provisions of 94, 96
Mines and Works Act (1911) 107
mining 22, 84, 104–5, 107, 109, 117, 183–4, 188, 190–1, 248, 261, 264, 316, 320
   coal 324
   colton 184
   conflict minerals 184–5
   contract labour in 108
   copper 184
   gender segregation of workforce 113–18
   gold 92, 184, 186, 281, 283
   platinum group metals (PGM) 23, 30, 33, 37, 46–7, 86, 89–90, 92, 95, 98, 104, 112, 121, 142, 265, 281, 285, 304, 316, 324, 354–6, 417
   silver 281
   tin 184, 281
   tungsten 184, 281
Mining Charter 108, 114
Mining Charter III 285
Mitsubishi 355
Modern Settings 142
Moldenhauer, Paul 277
Mongolia 283
Monsanto 134, 395–6
Morgenrath, Birgit
   Deutsches Kapital am Kap (2003) 67
Morgenthau, Henry
   US Treasury Secretary 278
Mosebetsane, Ntombizolile 51, 145, 169
Mosiane, Pinky
   rape and murder of 115
Mozambique 85
Müller, Gerd 318, 398
Müller, Hermann 277
multi-stakeholder initiative (MSI) 217–18
Myanmar 184

N

Nachtweh, Hans-Georg
   editor of *Der Spiegel* 66
Namibia 343
National Party 336
   electoral victory of (1948) 62, 70
National Union of Mineworkers (NUM) 47, 394
   members of 95
nationalisation 261–2
nationalism
   Afrikaner 65
Nazi Party 277
   members of 279
neoliberalism 173, 207, 248, 339, 344, 373, 393, 418
Nestlé 70
Netherlands 296–7, 300
   Hague, The 401
New York Times 136
New Zealand 187
Newmont Mining 318
Nicaragua 183
Nichol, Jim 271
Nigeria 69
Noki, Mgcineni 374
Non-Aligned Movement 228
non-governmental organisations (NGOs) 65, 147, 183, 185, 214, 216, 218, 245, 380, 382, 395

secular 74
Nooke, Günter 283
North Atlantic Treaty Organization (NATO) 282
Norway 229
Novartis 70

O

Open Budget Initiative 187
Open Government Partnership (OGP) 187
Orange 345
Organisation for Economic Co-operation and Development (OECD) 36, 184, 284, 399
  Guidelines for Multinational Enterprises 188–9
  Guiding Principles 34
  initiative on profit sharing (BEPS)(2015) 306
Organization of Petroleum Exporting Countries (OPEC) 69
other business enterprises (OBEs) 229
Ouattara, Alassane 344
Oxfam 395
Oxford University
  Kellogg College 225

P

Pakistan 242
  Ali Enterprises factory fire (2012) 240, 398
  Karachi 240–1
Pan Africanist Congress (PAC) 63
von Papen, Franz 278
Paradise Papers Scandal 345
Paris Agreement 269
Partnership for Sustainable Textiles 398
Paskert, Dierk 282
People's Global Action (PGA) 390
Perry, Joe 288
Peru 283
Petroleum Agreement 277–8
Philippines 183, 185–6
Plough Back the Fruits 31–3, 322, 324, 403
Poland
  opposition to fracking in 186
Population Registration Act (1950) 62
Pro! Africa Initiative 36, 324
Promotion and Protection of Investment Act (2015) 229
Protestant Business Leaders Working Group 174
Publish What You Pay (PWYP) networks 186, 266
Puerto Rico 299

Q

Qatar
  Doha 338

R

racism 78
  constitutionally based 78–9
Rajak, Dinah 34, 139
Ramaphosa, Cyril 48, 95, 313
Ramonet, Ignacio 346
Rau, Milo 40, 347
Räuschel, Jürgen
  BASF: The Anatomy of a Multinational Corporation 135
Rauschenbach, Rolf 136
responsibility 201–2
  conditions of 197–8
  face-to-face 200
  grounding of 199–200
  role-specific 198
  shared 198
Restitution of Land Rights Act 22 (1994) 319
Rheinmetall 67
Rights and Accountability in Development
  personnel of 225
RINA S.p.A. 240–1
Robinson, Mary 224
Rodney, Walter
  How Europe Underdeveloped Africa (1973) 313
Romania
  opposition to gold mining in 186
Rosa Luxemburg Foundation 322
Rougier 345
Rowland, Tiny 87
Royal Bafokeng Platinum 285
Royal Society for the Protection of Birds (RSPB) 217
Ruggie, John 213, 223–6, 233
Russian Federation 227–9, 340

S

Saage-Maaß, Miriam 207
Sadiki, Leon 374
Sankara, Thomas 345
SASOL 67
  establishment of (1950) 135
Schindler 70
Schröder, Gerhard 281
Second World War (1939–45) 63–4, 74, 135
  Nuremburg Trials (1948) 65
Sen, Amartya 344
Seoka, Bishop Jo 147–8, 163, 169
  speech at BASF Shareholder Meeting (2015) 130–1, 140, 173, 262
Shanduka Resources 95
Sharife, Khadija 347
Sharpeville Massacre (1960) 63, 86, 270
Siemens AG 358
Sibanye-Stillwater 317
Sikhala Sonke 321–2, 430
social audits 241–2
  critiques of 243–4, 247, 249
  quality control 246
  reports 244
Social Labour Plan (SLP) 49, 94, 248, 270, 314, 317
Society for Plant Breeding 288
SOLIFONDS 322
Solvay 242
Sontag, Susan 29, 365–6
South Africa 29, 32, 65–7, 69, 77, 89, 97–8, 105, 136, 138, 172, 187–8, 198, 222–4, 227, 229–30, 242, 264, 296, 304–6, 324, 417, 432
  apartheid 32–3, 38, 63–4, 66, 69–71, 74–5, 79, 86, 91–3, 106, 109, 113, 116, 134–6, 167, 202, 262, 336, 353
  Bophuthatswana 88–90
  Cape Town 353, 365
  Department of International Relations and Cooperation (DIRCO) 223, 229–30, 233
  Department of Labour 229
  Department of Mineral Resources 48, 229, 317
  Department of Trade and Industry 229
  Department of Water and Sanitation 229
  Eastern Cape 184, 358
  economy of 22, 32, 68, 370
  Gauteng Province 87
  income gap in 32
  Johannesburg 46, 84, 135, 259–60, 281, 312, 317, 369
  Marikana 23, 37, 47–50, 89, 96, 104, 119, 142, 188, 217, 263,

441

304, 322, 325, 416, 419, 430
North West Province 23, 87
Platinum Belt 23, 107, 216, 258, 353, 358, 396
Pretoria 130, 320
Rustenburg 88–9
sanctions targeting 63–6
Transkei 75
Witwatersrand 84–5
South Africa Foundation 134
South African Anglo American Corporation 87, 262
South African Commission of Inquiry 131
South African Communist Party (SACP) 48
  member of Tripartite Alliance 400
South African Council of Churches 24
South African Development Community (SADC) 343
  EPA of 342
South African Human Rights Commission 229
South African Public Investment Corporation 97
Soviet Union (USSR) 378
  Moscow 379
Soweto Uprising (1976) 63, 69
  political impact of 136
Spain
  Barcelona 135
Spivak, Gayatri 203
Standard Bank 266
Staples, Shelley 369
Stierwascher-Volkstanzgruppe 77
Strabag 358
Strauß, Franz-Josef 137
Sub-Saharan Africa Initiative of German Business (SAFRI) 283
Suchard 70
Süddeutsche Zeitung 353, 355
Sustainable Agriculture Network 241
Sweden 187
Swiss Apartheid Debt and Reparations Campaign (KEESA) 322
Swiss National Bank 70
Swiss National Fund 74
Swiss Statistical Office 70
Switzerland 33, 64, 67, 69–71, 79, 229, 296
  Davos 259
  Geneva 218

Zug 71, 74, 267
Syngenta 242

T
Tagesschau 352–3
Taiwan 75
Tambo, Oliver 324
Technip 345
Thailand
  Bangkok 135
Thelejane, Agnes Makopano 145, 169, 176
  family of 145
Thelejane, Thabiso 145
Third Reich (1933–45) 79, 135, 276
  Schutzstaffel (SS) 65
Together for Sustainability (TfS) 216, 242
Total 345
trade unions 48, 65, 136, 184, 214–17, 241, 317
  black 138
  repression of 223, 391
Transatlantic Trade and Investment Partnership (TTIP) 289, 396
Transkei Trade Union and Information Office 75
transnational corporations (TNCs) 25, 33, 51, 133, 138, 188, 218, 223–4, 226, 228–30, 336, 379, 395–400, 403
  South African view of 231
transnationalisation 396, 399
Treaty Alliance 230
Tripartite Alliance
  members of 400
Trump, Donald 318
Truth and Reconciliation Commission (TRC) 74, 356
Tuesday Circle
  as Collegium 290

U
United Kingdom (UK) 64, 97, 188, 225, 260
  Department for Environment, Food and Rural Affairs (DEFRA) 287–8
  London 312, 354, 369
  opposition to fracking in 186
United Nations (UN) 34–5, 69, 75, 77, 136, 212–13, 284, 306, 401, 403
  Code of Conduct for Transnational Corporations and Other Business Enterprises with Regard to Human Rights (2003) 213
  Commission on Human Rights 223
  Comtrade Database 305
  Conference on Trade and Development 226
  Environment Programme (UNEP) 183
  Forum on Business and Human Rights 225, 228
  General Assembly 64, 224
  Global Compact (UNGC) 31, 34, 140, 175, 189–90, 213, 259
  Guiding Principles on Business and Human Rights (UNGPs) 31, 35, 142–3, 188, 216, 223–8, 233, 398
  Human Rights Council (HRC) 213, 218, 222, 225–6, 229, 399
  Subcommission on the Promotion and Protection and Protection of Human Rights 223
  Resolution 26/9 (2014) 225–6
  Vienna Convention 224
  War Crimes Tribunal 401
  World Heritage Sites 190
  World Summit on Sustainable Development 259–60
United States of America (USA) 97, 134, 188, 279, 318, 338
  Alien Tort Claims Act 67
  Dodd-Frank Act 184, 189, 215
  New York 266
  Standing Rock Protests 186
  Washington DC 134, 289, 318–19
University of Pretoria
  Centre for Human Rights 229
University of the Western Cape
  Dullah Omar Institute 229

V
VENRO 214
Verheugen, Günter 65
Vestager, Magrethe
  EU Competition Commissioner 133
Via Campesina 392
Vienna Boys' Choir 77
Vietnam 379

Voest/Noricum 75
Volkswagen (VW) 136, 284, 312–13, 324, 348
  emissions scandal (2017–) 316–17, 395
  role in apartheid 38

W
Wacker 242
Wall, Diana 371–2
Weisman, Robin 321
Wellmer, Gottfried 67–8
  Deutsches Kapital am Kap (2003) 67
Welt am Sonntag 353
Werkstatt Ökonomie 65–6
Widows of Marikana 322
Witwatersrand University
  Centre for Applied Legal Studies (CALS) 229, 231–2

World Bank 37, 312, 315, 317–20, 322, 400
  International Finance Corporation 337
  Operation Directives on Resettlement of Indigenous Peoples and Cultural Property 319
  personnel of 318
  Structural Adjustment Programmes (SAPs) 336, 347
  Sustainable Development Report (2012) 319
World Trade Organization (WTO) 36, 335, 342, 347
  Africa Group 335
  Buenos Aires Ministerial Conference (2017) 335
  Doha Round (2001–) 338
  personnel of 339
  World Trade Report (2010) 338–9
Wurster, Dr Carl 279

X
Xstrata 74

Y
Young, Iris Marion 202

Z
Zattler, Jürgen 318
Zehle, Sybille 138–9
Zimbabwe 358
Zoellick, Robert
  President of World Bank 318
Zuma, Jacob 47
  resignation of 285
Zwane, Mosebenzi 285

443

Published in South Africa by Fanele, an imprint of Jacana Media (Pty) Ltd, in 2018
10 Orange Street
Sunnyside
Auckland Park 2092
South Africa
+2711 628 3200
www.jacana.co.za

© Rosa Luxemburg Stiftung, 2018

All rights reserved.
The content of the publication is the sole responsibility of the author(s) and does not necessarily reflect the position of Rosa Luxemburg Stiftung.

Sponsored by the Rosa Luxemburg Stiftung with funds of the Federal Ministry for Economic Cooperation and Development of the Federal Republic of Germany. This publication or parts of it can be used by others for free as long as they provide a proper reference to the original publication.

ISBN 978-1-928232-57-5

Layout by Shawn Paikin
Design concept by Tanja van de Loo
Editing by Russell Martin
Proofreading by Linda Da Nova
Index by Josh Bryson
Set in PT Serif 9/14pt
Printed by ABC Press, Cape Town
Job no. 003315

See a complete list of Jacana titles at www.jacana.co.za

This book was published in Germany in 2018 by Mandelbaum Verlag as *Zum Beispiel: BASF – Über Konzernmacht und Menschenrechte*
ISBN: 978-3-85476-565-3
Find out more about BASF and Lonmin at basflonmin.com

Credits

Concept
Maren Grimm
Jakob Krameritsch
Tanja van de Loo (assistance)

Contact zone chart
Jakob Krameritsch
Tanja van de Loo

Translation
For lingua·trans·fair:
Joanna Mitchell
Simon Phillips
Sally McPhail
Nivene Rafaat
David Beckett
Lyam Bittar
Cornelia Gritzner

Picture Proofs
Heiko Neumeister

Picture credits and video stills

Maren Grimm and Jakob Krameritsch
As well as
Victor Barro (221)
Britta Becker (293)
Asanda Benya (128)
Po-Ming Cheung (332)
Ende Gelände (410)
Gen-ethisches Netzwerk (274)
Fritz Hoffmann (16)
Thorsten Lapp, ARD/Panorama (58, 257 Mitte)
Sarah Lincoln (220)
London Mining Network (412)
Greg Marinovich (408)
One in Nine, Johannesburg (424)
Rasande (310, 420)
SADOCC-Archiv (76, 82)
Judy Seidman (10, 126, 254)
Tokolos Stencil Collective (376)
Widows of Marikana (160)
Zapiro (44)
Anonymous sources (Cover, flap, 1, 2, 329, 446–451)
in possesion of:
Markus Fiedler (155)
Anette Hoffmann (366, 368)

Thank you

The publishers would like to thank:
Janine, Phyllis & John Blignaut
Andreas Bohne
Carla Noever Castelos
Helle Døssing
Markus Dufner
Johannes Gelich
Juma Hauser
Anette Hoffmann
Fritz Hofmann
Lydia James
KASA – Kirchliche Arbeitsstelle Südliches Afrika
Thapelo Lekgowa
Tilman Massa
Paula Pfoser
Tobias Pilz
Graham Pote
Michael Reckordt
Birgit Reiter
Lotte Rieder-Fraunlob
Walter Sauer, SADOCC
Barbara Sennholz-Weinhardt
Richard Solly
Kai Zastrow
And the authors!

▶ **p. 446** Projection of TV images from the Marikana massacre on a Lonmin advertising board in Marikana West.
▶ **p. 447** Projection of the 'Remember Marikana' stencil of the Tokolos Stencil Collective onto a Lonmin company sign in Marikana, 2016.
▶ **pp. 448/449** Projection of TV images from the Marikana massacre onto the entrance area of BASF Holdings South Africa in Midrand near Johannesburg, 2016.
▶ **pp. 450/451** BASF – We create chemistry / Remember Marikana. Projection onto the entrance area of BASF South Africa (Pty) Ltd., Struandale near Port Elizabeth, 2016.

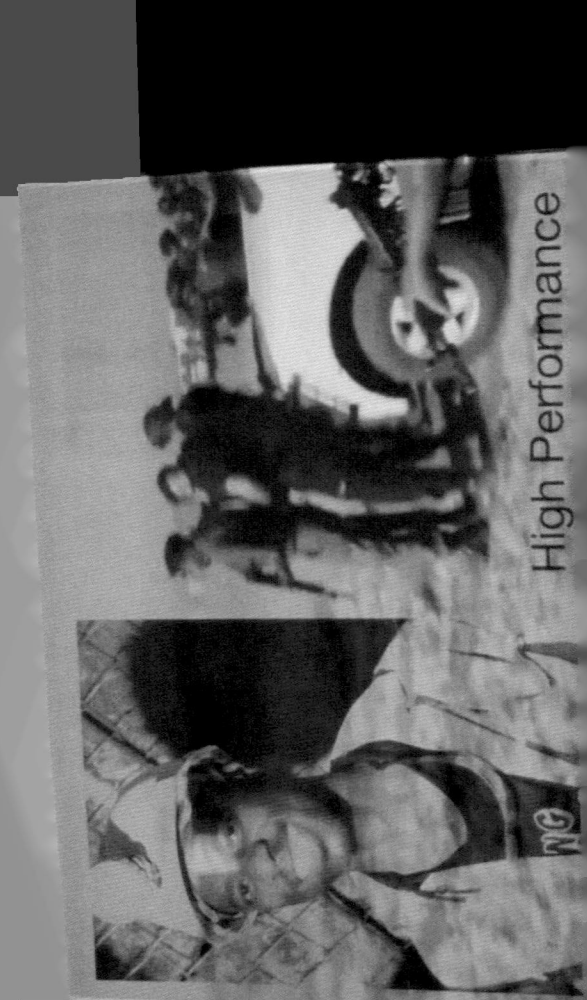

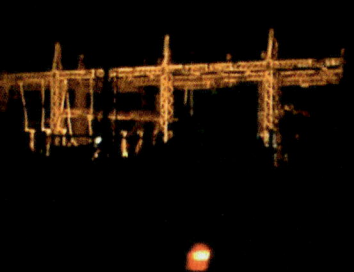